Theological Renewal
for the Third Millennium

Theological Renewal for the Third Millennium

A Kärkkäinen Compendium

VELI-MATTI KÄRKKÄINEN

Edited by
Patrick Oden and Andrew Ray Williams

Foreword by
Amos Yong

CASCADE Books • Eugene, Oregon

THEOLOGICAL RENEWAL FOR THE THIRD MILLENNIUM
A Kärkkäinen Compendium

Copyright © 2022 Veli-Matti Kärkkäinen. All rights reserved. Except for brief quotations in critical publications or reviews, no part of this book may be reproduced in any manner without prior written permission from the publisher. Write: Permissions, Wipf and Stock Publishers, 199 W. 8th Ave., Suite 3, Eugene, OR 97401.

Cascade Books
An Imprint of Wipf and Stock Publishers
199 W. 8th Ave., Suite 3
Eugene, OR 97401

www.wipfandstock.com

PAPERBACK ISBN: 978-1-6667-1354-1
HARDCOVER ISBN: 978-1-6667-1355-8
EBOOK ISBN: 978-1-6667-1356-5

Cataloguing-in-Publication data:

Names: Kärkkäinen, Veli-Matti, author. | Williams, Andrew Ray, editor. | Oden, Patrick, editor. | Yong, Amos, foreword.

Title: Theological renewal for the third millenium : a Kärkkäinen compendium / by Veli-Matti Kärkkäinen; edited by Andrew Ray Williams and Patrick Oden; foreword by Amos Yong.

Description: Eugene, OR: Cascade Books, 2022 | Includes bibliographical references and index.

Identifiers: ISBN 978-1-6667-1354-1 (paperback) | ISBN 978-1-6667-1355-8 (hardcover) | ISBN 978-1-6667-1356-5 (ebook)

Subjects: LCSH: Kärkkäinen, Veli-Matti. | Theology of religions (Christian theology). | Theology, Doctrinal. | Pentecostalism.

Classification: BX4827.K324 K37 2022 (paperback) | BX4827.K324 (ebook)

VERSION NUMBER 081022

Contents

Foreword by Amos Yong | ix

Acknowledgments | xiii

Encountering Veli-Matti Kärkkäinen:
  An Introduction from Two Directions | xv
  —By Patrick Oden and Andrew Ray Williams

Autobiographical Essay: Four Conversions | xxvii
  —By Veli-Matti Kärkkäinen

Part One: Methodology

CHAPTER 1
From a "Unitive" to a "Plural" Paradigm of Pneumatology:
An Interim Report of the State of Spirit(s) in Christian Theology | 3

CHAPTER 2
The Leaning Tower of Pentecostal Ecclesiology:
Reflections on the Doctrine of the Church on the Way | 19

CHAPTER 3
Teaching Global Theology in a Comparative Mode | 29

Part Two: Systematic Theology

CHAPTER 4
Divine Hospitality and Communion:
A Trinitarian Theology of Equality, Justice, and Human Flourishing | 43

CHAPTER 5
Divine Action in the World in
a Trinitarian-Pneumatological Framework | 59

CHAPTER 6
The Human Prototype:
With Jesus, We See What We Were Created to Be | 77

CHAPTER 7
Transformed, Freed, Empowered:
The Spirit's Work in the Gifting and Vocation of All Believers | 83

PART THREE: **Ecumenical Theology**

CHAPTER 8
Salvation as Justification and *Theosis:* The Contribution of
the New Finnish Luther Interpretation to Our Ecumenical Future | 101

CHAPTER 9
Sacraments and (Dis-)Unity: A Constructive Ecumenical Proposal
towards Healing the Divisions and Facilitating Mutual Recognition | 114

CHAPTER 10
Is the Spirit Still the Divine Line Between the Christian East and West?
Revisiting an Ancient Problem of *Filoque* with a Hope for an Ecumenical
Rapprochement | 133

PART FOUR: **Interreligious Theology**

CHAPTER 11
The Re-Turn of Religion in the Third Millennium: Pentecostalisms and
Postmodernities | 147

CHAPTER 12
How to Speak of the Spirit among Religions: Trinitarian *Prolegomena* for
a Pneumatological Theology of Religions | 169

CHAPTER 13
Dukkha and *Passio:* A Christian Theology of Suffering
in the (*Theravada*) Buddhist Context | 191

CHAPTER 14
Calvin and Religions | 212

PART FIVE: **Interdisciplinary Theology**

CHAPTER 15
Multidimensional Monism: A Constructive Theological Proposal
for the Nature of Human Nature | 231

CHAPTER 16
A Christian Vision of the "End" of Cosmos and Life: Towards a Constructive Eschatology for the Contemporary World | 254

CHAPTER 17
The Greening of the Spirit: Towards a Pneumatological Theology of the Flourishing of Nature | 270

Bibliography | 281

Index | 281

Foreword

I FIRST MET VELI-MATTI Kärkkäinen in March 1998 at a restaurant in Cleveland, Tennessee, where we were both attending the annual meeting of the Society for Pentecostal Studies (SPS). He was doing his *habilitation* at St. John's University in Collegeville, Minnesota, working with Killian McDonald at the time, and I had just started to write my doctoral dissertation at Boston University and was presenting my first paper at the scholarly conference. Our conversation was brief but enabled us to connect and then I noted a year later that he landed at Fuller Seminary.

During my PhD Research I realized that the two leading Pentecostal scholars, who were also ecumenists, were Cecil M. (Mel) Robeck and Veli-Matti, and after I landed my first teaching job at Bethel University Minneapolis, I was invited by North Central University, one of the Assemblies of God affiliated colleges, to teach one of their upper division theology courses on pneumatology. I was looking for a text introducing Pentecostal perspectives and didn't find one at hand. It was then that I contacted Veli-Matti and asked if I could bring together some of his essays and publish them in a book, which he consented to and I did.[1] I used the book for the next three years teaching that annual course.

Over the next decade, we continued to deepen our relationship. This included an essay that I wrote in about 2005, upon his coming close to completing publication of a series of textbooks that he had been writing as a result of teaching the basic theology sequence and electives at Fuller Seminary.[2] We wrote essays for books each other edited even as he also published reviews of various of my books and provided endorsements for a few others. We also co-edited a book together with Kirsteen Kim.[3]

---

1. See Kärkkäinen, *Toward a Pneumatological Theology*.
2. See my essay "Whither Evangelical Theology?," 60–85.
3. Kärkkäinen et al., *Interdisciplinary and Religio-Cultural Discourses on a Spirit-Filled World*.

I came to Fuller seminary in 2014 as professor of theology and mission in the School of Intercultural Studies (SIS) and also as the director of the PhD in intercultural studies program. That allowed us to spend much more time together on a more regular basis than before, although we used to joke around that we would still see each other as much if not more at conferences like SPS and AAR (American Academy of Religion) than we would on campus. In the summer of 2019 I became the dean of SIS and the SOT (School of Theology), and therefore became Veli-Matt's "boss." Of course, he was one of those I consulted before taking up this role, and he was very encouraging and has been, despite the challenges we have been facing as a seminary.

It quickly became very clear to me that unlike many prolific theologians, Veli-Matti has taught more than his fair share of masters theology courses over the last two decades, annually taking on one or two or even more courses as overloads. He has done this alongside mentoring many PhD students and doing so with attentiveness at both levels, each requiring very different but yet complementary pedagogical skill sets. In addition, he has faithfully and dutifully carried out his responsibilities as chair of the systematic theology department, which has included working with contingent faculty in the department, intervening when needed, reviewing and assessing their teaching, and being responsible for ensuring that our students receive excellent experience and formation in theology.

Both of us were raised in Pentecostal churches. My parents were Pentecostal preachers but both of our mothers were women of prayer, energy, and the fervor of the Holy Spirit. So much so that even if Finland and Malaysia (where we grew up) are two very different worlds, there is a sense in which we are not just "brothers from another mother," to use this colloquialism, but brothers-from-pentecostal-mothers! We would share about how our conversations with our mothers inevitably turned into receiving theological lectures from them motivated by their piety and their concern that in our theological speculation we would not meander too far from the truth.

There is also the sense in which we have become real partners, with a handful of others, in the forging of academic Pentecostal theology over the last thirty years. This has involved explaining Pentecostalism and pentecostal spirituality to others on the one hand and of translating ecumenical and even interreligious insights to the pentecostal world on the other hand. Nevertheless, our complementarity actually masks some deep differences that we have observed more clearly in the last year here at Fuller as we have engaged inter-departmentally (I joined him in systematic theology when I became dean) in some curricular revision conversations. As a result of his ecumenical formation at Helsinki and Collegeville, Veli-Matti is much more historically grounded in the theological and dogmatic tradition than

I, whereas my own predilections are more anticipatory and welcoming of the ongoing and dynamic adaptation of the tradition as it encounters new circumstances. This is of course not to say he is opposed to the development of theology, but it is to say that he respects the methodological contours of the dogmatic tradition in ways that are more difficult for me to appreciate. And to be sure, my Finnish Pentecostal (now also ordained by the Evangelical Lutheran Church of America) brother has been at the forefront of constructive theology, where he deploys particularly tools from the interdisciplinary conversation between theology and science on the one hand, and developments in comparative theology on the other. I, myself, have done some work in both of these areas but surely not as extensively as he has, even as my own sojourn has taken me across a variety of other arenas of exploration.[4] In short, I am more eclectic in my musings and less disciplined, while he, of course, has drilled down more deeply and in depth as a systematic and dogmatic theologian, as evidenced in his five-volume and 2,500-page magnum opus.

This book is a fitting update from the first collection of essays that I edited, introducing readers to the forging of Veli-Matti's constructive theology. Here, the various pieces are laid out in anticipation of the synthesis that we can now also enjoy. There is much more to come from his hand, but this volume provides a window into the making of the most significant multi-volume effort in dogmatic theology by one person, which at the beginning of the third decade of the twenty-first century no one would have thought possible. And no one else could have had such an expansive theological vision except for one who has had opportunity to lecture in every continent, who has lived extensively on three of them, and who has been as diligent in uncovering every theological nook and cranny as Veli-Matti Kärkkäinen.

Amos Yong
Dean, School of Mission & Theology
Fuller Theological Seminary, Pasadena California

---

4. The divergences are laid out in my essay, "The Many Tongues of the Spirit? Interpreting Veli-Matti Kärkkäinen's A Constructive Christian Theology for the Pluralistic World," in *The Dialogical Evangelical Theology of Veli-Matti Kärkkäinen*, 51-63.

Acknowledgements

WE ARE GRATEFUL TO the managing and permissions editors of the following journals and books for non-exclusive rights to reproduce these essays:

Chapter 1: "From a 'unitive' to a 'Plural' Paradigm of Pneumatology: An Interim Report of the State of Spirit(s) in Christian Theology." *Perspectives in Religious Studies* 41 (2014) 183–96.

Chapter 2: "The Leaning Tower of Pentecostal Ecclesiology: Reflections on the Doctrine of the Church on the Way." In *Toward a Pentecostal Ecclesiology: The Church and the Five Fold Gospel*, edited by John Christopher Thomas, 261–71. Cleveland: CPT, 2010.

Chapter 3: "Teaching Global Theology in a Comparative Mode." In *Teaching Global Theologies. Power and Praxis*, edited by Kwok Pui-lan et al., 45–53. Waco, TX: Baylor University Press, 2015.

Chapter 4: "Divine Hospitality and Communion: A Trinitarian Theology of Equality, Justice, and Human Flourishing." In *Revisioning, Renewing, and Rediscovering the Triune Center: Essays in Honor of Stanley J. Grenz*, edited by Jason Sexton, 135–53. Eugene, OR: Pickwick, 2014.

Chapter 5: "Divine Action in the World in a Trinitarian-Pneumatological Framework." In *Third Article Theology: A Pneumatological Dogmatics*, edited by Myk Habets, 441–62. Minneapolis: Fortress, 2016.

Chapter 6: "The Human Prototype: With Jesus, We See What We Were Created to Be." *Christianity Today* 56 (2012) 28–31.

Chapter 7: "Transformed, Freed, Empowered: The Spirit's Work in Gifting and Vocation of All Believers." In *Holy Spirit and Lutheran Identity*, edited by Chad Rimmer, 197–210. Geneva: Lutheran World Federation, 2020.

Chapter 8: "Salvation as Justification and Theosis: The Contribution of the New Finnish Luther Interpretation to Our Ecumenical Future." *Dialog* 45 (2006) 74–82.

Chapter 9: "Sacraments and (Dis-)Unity: A Constructive Ecumenical Proposal towards Healing the Divisions and Facilitating Mutual Recognition." In *Come, Let Us Eat Together: Sacraments and Christian Unity*, edited by Marc Cortez and George Kalantzis, 200–18. Downers Grove, IL: InterVarsity, 2018.

Chapter 10: In *The Trinity: Global Perspectives* by Veli-Matti Kärkkäinen, 44–59. Louisville: Westminster John Knox, 2007.

Chapter 11: "'The Re-Turn of Religion in the Third Millennium': Pentecostalisms and Postmodernities." *Svensk Missionstidskrift* 95 (2007) 469–95.

Chapter 12: "'How to Speak of the Spirit Among Religions': Trinitarian Prolegomena for a Pneumatological Theology of Religions." In *The Work of the Spirit: Pneumatology and Pentecostalism*, edited by Michael Welker, 47–70. Grand Rapids: Eerdmans, 2006.

Chapter 13: "Dukkha and Passio: A Christian Theology of Suffering in the (*Theravada*) Buddhist Context." In *Global Renewal, Religious Pluralism, and the Great Commission: Towards a Renewal Theology of Mission and Interreligious Encounter*, edited Amos Yong and Clifton Clarke, 97–116. Lexington: Emeth, 2011.

Chapter 14: "Calvin and Religions." In *John Calvin and Evangelical Theology: Legacy and Prospect*, edited by Sung Wook Chung, 266–83. Louisville: Westminster John Knox, 2009.

Chapter 15: "'Multidimensional Monism': A Constructive Theological Proposal for the Nature of Human Nature." In *Neuroscience and the Soul: The Human Person in Philosophy, Science, and Theology*, edited by Thomas M. Crisp et al., 221–27. Grand Rapids: Eerdmans, 2016.

Chapter 16: "A Christian Vision of the "End" of Cosmos and Life: Towards a Constructive Eschatology for the Contemporary World." In *The Interface of Science, Theology, and Religion. Essays in Honor of Alister E. McGrath*, edited by Dennis Ngien, 137–53. Eugene, OR: Pickwick, 2018.

Chapter 17: "'The Greening of the Spirit': Towards a Pneumatological Theology of the Flourishing of Nature." In *Blood Cries Out: Pentecostals, Ecology, and the Groans of Creation*, edited by A. J. Swoboda, 83–97. Eugene, OR: Wipf & Stock, 2014.

Encountering Veli-Matti Kärkkäinen

An Introduction from Two Directions

BY PATRICK ODEN AND ANDREW RAY WILLIAMS

THE FIRST DIRECTION: PATRICK ODEN

UP UNTIL MY (PATRICK) second year of seminary, my interest in systematic theology was, well, not very strong. In my first year of seminary studies, I learned I was capable at this important topic—likely due to a lot of formal and informal study of church history in my undergraduate years. The problem was that theology didn't particularly resonate with my questions and background. My exposure up to that point indicated it was rather univocal and had a narrow template of development and narrow range of invited contributors. If you were in that group, it really made sense, but if not, it was more of a learn, absorb, repeat kind of process.

Coming from a Southern Californian, Wesleyan-Pentecostal background with family involved in multicultural ministries well before it was encouraged, I had so many different streams of influences, voices, traditions, and a burgeoning passion for the integration of theology and ministry that I couldn't quite navigate since most authorities pushed one way or another. Theology, I felt more than could yet reason, had to mean something to real lives. I needed resources that reflected the many directions of the Holy Spirit's work in this world, and for the most part what I had been exposed to were talking from very different traditions and contexts. I went into my second year of seminary exhilarated and discouraged, wanting to find new directions that resonated with the historic church in all its diversity, and contemporary challenges in all their complexity, and contemporary society in all of its global and cultural diversity. I yearned for some kind of intellectual direction besides the status quo models.

With that in mind, and with a growing interest in deepening my Pentecostal side, I signed up to take a theology elective on pneumatology with a relatively new-to-Fuller theologian named Vel-Matti Kärkkäinen (VMK). Even though I grew up in the church and was a Biblical and Theological Studies major at Wheaton (along with a history major), I never had a class, or even read a book, on the Holy Spirit. Not uncommon in the turn-of-the-millennium days. From the very first day, from that very first look at the syllabus and my classmates, I knew it was going to be a life-changing moment. The overall approach of the course wasn't unique, a lot of assigned reading with substantive lectures taking the majority of class time, and a variety of papers, from short books reviews to a longer research essay, taking up most of the time outside of class.

The approach was familiar, the content and method was entirely new, and I've never been the same since. It wasn't a big class, maybe ten or eleven students, but in this group, there was at least one person from each of the inhabited continents. Diversity of experiences and contexts was built in to the discussions, something that wasn't happenstance, but indeed expressive of how VMK invites a broad range of students into conversation. This diversity wasn't just limited to the students. The readings were more diverse than I'd encountered before, including a wide array of traditions and perspectives, contributing toward a truly global sense of the work of the Holy Spirit and interpretation about the Holy Spirit. In this way, I was getting an education that could not be matched by hardly any other institution in the world.

More than just a class for me, this was in fact a kind of awakening. When I started, I was interested in the Holy Spirit and only vaguely interested in systematic theology. By the time I was done with that quarter, a new passion took root in me that has never really left. I had no idea that theology could be like this, inviting and expressive, drawing from many different traditions rather than pitting traditions against each other, and an openness to learn, even if not always agree, with an ever-widening pool of conversation partners. This class sparked a journey of discovery for me and at every point VMK combined a rare rigorous expectation with delighted encouragement. I was awakened to a lot of content about theology but also a way of doing theology that in my then ignorance didn't seem unusual. It was just how theology was being taught. I came to realize how unique this approach is, but by the time I realized this, it was too late for me. I was hooked into this methodology and it took shape in my writing and research and even my continuing journey of faith.

After that class, I took general systematic theology course with VMK and then a directed reading with him on the work of the Holy Spirit in the Eucharist, the latter being especially formative and a great chance to have more in-depth interaction with him at a crucial point of my academic development. Four years after finishing my MDiv, I returned to VMK's classroom to audit a doctoral class on Moltmann's theology. Once again, VMK's approach did something in me and to me at a key intellectual, spiritual, and vocational point in my life. I was auditing but ended up doing multiple presentations and a long research paper. Something about VMK got me doing all the work for its own sake, not for credit or checking boxes. I had been reading through the Philokalia in this season, and this class resonated a similar deep love of the beauty of God's work into my life.

In that class, I discovered more about Moltmann's theology, reading through all his major works, while also realizing even more deeply the interesting method that was behind the whole course. This method, the way VMK approaches both theology and teaching, has been more fully explored in his many texts over the years, especially in his monumental five volume *Constructive Christian Theology for the Pluralistic World*, but for me it was my entryway into theology and continues to shape how I think about the theological task and how I look to learn from wide and diverse resources in order to better come to terms with God's person and work in history and in the present.

More than a method and a task, all of which will become ever more clear in the following pages, in my now over twenty years as a student and colleague with VMK, I have picked up a few other insights about his approach that may not be as evident in his essays and books—though are always present. VMK is immensely passionate about learning about God and sharing this learning with others in all kinds of settings. His is a very rigorous, informed theology to be sure, but he has the heart and passion of a pastor and evangelist. Theology is more than a topic of study for VMK. I am still continually struck by how much delight he has in the theological journey itself. This delight is contagious and expansive, always willing to learn and listen, to discover new threads of experiences, and to empower women and men who are coming with their own questions and learning. That has made him into a wonderful scholar and teacher.

Some scholars want to have followers or disciples; some want their own egos massaged. VMK, in contrast, is eager to learn and see others thrive in this journey of discovery. It really is a sense of delight, which comes out in the joy of new conversations and insights and successes of students and colleagues. It also comes out at times as a wry sense of humor that can take many students off guard. I have many wonderful experiences learning in the courses and seminars I shared with VMK, but my prized memories are those times we caught each other's eyes with a quiet, shared funny insight or shared a quick quip. Having a sense of humor wasn't encouraged by the early monastics but I've learned again and again it really is a mark of someone who knows and loves God with inviting freedom.

This approach to learning and teaching underlies how his theological method has taken more specific shape over the years, coming to ever more honed method, though as wide-ranging in scope as ever before in ever new directions. I'm reminded of something he said way back in that first pneumatology class I had with him. By nature of the discussion, he covered the work of Pannenberg and Moltmann quite a bit, leading some students to comment, with a sense of humor, each time they were discussed (virtually every class in one way or another). "Ah, here's Herr Pannenberg!" In good natured acknowledgment, he also added that every theologian should know either Pannenberg or Moltmann well, both because of their immense theological contributions but also because of their prolific interactions with church history, historical and contemporary theologians, as well as many other resources. I have spent much of the last twenty years studying both and have come to realize how much VMK exemplifies each of their best qualities.

Pannenberg's intent, as his interpreters have sometimes said, was to know everything about everything. Because God is the creator of all, there is no field outside the scope of theology. This isn't meant to put everything beneath theology, more to show the wideness of conversations that can and should be had in order to understand God and God's work ever better. Pannenberg saw the need to engage in other fields, mastering scholarship in diverse topics, always gaining more and more insight into how God works in this world as he engaged these sources. Moltmann, in comparison (not really contrast), had an encyclopedic knowledge himself, involved in almost every major theological discussion of the twentieth century, yet his goal was to address challenges, frictions, to, in a curious roundabout way, make a practical impact in the church and in this world. In other words, he knew that theology, if it were to speak of the living, active God, had to have integrity with our lived experiences and be confronted by our hurts, fears, terrors.

Like Pannenberg, VMK does not approach theology as a narrow sphere of isolated knowledge, coherent only within its own structure and language. Instead, theology is an expansive exploration, covering as much ground as existence itself, always inquisitive, seeking to understand each facet through learning and conversation with experts. Each aspect of human reality is invited into this discussion, each aspect a field of wondrous opportunity to discover something new, make connections with theological insights, expanding our awareness of God, the world, and ourselves all the while.

While the quest to know everything about everything is never achievable—there's more than we can ever know and always new knowledge being developed—it shapes theology toward curiosity and dialogue. Instead of seeking domination, one field over another, one scholar over the next, the goal is learning itself, in the best tradition of European salons, where the best and brightest talk with each other, with a rapturous crowd listening in, taking notes, relaying the conversation to others. Indeed, that latter is how I see my own role in this present project, excited about conversations I've listened into and wanting others to realize how much good wisdom can be found in these sessions (nicely bound together in essay form).

While Pannenberg gathered together a wonderful set of conversation partners and knowledge about every field he could reach, he was not as concerned with the practical impact of theology nor the global conversations taking shape in all sorts of places and all sorts of languages. Even the church was rather remote, maybe even theoretical, as a matter of theological assessment. With Moltmann, however, we find both the practical and the global as significant areas of conversation, all while approaching these, and the church itself, from a thoroughly systematic and constructive direction. Like Moltmann, VMK has long been interested in the life of the church, serving it as a minister and as a missionary, and spending the majority of his professional career training young ministers and other leaders at Fuller Theological Seminary. At every point this interest has taken on a global and polyvocal character. While diversity and inclusion are now prioritized in higher academics, and primarily oriented along certain sociological schemas, this is a relatively recent shift and one in which there is a lot more outward support for than underlying values (as can be shown in looking at syllabi that aren't intended to be shared with accreditation committees or administration vice-presidents). For VMK, this interest in diverse and global conversations arises out of his own theological method, needing no outward push or impetus to drive it. Indeed, his continued push for global conversations had been resisted by many in the field (and at our own institution). Now, well into an era of celebrated diversity, VMK has continued farther than almost anyone in showing how thoroughly and constructively this global, inter-religious, interaction provides a richness of theological insight.

It is these ways—how VMK emphasizes a coherent and inclusive theology that invites dialogue in an always hospitable manner—that contribute to what really is a new method for theological development. This method is not closed off in combative or fearful isolation, nor policed within in artificially narrowed boundaries. It is open to the world's learning and perspectives, because God too is open, inviting, hospitable, coherent, inviting peoples from all over the world into communion, never forced while never passive. And here in this reflection of God's mission I find another striking aspect in common with Moltmann and Pannenberg: a deep, residing love for the salvific work of Christ and passion for the power of the transformative presence of the Holy Spirit. More than the content I've learned from VMK, I have been shaped by his heart and inviting approach, which have been experiences of the Gospel throughout key points in my life. In this, VMK exemplifies the best of not only Christian theology but also of Christian Evangelicalism. Not in its narrow, politicized American sense, but in the global expression of men and women who have been deeply shaped by the Scriptures and are committing their lives to the spreading of hope and love throughout their contexts. This is a Pentecostal faith, in which vocation and charisms can become intertwined and serious study is invested with joy and hope.

That joy, that hope, that celebration and delight in truth, that dogged persistence in pushing against conventions that exist in narrow, limiting ways for their own sake inspired my entry into the advanced study of theology, has shaped how I see theology taking shape around the world, and has been a spiritual and pastoral encouragement to me in some of my lowest moments and in my successes. The rich pastoral heart of VMK that expresses itself in magisterial expertise and wry humor is a model for me of what theology is at its best and how theology can take the lead in bringing transformative community and resurging coherent pursuit of truth into a world that so desperately needs both.

In the essays that follow, you will discover the intellectual journey that led to new vistas and connections, feeding into his five volume systematic series. At each point, I want you to also remember that the man who wrote these, who continues to explore and gather conversations all over the world, is deeply, passionately, actively committed to the Gospel in the fullest and deepest meaning of that great commission given to us as disciples of the living Christ.

THE SECOND DIRECTION: ANDREW RAY WILLIAMS

I (Andrew) first encountered Veli-Matti Kärkkäinen's work in a pneumatology course taken in my first year of seminary studies.[5] Through taking other

---

5. See Kärkkäinen, *Pneumatology*.

theology courses, I would soon discover that in addition to pneumatology, VMK had also published textbooks on the doctrine of God, Christology, ecclesiology, theology of religions, among others. However, like many seminary students, the extent to which I engaged VMK's work was limited to his textbooks.

In 2015, when I began writing my master's thesis on Pentecostal ecological theology, I stumbled upon one of VMK's constructive essays in an edited volume relevant to the subject matter. Not only was the essay germane to the topic I was researching, but the essay's emphasis upon mining pneumatological resources to address the pertinent issues resonated with my own Pentecostal sensibilities.[6] Soon I would discover VMK's *Creation and Humanity* (2015), in which he expands his discussion on ecological and environmental theology. After purchasing a copy and utilizing his insights for my thesis, I began engaging other sections within the volume previously unread.

Earlier in seminary I had been assigned readings from two of VMK's chief dialogue partners, Wolfhart Pannenberg and Jürgen Moltmann. In fact, I had largely decided to write on ecological theology due to Moltmann's influence on my own thinking. However, in VMK's work, I witnessed how these seminal thinkers could interact with an incredibly broad and diverse set of interdisciplinary voices—many voices that I had not yet considered. Therefore, after finishing *Creation and Humanity*—the third volume of his monumental five volume, *Constructive Christian Theology for the Pluralistic World*—I soon read the two previously released volumes, *Christ and Reconciliation* (2013) and *Trinity and Revelation* (2014), and later *Spirit and Salvation* (2016).

In the Fall of 2016, I enrolled in my PhD program at Bangor University (Wales, UK), writing on water baptism in the Pentecostal tradition.[7] During this time, I eagerly awaited the release of VMK's fifth and final volume, *Hope and Community* (2017). Because VMK shares in the spiritual inheritance of two church traditions, namely Lutheran and Pentecostal, I expected that VMK's sacramental insights would be valuable to my own constructive efforts. Since my own project sought to construct a Pentecostal theology of water baptism that was resourced and oriented by the Pentecostal resources, while also engaging in critical conversation with ecumenical sources, I believed I was likely to find VMK's sacramental perspectives instructive.

---

6. Ironically, this essay is included within this volume. See Kärkkäinen, "Greening of the Spirit."

7. See Williams, *Washed in the Spirit*.

Following its release, I found myself incorporating concepts into my thesis gleaned from *Hope and Community*.

However, my interest in and appreciation for VMK's theology goes beyond his contributions to these two research areas. Beginning when I was a student and continuing on into my current work as a pastor and professor, I have found myself exhilarated by VMK's thought. Following his five-volume project, I began reading much of his earlier constructive work and realized how much of his early contributions to Pentecostal theology set the stage for developments I have taken for granted as a young Pentecostal scholar. Further, I have also been able to discern the development of his theology, first establishing himself as one of the leading Pentecostal voices in the academy, and more recently working toward an ecumenical rather than merely a confessional theology.

His epic five-volume systematics, for example, is unique in that it puts forward all foundational Christian doctrines, including the present global and contextual voices, while also placing Christian doctrines into dialogue with four other living faiths—Judaism, Islam, Buddhism, and Hinduism. And yet, his employment of a distinctly dialogical and hospitable methodological vision for theology is represented not only by placing key Christian doctrines in conversation with a variety of other religious perspectives, but also by spending time in dialogue with the natural sciences, secularism, among others. Following Wolfhart Pannenberg, VMK proposes that "theology's domain is wide and inclusive, not only of the spiritual but also of the secular, not only the church but also the world, including science and culture."[8] VMK also follows Thomas Aquinas's vision in viewing *everything* through a theological lens, since the object of theology is God and everything in relation to God. Moreover, VMK's interreligious approach makes his work not only one of systematic/constructive theology, but also of comparative theology.

In my own estimation, VMK's inclusive, interdisciplinary methodological visions rightly urges the Christian church and academy towards a more holistic Christian vision of the world—one that is in continual dialogue with a variety of religious and non-religious perspectives. His theology is consciously marked by both innovation *and* orthodoxy. Put another way, his work is willing to learn from an astoundingly wide range sources in a conversant style, while also staying rooted within the broad dogmatic tradition of Christian theology. While one can sense VMK's desire to urge doctrine forward through interdisciplinary endeavors and situating it

---

8. Kärkkäinen, *Christian Theology in the Pluralistic World*, 4.

within new contexts, he also deeply informed by the theological and dogmatic tradition.

In these ways, VMK's theology is anticipatory of the way theology will most likely be done into the future of the third millennium. Though much of evangelical theology is still following the agenda of Euro-North American scholars, the explosive growth of global church in the majority world will soon (hopefully) have a greater impact on the kinds of conversations theologians are having. Due to the changing landscape of Christian evangelicalism—moving from a North American phenomenon to a more global one—Christian theology will continue to spread and speak from a variety of contexts. An ecumenical, interdisciplinary, and interreligious orientation will become the norm, rather than the exception, one might presume.

This makes VMK's theology all the more significant and pertinent at the turn of the third decade in the twenty-first century. Though VMK's constructive endeavors have received much acclaim, I still sense that his work has yet to fully be appreciated to the degree it ought to be. In my estimation, VMK's current contributions place him in the company of the leading Christian theologians of our time.

This conviction undergirds the purpose of this volume. Rather than having a volume that merely gathers otherwise easily accessed material, this book seeks to provides an entryway to those interested in VMK's constructive works, yet do not know where to "place" him in theological contexts, as well as providing a useful window for those who are familiar with his systematics but would benefit from additional material they might not otherwise know about or are able to access. My own desire is that this volume helps others further appreciate the rich theological contributions of VMK.

I have been afforded the unique opportunity to have been gifted with incredible theological mentors. In seminary, Mark J. Cartledge served as my master's thesis supervisor, developing me into someone who could move into PhD studies. Further, Chris E. W. Green, my *doktorvater*, guided me into becoming a theologian in my own right. And while I have never formally studied under Veli-Matti Kärkkäinen, I consider him a formative "mentor from afar." Through his wide corpus, I have been spiritually enriched and theologically challenged.

APPROACHING THIS BOOK

Amos Yong has stated that Veli-Matti Kärkkäinen has become "one of the more important theologians to be reckoned with in our time."[9] This

9. Yong, *Dialogical Spirit*, 121.

becoming has developed over the course of many decades with prolific contributions in essays, monographs, lectures, and other mediums. In an early recognition of his developing contributions, Yong edited a volume titled *Toward a Pneumatological Theology: Pentecostal and Ecumenical Perspectives on Ecclesiology, Soteriology, and Theology of Mission*, which was published in 2002. In that work, we already see the trajectory of Kärkkäinen's research project taking shape. Since that volume was published, Kärkkäinen has continued his prolific efforts, culminating in his five-volume *Constructive Christian Theology for the Pluralistic World* and continuing even still.

The goal of this present text is to take up where Yong's volume ended, to offer a curated selection of Kärkkäinen's essays from between 2006 and 2020. There are two kinds of readers we have in mind. First, this volume offers an accessible introduction to Kärkkäinen's diverse contribution for readers who are only familiar with his popular survey texts or are new to his work overall. Second, for those familiar with his theology, this volume provides insights into the journey his theological contributions have taken over the last fifteen years and serves as a kind of intellectual storyboard leading into his five-volume constructive systematics.

Given his wide-ranging interests and prolific contributions, the challenge for us was not to find material but to look through his extensive publications and select essays that offer a representative sample of his theological priorities. With this in mind, we have selected essays that fit into five sections. The first section relates to Kärkkäinen's method. Without understanding his distinct and intentional way of engaging both theology and theological education (in teaching, writing, and researching), it can seem that Kärkkäinen's work does not have a clear order to it. There is certainly a method to his madness, and this method potentially is one of the most constructive aspects of his work, pointing toward and exemplifying the way theology will be developed in coming decades and beyond in global settings. The second section provides examples of his writing on key topics in systematic theology. Those who only know his work from his surveys or who have only a surface reading of his writings have sometimes claimed Kärkkäinen primarily summarizes the work of others and lacks his own distinct constructive insights. This assumption misses how Kärkkäinen's rigorous attention to established theological contributions actually leads into his own unique and stimulating proposals.

The third section provides a glimpse into his ecumenical writings, emphasizing his hospitable and dialogical efforts in seeking conversation with those across church traditions. In the fourth section, the hospitable and dialogical approach looks outside of Christianity, engaging with the insights and contributions of other religions. This deeply integrated interreligious dialogue may be one of the most distinctive elements of the five-volume *Constructive Christian Theology for the Pluralistic World* and worth much more attention in his ground-breaking approach. Finally, in section five, we include essays that highlight his interest in science and human nature, showing how his theology is informed by conversations with diverse fields and have both practical and intellectual insights.

These sections are far from comprehensive, and we agonized over the many worthwhile essays we could not include, but they do offer a wide-ranging taste of Kärkkäinen's trajectory that we hope will inspire more research into his work and ever more attention to his important constructive contributions to global twenty-first-century theology.

Autobiographical Essay
Four Conversions[10]

By Veli-Matti Kärkkäinen

DIFFERENTLY FROM THE MODERNIST universalizing tendency, similarly to Moltmann—and in a radical departure from Pannenberg (to use these two well-known scholars as tokens)—I am convinced that the content and form of Christian theology is shaped by one's life-story, including one's broader communal and socio-cultural environment. A useful way to introduce myself as the author behind the essays in this collection is to highlight four subsequent "conversions" in my life:

Having been born and raised in Finland, I share the religious legacy of two church traditions, namely Lutheran and Pentecostal. Baptized and confirmed in the Lutheran Church and having found another spiritual home (via the influence of my pious mother) in Pentecostalism, I used to live comfortably a "double" spiritual life. Though now an ordained Lutheran minister—by the Evangelical Lutheran Church in America, assigned to serve as an associate pastor for the Finnish-Lutheran Church in California and Texas—I also continue to embrace Pentecostal-Charismatic Christianity. A citizen of Finland, beginning from my childhood, I also continue drinking from the wells of the Eastern Orthodox tradition; the Greek Orthodox Church in Finland (under the Patriarchate of Constantinople rather than Moscow, is the other "state church" alongside the Lutheran Church).

This personal and family background helps explain why I chose ecumenics as the major in my doctoral and post-doctoral (*Habilitationsschrift*) studies at the University of Helsinki under the late Lutheran expert

---

10. This essay is a slightly edited excerpt from my publication: "Constructive Christian Theology," 370–78.

Professor Tuomo Mannermaa. Having first studied behavioral sciences and philosophy in my native land and having started lecturing on those disciplines in my twenties at the University of Jyväskylä, I finished another Master's degree in theology at Fuller Seminary in Pasadena, CA where I have taught systematic theology for over twenty years at the time of this writing.

After two years of pastoring, the church sent me to Thailand to teach theology (in Thai!) with my family. Soon after, I registered as a doctoral student in Helsinki—and this takes me to my first conversion, namely the ecumenical one. Alongside the influence of my own spiritual background, on the "mission field" I noticed how urgent it is to work for the sake of the unity of the church if the Christian Gospel hopes to have any credibility among people of other faiths. How extremely strange it seemed to me to have Christian ministers from other countries bring to the majority Buddhist (and minority Muslim) land their own narrow-minded ecumenical prejudices and fights! Wisely my *Doktorvater* sent me to study for a full year with the Benedictines in the USA under the famed patristic scholar and ecumenist Fr. Kilian McDonnell. Living with my family on the campus of St. John's (Collegeville, Minnesota) in a fellowship with an ecumenically diverse group of international scholars, being tutored by the Benedictines, and participating in the daily spiritual exercise of monks and nuns, enriched my spiritual life and theological outlook immensely.

At the same time, another conversion, which I call "global," had emerged in my mind. Having already had a couple of moves between cultures, first from a Nordic country to California and then, after a couple of years back in my native land, to South East Asia, these moves began to make me suspicious of the narrow and naïve European(-American) White Male directed theology—a challenge which I first picked up at Fuller in my student years. While in no way undermining what I was taught by my European mentors, I also started a long journey towards an intentionally inclusive, diverse, and pluralistic way of theological thinking.

This takes me to my third conversion, namely the interreligious one. Eventually I noticed that there is actually no radical gap between ecumenism and interfaith work. Listening to the Other, sharing about one's own identity, and seeking to cultivate a hospitable and welcoming posture are virtues necessary to both. I eagerly began a grassroots-level immersion into Theravada Buddhism, living and teaching at the time in the world-center of that religion, Thailand. Later, after a six year-tenure as the Theological College Principal in Finland, I joined Fuller faculty in 2000, and there continued a meticulous self-study of some living faiths. That work continues to this day.

Joining Fuller (while continuing my then newly received appointment in Helsinki as the Docent of Ecumenics) took me to my fourth and (at the time of this writing) final conversion. It had to do with an interdisciplinary orientation, prompted and guided by many fine colleagues at Fuller, such as Professor emerita Nancey Murphy, a world-renowned philosopher and theology-science expert, as well as Professor Warren Brown, a noted neuropsychologist. As much as I resisted the call to make this shift—even if I had already earned a graduate degree in behavioral sciences early in my academic career—it turned out to be not only inevitable but a great opportunity. But it was and still is a painful transition for a humanist; even to learn the language of natural sciences and, say, neurosciences, is demanding and complex.

All four of these conversions—the interdenominational, intercultural, interreligious, and interdisciplinary—have made me the kind of theologian and minister I am and they have also helped shape and direct my theological work.

Alongside the four conversions, what has really helped shape my life—both the academic life and the pastoral life (Associate Pastor for the Finnish Lutheran Church in California and Texas)—is my family. With my wife Anne, married since 1980, and our two daughters, both of them mothers with families of their won, Nelli-Maaria (living now in Finland) and Maiju-Karoliina (in Los Angeles), I have had the opportunity to live on three different continents. We have learned new languages, have tried to cope with unexpected cultural differences, and have travelled accross the world—literally! Nothing gives me more joy and energy than daily morning coffee moments in bed with a devotional with my wife; or conversations during the day about various matters; or the moments spent with our three grandchildren living on two continents, observing them to grow and hearing them ask endless number of questions. Family life. *Koinonia*, communion.

PART ONE

Methodology

CHAPTER 1

From a "Unitive" to a "Plural" Paradigm of Pneumatology

An Interim Report of the State of Spirit(s) in Christian Theology

FIRST WORDS: IN SEARCH OF A NEW PARADIGM

THE PURPOSE OF THIS essay is twofold.[1] First, I wish to take a wide critical survey of the most current developments in pneumatology at the global and ecumenical level. Second, I would like to suggest a constructive "turn" from what I call a "unitive" paradigm in which only one Spirit (of God) is considered, while the rest of the spiritual realities are dismissed, to a "plural" paradigm. The latter accounts for the Spirit of God within a highly pluralistic cosmology with many (other divine) spirits, powers, and spiritual realities.[2] Cultural and religious plurality, the rise of postmodern philosophies, as well as transformations in scientific paradigms are all contributing factors to this change of outlook. The term "interim report" suggests that this is a work in progress. My continuing pursuit of a proper paradigm for pneumatology is fueled by two observations.

On the one hand, there are exciting and exhilarating developments underway that point to the *transformation* of Christian pneumatology. This

---

1. This essay builds on and draws heavily on my "Spirit(s) in Contemporary Christian Theology," 29–40. See also my *Spirit and Salvation*.

2. Kirsteen Kim speaks of the same distinction using the terms "one-spirit" and "many-spirit" pneumatologies and cosmologies. Kim, "Potential of Pneumatology for Mission in Contemporary Europe," 338.

promise lies in the robust and intentional desire to widen and make more inclusive the theological understanding of the ministry of the Spirit. In that wider and more inclusive outlook—while not leaving behind traditional topics such as the Trinity, Scripture, and salvation—the Spirit is also connected with topics such as creation, humanity, and eschatology, as well as political, social, environmental, and other "public" issues. This is a great corrective to tradition. Although one must resist the temptation to describe the pneumatological tradition in too uniform and homogenous terms—for the simple reason that there is already in the history of pneumatology dramatic differences, divergences, and surprises—it is also the case that by and large pneumatology has too often been bound within certain theological, ecclesiastical, and cultural strictures: that is, European and later European-American, male-driven, ecclesiastical-sacramental, individualistically oriented "spiritualist" priorities.

In the past the doctrine of the Spirit was mainly—even though, of course, not exclusively—connected with topics such as the doctrines of salvation, the inspiration of Scripture, some issues of ecclesiology, as well as individual piety. With regard to the doctrine of salvation, the Spirit represented the "subjective" side of the reception of salvation whereas Christology formed the objective basis. In the doctrine of Scripture, the Spirit played a crucial role in both inspiration and illumination of the Word of God. In various Christian traditions, from mysticism to Pietism to Classical Liberalism and beyond, the Spirit's work was seen mainly in relation to animating and refreshing one's inner spiritual life. While ecclesiology was usually built on christological foundations, the Spirit was invoked to animate and energize already existing structures. At times the Spirit was connected with various ministries in the church, as well as its prayer life and with sacraments—a connection made as a rule in the Christian East. In other words, the role of the Spirit in traditional theology was quite reserved and limited. It is this reductionism that has been challenged in many ways by contemporary pneumatologies. All of these changes are to be commended.

On the other hand, however, it seems to me that by and large "mainline" Christian pneumatologies are still imprisoned in the paradigm of a "unitive" pneumatology. Other spirits, powers, and energies are not seen as worthy of academic discussion and inclusion in respectable pneumatological presentations. A recent personal experience of that kind of "bound" pneumatology may illustrate this malaise. An anonymous reviewer of one of my recent manuscripts affirmed the careful and detailed historical and systematic study of the development of Christian doctrine of the Spirit but then complained harshly that, first, the global and contextual views do not merit inclusion in that prestigious theological collection and, second, even more importantly, the discussion of non-Christian—"pagan"—interpretations of the spirit in African folk religions, Islam, and various Hindu and Buddhist movements must be deleted.

Why so? What are the reasons for continuing to stick with the unitive paradigm? Among other things, it has to do with the continuing hegemony of the Enlightenment epistemology according to which everything *non*-natural in religiosity should be dismissed—an idea that hardly sounds "natural" to most Christians, or even most people of the world! This omission of "supernatural" powers and spirits of course stands in marked contrast to the beginnings of the Christian tradition when, in keeping with the worldview of the ancients, the world was filled with spiritual powers. Just consider the cosmology of the New Testament, whether Jesus's own ministry or the worldview of the Apocalypse, and you get the picture. Christian tradition until the times of the Enlightenment—and in some quarters beyond that—continued to take for granted plural cosmologies and pneumatologies. Rightly, the historian of dogma Jaroslav Pelikan notes:

> Christian apocalypticism reflected a supernaturalistic view of the world, which Christian believers shared with other religious men of antiquity.... "Traffic was heavy on the highway between heaven and earth. God and spirits thickly populated the upper air, where they stood in readiness to intervene at any moment in the affairs of mortals. And demonic powers, emerging from the lower world or resident in remote corners of the earth, were a constant menace to human welfare. All nature was alive—alive with supernatural forces."[3]

True, there is no returning to the outdated premodern worldview (that is the correct persistent claim of scholars such as Walter Wink). That said, however, the radical changes in philosophy, sciences, and our globalized world have also helped us see the deeply reductionist and forced nature of the Enlightenment epistemological strictures. The rediscovery of the plural paradigm of considering the Spirit/spirits/powers in Christian pneumatology does not have to be a return to a lost idyllic mindset of pre-Enlightenment times. Rather, it is a robust and courageous re-turn to a more complex, plural, and multilayered account of reality in the midst of which the Spirit of the Almighty God is at work in innumerable ways. While not a great admirer of postmodernism (for the simple reason that I have a hard time understanding what we are talking about when speak of "postmodernism"—and its advocates do their best to deepen the ambiguity!), the shift

---

3. Pelikan, *Emergence of the Catholic Tradition (100–600)*, 132; he quotes from Case, *Origins of Christian Supernaturalism*, 1.

in outlook may be useful. Whereas modernity celebrated unity, oneness, and homogeneity, postmodernity embraces "the growing fascination with 'the other.' The tendency to celebrate the different and suspect the same, to prefer *heteron* over *tauton*, *aliter* over *idem*, the alien over the identical, may be one of the defining peculiarities" of our age.[4] In this kind of pluralist milieu, religious sensibilities, including pneumatological, may have a better place to flourish. Whereas in the past "scientific modernity and traditional religion" were formative forces, nowadays—even with the diminishing of organized religion in the Global North—"experientialism" is on the rise and a part of the global religious resurgence, claims Harvey Cox.[5] We could add that this development is happening not only in Christianity but also in some other religions.[6]

We have already started pointing to directions that may be helpful in finding resources for a reworked pneumatological paradigm. In my own work I have found the following ones promising and at the same time invitations for deeper scrutiny:

- Postmodern sensibilities in the Global North
- A diverse group of studies and approaches that includes postcolonialism, the study of "powers," the importance of "Intimations of Transcendence,"[7] among others
- New ways of tapping into transformations underway in the dominant scientific paradigm, particularly with regard to the conception of cosmology[8]
- Theologies from the Global South[9]
- Emerging global Pentecostal/Charismatic theologies[10]

The rest of the essay will seek to assess critically and sympathetically the state of contemporary global theological reflection on the spirit(s) with a view to assessing the potential and the obstacles on the way towards a plural

---

4. Shults, "Theological Responses to Postmodernities," 1.
5. Cox, *Fire from Heaven*, 299–301.
6. See, e.g., Hossein, *Islamic Spirituality*.
7. See Wiebe, *God and Other Spirits*.
8. For a highly constructive proposal, see Yong, "Spirit-Filled Creation?," 173–225.
9. I have been helped by, among others, Kalu, "*Sankofa*," 135–52; Onyinah, "Deliverance as a Way of Confronting Witchcraft in Contemporary Africa," 181–202; for a wider source, see Kim, *Holy Spirit in the World*.
10. See my "Introduction," xiii–xviii.

paradigm. In order to help manage the wide and diverse perspectives and contributions, let us organize the discussion into four interrelated layers:

- Spirit(s) in the Cosmos
- Spirit(s) in Creation
- Spirit(s) in Society
- Spirit(s) in Salvation

THE SPHERES OF THE SPIRIT(S)

Spirit(s) in the Cosmos

Beginning the investigation with the role of spirits in the cosmos is to begin where the unitive paradigm—ironically—has been the most persistent in post-Enlightenment pneumatologies. Whereas premodern Christians and other religionists used to exorcize demons and spirits from human persons, post-Enlightenment scholars excised from the theologian's vocabulary all talk about the spiritual realities in the cosmos. The stated reason was that for the scientifically informed person any talk about spiritual realities such as demons, evil spirits—or even good spirits or angels—is simply impossible. One can see here the deep irony in that at the same time those theologians, unless they were completely "secularized," continued speaking of one "Absolute Spirit," God, the Spirit. In other words, theologians failed to see that positing this Big Spirit certainly violates the scientific paradigm even more than speaking of little spirits, as it were.[11]

It is not that all theologians were silent about spiritual beings that may inhabit the cosmos—even though many were! It is more about selectivity and denial. A striking example here is the pneumatology of Jürgen Moltmann. His profound and groundbreaking imagination of a "holistic pneumatology" in the celebrated *The Spirit of Life: A Universal Affirmation* is completely silent about anything referring to evil spirits, demons, or even angels![12] Even his extended treatments of suffering, ecological disasters, and

---

11. Behind the reluctance to speak of spiritual beings is also the rise in the twentieth century of various types of naturalisms—indeed, currently, one should speak of naturalisms (in the plural) because there are various types. For a detailed theological analysis and assessment, see my *Creation and Humanity*, ch. 2.

12. As the original German subtitle of his pneumatological magnum opus has it, *Eine Ganzheitliche Pneumatologie*; unfortunately the English translation does not capture this and gives a somewhat misleading idea: Moltmann, *Spirit of Life*.

socio-political injustices do not inspire any thinking on spirits and powers.[13] Yet this all happens in the context of seeking to loosen the Spirit from pietistic, ecclesiastical, and cultural strictures. Although Karl Barth provided one of the most profound contemporary discussions of angelology, he also saw the topic of the demonic and powers so inconsequential to theology that it sufficed to take a "quick, sharp glance" at it.[14] Paul Tillich speaks of the demonic in pneumatology as part of "Life and Its Ambiguities,"[15] but it stays at a very generic level. Pannenberg's world-embracing theological system knows no evil or demonic spirits, although quite interestingly he includes a short discussion on angels as seen through the pneumatological metaphor of "force field."[16] Even the criteria for the discernment of the spirit(s) are by and large missing in contemporary pneumatologies.[17] In sum: the leading contemporary theologies in the Global North follow almost exclusively the unitive paradigm.[18]

We have to turn to the theologians of the Global South to get some help in imagining a cosmos with diverse spirits, spiritual powers, spiritual realities.[19] According to the grand old man of African theologies, John Mbiti, on that continent:

> the universe is composed of visible and invisible parts. It is commonly believed that, besides God and human beings, there are other beings who populate the universe. These are the spirits. There are many types of spirits. God is their Creator, just as he is the Creator of all things. The spirits have a status between God and men, and are not identical with either. But people often speak about them in human terms, or treat them as though they had human characteristics such as thinking, speaking,

---

13. One reviewer of the *Spirit of Life* who obviously had studied the work in much detail, reports that for Moltmann it suffices to refer to evil spirits in passing in a couple of footnotes! Stibbe, "British Appraisal," 13.

14. Barth, *Church Dogmatics*, 3:369–531 (519).

15. Tillich, *Systematic Theology*, 3:102–106. As is well known, in the first volume of his *Systematic Theology*, Tillich also speaks of the demonic in terms of archetypes of depth psychology and in reference to an awareness of the suprahuman power of the demonic in literature.

16. Pannenberg, *Systematic Theology*, 2:102–9.

17. As noted concerning Moltmann's *Spirit of Life*, by Chan, "'Asian Review,'" 39. See further Tony Richie, "Demonization, Discernment, and Deliverance in Interreligious Encounter," 171–86.

18. For a critique and constructive proposal, see Bradnick, "Spirits and the Stars," 213–26.

19. For sample of representative texts with comments, see Kärkkäinen, *Holy Spirit and Salvation*, chs. 15 (Africa), 16 (Asia), and 17 (Latin America).

intelligence and the possession of power which they can use as they will. Because the spirits are created by God, they are subordinate to him and dependent on him, and some of them may be used by God to do certain things.[20]

That observation is not limited to Africa, but is also true in most Asian contexts.[21] In many locations of the Global South—radically differently from the post-Enlightenment Global North—"Myriads of spirits are reported . . . but they defy description almost as much as they defy the scientist's test tubes in the laboratory."[22] While mysterious and never totally exposed to human knowledge, the spirits are also particular and specific, as in many Asian lands: "The cult of the spirits and cosmic forces as the Bons (Tibet), Devas (South Asia), Nats (Burma), Phis (Thailand, Laos, Cambodia), the ancestral spirits (in the Confucian cultures of China, Korea, Vietnam, the Kalash in Pakistan) and the Kami (Japan) are an essential element of the spirituality of primal religions."[23]

Differently from Europe and North America, in the African context religion permeates all of life (very much similarly to the Asian and Latin American contexts).[24] Again, unlike believers in the Global North, where faith may often be mainly a matter of cultural alignment, rational believing, or pietistic cultivation, those Christians in the Global South, who live surrounded by the powers, invoke the power of the Holy Spirit as their resource and shield.[25] Here is a reason for the rapid "Pentecostalization" of Africa and the rapid advancement of Pentecostal/Charismatic spiritualities in other global contexts. Local theologians are prone to remark that this development is hardly surprising in light of the "secularizing" tendencies of much of theology imported from the Global North.[26]

Part of the cosmic orientation of all traditional and most contemporary cultures in the Global South involves deep and wide interaction between religions, which includes the discernment of spirits of religions. The Confucian concept of *ch'i* aptly illustrates the cosmic dimension of the Spirit of God, animating and vitalizing all life, including the material body.[27] Other interesting connections between the *ch'i* and the Holy Spirit have been

20. Mbiti, *Introduction to African Religion*, 70.
21. Lak, "Preface," vi.
22. Mbiti, *African Religions and Philosophy*, 78.
23. "Spirit at Work in Asia Today," 23.
24. Mbiti, *African Religions*, 2.
25. Imasogie, *Guidelines for Christian Theology in Africa*, 81.
26. Imasogie, *Guidelines for Christian Theology in Africa*, 81.
27. Lee, *Trinity in Asian Perspective*, 95–96.

recently discerned by the Korean theologian Koo D. Yun.[28] The work comparing the Mahayana Buddhist notion of *Sunyata* and the Christian concept of the Holy Spirit by another Asian American theologian, Amos Yong, belongs to the same genre.[29] Or think of the similarities and differences between the Shintoistic pantheistic traditions in Japan and some panentheistic Christian pneumatologies.[30] And so forth.

Spirit(s) in Creation

Although pneumatological cosmologies and discussion of powers is missing in much of mainline theology of the Global North, significant advances have been made in linking the Spirit of God to creation. This has happened both as a result of the rediscovery of biblical-theological resources and a robust engagement between theology and natural sciences. Rightly, the Roman Catholic feminist theologian Elizabeth Johnson remarks:

> Of all the activities that theology attributes to the Spirit, the most significant is this: the Spirit is the creative origin of all life. In the words of the Nicene Creed, the Spirit is *vivificantem*, vivifier or life-giver. This designation refers to creation not just at the beginning of time but continuously: the Spirit is the unceasing, dynamic flow of divine power that sustains the universe, bringing forth life.[31]

Not that this is a new and novel theological insight in itself; just consider for example the rich metaphors employed in medieval mystical traditions such as Hildegard of Bingen's "Greening" of the Spirit and St. Bernard of Clairvaux's "living water"[32] or the hymn to the Spirit, the Creator, attributed to none other than Thomas Aquinas, which speaks highly poetically of the Spirit's creative power throughout the cosmos.[33] What makes the current rediscovery of the Spirit's creative agency significant is that it puts the whole

---

28. Yun, *Holy Spirit and Ch'i (Qi)*.

29. Yong, *Pneumatology and the Christian-Buddhist Dialogue*.

30. Inoue, "Spirit and Spirits in Pantheistic Shintoism," 55–70.

31. Johnson, *Women, Earth and Creator Spirit*, 42. The late Canadian Baptist Clark Pinnock says the same in this way: "There is a cosmic range to the operations of the Spirit, the Lord and giver of life. . . . Spirit is the ecstasy that implements God's abundance and triggers the overflow of divine self-giving. Power of creation, the Spirit is aptly named 'Lord and giver of life' in the Nicene Creed. . . . The universe in its entirety is the field of its operations." See Pinnock, *Flame of Love*, 49–50.

32. See Dreyer, "Advent of the Spirit," 123–62.

33. In Donahoe, *Early Christian Hymns*, 156–59.

ministry, role, and work of the Spirit in a robust cosmic, evolutionary, and scientific context. Seeking to capture some of the rich potential of creational pneumatology, Moltmann, the most noted constructive theologian in that respect, employs a number of metaphors—some old, some new—to highlight the Spirit's creative presence in the world:[34]

- The formative metaphors: the Spirit as energy, as space, and as Gestalt
- The movement metaphors: the Spirit as tempest, as fire, and as love
- The mystical metaphors: the Spirit as source of light, as water, and as fertility

Theological imagination from the Global South has added many more important metaphors in theologians' desire to capture the many roles of the Spirit in the cosmos and creation. The Korean-born J. Y. Lee speaks of "[c]loth as a metaphor of the Spirit [that] protects and sustains all things on earth. Unlike the shield, a masculine metaphor of protection, it is closely associated with a feminine image in Asia. Women weave cloth and use it for the protection and decoration of the body." And, drawing also from the rich Confucian traditions, he continues: "The Spirit as *ch'i* also weaves through the entire cosmos and gives life. The Spirit is a weaver and a protector of all things on earth, for cloth is the symbol of her presence." Lee continues employing metaphors of mother, both human and animal, even a "kettle" related to cooking, "creating" food, and concludes: "In fact, the Spirit as *ch'i* is the vitality of the material principle, and the nourishment of soul is, in fact, the nourishment of the body."[35] These and many biblical ways of speaking of God in relation to the world through the Spirit operate with the idea of an "incomparable divine *presence*."[36]

The return to the biblical account of the *ruach Yahweh* as the life-principle, not detached from but rather energizing and supporting all life of the cosmos, including the physical/material, helped theology to build an engaging bridge with the scientific account of evolution and life.[37] While theologically not fully satisfactory in all accounts, Hegel's concept of the Spirit comes closer to the biblical understanding as the "term (*Geist*) combines the concept of rationality reflected in the English word 'mind' with

---

34. Moltmann, *Spirit of Life*, ch. 12.
35. Lee, *Trinity in Asian Perspective*, 104.
36. Shults, *Reforming the Doctrine of God*, 36.
37. See the important discussion in Moltmann, *Spirit of Life*, 40.

the dimension of the supermaterial bound up with our term 'spirit' . . . , an active subject, an activity, or a process."[38]

Working from these cues, Pannenberg has famously argued that the biblical notion of "God as spirit" might have consonance with the current scientific view of life as the function of "spirit/energy/movement," expressed as the concept of (force-)field.[39] "The presence of God's Spirit in his creation can be described as a field of creative presence, a comprehensive field of force that releases event after event into finite existence."[40] While contemporary physics definitely sees no need to resort to Divine Spirit to explain its fields, Pannenberg sees here—in keeping with the metaphysical origin of the field concept in ancient Greek philosophy in that *pneuma* was considered to be a very fine stuff that permeated all the cosmos and held everything together—an opening for a metaphysical, theological explanation.[41] The conception of the Divine Spirit in terms of "incomparable divine presence" or even as the "field" goes well with Moltmann's conception of Spirit as the creative Spirit of Life.[42] He expands the traditional idea of the "fellowship of the Spirit" to encompass the whole "community of creation" from the most elementary particles to atoms to molecules to cells to living organisms to animals to human beings to communities of humanity. In this "fellowship as process," all human communities are embedded in the ecosystems of the natural communities and live from the exchange of energy with them.[43] The cosmos is an interconnected web of creatures, big and small, brought to life and sustained continuously by the Divine Spirit.

However, something is missing here—not surprisingly in light of the observations above: The role of spirits and powers is not considered in these creation theologies of the Global North. Amos Yong rightly wonders if contemporary theologies, including religion-science conversations, are "[o]pen

38. Grenz, *Theology for the Community of God*, 82.

39. Pannenberg, "God as Spirit—and Natural Sciences," 783–94.

40. Pannenberg, *Introduction to Systematic Theology*, 194. The well-known critique by the physicist-priest Polkinghorne of some aspects of Pannenberg's use of "field" from M. Faraday (which, of course, has been quite radically revised since) does not materially invalidate his theological approach. Polkinghorne, "Wolfhart Pannenberg's Engagement with the Natural Sciences," 151–58. For a similar critique but also a highly creative constructive proposal, see Morales, "Vector Fields as the Empirical Correlate of the Spirit(s), 227–42.

41. Pannenberg, *Systematic Theology*, 2:81.

42. Moltmann, *God in Creation*, 9–13 (9). In the Christian East, more so than in the West, both in tradition and in contemporary theology, the linking of the Spirit with creation has been a rule and custom. For profound statements by the Russian-born Sergius Bulgakov, see *Comforter*, 220.

43. Moltmann, *Spirit of Life*, 225–26.

enough for proposing in the theology and science conversation a consideration of a spirit-filled cosmos?"[44] Hence, we have the challenge of how well plural pneumatologies might engage scientific interpretations of creation.[45] Some cautious attempts have been slowly taken by such leading experts as Philip C. Clayton;[46] the end results are yet to be seen.

Spirit(s) in Society

Not for nothing did the American Roman Catholic pneumatologist Fr. Kilian McDonnell, OSB, already decades ago, lament that both in "Protestantism and Catholicism, the doctrine of the Holy Spirit, or pneumatology, has to do mostly with private, not public experience" and that therefore pneumatology has lost connection with the rest of the world and life. Hence, in contemporary theology a definite turn is needed from "a theology of the Word to a theology of the World."[47] In that outlook, history, not only salvation history, is the sphere of the Spirit as well.[48]

Improvements to widen and make more inclusive the sphere of the Spirit, as already mentioned, are underway and are significant. Along with the sphere of creation, contemporary theology is also seeking ways to rediscover the role of the Spirit and spirits in history,[49] politics,[50] economics,[51] as well as the arts and entertainment.[52] Other significant similar efforts relate to integrating the Spirit into care of the environment,[53] gender equality,[54]

44. Yong, *Spirit of Creation*, 179. See also his analysis of common hermeneutical approaches to "the powers": *In the Days of Caesar*, 139–45.

45. Consider also the important emerging discussion of a program that has many intentions in common with what is called here plural cosmologies: Keller and Schneider (Eds.), *Polydoxy*. Also noteworthy are attempts by some Native people to create plural cosmologies, e.g., Cousins, "Mountains Made Alive," 497–510.

46. Clayton, "Spirit in Evolution and in Nature," 187–96.

47. McDonnell, "Determinative Doctrine of the Holy Spirit," 142. Thus the title of his recently released landmark work, *The Other Hand of God: The Holy Spirit as the Universal Touch and Goal*.

48. See Kovel, *History and Spirit* and the essay by Patrick Oden in this volume.

49. See Oden, "Chaos or Completion," 71–84.

50. Kim, "Spirits of the Political," 125–40.

51. Wariboko, "Spirits and Economics," 141–54.

52. Johnston, "Art and the Spiritual," 85–96

53. I construct a pneumatologically loaded theology of the flourishing of nature in my *Creation and Humanity*, ch. 8. For a more radical, semi-pantheist proposal, see Wallace, "Christian Animism, Green Spirit Theology, and the Global Crisis Today," 197–212.

54. Johnson, *She Who Is*; Prichard, *Sensing the Spirit*.

work,⁵⁵ and politics, including socio-political liberation and equality.⁵⁶ Some postcolonialists have joined the effort, claiming that "it will be necessary to understand immigration history, racism, hybridity, and hyphenated reality to get a glimpse of how a new pneumatology can emerge and address the issues of domination and imperialism in our context."⁵⁷

Historically it is good to note that these attempts to widen the sphere of pneumatology were importantly prepared by the earlier generation of theologians. Just consider Tillich's life- and culture-affirming theology in general and pneumatology in particular.⁵⁸ His profound discussion of "Life in Spirit" (third volume of *Systematic Theology*) expands and widens the Spirit's horizon from the inorganic to organic to personal to ecclesiastical to all the dimensions of society—arts, culture, or politics.⁵⁹ In all of this, Tillich considers the meaning of "The Spiritual Presence" in the human spirit, religion, culture, and morality, not to ignore Christology and the church! Similarly to his Lutheran colleague, the Dutch Reformed Hendrikus Berkhof attempted a powerful revision of his own tradition's theology in light of the heritage of Classical Liberalism and the new challenges of the twentieth-century context, envisioning the Spirit as the "vitality" of God, "God's inspiring breath by which he grants life in creation and re-creation."⁶⁰ Behind this attempt to loose the Spirit of God is the important line of the Reformed theological tradition going back to Abraham Kuyper⁶¹ and of course ultimately to Calvin and other early Reformers.

This is all good and significant, but the question arises: what about the powers and spirits? Again, mainline theologians, including feminists, other liberationists, and post-colonialists, do not have much to offer in terms of the plural paradigm. Walter Wink's program of "powers" is a delightful exception to this rule. New Testament scholar Wink argues that the powers are "the spiritualities of institutions, the 'within' of corporate structures and the inner essence of outer organizations of power." The outer aspect consists of "political systems, appointed officials, the 'chair' of an organization, laws. . . ."⁶² Although Wink definitely rejects the identification of these

---

55. Volf, *Work in the Spirit*.

56. Müller-Fahrenholz, *God's*; Comblin, *Holy Spirit and Liberation*.

57. Kim, *Holy Spirit, Chi, and the Other*, 2.

58. McDonnell, "Determinative Doctrine," 155.

59. Tillich, *Systematic Theology*, 3:14–15; this first chapter, at the beginning of his pneumatology, is titled "Life and Its Ambiguities."

60. Berkhof, *Doctrine of the Holy Spirit*, 14.

61. For a brief consideration of Kuyper's pneumatology, see Kärkkäinen, *Holy Spirit and Salvation*, 252–58.

62. Wink, *Naming the Powers*, 5.

powers with the traditional notion of "angels," "principalities and powers," as well as "Satan," for him, the powers, however, are "real." They are social, cultural, political, financial, global powers. If so, they must be "redeemed": originally the powers were good but became evil. The key to redeeming the powers is in the Jesus-kind of lifestyle: nonviolent, peaceful, and free. That is set against the "Domination system of the Powers" of the world.[63] Wink's strategy of "redeeming powers" is thus radically different from the biblical custom of exorcism—still prevalent in quarters of the Roman Catholic Church and among many Pentecostal/Charismatic Christians and a number of Global Church Christian communities.

We should commend Wink for a great service in exposing the modernist reductionism in a theological denial of powers. His desire to tackle the biblical text in light of Christian tradition and the post-Enlightenment world is to be acknowledged. What bothers me most is Wink's totally nonmetaphysical interpretation of powers. Whatever one thinks of the status of metaphysics in contemporary theology and philosophy, denying all metaphysical implications of the Christian idea of powers is unacceptable to me. The American Open Theist Gregory Boyd rightly critiques Wink and those likeminded, reminding us that not only in the biblical world but also in ancient cultures at large, as well as in the global cultures outside the North, people take spiritual realities as metaphysically real. In that outlook, "the good and evil, fortunate or unfortunate, aspects of life are to be interpreted largely as the result of good and evil, friendly or hostile, spirits warring against each other and against us," without at the same time denying "that evil is also a reality of the human heart and of human society."[64] While many of us would like to soften Boyd's overemphasis on a "warfare" mentality—which certainly, against his contention, is not the dominant model even in Scripture—the comment makes the needed plea for resisting the reductionism of modern theology. Why should we, following Wink, juxtapose the traditional (including its contemporary applications) "literal" understanding—despite its many problematic applications and experiences and its individualistic orientation—with the totally nonmetaphysical one? Couldn't a plural cosmology have them both?

---

63. Wink, *Engaging the Powers*; see p. 44 for the chart contrasting the two systems.
64. Boyd, *God at War*, 19. For a succinct summary of his argumentation, see ch. 1 in Boyd, *Satan and the Problem of Evil*.

Spirit(s) in Salvation

In traditional theology, *ordo salutis*, the "order of salvation," is the part of pneumatology that discusses in detail the interrelated aspects—or "steps," as it were—of the reception by men and women of the salvific benefits wrought by the Triune God. As mentioned, Christology represents the "objective," whereas pneumatology the "subjective" work of salvation. As a corrective, Moltmann's revisionist pneumatology argues forcefully—and rightly in my mind—that the beginning point of the *ordo salutis*, rather, is the holistic, ever-present, cosmic, and earthly Spirit of God. There is no place for dualism between earthly/spiritual, sacred/secular, individual/communal, and so forth.[65] The Spirit of God supports life and resists life-destroying acts and attitudes,[66] and everywhere facilitates liberation and inclusion.[67] It does not suffice to speak of "new birth" as a personal experience alone; it also has to do with the hope for the "rebirth" and renewal of the whole cosmos. Justification is as much about walking justly in the renewed mindset as about the forgiveness of sins. Sanctification is not merely about abstaining from sin but also about sanctity and honoring of life. Liberation, inclusivity, and human flourishing—both in happiness and sickness—are key values. Moltmann joins hands with a number of different types of liberation theologies as in them salvation can never be "spiritual" in a way that leaves behind the material, social, political—the "mundane."[68] It is not about leaving behind spirituality but rather living out a *Spirituality of Liberation*, to cite an important book title by Jon Sobrino, which as the subtitle puts it, leads *Toward Political Holiness*.[69]

For such renewed, healed, and empowered life to flourish, the Spirit's role as "The Charismatic Powers of Life" should be rediscovered.[70] To charismatic effects belongs freedom from bondage under the powers and healing, whether physical or mental. Similarly, empowerment and gifting are the workings of the charismatic energies. Here again, much help can be gained from the pneumatologies of the Global South. An important part of some African theologies is a distinctive "Spirit-Christology"[71] that "shows Jesus'

---

65. Moltmann, *Spirit of Life*, 84.
66. Moltmann, *Spirit of Life*, 86.
67. Moltmann, *Spirit of Life*, 101.
68. See Comblin, *Holy Spirit and Liberation*, 94–95, 99.
69. Sobrino, *Spirituality of Liberation*, 49.
70. Title of ch. 9 in Moltmann, *Spirit of Life*.
71. Bediako, *Christianity in Africa*, 176. For Spirit-Christologies and their implications, see Kärkkäinen, *Christ and Reconciliation*, ch. 8.

power over the world of spirits and his connectedness to the Holy Spirit."[72] Salvation in this outlook includes physical and mental healing as well as deliverance from evil powers and spirits.[73]

Where much work awaits Christian theologians is the careful engagement of other faith traditions and their visions of salvation.[74] Only then are we opening up to the demands and horizons of a truly plural pneumatological paradigm.

IN LIEU OF CONCLUSIONS: TASKS FOR THE FUTURE

In order for the pneumatological discourse of the mainline Global North to overcome its limitations and omissions, it needs a robust interdisciplinary and intercultural collaboration. To that matrix belongs also a sustained dialogue with scholars in various sciences. There is a new paradigm for understanding the nature of "matter" emerging among scientists, the form of which is yet to be seen. We already know that what in the past we took as "matter" is rather energy and movement. Theology should not naively assume, however, that this more elusive and less concrete way of envisioning what the world is made of would necessarily be an asset to religion, let alone to Christian theology. On the other hand, the move away from the modernist, somewhat static and fixed conception of reality towards a more becoming-oriented, complex, and "spirited" worldview at least makes room for diversity of interpretations.

Contemporary pneumatology is also badly in need of consultation with the theologians of the Global South. Interaction between theologians from North and South would facilitate comparing notes on the many promising advances regarding the loosing of the Divine Spirit, particularly with regard to the created reality and various segments of society.

A continuing robust dialogue with other living faiths and their pneumatologies and cosmologies may further fund Christian attempts to revise its own theological canons. However, I do not see much promise in the naive pluralistic theologies that not only dismiss the distinctive claims of Christian tradition but also deny the otherness of the religious Other. That tactic hardly represents hospitality. It is violence. We thus have the continuing deep and wide *theological* task: having made the move from a unitive to

---

72. Goergen, "Quest for the Christ of Africa."

73. See the important study by Oladipo, *Development of the Doctrine of the Holy Spirit in the Yoruba (African) Indigenous Christian Movement*.

74. See Part 2 of my *Spirit and Salvation*. For salvific resources in other religions, see my *Christ and Reconciliation*, ch. 15.

plural pneumatologies and cosmologies, we must negotiate carefully the relation between the Spirit of God and other powers. While there is a lot of enthusiasm concerning the shift to plural pneumatologies, in some instances the move itself is celebrated to the point that the contours of a distinctively *Christian* theological understanding of the Divine Spirit are blurred. The same task of course awaits pneumatologists from other traditions—Jewish, Islamic, "secular," and others. A truly pluralist pneumatological paradigm facilitates distinctive identities of traditions and their continuing, mutually learning encounters. After all, *spiritus ubi vult spirat* (John 3:8).

CHAPTER 2

The Leaning Tower of Pentecostal Ecclesiology

Reflections on the Doctrine of the Church on the Way

FIRST WORDS

I HAVE BEEN TO too many conferences and symposia in which responses, rather than being responses to other presentations, have been self-contained constructive proposals with little or no relation to the task given originally to the speaker. Hence, as soon as I was invited to serve as one of the respondents to the presentations at this conference, I decided to do just that, namely *to respond*.

I was also helped by the circumstances. For the past six weeks I have been travelling with my wife in various parts of Europe and have received the conference presentations by email sporadically. Literally, I have been reading and reflecting on them on the way. Traveling from one country to another, I have been reminded of the journey-like nature of all theology, including the theology of the church. As long as theology is *in via*, it has the potential for development, self-correction, and learning.

Moreover, as I visited the Leaning Tower of Pisa in Italy, it appeared to me that that monument may provide me with an appropriate metaphor: similarly to that leaning tower, Pentecostal theology has been leaning in certain directions from the beginning. What makes the tower of Pisa an interesting photography target is that it seems to be leaning no matter from which angle you are looking at it! Now it is time to find out what these directions have been and why it is that a *leaning position*—rather than a fixed one—may be to the advantage of this incipient doctrine of the church. In other words, in light of the presentations given in this conference, I seek to discern the directions in which Pentecostal ecclesiology has been and is currently leaning.

Peter Althouse succinctly describes the current status of Pentecostal ecclesiology; his evaluation serves as the springboard for further developments as well: "Although Pentecostalism is now over a century old, its theology of the church is sorely underdeveloped. In practice, Pentecostal churches eclectically borrow from other theological traditions and apply their practices in pragmatic and technical ways, but with little understanding of their philosophical and theological implications."[1] That said, it is also true that tentatively and nonthematically, Pentecostal ecclesiology contains a lot of promise as its core values are being rediscovered, developed, and fine-tuned.

In my response, I will first offer some remarks on directions and developments taken by the conference contributors when it comes to various aspects of the Fivefold-Gospel-driven ecclesiology. In the second part, I will seek to give some advise as to what kinds of tasks lie ahead of us as we continue constructing an authentic ecclesiology, whether based on the Full Gospel scheme or not.

LOOKING AT THE LEANING TOWER FROM FIVE ANGLES

With Chris Thomas, I was at a World Council of Church's consultation on mission in Santiago de Chile in 2003. In one of the many personal conversations, Chris turned to me and said, "Veli-Matti, we should do something more about constructing a Fivefold-Gospel-based Pentecostal doctrine of the church." As soon as I heard this, I knew such a task is important and relevant for Pentecostal theologians. I also knew that Chris and others had already labored in that field. Since that conversation, the thought has never left me, and in my teaching of systematic theology at Fuller Theological Seminary, the University of Helsinki, and elsewhere, I have routinely mentioned that Pentecostal ecclesiology could be developed along these lines—but that that work has only been initiated and that I do not know what its results will be!

However, against my initial high hopes concerning the potential of the Fivefold Gospel as the basis for an ecclesiology, a number of doubts and

---

1. Althouse, "Ascension—Pentecost—Eschaton," 225.

questions have arisen in my mind. Ken Archer helpfully lists the typical challenges faced by any effort to build ecclesiology on the foundations of the Full Gospel scheme: "[I]t does not address all the theological loci. Or that the Fivefold gospel can no longer function in the same way as it did in the early classical period of Pentecostalism. Furthermore, some argue that we must speak of Pentecostalisms not Pentecostalism and such a work would be too narrow and only be representative of a narrow USA version of Pentecostalism."[2] Furthermore, with reference to my own writings, Archer rightly notes that "interestingly, even though he affirms the Fivefold gospel as important for informing and shaping ecclesiology, he never explains how it does so."[3] "Similarly," Archer writes, "Frank Macchia never identifies or explains the fivefold marks of the church beyond reasserting the Fivefold gospel. How does the Fivefold gospel shape ecclesiology beyond offering a Pentecostal commentary upon the marks of the church mentioned by the Nicene-constantinopolitan Creed?"[4]

At this point of investigation, I think it is premature to pass a final judgment with regard to whether an effort to build an ecclesiology on the basis of the Fivefold Gospel is feasible or not. That assessment can only be made once we have more materials in place. What helps us in this discerning process is to highlight some of the directions—leanings, if you will—along which Pentecostal theologians in this conference have developed main themes of the Full Gospel. Let me make four brief observations to that effect:

First, I am encouraged by the way Jesus's role as Redeemer and Sanctifier has been developed in these presentations. Rather than delving into the typical debates about justification or sanctification, typical in much of Evangelical and Protestant theologies, these writers aim at an inclusive, holistic, and socially-politically relevant account of salvation. In this regard, I find Archer's preference for "Pentecostal *Soteriological* Ecclesiology"—instead of the typical *charismatic* ecclesiology—quite intriguing and promising. Those two ecclesiologies are complementary and belong to the texture of Pentecostal spirituality. I look forward to hearing more about that in the future. Matthias Wenk's search for "a theology of holiness that would help combat the dangers of individualism so rampant in many forms of Pentecostalisms" highlights the biblical link between holiness and community, including the principle of inclusiveness, as well as holiness and ethics at the personal and

2. Archer, "Fivefold Gospel and the Mission of the Church," 32.
3. Archer, "Fivefold Gospel and the Mission of the Church," 26.
4. Archer, "Fivefold Gospel and the Mission of the Church," 28.

communal levels.⁵ According to him, "From its very beginning Pentecostalism was known for its inclusive power, its potency in overcoming ethnic, gender and social barriers between people."⁶ Dario López's subtitle, "The God of Life and the Community of Life," is indicative of the desire of several contributors to expand and make more inclusive Pentecostal pneumatology and ecclesiology, especially the vision for the Pentecostal understanding of the church as liberationist, in search of justice, equality, and credible public witness.⁷ The figure of J. Moltmann looms large behind several presentations—even where his name is not mentioned. These inclusive soteriological visions as the context for ecclesiology offer a shining example of the right direction in which Pentecostal ecclesiology could be leaning—and at times is leaning—as long as it is not taken over by the opposite forces. Wynand de Kock does a valuable service to Pentecostal theology by highlighting the significance of two competing hermeneutics in the Pentecostal understanding of redemption. One is communal, turned towards inclusivity, openness to the world, and life-affirming; the other one is individualistic, exlusivistic, escapist, and blind to social implications such as racism and sexism.

Second, the two essays on Jesus's role as Spirit-Baptizer by Daniela Augustine and Simon Chan were the biggest surprises in terms of what I anticipated.⁸ Rather than focusing on typical Pentecostal themes related to Spirit-baptism and the "initial evidence," these essays focus on constructing a pneumatological ecclesiology in the context of ecumenical discussion, particularly drawing from Orthodox writers. That approach has huge ecumenical implications. Those developments resemble in many ways Macchia's groundbreaking work on expanding and making more comprehensive the notion of Spirit-baptism in his landmark work *Baptized in the Spirit*. In many ways, these two essays could have joined the lead article of Archer in providing a wider perspective and context for reflections on Pentecostal ecclesiology.

Third, Kimberly Alexander's idea of "The Healing Home Model" reminds me of Luther's idea of the church as the hospital for the incurably sick.⁹ Luther's theology was based on the idea of the Christian as the "Christ" to the neighbor because of the presence of Christ in the Spirit through faith (*in ipsa fide Christus adest*). This idea has an affinity with the Eastern

---

5. Wenk, "Church as Sanctified Community," 104.

6. Wenk, "Church as Sanctified Community," 105.

7. López Rodriguez, "Redeeming Community," 69–83.

8. Augustine, "Empowered Church," 157–82; Chan, "Jesus as Spirit-Baptizer," 139–56.

9. Alexander, "Pentecostal Healing Community," 183–206.

soteriological concept of participation and union, a theme mentioned by Archer,[10] among others. Furthermore, Alexander's linking of healing to the Eucharist is a theme well worth further exploration; it is an ancient belief of Christians that whatever other forms of healing there might be, the Table of the Lord is healing medicine not only to the "soul" but also to the body.[11] Importantly also, both Alexander and Opoku Onyinah question the ruling modernist epistemological model, which has helped much of mainline Christian spirituality miss the notion of healing, exorcism, and other miraculous works of salvation. For Onyinah the African cultures' openness to healing and "spiritual dimensions" serves as a critique of Western reductionism,[12] whereas for Alexander's American context, postmodernity is the reminder of the limits of the Enlightenment-based ideology. A proper theology of healing also calls for a robust theological anthropology, a theme yet to be developed by Pentecostals. Listening to the voices from the Global South helps Western Pentecostals seek a theological account of the human being and God's salvific vision, which in a nonthematic way was present in early Pentecostalism but which has subsequently been in danger of being forgotten.

Fourth, new directions are also being sought in the two essays focused on Jesus's role as the Soon-Coming King. In what I find probably theologically the most pregnant statement of the relationship between the Triune God, eschatology, and the church, Macchia writes:

> Eschatology thus qualifies the life and ministry of the church precisely because the church is constituted by the Spirit. The church does not administer Spirit baptism, Spirit baptism administers the church. Moreover, the church is not founded by Christ and the apostles and then granted the Holy Spirit as an added bonus or supplemental gift. The church is rather constituted by the outpouring and presence of the Spirit.[13]

In other words, the church is not first established by Christ and then—in an analogy of the Christmas Tree—decorated by the tinsel of the Spirit to make it more appealing. Rather, the pneumatological moment is as important as the christological one. The Father uses the two hands—Christ and the Spirit—in all aspects of his work in the world, including the church. This triune movement into which the church is graciously called and included is eschatological: the Father is showing himself to be faithful to his creation

---

10. Archer, "Fivefold Gospel and the Mission of the Church," 16.
11. Alexander, "Pentecostal Healing Community," 198–99.
12. Oniyah, "Pentecostal Healing Communities," 207–24.
13. Macchia, "Church of the Latter Rain," 249.

as he redeems eternal promises made in Christ in the power of the Spirit. Hence, eschatology is about the kingdom of God, the righteous rule of the Triune God. Pentecostal theology has been leaning towards this orientation since its inception as it envisioned salvation in terms of the Full Gospel. However, it lost this inclusive and comprehensive vision as it aligned itself with conservative Protestantism.

Materially, the same trinitarian eschatological approach is present in the opening sentence of Althouse's essay. He incorporates into his reflections the important role of *ascension* of Christ, a theme too often missed by Pentecostals: "The gift of the Spirit promised in the ascension of Christ and fulfilled in the Spirit's descent, inaugurated the church as the people of God under the eschatological reign of the Lord Jesus Christ (Acts 2:2–4)."[14] Indeed, ascension rather than resurrection is the "climax of Jesus' history."[15] It is the ascended Christ who is the agent of the Pentecostal pouring out of the Spirit as the harbinger of the end times. No other contemporary theologian has developed the theme of ascension as powerfully as Karl Barth, whose insights are offered in the last part of his *Church Dogmatics* (IV/1). Macchia, Althouse, and other Pentecostal theologians who are familiar with Barth could draw valuable lessons from his masterful exposition.

Having looked briefly at the ways conference presentations are developing key themes of the Fivefold Gospel ecclesiology, let me acknowledge and challenge Archer's proposal, based on the earlier work of Thomas that seeks to integrate the fivefold ministry gifts of Christ (Eph 4:11–13) and sacraments:[16]

- Jesus is the Savior. The church as the Redeemed Community and the ecclesiastical sacramental ordinance is Water Baptism. To this I would add apostles and the *apostolic* function of the community.

- Jesus is the Sanctifier. The church as a Holy Community and Footwashing is the ecclesiastical sign. To this I would add teachers and the *teaching* function of the community.

- Jesus is Spirit Baptizer. The church as a Charismatic Community and the ecclesiastical sign is Glossolalia. To this I would add the prophets and the *charismatic* function of the community.

- Jesus is the Healer. The church as a Healing Community with the ecclesiastical sign of praying for the sick with the laying on of hands

---

14. Althouse, "Ascension—Pentecost—Eschaton," 224.
15. Althouse, "Ascension—Pentecost—Eschaton," 229.
16. See Thomas, "Pentecostal Theology in the Twenty-First Century," 3–19.

and anointing with oil. To this I would add pastors and the *pastoral* function.

- Jesus is Coming King. The church as a Missionary Community with the Lord's Supper serving as the ecclesiastical sign. To this I would add the evangelists and the *evangelistic* function of the community.

My questions to Thomas include these: (1) I need help in discerning the logic of the linking of Jesus's various roles with specific sacramental signs; or else, this link seems to me somewhat artificial and haphazard. (2) The way sacraments and gifts are mixed in this scheme calls for clarification. For example, what is the basis for linking footwashing with the teaching gift? (3) How is *glossolalia* to be understood as the "missionary sign"? Aren't all the gifts "missionary" signs, say, healing and words of wisdom? With regard to Archer's expansion of Thomas's scheme, I will add a few more questions: (4) The list of "offices" or gifts of ministry listed in Ephesians 4 hardly is a comprehensive list, any more than any of the lists of the gifts. Even if it were, the logic of linking these offices with specific dimensions of ecclesiology calls for more explanation. Just to take one example: Isn't the apostolic task of the church much more comprehensive than that related to salvation and water baptism?

TASKS FOR THE DEVELOPMENT OF PENTECOSTAL ECCLESIOLOGY

Robust Trinitarian Theology

The first urgent task for Pentecostal ecclesiological work, already started in several essays, is a robust trinitarian vision for the church. This plea was made passionately by Chan. Similarly, de Kock reminded us of the ancient idea, prevalent especially in Eastern theology, of the church as the image of the Trinity and the implications of the perichoretic indwelling of persons into an inclusive view of redemption.[17] Above, I mentioned the important contributions to this theme by Macchia and Althouse.

Now, why is a robust trinitarian theology so essential to the task of constructing an ecclesiology? In my understanding, trinitarian theology offers resources for several interrelated tasks. Let me just outline three of those:

---

17. de Kock, "Church as a Redeemed, Un-Redeemed, and Redeeming Community," 52.

1. The Whole History of Jesus: A Trinitarian Spirit-Christology helps rediscover the whole history of Jesus as the background and power for the coming to being and continued existence of the church. What ancient creeds miss in their otherwise healthy trinitarian orientation is the lack of focus on the earthly life of Jesus. As Moltmann pointedly remarks, in the creeds, between the clauses "conceived of the virgin Mary" and "suffered under Pontius Pilate" there is only a comma! The teachings, healings, exorcisms, invitation to sinners and outcasts, baptism with the Holy Spirit, and inauguration of the kingdom are left out. Pentecostal Spirit-Christology, with its accent on Jesus as Healer and Baptizer with the Spirit, could be a God-sent corrective. The full force of that rediscovery just needs to be added to ecclesiology.

2. Spirit-Christology: Against misunderstandings prevalent among poorly informed observers of Pentecostalism, the Pentecostal movement does not represent pneumatocentrism. Its distinctive feature is a thoroughgoing Spirit-Christology. I am using the term Spirit-Christology in a nontechnical sense, meaning that I do not mean by it any specific type of Spirit-Christology as those are available in contemporary theology. I simply mean the integral, robust mutual conditioning of the work of the Son and Spirit throughout the Gospels and its development in much of patristic theology, both Eastern and Western. In everything that the Son does, the Spirit is present and an agent and vice versa—and this in a healthy trinitarian context.

3. The Role of the Father: Trinitarian theology may also help Pentecostal theology and ecclesiology rediscover the importance of the first article of the creed, that on the Father and the Father's work in creation and in the world. There is some truth to the claim of the Anglican charismatic Tom Smail, noted by Chan, who speaks of *The Forgotten Father* in much of Pentecostal theology. Chan's suggestion of turning to Orthodox trinitarian understanding in which the monarchy of the Father is at the center is worth exploring; most Pentecostals so far have been turned on by social trinitarianism. Be that as it may, trinitarian theology fosters a robust creation theology. Creation theology, in part, strengthens holistic theology and ecclesiology. The following statement by Althouse sounds very promising to me: "Creation itself is the focus of hope for its eschatological renewal in that the Spirit depicted as a 'violent wind [that] came from heaven and filled the whole house', alludes to the creation narrative of Genesis when the Spirit of God (wind) broods over the waters (Gen. 1.2)."[18]

---

18. Althouse, "Ascension—Pentecost—Eschaton," 224.

Communion Ecclesiology

If there is any theme in contemporary ecumenical ecclesiological discussion about which there is virtual unanimity, it is the importance of *koinonia*, communion. Under the guidance of the Orthodox John Zizioulas, current theology has rediscovered the biblical and patristic notion of the church as *koinonia*. In Pentecostal parlance, this is called the church as the *fellowship*. Now, the English term "fellowship" is of course shallow and almost meaningless. But as a translation from the biblical term *koinonia* it is, as *Lumen Gentium* # 9 says, a powerful claim according to which God did not intend to save persons as individuals but rather as a bonded people. The beginning chapters of the Book of Acts, dear to Pentecostals, provide us with a powerful resource. In the long-standing international dialogue between Roman Catholics and Pentecostals, a landmark document was produced, titled *Perspectives on Communion*. It makes great reading for both Pentecostals and others.

Trinity and communion belong together. The eternal love relationship between Father, Son, and Spirit represents the primary mode of communion. As Zizioulas says, the Christian God does not exist first as "one" but as three, persons-in-relation. The church is the image of God. A trinitarian communion theology is the best medicine for the rampant individualism of the cultures of the Global North.

Theology of Charisms and the Charismatic Structure of the Church

In the conference presentations, surprisingly, there is a conspicuous lack of discussion on charisms as an integral part of the life and mission of the church as well as development of the theme of the charismatic structure of the church. Macchia begins that discussion with reference to Hans Küng's highly important insights in his landmark work *The Church*. Much more is needed in this area in order for a robust theology of charisms to emerge.

A fruitful way—again in keeping with a trinitarian Spirit-Christology—is the link between not only charisms and Pentecost but also charisms and the *ascension* of Christ, a theme opened up by Althouse. According to Eph 4, it is the ascended Christ who gives gifts to the church, gifts having to do with church offices. Ernst Käsemann, the former-generation NT scholar, famously claimed that these gifts—call them also charisms—are nothing less than participation in the power and continuing ministry of the ascended Christ in the church. Hence, the gifts, offices, charisms are both christological and pneumatic in nature.

BASIC QUESTIONS OF THE ECCLESIALITY OF THE CHURCH

Behind the question of the ecclesiality of the church is simply the question of what makes the church, church, i.e., the conditions of the church. Free Churches, among which Pentecostalism is usually counted, have a vastly different interpretation from both the Roman Catholic and Orthodox Churches; and there is a different orientation even between Free Churches and Mainline Protestants. The questions of sacraments and episcopacy loom large in those debates.

Part of this discussion is the question of the marks of the church, a theme mentioned briefly by Daniel Castelo and Augustine.[19] Archer refers to Macchia's idea of the basic features of the Fivefold Gospel as the "ecclesiological marks."[20]

A number of potentially fruitful themes emerge out of the investigation into the marks of the church. Let me just mention two: (1) It could be claimed that apostolicity is a defining feature of Pentecostal spirituality and ecclesiology. It is not for nothing that from the beginning Pentecostals have often identified themselves as *apostolic* churches. Apostolicity for Pentecostals means continuity with the apostolic church of the Book of Acts. (2) It may be the case that what other traditions, particularly Roman Catholics, call "catholicity," in Pentecostal parlance is called the Full Gospel, i.e., a Gospel that is "whole," not lacking anything, as the Greek term literally says.

I find Castelo's "turn" to imagination as a way of doing ecclesiology a most intriguing and promising move. What other "method" would fit in so smoothly with the continuing, Spirit-led reflection on the nature and mission of the Christian community for the movement born of the Spirit!

---

19. Castelo, "Improvisational Quality of Ecclesial Holiness," 87–104.
20. Archer, "Fivefold Gospel and the Mission of the Church," 28.

CHAPTER 3

Teaching Global Theology in a Comparative Mode

THE PURPOSE OF THIS chapter is to reflect on and resource attempts to revamp the teaching of systematic/doctrinal/constructive theology in a way comparative in nature. I am approaching the task of making theological education more globally sensitive through the lens of interfaith relevance and religious plurality. To further trim down my canvas, I am working from the perspective of my own academic field, which is systematic (/doctrinal/ constructive) theology. Along with standard systematic theology courses, in which I engage every major doctrinal locus with some relevant insights from other religions, I also co-teach a graduate-level comparative course titled "World Religions in Christian Perspective." That course consists of about two-thirds basic introduction to fundamental teachings and traditions of Islam, Buddhism, and Hinduism, and one-third engaging with Judeo-Christian teachings. The latter course naturally leans much more easily to a comparative mode. What is, however, a much wider and deeper challenge to universities, divinity schools, and seminaries (which already are offering separate courses on world religions) is the willingness to reconsider all theology courses from the perspective of religious plurality. Approaching the topic from my own discipline, I also understand that there are specific concerns and issues pertinent to biblical and historical studies as well as ministerial courses. I leave that refinement to my colleagues.

In order to locate my reflections, let me share briefly how I came to be convinced of the necessity of teaching theology in a comparative mode. Personal narratives as the way of introduction go beyond niceties and are therefore an integral part of doing theology. While finishing my theological education in Europe, focusing on Ecumenics and following a typical Continental model with a heavy emphasis on studying theological traditions, I moved with my family to Thailand to teach theology for Asian students. As a naive and eager fledgling theologian in a new environment, I thought it necessary to first learn the language in order to gain a deeper access to the culture. Beginning to teach theology in Thai for Thai students was quite a bit of a learning experience as well. Later, returning to Europe for a few years, I continued rethinking the challenge posed by global diversity and religious plurality. My training in ecumenics focused much on learning how to dialogue with and encounter the Other. This led to a commitment to long-term work with the World Council of Churches (WCC) both in inter-Christian and interfaith "Ecumenics"; although often kept at arm's length from each other, these two have much in common and feed each other. After moving to teach in the United States more than a decade ago while continuing my post also at the University of Helsinki, I became engaged in enterprises such as the Association of Theological Schools (ATS) interfaith education project. This has helped me compare notes and learn from distinguished colleagues and sister schools. At the same time, my international doctoral students have further taught me valuable lessons about diversity.

The structure of this chapter consists of three sections. The first part seeks to reorient the task and meaning of theological education in light of religious plurality. Based on this challenge, the second part is devoted to reimagining the implications for theological education that adopting such a comparative, dialogical mode would have. The final part highlights a number of different types of resources I have found useful, both in terms of pedagogy and sources. Knowing that my colleagues in their chapters are presenting a number of other resources, I will focus on those with which I am most familiar, produced by the processes in which I have had an opportunity to participate over the years.

RE-ORIENTING THEOLOGICAL EDUCATION

A current document-in-the-making sponsored by the World Council of Churches, "Religious Plurality and Christian Self-Understanding," reminds us of the most prominent challenge the Christian church faces in the beginning of the third millennium:

> Today Christians in almost all parts of the world live in religiously plural societies. Persistent plurality and its impact on their daily lives are forcing them to seek new and adequate ways of understanding and relating to peoples of other religious

traditions . . . All religious communities are being reshaped by new encounters and relationships . . . There is greater awareness of the interdependence of human life, and of the need to collaborate across religious barriers in dealing with the pressing problems of the world. All religious traditions, therefore, are challenged to contribute to the emergence of a global community that would live in mutual respect and peace.[1]

Prophetically anticipating the future that lay ahead, Paul Tillich is reported to have confessed, just few days before his death, that if he had the opportunity to rewrite his three-volume *Systematic Theology*, he would do so engaging widely with other world religions. This was due to his brief exposure at the end of his life to some forms of Japanese Buddhism, as well as the influence of his famed Romanian religious studies colleague, Mircea Eliade.[2] One wonders what Tillich's *magnum opus* would have looked like had he been given a chance to rewrite it with religious plurality in mind. What's more, how different would the rest of the presentations of Christian doctrine, ethics, and philosophy have been if they had been written with the same goal in mind! The fact is that even in the beginning of the third millennium one cannot find any full-scale presentations of Christian doctrine or ethics in which other faith traditions are an integral part of the discussion along with the best of Judeo-Christian tradition.[3]

While there is no need for finger-pointing, we theological educators bear much of the responsibility for this state of affairs. Hence, the menu for training Christian theologians and ministers for the diverse global world needs to be expanded in a way that makes learning about and comparing Christianity with the religious Other an integral part of the task. This is more than merely taking elective—or even a couple of mandatory—courses in world religions, the importance of which in itself should not be understated. (I take it for granted that every divinity school requires at least a minimum of courses about other religions as part of the standard curriculum.)

Contributions from three interrelated academic fields of inquiry are needed to enrich, challenge, and reshape the current theological pedagogy and content, namely comparative religion/religious studies, theology of religions, and comparative theology. Comparative religion (along with the related but distinct fields of the history of religions and other disciplines in religious studies, phenomenology of religions, and social scientific study

---

1. "Religious Plurality and Christian Self-Understanding," #2, 3.

2. Tillich, *Future of Religions*, 91.

3. My own long-term project, *Constructive Christian Theology for the Pluralistic World* (2013–2017) seeks to correct that lacuna.

of religions) seeks to identify, analyze, and compare "ideas, words, images and acts, historical developments—as found in two or more traditions or strands of tradition."[4] Christian theology of religions seeks to reflect critically and sympathetically on the theological meaning of religions in the economy of God.[5] "Theology of religions is that discipline of theological studies which attempts to account theologically for the meaning and value of other religions. Christian theology of religions attempts to think theologically about what it means for Christians to live with people of other faiths and about the relationship of Christianity to other religions."[6] While in principle there could be theologies of religions from the point of view of any religion (for example, Islam), the Christian tradition has so far excelled in this enterprise.[7] Theology of religions, however, can get us only so far for reasons that are well known, such as that it tends to stay at too generic a level, and that it may fail to engage the Other from the perspective of that Other's tradition, and so forth.[8] Hence, in recent years, a complementary and more focused way of engaging in mutual dialogue among religious traditions has been attempted under the rubric of comparative theology, which, on the one hand, builds on the discipline of comparative religions that seeks to compare theologies from different religious traditions, and on the other hand, is a theological enterprise that studies two or more religious traditions by focusing on certain specific topics from the perspective of a certain confession.[9] In sum, comparative theology gleans resources not only from Christian theology and theology of religions but also from comparative religion.

RE-IMAGINING THEOLOGICAL EDUCATION

But is a comparative and dialogical approach feasible and useful? Doesn't it rather lead into confrontation and violence? Shouldn't the academic

---

4. Clooney, *Comparative Theology*, 9.

5. The Roman Catholic Jacques Dupuis preferred to name it "theology of religious pluralism." See his monumental work, *Toward a Christian Theology of Religious Pluralism*.

6. Kärkkäinen, *Introduction to the Theology of Religions*, 20.

7. For discussion of Muslim theology of religions in dialogue with Christian traditions, see the work of my former doctoral student Lewis Winkler, *Contemporary Muslim and Christian Responses to Religious Plurality*.

8. For a penetrating critique of theology of religions, see Fredricks, *Faith among Faiths*; Schebera, "Comparative Theology," 7–18.

9. Tracy, "Comparative Theology," 446.

preparation of religious professionals rather have the goal of negating differences among faith traditions as a way to a pluralistic society?[10]

Whereas comparative religion seeks to be "neutral" with regard to faith commitments and to look "objectively" at the features of religious traditions, North American Catholic theologian Francis X. Clooney, the leading expert in comparative theology, asserts that this field—which is "*comparative* and *theological* from beginning to end—marks acts of faith seeking understanding which are rooted in a particular faith tradition but which, from that foundation, venture into learning from one or more other faith traditions. This learning is sought for the sake of fresh theological insights that are indebted to the newly encountered tradition/s as well as the home tradition."[11] Comparative theology is robustly Christian theology and is committed to its traditions and its contemporary expressions.

There is, thus, a deep built-in dynamic between unwavering commitment to one's own tradition and a bold openness to dialogical engagement and learning from others. "In our religiously diverse context, a vital theology has to resist too tight a binding by tradition, but also the idea that religious diversity renders strong claims about truth and value impossible."[12] Hence, comparative theology, similarly to Christian theology—as long as it is both *Christian,* rather than a "pan-religious" mixing of aspects of insights from here and there,[13] as well as *theological,* rather than a sociological description of church practices or merely an analysis of human interpretations of human religiosity—is both an act of faith and a spiritual practice.[14] In this way, it does not deny or compromise its status as an academic discipline which follows the strict procedures and principles of any similar academic field in the humanities.

An important part of this task is to "inscribe within the Christian theological tradition theological texts from outside it, and to (begin to) write Christian theology only out of that newly composed context."[15] Unlike the

10. This section as a whole depends heavily on my *Christ and Reconciliation,* 21–29.

11. Clooney, *Comparative Theology,* 10. "Comparative theology must not be confused with comparative religion, since faith is a necessary and explicit factor in the former and not in the latter, where its influence might even be ruled out. But the fields need not be separated entirely, since comparative theology still has to measure up to expected disciplinary standards regarding the religions being compared" (12).

12. Clooney, *Comparative Theology,* 8.

13. This is the fallacy of Smart and Konstantine, *Christian Systematic Theology in a World Context,* whose work seeks to develop a Christian-based more-or-less generic account of some key doctrinal themes. For a discussion and critique, see Kärkkäinen, *Trinity,* ch. 16.

14. For fine insights, see Clooney, *Comparative Theology,* 10–11.

15. Clooney, *Theology after Vedānta,* 7.

theology of religion's more generic approach, comparative theology makes every effort to undertake a detailed consideration of topics in diverse religious traditions. "It is detailed, deeply reflexive, self-corrective in the course of its own investigation, even in regard to its basic questions, methods, and vocabulary."[16]

One may hear the objection that it is only Christianity (and perhaps Judaism) that is "theological" strictly speaking. While it is true that as an academic discipline "theology" is by and large limited to the Christian sphere,[17] this is not to deny that in some qualified sense it is appropriate and useful to speak of "theologies" of different living faiths. Clooney makes the compelling case for such an opinion. He argues for "Hindu theology and Hindu comparative theology, though without arguing that 'Hindu theology' is exactly like Christian theology."[18] Hence, he states that his choice of texts from various Hindu traditions presume the possibility of making theological comparisons because "Hindu traditions such as Mimamsa[19] and Vedanta are best described as 'theological.'" Furthermore, not only is it the case that the faithful in each tradition have a "faith," but it is also true that, to a growing extent, they are aware of the growing diversity and thus the need to engage others.[20]

Scholars engaged in the enterprise of comparative theology come from two different backgrounds.[21] Some are trained as scholars of religions with the openness to learning about theology, while others are versed in theology with the desire to become acquainted with basics of other religions. An example of a theologian who has robustly taken the comparative approach is the former Oxford University divinity professor Keith Ward, who has launched the most ambitious and wide-reaching project in comparative theology ever attempted by a theologian. His four-volume work focuses on revelation, creation and God, human nature, and community, and seeks to develop a robustly Christian account of these four key loci in intense and detailed dialogue with Judaism, Islam, Buddhism, and Hinduism. He rightly describes his project as "a systematic Christian theology, undertaken

---

16. Clooney, "Comparative Theology," 521–22.
17. See Moltmann, *Experiences in Theology*, 43.
18. Clooney, *Comparative Theology*, 78.
19. A liturgical ritual tradition in Hinduism.
20. Clooney, *Comparative Theology*, 78.
21. For an up-to-date and highly useful mapping out and analysis of the most important contributions to comparative theology, see Clooney, *Comparative Theology*, ch. 3.

in a comparative context."[22] In other words, it is an "open orthodoxy," a faithful, open-minded, and developing construction of Christian faith.[23]

Systematicians and other theologians of course face the great challenge of overcoming lacunae in the detailed knowledge of religions. For example, Ward admits throughout his project that his knowledge of religions is limited in that it is based on careful reading of texts, along with some important personal contacts. In my case, only Buddhism—Theravada tradition, to be more precise—is familiar at a more personal and experience-based level from the years I spent in Thailand as a teacher of Christian theology. Despite the fact that I am fluent in Thai and can thus read many Buddhist writings inaccessible to Western scholars, I still woefully remain an outsider. However, having firsthand exposure to one specific tradition should also transfer to the way one studies other traditions. As a continuing student of Hinduism, Islam, and Judaism, I read their texts differently from the way I did before my exposure living with Buddhists as a young theologian.

In order for the comparative approach to be *comparative*, and hence useful and interesting, one has to resist the modernist fallacy of the "common core" and "rough parity" of religions. Modernist ideology does not honor the Otherness of the Other and thus fails to prepare the student for our diverse and pluralistic world. A truly dialogical mode, rather than denying differences, is an essential asset in the pursuit of truth and conviction. As the German systematician Jürgen Moltmann underlines: "Dialogue has to be about the question of truth, even if no agreement about the truth can be reached. For consensus is not the goal of the dialogue. . . . If two people say the same thing, one of them is superfluous. In the interfaith dialogue which has to do with what is of vital and absolute concern to men and women—with the things in which they place the whole trust of their hearts—the way is already part of the goal."[24] Moltmann rightly says that only those people are capable of dialogue—or "merit dialogue," as he puts it—who "have arrived at a firm standpoint in their own religion, and who enter into dialogue with the resulting self-confidence."[25] Thus, Moltmann continues, "it is only if we are at home in our own religion that we shall be able to encounter the religion of someone else. The person who falls victim to the relativism of the

---

22. Ward, *Religion and Community*, 339.

23. See further, Ward, *Religion and Revelation*, 1–2. The remaining two volumes are *Religion and Creation* and *Religion and Human Nature*.

24. Moltmann, *Experiences in Theology*, 19–20.

25. Moltmann, *Experiences in Theology*, 18.

multicultural society may be capable of dialogue, but that person does not merit dialogue."[26]

Engaging not only the cultural diversity within the vastly globalizing Christian church, but also the religious diversity, is a laborious and in many ways annoying project, as it takes theologians not only to the edge of their intellectual capacities but also of their emotional comfort zone. Clooney puts it well:

> If we are attentive to the diversity around us, near us, we must deny ourselves the easy confidences that keep the other at a distance. But, as believers, we must also be able to defend the relevance of the faith of our community, deepening our commitments even alongside other faiths that are flourishing nearby. We need to learn from other religious possibilities, without slipping into relativist generalizations. The tension between open-mindedness and faith, diversity and traditional commitment, is a defining feature of our era, and neither secular society nor religious authorities can make simple choices before us.[27]

RE-SOURCING THEOLOGICAL EDUCATION

How do we go about revamping theological education with the goal of developing a dialogical, comparative mode? Regarding pedagogical moves, I have found the following ones useful: First, nothing beats the effort to provide students with access to either grassroots personal encounters with people of other faiths or, if that is not possible, at least with visits to sacred places or otherwise meaningful sites of other religions. For me, living in a cosmopolitan area such as Los Angeles, California, facilitating both efforts is not too difficult. While of course a more sustained face-to-face relationship with a person or group from other faith traditions is the desired form of encounter, even well-planned visits to mosques, temples, and shrines, with a presentation from the representative(s) of the Other and an opportunity to ask questions is highly useful. I have found that often students are very enthusiastic about opportunities to visit the sacred site of another religion—not infrequently for the first time in their lives. Because of this, they often go beyond the required minimum and begin to seek out contacts on their own.

Second, I make sure that the students are not only reading *about* another faith tradition but also read at least a minimum amount in the

---

26. Moltmann, *Experiences in Theology*, 18–19.
27. Clooney, *Comparative Theology*, 7.

scriptures of other traditions themselves, whether these be their primary sources such as the Qur'an, Tipitaka, or Vedic texts, or secondary texts such as Hadith or Bhagavad-Gita. Not without basis does Timothy C. Tennent, a distinguished American theological educator with intimate knowledge of the religious diversity in the subcontinent of India, observe: "In the West, it is rare to find someone who has more than a cursory knowledge of the sacred texts of other religions. In contrast, because Christians in the Majority World are often in settings dominated by other religions, it is not uncommon to meet a Christian with a Muslim, Hindu, or Buddhist background who has an intimate knowledge of another sacred text."[28] I fear that not only the theological students and professionals in the Global North, but also those in the South are illiterate in the texts of other faiths: as is well known, for many, becoming a Christian means leaving behind everything in the old religion and its practice. Be that as it may, I know from experience that most students find reading the scriptures of other traditions very challenging. The reasons are many: neither the Qur'an nor Vedas has a plot; Hindu and Buddhist scriptures are so exceedingly vast that even to begin locating something is almost impossible for the beginner; terminology and forms of expression are also very different; and so forth. This means that students need quite a bit of guidance in selection and comprehension. Fortunately, access to the scriptures is easy in this Internet age.[29] Third, along with scriptures, I try to find at least some readings by representative contemporary "theologians" of other faith traditions. Fourth, as much as possible, I try to get visiting presenters from other faith traditions.

There are a slowly growing number of resources that offer guidance and inspiration, as well as primary and secondary sources. Let me highlight here the two main processes and projects with which I am most intimately familiar. First, in recent years the WCC has launched significant efforts to bring together resources that the global church can use for the training of theologians and ministers in various locations. Under the rubric "Ecumenical theological education,"[30] the production of *The Handbook of Theological*

---

28. Tennent, *Theology in the Context of World Christianity*, 55.

29. All important Hindu scriptures can be found on the Sacred Texts website: www.sacredtexts.com. Some (mainly Mahayana) Buddhist texts can likewise be found there, and a major part of the necessary portions of the Tipitaka (Theravada) is available on the website Access to Insight: Readings in Theravāda Buddhism: www.accesstoinsight.com. The Qur'an (with several modern versions) can be easily found, e.g., at ALTAFSIR.COM: http://altafsir.com, and much of Hadith is available in the Hadith Collection at http://www.hadithcollection.com/.

30. See "Ecumenical Theological Education," http://www.oikoumene.org/en/what-we-do/ecumenical-theological-education.

Education in World Christianity (2010) was a massive enterprise.[31] Far more than just a listing of schools and institutions, the manual is an indispensable means of connecting and being informed. A promising start has also begun through an earlier project named "Teaching Christianity in Dialogue with Other Faith Traditions,"[32] which has produced some fruit so far and carries a lot of potential. Also useful is the programmatic statement "Magna Charta on Ecumenical Theological Education in the 21st century—ETE reference document,"[33] which includes interfaith preparedness as one of the key themes for global theological education and looks for projects and collaboration. Another related ecumenical enterprise is the huge "Global Digital Library on Theology and Ecumenism,"[34] with currently more than 65,000 essays and documents, reference works, journals, and special collections on ethics, theology, ecumenism, and interreligious dialogue. Indeed, that online site may well be the most resourced collection of materials for teaching theology and ethics in a pluralistic, globalizing world.

The second major set of resources has to do with the various programs organized by and related to the Association of Theological Schools (ATS) in North America. Another recent addition is the highly useful resource titled *Christian Hospitality and Pastoral Practices in a Multifaith Society* (2012).[35] It is an offshoot from a multiyear process titled "Christian Hospitality and Pastoral Practices,"[36] which initiates new courses and programs particularly with ministerial training in mind. Some of the many representative seminary-based funded initiatives that can be explored for resources, insights, and experiences include:

---

31. Werner et al., *Handbook of Theological Education in World Christianity*. For the work done around the *Handbook* in the Edinburgh 2010 Centennial Process, see "Theological Education and Formation," http://www.edinburgh2010.org/en/study-themes/main-study-themes/theological-education-and-formation.htm.

32. "Teaching Christianity in Dialogue with Other Faith Traditions," http://www.oikoumene.org/en/resources/documents/wcc-programmes/interreligious-dialogue-and-cooperation/christian-identity-in-pluralistic-societies/teaching-christianity-in-dialogue-with-other-faith-traditions.

33. "Magna Charta on Ecumenical Theological Education in the 21st century," http://www.oikoumene.org/en/resources/documents/wcc-programmes/education-and-ecumenical-formation/ete/wcc-programme-on-ecumenical-theological-education/magna-charta-on-ecumenical-theological-education-in-the-21st-century-ete-reference-document.

34. "Global Digital Library on Theology and Ecumenism," http://www.globethics.net/web/gtl/globetheolib.

35. Graham, *Christian Hospitality and Pastoral Practices in a Multifaith Society*, 1–10.

36. "Current Initiatives," http://www.ats.edu/resources/current-initiatives/christian-hospitality-and-pastoral-practices.

- "Taking Interfaith Off the Hill" (Andover Newton Theological School)[37]
- "Educating Clergy for a Multifaith World" (Hartford Theological Seminary)[38]
- "The Pastoral Practice of Christian Hospitality as Presence in Muslim-Christian Engagement: Contextualizing the Classroom" (Luther Seminary)[39]
- "Christian Hospitality and Neighborliness: A Wesleyan-Pentecostal Ministry Paradigm for the Multi-Faith Context" (Pentecostal Theological Seminary)[40]

Other initiatives based at theological schools include Auburn Seminary's long-term labor of developing multifaceted and creative interfaith teaching and learning resources, including *Beyond World Religions: The State of Multifaith Education in American Theological Schools* (2009).[41] I have personally benefited from looking at resources prepared by scholars from other religions who are beginning to experiment with interfaith programs. An interesting task for a Christian theological educator is to reflect on the distinctive challenges a Jewish colleague faces when organizing interfaith programs in a Christian school![42]

APPEAL FOR A DIALOGICAL, COMPARATIVE MODE OF TEACHING THEOLOGY

As argued in this chapter, for theological education in the third millennium to redeem its promise requires a radical re-formation of content, approach, and resources. Other chapters in this book highlight related challenges in meeting globalization. The present chapter has focused on the dialogical and comparative aspect of the pedagogical task, with a stated focus on religious plurality.

The dialogical approach, however, is not limited to interfaith pedagogy. It is, however, the preferred mode of discussion, teaching, and learning

---

37. Mobley, "Taking Interfaith Off the Hill: Revelation in the Abrahamic Traditions."
38. Roozen, "Curriculum Development Project."
39. Hess, "Pastoral Practice of Christian Hospitality."
40. Han, "Christian Hospitality and Neighborliness."
41. "Research: Multifaith Education in Seminaries," http://www.auburnseminary.org/seminarystudy/.
42. Baird, "Case for Multifaith Education."

for everything in divinity and religious studies. It calls for mature convictions and also a childlike openness to learn. It requires affirming one's own identity and willingness to be reshaped by new encounters. This theological vision is supremely captured in Moltmann's pointed statement:

> [T]ruth is to be found in unhindered dialogue. Fellowship and freedom are the human components for knowledge of the truth, the truth of God. And the fellowship I mean here is the fellowship of mutual participation and unifying sympathy... This free community of men and women, without privilege and without discrimination, may be termed the earthly body of truth... [I]t is only in free dialogue that truth can be accepted for the only right and proper reason—namely, that it illuminates and convinces *as* truth. Truth brings assent, it brings about change without exerting compulsion. In dialogue the truth frees men and women for their own conceptions and their own ideas... Christian theology would wither and die if it did not continually stand in a dialogue like this, and if it were not bound up with a fellowship that seeks this dialogue, needs it and continually pursues it.[43]

---

43. Moltmann, *Trinity and the Kingdom of God*, xii–xiii (emphasis in the original).

PART TWO

Systematic Theology

CHAPTER 4

Divine Hospitality and Communion

A Trinitarian Theology of Equality, Justice, and Human Flourishing

INTRODUCTION: "TRINITY IS OUR SOCIAL PROGRAM"—OR IS IT?

TESTIMONIES TO THE INDISPENSABILITY and "usefulness" of the doctrine of the Trinity can be easily found in contemporary theology from across the ecumenical spectrum. To the Eastern Orthodox John Zizioulas, "Trinitarian theology has profound existential consequences,"[1] and to the late (United) Reformed Colin Gunton, "much, indeed everything depends on the way that that particular doctrine [of the Trinity] is articulated."[2] The Baptist Millard J. Erickson mentions no less than twelve reasons for the importance of this doctrine, many of them "practical."[3] And so forth. Certainly the late Stanley Grenz believed not only in the indispensability of that doctrine but also everywhere reflected on its implications for communal and personal life. Just consider the title of his widely used textbook *Theology for the Community of God*.[4] Indeed, having used that book of Stan's for years as an integrative introductory text in systematic theology classes, I recall more than one student making a remark like this: "Why is it that with every theological topic we also end up asking what are the implications for the community?"

1. Zizioulas, "Doctrine of God the Trinity Today," 19.
2. Gunton, *One, the Three and the Many*, 149.
3. Erickson, *God in Three Persons*, 29.
4. Grenz, *Social God and Relational Self*.

So it appears that the doctrine of the Trinity "works" in terms of everyday life benefits—at least a good one does. But is it supposed to "work"? Is the doctrine of the Trinity meant to be a tool for liberation and equality? Are we even supposed to inquire into the "practical" implications of the most revered and mysterious article of our faith, the Trinity? Doesn't that kind of inquiry necessarily lead to, so to speak, a *liberation theology "from below"*—a superficial theology of God put in the service of human social needs? No, it does not have to. Indeed, the present essay is not meant to be an exercise in such a "from-below liberationist theology." Let me list some reasons why not:

To begin, the Trinity in the first place was never meant to be primarily a model for human relations; it is a statement about God![5] Second, as an affluent white European male theologian—living in the entertainment metropolis of the world, the City of Angels in California—I am hardly qualified to speak of liberation of the oppressed! The third reason this essay is not an exercise in a distinctively liberation theology is that I firmly believe that *all* good theology should have a liberationist impulse embedded in its deep structure. Although I applaud the indispensable contributions of *liberation* theologies (from Latin America, Africa, and say, the perspective of women and other marginalized human beings), I also think that only when the motif of liberation at all levels is adopted as an integral theological theme can Christianity be in a place to make a difference in real life.

The final reason this essay is not an exercise in (liberation) theology *"from below"* is that as much as there is correspondence between the divine and human communities, the differences are even more profound. While affirming the turn to communion theology and its implications for inclusivity, relationality, and belonging, contemporary theology also has to exercise healthy self-criticism. The basic concern boils down to this question: how should we imagine the correspondence, or how much can we claim to learn from the "divine society" for the sake of human societies? A basic similarity has to be assumed, if for no other reasons than because humanity exists as *imago Dei*. However, this correspondence even at its best is partial and fragmentary for the obvious reasons that whereas the divine life is uncreated and infinite, the human is not, and whereas the divine life is perfect, the human is not. And so forth. Hence, the saying "The Trinity Is Our Social Program" has to be handled with great care.[6] The Roman Catholic Brazilian Leonardo Boff's approach serves here as a useful model. Unlike most

---

5. See further, Grenz, *Rediscovering the Triune God*, 130–31; Cunningham, *These Three Are One*, 51–53 especially.

6. For an important discussion of the limitations of the correspondence, see Volf, "'Trinity Is Our Social Program,'" 403–23.

Liberationists, he wishes to begin "from above" even when the goal is to develop a socially and politically relevant Liberation program: "The Trinity is not something thought out to explain human problems. It is the revelation of God as God is, as Father, Son, and Holy Spirit."[7] Rather than *praxis* being the matrix out of which trinitarian communion theology emerges and whose well-being it serves, the order must be the reverse.

With these warnings and caveats in mind, let me first review briefly what the talk about God as communion means and how that is related to the notion of hospitality, the source of gifts essential to flourishing human life, whether individual or social. Thereafter, I will attempt three excursions into specific issues—how we could best think of the formation of human communities, questions of justice and equality, and the topic of human flourishing—through the lens of a trinitarian communion theology of hospitality. Needless to say, this essay is suggestive and exploratory and meant to inspire conversation rather than attempt any last word.

GOD'S LIFE AS COMMUNION AND HOSPITALITY

To say that that One God exists as Father, Son, and Spirit is to say communion—personal and eternal communion of the three. The turn to a relational understanding of personhood at large has helped rediscover communion theology.[8] The Orthodox John Zizioulas's formative collection of essays with a telling title, *Being as Communion* (1985),[9] has become a clarion call for contemporary theologians. The main thesis of Zizioulas's theology is simple and profound: God is not first "one substance" and only then exists as "trinity"; rather, the "Holy Trinity is a *primordial* ontological concept and not a notion which is added to the divine substance."[10] In other words, "the substance of God, 'God,' has no ontological content, no true being, apart from communion," mutual relationships of love.[11] God's being coincides with God's personhood, which cannot be construed apart from communion.[12] Biblically that is expressed by the idea of God as "love," which is "*constitutive*

---

7. Boff, *Trinity and Society*, 3.

8. See Grenz, *Social God*, 3–14.

9. Zizioulas, *Being as Communion*; see also his "Human Capacity and Human Incapacity," 401–47.

10. "In the Beginning Is Communion," chapter title in Boff, *Trinity and Society*, 9.

11. Zizioulas, *Being as Communion*, 17.

12. Zizioulas, "Teaching of the 2nd Ecumenical Council on the Holy Spirit in Historical and Ecumenical Perspective," 37.

of His substance, i.e., it is that which makes God what He is, the one God."[13] Hence, God is person as a community of three persons. God's being coincides with God's *communal* personhood. While there are of course varieties of communion theologies on the contemporary scene, the foundational intuition is that, rather than the individual, the ultimate reality is the communion, personhood, belonging, reflecting the life of the Triune God.

While communion theology—and the social analogy[14]—has been embraced widely in contemporary theology, not all appropriate it similarly. Whereas Zizioulas as an Orthodox theologian conceives it hierarchically, making the Father the source (*aitia*) of the Trinity,[15] the Reformed Jürgen Moltmann and a number of contemporary female theologians have passionately argued for an equalitarian notion of communion.[16] Several leading women theologians have reminded us that to the notion of communion belong the principles of mutuality and relationality: "God, too, lives from and for another: God the Father gives birth to the Son, breathes forth the Spirit, elects the creature from before all time . . . God's rule is accomplished by saving and healing love."[17]

Communion theology brings God and world, God and humanity, close to each other. Whether or not you call it panentheism is not the point.[18] The point simply is this: Behind the appreciation of the communion nature of God is the intuition that while distinct, God and world do not represent two totally different realities; they are intertwined. An older static conception of reality is giving way to a more dynamic one in which "categories such as history, process, freedom, and so on, then dynamism, interplay of relationships, and dialectics of mutual inclusiveness make their appearance." In that kind of worldview, the world poses itself as the "receptacle of God's self-communication" and "begins to belong to the history of the triune God."[19] While God remains God and the world remains the world, they are not separate from each other.

---

13. Zizioulas, *Being as Communion*, 46 (italics in the original); see also Zizioulas, "Human Capacity," 410.

14. For a historical look, see Kärkkäinen, *Trinity*, ch. 4.

15. Zizioulas, *Being as Communion*, 41; see also Zizioulas, "On Being a Person," 41.

16. Moltmann, *Trinity and the Kingdom of God*, 17–19; 191–92; Johnson, *She Who Is*, 222.

17. LaCugna, *God for Us*, 383; see also Baker-Fletcher, *Dancing with God*.

18. Recently I have advocated a new way of conceiving the God-world relationship, namely, in terms of "Classical Panentheism," a combination of Classical Theism and contemporary forms of panentheisms. See my *Trinity and Revelation*, ch. 10.

19. Boff, *Trinity and Society*, 112–13.

Such an intimate communion theology may best capture the infinite hospitality of God. Theology then, following the Feminist Letty M. Russell, becomes an exercise in "reframing the idea of hospitality through identifying characteristics of God's gift of welcome."[20] To speak of God is to speak of giving, gift, hospitality. No one else in the history of theology has spoken of this theme as powerfully as Martin Luther. In his profound theology of love, based on the theology of the cross, the Reformer proclaims: "Rather than seeking its own good, the love of God flows forth and bestows good."[21] God's love seeks that which is worthless in itself and donates not only gifts but one's self.[22] At the cross, God's self-giving, the most profound act of hospitality, came to expression.[23] Indeed, according to the Reformer, the divinity of the Triune God consists in that "God gives" himself. The essence of God, then, is identical with the essential divine properties in which he gives himself, called the "names" of God: Word, justice, truth, wisdom, love, goodness, eternal life, and so forth. God is, as Luther put it, the "whole beatitude of his saints"; the name of God donates God's goodness, God himself; the spiritual goods are God's gifts in the Christian.[24] The doctrine of the Trinity expresses profoundly this grammar of giving and hospitality: sent by the Father, the Son unites to himself in the power of the Spirit what was separated.

But is this too good to be true? Not without reason is the whole possibility of hospitality and gift questioned by many contemporary thinkers, from the Jewish Emmanuel Levinas to the late French philosopher Jacques Derrida. Well known are the severe reservations of Derrida concerning the gift and hospitality. His *Given Time* is a massive attempt to deconstruct the whole notion of the possibility of gift.[25] The reason is simply this: in our world, there is no way of giving a gift without the expectation of some kind of reciprocity. Derrida demands absolute unconditionality of a true gift and goes so far in his insistence on "unconditional hospitality" that he advises us to "say yes to who or what turns up, before any determination, before any anticipation, before any identification,"[26] even if the guest "may be the devil"![27]

20. Russell, *Just Hospitality*, 77; on "reframing," see Lakoff, *Don't Think of the Elephant*, 15.

21. Luther's *Works* 31:57 (Heidelberg Disputation, thesis #28).

22. Mannermaa, *Kaksi rakkautta*, 9–11.

23. An important discussion of the theme can be found in Newlands and Smith, *Hospitable God*.

24. Luther, *Psalmenvorlesungen*, 454, 4–10; 158, 18–19; 303, 20–26.

25. Derrida, *Given Time*: 1; Dufourmantelle and Derrida, *Of Hospitality*.

26. Dufourmantelle and Derrida, *Of Hospitality*, 77.

27. Derrida, "Hospitality, Justice, and Responsibility," 70.

Derrida is of course right about the fact that in our kind of world—finite and sinful—absolutely unconditional hospitality is impossible for men and women. Derrida's skepticism, however, must be qualified and put in perspective. First, there is a difference between human and divine hospitality and gift-giving. While the former is limited and imperfect, the latter is absolute and possible. Only the divine gift can be a "pure gift."[28] Second, when it comes to human hospitality, only with the coming of the eschatological kingdom it is possible for men and women to participate in hospitality without the limits of the fallen world. Third, granted that in the meantime we have to be content with less than absolute standards for gift and hospitality, it still is far better to give a gift and show hospitality even in an imperfect form than take away from others, be complacent, or just ignore the other. The same "already"–"not-yet" dynamic characterizes all Christian existence.

In an important recent study, *The Hospitable God*, George Newlands and Allen Smith note that "[t]hough we may not find the word 'hospitable' on every page of the doctrinal tradition about God, we suggest that hospitality provides a summative term which may express eloquently affirmations and concerns which lie at the heart of the Christian gospel. Hospitality reflects the understanding of God, and of the shape of service to God and to our fellow human beings, that is central to other major world faiths."[29] Consequently, "Hospitality is not optional for Christians, nor is it limited to those who are specially gifted for it. It is, instead, a necessary practice in the community of faith."[30]

Any talk about hospitality, however, raises the question of whether it "sound[s] dangerously like a particularly comfortable religious title, a coffee table Christianity to soothe away the cares of the actual world in which we live."[31] True, *hospitality* can be easily abused—similarly to *love* and *mercy*—yet in light of biblical revelation, the opposite is the case: "hospitality carries risks," it includes sacrifice, self-giving, discipleship, turning to others.[32] Indeed, in Christian tradition, "it is the hospitality of cross and resurrection. It acts often in spite of unpalatable reality. It arises as a protest against rights violations, a hope against hope . . . The hospitality of God is dynamic. It invites active human commitment in reciprocal, specific, sensibly executed

---

28. See the important discussion in Tanner, *Economy of Grace*, 58, 63.
29. Newlands and Smith, *Hospitable God*, 22.
30. Pohl, *Making Room*, 31.
31. Newlands and Smith, *Hospitable God*, 3–4.
32. See further, Newlands and Smith, *Hospitable God*, 4.

hospitable action."³³ Letty Russell aptly characterizes some key features of the divine hospitality: "In the Bible, God's welcome—hospitality—has at least four overlapping central components: (1) unexpected divine presence; (2) advocacy for the marginalized; (3) mutual welcome; and (4) creation of community."³⁴ The radical nature of hospitality is intensified in light of the fact that we live in a world that often is not hospitable.³⁵

HOSPITALITY AND COMMUNITY OF EQUALS

Famously, Jürgen Moltmann has juxtaposed what he calls "monotheism," which for him is nothing less than "monarchism,"³⁶ whether it manifests itself in politics³⁷ or church life,³⁸ with Christian trinitarianism, a theology of communion. In his view, nontrinitarian "monotheism" supports domination and abuse of power, whereas trinitarian imagination supports equality, fairness, and mutuality.³⁹ The way to combat the hierarchical and power-laden way of life for Moltmann is to imagine the trinitarian God as a "community of equals, vulnerable and open to the human suffering, who experiences this suffering in himself."⁴⁰ Trinity is not a hierarchical entity, but rather a fellowship of persons: "We understand the scriptures as the testimony to the history of the Trinity's relations of fellowship, which are open to men and women, and open to the world."⁴¹

Indeed, at the heart of trinitarian communion theology is the insistence on the Trinity as a dynamic, lively symbol. That approach wishes to replace the derivationist, subordinationist, and hierarchical ways of conceiving the Triune God with a relational, equalitarian, and inclusive way, one that is "a relational pattern of mutual giving and receiving."⁴² As the moderate Roman Catholic Feminist Elizabeth Johnson succinctly puts it, "The symbol of the triune God is the specific Christian shape of monotheism."⁴³ It speaks

---

33. Newlands and Smith, *Hospitable God*, 9.
34. Russell, *Just Hospitality*, 82.
35. Newlands and Smith, *Hospitable God*, 13. For an important discussion, see Caputo and Scanlon, *God, the Gift and Postmodernism*.
36. Moltmann, *Trinity and the Kingdom*, 191. See also 130.
37. Moltmann, *Trinity and the Kingdom*, 192–200.
38. Moltmann, *Trinity and the Kingdom*, 200–202.
39. Similarly Boff, *Trinity and Society*, 139–40.
40. Matei, "Practice of Community in Social Trinitarianism," 217.
41. Moltmann, *Trinity and the Kingdom*, 19; see also 17–18 and 191–92.
42. Johnson, *She Who Is*, 194–97 (196).
43. See further, Johnson, *She Who Is*, 211.

of "one God who is not solitary God but a communion of love."[44] For such a discourse, essential values are the following three: First, the symbol of trinitarian communion speaks of mutual relationality. The Triune God can be spoken of with the help of the metaphor of friendship, which is the "most free, the least possessive, the most mutual of relationships, able to cross social barriers in genuine reciprocal regard."[45] Second, the symbol of the Triune God speaks of radical equality. The Christian symbol of the Trinity for Johnson bespeaks a community of equals with patterns of differentiation that are nonhierarchical.[46] Third, the symbol of the Trinity speaks of "community in diversity," expressed in classical theology with the term *perichoresis*, a picture of an eternal divine round dance.[47]

An integral communion theology may help overcome the rampant individualism of much of modern theology, particularly in the Global North. The Cuban-born Justo González claims that this is one area in which Euro-American theology needs to be mentored and corrected by the theologies of the Global South, in this case by the Hispanic tradition for which "[t]he best theology is a communal enterprise," as opposed to "Western theology—especially that which takes place in academic circles—[that] has long suffered from an exaggerated individualism. Theologians, like medieval knights, joust with one another, while their peers cheer from the stands where they occupy places of honor and the plebes look at the contest from a distance—if they look at all." Communion theology and theology done by and in the community, in contrast, "will not be a theology of theologians but a theology of the believing and practicing community."[48]

The rampant individualism of much of Western theological tradition is not politically innocent, argues the Uruguayan Jesuit Juan Luis Segundo. According to his analysis, Christian tradition's replacement of the biblical and patristic communion orientation is not only a historical matter, stemming from Greco-Roman and particularly European Enlightenment-based cultures; it is also ideological at its core. The Western cultural emphasis on the "private" underwrites the capitalistic economy with its protection of the individual's rights, particularly economic. In this outlook, God was looked to as the "private" *par excellence*. This, in turn, is nothing other than

---

44. Johnson, *She Who Is*, 222.
45. Johnson, *She Who Is*, 216–18 (217).
46. Johnson, *She Who Is*, 219.
47. Johnson, *She Who Is*, 220.
48. González, *Mañana*, 29–30.

"shift[ing] onto God the features wherewith the individual feels he can find self-fulfillment in a society based on domination."[49]

As mentioned above, the correspondence between the divine communion and human communities is partial and suggestive. But even then, it has to be taken seriously. As Boff succinctly puts it, "Human society is a pointer on the road to the mystery of the Trinity, while the mystery of the Trinity, as we know it from revelation, is a pointer toward social life and its archetype. Human society holds a *vestigium Trinitatis* since the Trinity is 'the divine society.'"[50] This is not to hide the obvious fact that indeed all theological claims—as analogues, metaphors, symbols—derive from human experience and utilize tools available in human cultures. There is no "God's point of view" available to us.[51] Rather, the methodological caution has everything to do with the danger of making theological doctrine a cheap tool for fixing human problems at the theologian's wish. In this outlook, rather than being a social program, the trinitarian divine communion serves "as a source of inspiration, as a utopian goal . . . [for] the oppressed in their quest and struggle for integral liberation."[52]

Systematic theology also has to negotiate carefully and dynamically the complicated question of the hierarchy in the divine life. Christian tradition until recently and Eastern Orthodox tradition even today insists on the primacy of the Father and hierarchy.[53] For Zizioulas, in the Divine Hierarchy, there is reciprocity if not symmetry. Reciprocity means that Spirit and Son are the "presupposition of [the Father's] identity."[54] On the other side, the Son and Spirit exist only through the Father; the Father is the "ground" of God's being.[55] Moltmann could not disagree more vehemently. Similarly, most female theologians and other Liberationists simply dismiss the whole idea of any kind of hierarchy in the divine communion. Wolfhart Pannenberg steers a middle course that seems most appealing to the current project. On the one hand, he rejects the role of the Father as the "source" of

---

49. Slade, "Theological Method of Juan Luis Segundo," 68.

50. Boff, *Trinity and Society*, 119.

51. Boff, *Trinity and Society*, 112.

52. Boff, *Trinity and Society*, 6–7.

53. A main reason for Zizioulas to insist on the primacy of the Father (apart from his desire to align with Christian tradition, particularly that of the Christian East) is his understanding that this is the only way to secure the "personal" basis of the Trinity, as the Father is person. The alternative would be an "ontology of substance," i.e., a nonpersonal basis. See Zizioulas, "Teaching of the 2nd Ecumenical Council on the Holy Spirit," 36n18. For a helpful comment, see Volf, *After Our Likeness*, 79.

54. Quoted in Volf, *After Our Likeness*, 78.

55. Zizioulas, *Being as Communion*, 89.

the Trinity, insisting on the mutual—although highly distinct—dependency of each trinitarian person on others for their deity. On the other hand, in keeping with tradition, he affirms the monarchy, albeit not in a way that would violate the principle of mutuality or subordinate the Son and Spirit.[56] It seems to me this is the most nuanced and theologically most sustainable way of conceiving the dynamic relationality and communion of the trinitarian life. It also helps systematically negotiate the biblical data, which unabashedly seems to assign to the Father the role of primacy in the godhead. This primacy—monarchy—following Pannenberg, however, does not have to lead to hierarchy nor asymmetrical relations. In this eternal trinitarian life of love, there is mutual conditioning, respect, and honoring. Diversity is being affirmed in strict unity. Could one imagine anything more appropriate as an inspiration and critique for human relationships and communities?

HOSPITALITY AND ADVOCACY OF JUSTICE

In his brilliant and striking manner, the African American Robert McAfee Brown notes that in the Bible "justice" appears to be God's middle name![57] Following Russell, we "understand hospitality as the practice of God's welcome, embodied in our actions as we reach across difference to participate with God in bringing justice and healing to our world in crisis."[58] Recall also her note above that among the several features of the divine hospitality is "advocacy for the marginalized."[59] Hospitable constructive theology not only advocates inclusivity and equality, it also makes every effort to actively promote liberation and freedom. While the task of hospitality as advocacy has been, and continues to be, the major focus of Liberation theologies of various stripes, it is essential, as mentioned, for the current constructive theology to remind us of the fact that at its core all Christian theology is "liberation theology." As long as liberation is merely an "added thing," an auxiliary element, it can be sought or dismissed—and the theological task continues as it is. However, the gospel means liberation at all levels.[60] The God of the Bible is committed to liberation. "God is God who saves us not through his domination but through his suffering . . . And it is thus that

---

56. Pannenberg, *Systematic Theology*, 1:324.

57. Brown, "'Preferential Option for the Poor' and the Renewal of Faith," 10. I am indebted to Russell, *Just Hospitality*, 106.

58. Russell, *Just Hospitality*, 2; for an extended discussion of "just hospitality," see ch. 5.

59. Russell, *Just Hospitality*, 82.

60. Boesak, *Farewell to Innocence*, 9.

the cross acquires its tremendous revelatory potential with respect to God's weakness as an expression of his love for a world come of age."[61]

Although "praxis" *per se* cannot of course be made uncritically the basis for doing theology, neither can it be ignored. Theology does not happen in a vacuum. All theology is contextual in the sense that it is shaped and lived out in a context. From a Liberationist perspective, this praxis is not merely the common human experience, but more specifically the human experience and reality of the poor, the despised, the marginalized, those without opportunities. This is the specific "praxis" of theology.[62] The adoption of "praxis" as the point of departure for God-talk does not of course mean sidetracking biblical revelation and Christian tradition. Rather, it means an intentional and robust dialectic between critical theological reflection in a specific context and in light of action to address impending needs and challenges.[63]

The African American senior theologian James Cone reminds us that the context of praxis in Black theology is the experience of Blacks in the United States. Consequently, "Black theology ... [is] the affirmation of black humanity that emancipates black people from white racism, thus providing authentic freedom for both white and black people. It affirms the humanity of white people in that it says NO to the encroachment of white oppression." This is an important affirmation of Black praxis as a point of departure into liberative speech about God. However, it has to be qualified and complemented by two critically important points. First, even such a specific point of view as "Black experience" is not an unnunaced, generic phenomenon. This Black experience may be different for African American *women* than for men. This is what the Womanist theologians argue. Delores S. Williams wishes to replace her male counterparts' focus on Exodus as the paradigmatic narrative of God's liberative work with the Genesis story of Hagar, the dismissed slave woman. Whereas in the Exodus narrative liberation stands in the forefront, in Hagar's story survival is the key; God participates in Hagar's and her child's survival.[64] What is most instructive in the Hagar story—and paradigmatic for Black women—is that Hagar is the only person in the Bible attributed with the power of naming God (Gen 16:3). Not that she does not use the designations for God used by Abraham and Sarah, her oppressors, but she also gives God a new name, *El Roi*, "God of seeing."[65]

61. Gutiérrez, *Essential Writings*, 39.
62. See Chopp, "Latin American Liberation Theology," 412.
63. On the "hermeneutical circle," see Segundo, *Liberation of Theology*, 9.
64. Williams, *Sisters in the Wilderness*, 5.
65. Williams, *Sisters in the Wilderness*, 20–27.

The main point for this discussion is simply this: The nature and conditions of liberative speech about God vary in different contexts. This is not to pit one discourse of God against others. It is to make room and facilitate diverse, mutually enriching, and specific conversations.

The second qualification for Cone's methodology of beginning from Black praxis has to do with the principle of complementary inclusivity, lest the discourse—in this case Black speech about God—become exclusive and even violent, as it did with the young Cone.[66] The limitation of hospitality to only one race, the Blacks (or, alternatively, to whites or others), has to be rejected as violence. Hence, the mature Cone's conciliatory and hospitable note of an inclusive nature about paying theological attention to "color" should be affirmed. Utilizing Paul Tillich's concept of the symbolic nature of theological talk, he says, "The focus on blackness does not mean that *only* blacks suffer as victims in a racist society, but that blackness is an ontological symbol and a visible reality which best describes what oppression means in America."[67] Always conciliatory in his approach, another African American theologian, James H. Evans, maintains that in Black theology God is experienced as impartial, "no respecter of persons" (Acts 10:34). In a world of injustice, African Americans have put their faith in the One who deals justly with them, but not only with them but also with whites.[68] The expression "inclusive partisanship" of the God of the Bible, utilized by Liberationists from various contexts, including female theologians of Hispanic origin[69] working in the context of emerging *Mujerista* theologies[70] and theologians from the context of the First Nations of North America,[71] helps avoid exclusion and foster liberative inclusivity. God's preference for a particular group of people—be it Blacks, Hispanics, Asians, or white Europeans—is not meant to exclude others.[72]

Meaningful and healthy human life requires not only belonging to community but also equality and justice, as well as a sense of self-worth. That kind of life is best described in terms of human flourishing.

---

66. Cone, *Black Theology of Liberation*, 111.
67. Cone, *Black Theology of Liberation*, 7.
68. Evans, *We Have Been Believers*, 67–76.
69. See Rodríguez, *Racism and God-Talk*.
70. See Isasi-Díaz, *En la Lucha* [In the Struggle].
71. See Warrior, "Canaanites, Cowboys and Indians," 261–65.
72. This tendency was evident in Cone's early theology.

HOSPITALITY AND HUMAN FLOURISHING

Cartographing the cultural changes across two millennia, the famed Canadian philosopher Charles Taylor, in *A Secular Age,* makes a sweeping statement: "Every person, and every society, lives with or by some conception(s) of what human flourishing is: what constitutes a fulfilled life? What makes life really worth living? What would we most admire people for?"[73] During the past five hundred years, the overall framework for such reflection has dramatically changed as there are two main options, radically different from each other: religion or what Taylor calls "exclusive humanism." These two frameworks articulate the quest for human flourishing in totally different ways:

> Does the highest, the best life involve our seeking, or acknowledging, or serving a good which is beyond, in the sense of independent of human flourishing? In which case, the highest, most real, authentic or adequate human flourishing could include our aiming (also) in our range of final goals at something other than human flourishing... It's clear that in the Judaeo-Christian religious tradition the answer to this question is affirmative. Loving, worshiping God is the ultimate end. Of course, in this tradition God is seen as willing human flourishing, but devotion to God is not seen as contingent on this. The injunction "Thy will be done" isn't equivalent to "Let humans flourish," even though we know that God wills human flourishing.[74]

The senior American theologian David H. Kelsey rightly notes, "Christian theology has a large stake in making it clear that its affirmations about God and God's ways of relating to human beings underwrite human beings' flourishing." Not only outspoken atheists and critics of religion but also many popular mindsets of the contemporary world share the "widespread and deep suspicion that Christians magnify God and God's power and dominion by systematically minimizing human beings, making them small, weak, and servile—anything but flourishing." Hence, the "challenge to Christian theology has been to develop conceptual and argumentative strategies by which to show that, properly understood, human flourishing is inseparable from God's active relating to human creatures such that their flourishing is always dependent upon God."[75]

---

73. Taylor, *Secular Age*, 16.
74. Taylor, *Secular Age*, 16–17.
75. Kelsey, "On Human Flourishing," 1.

Mindfulness of the importance of human flourishing, however, should not lead us to replace the theological concept of "salvation" with mere "flourishing"[76] as the late British Feminist philosopher-theologian Grace Jantzen wants to do. There are two problems here. First, as argued above, to make religion (or God) a function of serving human needs is a failing enterprise; ultimately, it ends up serving neither humanity nor the cultivation of genuine religiosity. Second, and more importantly for this discussion, it can be argued that salvation and flourishing are rather an integral part of the one pluriform, holistic Christian vision, namely, hope for the life to come and a fulfilling, meaningful life on this earth. Not only "flourishing," as Jantzen one-sidedly claims,[77] but also the Christian holistic vision of salvation includes both physical and spiritual, earthly and mental, this-worldly and otherworldly dimensions.

True, in Christian tradition—as well as in other religious traditions (and perhaps, differently, even in secular utopias)—there are plenty of instances in which the idea of flourishing in this life has been lost because of concentrating merely on hope for the life to come. But how many contemporary theologians are there who would consider that kind of "eschatology" genuine and balanced *Christian* hope? On the other hand, in the final analysis, the power of the classical Christian hope for this life is grounded in the coming eschatological redemption and new creation wrought by the same faithful and loving God who is also the Creator and Provider. If religion were merely a matter of flourishing in this life, even the most flourishing life would not have any lasting significance, particularly when put in the vast cosmic perspective in which human life, as a "last minute" phenomenon in the almost fifteen-billion-year history of the universe's evolution, is an utterly tiny and insignificant thing. Similarly, following the logic of the outdated and rejected Classical Liberal Quest, Jantzen[78] also seems to make Jesus merely a fine example of life lived to its fullest without any notion of sin and need for salvation, which seems to the systematic theologian an utterly naive and unnuanced claim.

What kind of view of God supports and underwrites the goal of human flourishing? It is *theologically* "Christocentric," Kelsey explains:

> in the sense that it is in large part generated out of, and governed by, reflection on implications concerning God of Christian claims that the God who relates to created human beings also relates to them to draw them to eschatological consummation

---

76. Jantzen, *Becoming Divine*, 160–61.
77. Jantzen, *Becoming Divine*, 166–67.
78. Jantzen, *Becoming Divine*, 162–63.

and, when they are estranged from God, to reconcile them to God, by giving them Godself in an exceedingly odd way, namely, in the concrete personal life and particular personal identity of Jesus of Nazareth.[79]

Robustly trinitarian theology adds to that the presence of the ever-present, life-giving, life-supporting, and energizing Spirit of God. What is there in this classical picture of the Christian God that would frustrate human flourishing, one should ask? On the contrary, there is much that bespeaks flourishing; that much can be said without making the doctrine of God a cheap function of human interests. If human beings are creatures of God, then where else could they find the fulfillment of their deepest desires? The divine hospitality alone can deliver the promise.

It is highly significant that it is in his study *The Trinity*—dealing with the doctrine of God—that St. Augustine penned these famous words: "God is the only source to be found of any good things, but especially of those which make a man good and those which will make him happy; only from him do they come into a man and attach themselves to a man."[80]

A CLOSING WORD

A few years before his untimely passing away, Stan Grenz articulated wonderfully the meaning of the doctrine of the Trinity in relation to faith and human life:

> Stating the matter simply, "community" is central to my theological thinking because I am convinced that it is both at the heart of the biblical narrative and speaks clearly to the contemporary context. More specifically, I would add that community is crucial because it arises out of the very essence of God. At the heart of Christian theology is the doctrine of the Trinity, which declares that God is not only the one who enters into relationship with creation, and hence relates to us in time. Rather, God is internally relational within the Godhead, and hence eternally relational. Moreover, the Christian teaching declares that God is a trinity, rather than merely a binity; God is three-in-one. This suggests that mere one-to-one relationality does not exhaust the essence of God. Instead, the one God of the Bible is the fellowship of Father, Son, and Holy Spirit, to cite the traditional

---

79. Kelsey, "On Human Flourishing," 3–4.
80. Augustine, *On the Trinity* 13.10, cited in Volf, "Human Flourishing," 4.

Trinitarian terminology. In short, the God revealed in Jesus is communal, or community.[81]

Ascending "from below," as it were, from the signs of the gracious presence of the Triune God in the economy of salvation to glimpses into the nature and "personhood" of the one God—Father, Son, Spirit—yields indeed a beautiful picture of community, relationality, equality. Name it Gift or Love or—as often done nowadays—Hospitality, it all speaks of the infinite fountain of goodness. God the Giver is also the divine gift.

Theology—thinking after God—at its best, therefore, may become an act of hospitality, giving and receiving gifts, reflecting the Christian vision of the Triune God as the Giver and Sustainer of Life. The basic Greek verb *didomi* appears over 400 times in the New Testament. It is used of both human and divine giving, and it encompasses all levels from the most concrete to the most abstract.[82] The Finnish ecumenist Risto Saarinen aptly notes, "In religious life, giving can also be portrayed as divine action. God is the supreme giver, whereas human persons remain receivers."[83]

For the constructive theologian in search of such a vision of hospitality, the word of advice from Moltmann is in order: it is a call to "the fellowship of mutual participation and unifying sympathy," looking for a "free community of men and women, without privilege and without discrimination . . . the earthly body of truth." According to Moltmann, "Christian theology would wither and die if it did not continually stand in a dialogue like this, and if it were not bound up with a fellowship that seeks this dialogue, needs it and continually pursues it."[84] That kind of hospitable dialogical pursuit of truth reflects—albeit dimly and in a less than perfect way—the nature of the Divine Truth.

---

81. Grenz, "Community & Relationships."
82. For an insightful discussion, see Saarinen, God and Gift, 36–45.
83. Saarinen, *God and Gift*, 1.
84. Moltmann, *Trinity and the Kingdom*, xii–xiii (emphasis in the original).

CHAPTER 5

Divine Action in the World in a Trinitarian-Pneumatological Framework

DIVINE ACTION IN THE WORLD—WHAT IS AT STAKE FOR THEOLOGY?

IN ADDITION TO THE original work of creation and continuous creation, the Christian Scriptures—in sync with Jewish and Islamic traditions—are filled with accounts of divine acts in the world, not only in "salvation" history but also in universal history. They are so many and varied that one hardly needs to begin to compile a list. Indeed, all the way from the Fathers until the advent of modern science, the "mighty acts" of God were taken for granted. It simply was assumed that the God who had created the world in the first place, not only has the prerogative to "maintain" and guide it according to eternal divine purposes (general providence) but also to continue acting in history and nature—even to the point of responding to prayer and working out miracles (special providence).

So, what is the challenge to theology today? Philip Clayton, a leading expert in science-theology dialogue, puts it succinctly:

> Physical science, it appears, leaves no place for divine action. Modern science presupposes that the universe is a closed physical system, that interactions are regular and law-like, that all causal histories can be traced, and that anomalies will ultimately have physical explanations. But traditional assertions of God acting in the world conflict with all four of these conditions: they presuppose that the universe is open, that God acts from time to time according to his purposes, that the ultimate source

and explanation of these actions is the divine will, and that no earthly account would ever suffice to explain God's intentions.[1]

Not surprisingly, this dilemma became evident even to the pioneers of modern science. However, Newton and other believing scientists still felt compelled because of religious reasons to combine the mechanistic-determinist view of the world with real divine acts. Although they were willing to live with the unresolved problem, later modern scientists were not; that uneasy relationship was soon torn apart. Evolutionary theory with its focus on chance further helped make divine acts obsolete. Any notion of free agency in a world ruled by determinism and causal closure (which of course leads to reductionism) is extremely difficult as a concept.[2]

Modern theology had several options in this situation, none of them, however satisfactory or fruitful. To simplify a complicated matter, a bifurcation emerged: whereas Conservatives continued the affirmation of divine acts without concern for science, Liberals virtually left behind any factual notion of divine acts as they were conceived to be merely subjective responses to religious influences (Schleiermacher).[3] In other words, if any notion of an objective ("real") divine act entails intervention by God in the world, which is supposed to function according to the divinely set laws, it looks like the only alternative is to speak of subjective divine acts, that is, personal religious responses. That would certainly not contradict science, but then, theologically speaking, it would make meaningless the whole idea of God's works in nature and history. Even the Neo-orthodox attempt to salvage divine acts did not produce an alternative. With all their resistance to Classical Liberalism, they continued subscribing to the "nature-history" dualism, that is, science investigates the happenings in nature and humanities the domain of human affairs. That of course led to removing God and his acts from the realm of the sciences.[4]

So, is there a way out of this impasse? Dissatisfied with options available, a growing group of leading theologians and believing scientists are aiming at a third alternative that, while sensitive to the necessity (for biblical-theological reasons) of affirming divine acts, wishes to do so in a way that would not contradict physical sciences. Unprecedented theological

---

1. Clayton, "Impossible Possibility," 249.

2. See further, Peacocke, *Theology for a Scientific Age*, 139–40.

3. For a detailed history and discussion, see Murphy, *Beyond Liberalism and Fundamentalism*.

4. A prime example is Gilkey, "Cosmology, Ontology, and the Travail of Biblical Language," 194–205. Other similar interpretations can be found in R. Bultmann, G. Kauffman, and M. Wiles, among others.

advances have been made during the past decades, particularly under the leadership of the long-term international "Scientific Perspectives on Divine Action" interdisciplinary project co-sponsored by the Center for Theology and Natural Sciences (Berkeley, California) and the Vatican Observatory (Vatican City).[5] The key theological-philosophical approach advocated by the project is known under the somewhat cumbersome nomenclature "Non-Interventionist Objective Divine Action" (NIODA).[6] That proposal seeks to "view special providence as consisting in the *objective* acts of God in nature and history to which we respond through faith *and* we can interpret these acts in a *non-interventionist* manner consistent with the natural sciences." In other words, it is able to "believe credibly that God really did do what the Bible testifies to."[7]

The current essay takes its point of departure in the promise of the NIODA project. It does so by both affirming its main intent and sympathetically critiquing NIODA's liabilities and limitations. The main goal of the essay is to locate NIODA in a robust trinitarian-pneumatological framework in order to save it from some potential problems (to be identified below) and to make it more satisfactory for (systematic) Christian theology of divine providence and continuing creation.

I will first introduce the conditions and possibility of NIODA with regard to negotiating the dilemma about divine action described above. Thereafter, I will subject NIODA under a sympathetic critical assessment by focusing on theological (rather than scientific) aspects. Finally, I will seek to offer a constructive proposal with a view towards pneumatological and trinitarian conditions and implications.

THE CONDITIONS AND POSSIBILITY OF NON-INTERVENTIONIST OBJECTIVE DIVINE ACTS

The "Openness" of Nature

The goal of NIODA is to reaffirm divine acts without the fear of divine intervention. Particularly, it seeks "to speak about special divine acts in which God acts objectively in an unusual and particularly meaningful way in,

---

5. An assessment of the twenty-year interdisciplinary work on divine action with major volumes of publications is Russell, Murphy, and Stoeger, *Scientific Perspectives on Divine Action*.

6. See Russell, "Challenges and Progress in 'Theology and Science,'" 3–56; Clayton, "Toward a Theory of Divine Action," 85–110.

7. Russell, *Cosmology*, 112 (emphasis original).

with, and through events which serve to mediate God's action."[8] Its main architect, the physicist-theologian Bob Russell underlines that NIODA is not meant as an attempt to explain how exactly God acts, let alone prove that God acts. Rather, NIODA explanations seek to reconcile the conditions of non-interventionist divine acts vis-à-vis current scientific understanding. Nor is NIODA another version of the God-of-the-gaps. Rather than focusing on the gaps in our knowledge (which will probably be filled by new scientific discoveries), NIODA instead relies on what we currently know.[9]

What makes NIODA possible is the radical transformation of the scientific worldview in the twentieth century as the result of the shift away from the semi-mechanistic and dualistic Newtonian cosmology to relativity theories, quantum theory, and related developments.[10] Rather than steady, mechanistic, and dualistic, the workings of cosmos bespeak for relationality, interdependence, dynamism, evolvement, and complexity. What quantum theory reveals is that not only at the smallest, subatomic level (where it primarily functions), but also at the macro-level, nature reveals surprises, irregularities, and unpredictability. This is not to say that nature acts unlawfully; the laws of nature are still in place and natural phenomena are (relatively speaking) deterministic, otherwise no scientific observations would be possible. What the unpredictability means is that determinism is not ironclad and that—according to the major (Copenhagian) interpretation of quantum theory—natural processes and events are probabilistic in nature. The lack of exact results is not a matter of weakness of measurement, but an inherent feature of the reality studied.[11]

This kind of world is open rather than closed in nature. In the open universe, the process of emergence is constantly at work. The basic definition of *emergence* is "that new and unpredicatable phenomena are naturally produced by interactions in nature; that these new structures, organisms, and ideas are not reducible to the subsystems on which they depend; and that the newly evolved realities in turn exercise a causal influence on the parts out of which they arose."[12] A theologically and eschatologically significant observation is that "[e]mergence at all levels of being, and not just at those of life and mind, requires that nature possess an anticipatory rather than simply a cumulative character. It must be open to a domain of

---

8. Russell, *Cosmology*, 117.

9. See Russell, *Cosmology*, 125–29.

10. For a succinct listing, see Russell, *Cosmology*, 117–19.

11. See further, McGrath, *Scientific Theology*, 2:83–85; Russell, "Quantum Physics in Philosophical and Theological Perspective," 343–74.

12. Clayton, *Mind and Emergence*, vi; for the history, see ch. 1.

potentiality that makes a quiet entrance—from the future as it were—and thus opens up the otherwise unbending fabric of things to the later-and-more."[13] In other words, there is a dynamic tension between increasing entropy and the higher structuring. "In its dependence all creaturely reality is subject to the fate of destructuring, of dissolution according to the law of entropy. Because of the openness of process structures to future events, however, new structures are constantly formed, since processes take place in open rather than closed systems."[14]

A Multi-faceted and Complex Account of Divine Action

In keeping with the complexity and multi-level nature of the cosmos, NIODA's notion of divine action is multifaceted, not only because it encompasses both objective and subjective dimensions as argued, but also because it allows for divine action to happen directly (without having to perform any prior act) or indirectly (by setting into motion a sequence of events) as well as in either a mediated way (God acting in, with, and through the existing processes) or in an immediate way (*ex nihilo*).[15] The simultaneous establishment of various types of causalities is superior to the tendency to reduce it to only one type, typically the bottom-up approach, which refers to the effects of the lower on upper levels. Along with that we need to acknowledge other forms of causality and influence:

- "'Top-down' refers to God's action at a higher epistemic and phenomenological level than the level of the effects," such as when mind causally influences brain (and therefore the whole human being).[16]

- 'Whole-part' causality or constraint refers to the way the boundary of a system affects the specific state of the system," as God is the "boundary of the universe itself," leading up to certain states and processes.

- "Lateral" causality refers to effects at the same epistemic level as their causes, but at the end of the causal chain (as in biology, biological effects).[17]

---

13. Haught, *Is Nature Enough?*, 86.
14. Pannenberg, *Systematic Theology*, 2:112.
15. Russell, *Cosmology*, 122.
16. For a thoughtful and cautious clarification and questioning of some of the premises behind Peacocke's and others' use of downward causation (and emergence), see Murphy, "Emergence, Downward Causation, and Divine Action," 111–31.
17. Russell, *Cosmology*, 124.

Along with the top-down, the whole-part influence model is another way to speak of God's influence on the world without interrupting the regularities set up by the same God;[18] this is particularly important in complex systems.[19] The notion of information is useful for speaking of the influence of the environment or large system on various levels.[20] What is striking is that even in dissipative systems far from equilibrium, large-scale patterns may appear in spite of random motions of the units; this is what is aptly called "order out of chaos."[21]

Theologically speaking, the model is based on the recognition that the omniscient God uniquely knows, across all frameworks of reference of time and space, everything that is possible to know about the state(s) of all-that-is, including the interconnectedness and interdependence of the world's entities, structures, and processes. Because the "'ontological gap(s)' between the world and God is/are located simply *everywhere* in space and time, God could affect holistically the state of the world (the whole in this context) . . . This unitive, holistic effect of God on the world could occur without abrogating any of the laws (regularities) which apply to the levels of the world's constituents."[22]

Divine Action and a Chastened Interpretation of Determinism

One of the openings for divine action is "ontological indeterminism," that is, regular, natural processes are not totally deterministic, they are rather statistical or probabilistic. Hence, *pace* Laplace, there is no way to fully predict all processes of nature, not only because we do not know enough but also because indeterminism describes natural processes.[23] Among science-theology scholars, both quantum theory and chaos theory have been widely investigated concerning indeterminism, that is, their capacity to provide a meaningful opening for divine action.

Quantum theory helps explain bottom-up causality as it claims (in its major Copenhagen interpretation) that events and processes at the

18. Peacocke, "Sound of Sheer Silence," 235–40 particularly; Peacocke, *Theology for a Scientific Age*, 157–60.

19. For an accessible explanation, see Murphy and Ellis, *On the Moral Nature of the Universe*, 22–32; see also Murphy and Brown, *Did My Neurons Make Me Do It?*, 57–62.

20. Peacocke, "Sound of Sheer Silence," 220–29.

21. Prigogine and Stengers, *Order Out of Chaos*. "In dissipative systems order can indeed result from chaos. The requirement is that energy must enter the system in order for this to occur." Richard Carlson (private email communication, 9/7/2013).

22. Peacocke, "Sound of Sheer Silence," 236.

23. See also Russell, *Cosmology*, 120–21.

subatomic level are to some extent indeterministic and hence probabilistic. In that sense, the future is ontologically open, "influenced but *under*determined by the factors of nature acting in the present." Hence, we speak of potentialities and actualities.[24] The theologian who utilizes quantum theory is not implying that the subatomic level is the only one at which God works; recall the multifaceted nature of divine action discussed above.[25] Furthermore, the theologian must be careful not to make God a "natural cause." While deeply involved in natural processes, God also supremely transcends the created order, even in the deepest immanence.[26] And again, quantum theory is not creating another form of the God-of-the-gaps. Rather, indeterminacy has to do with what are called "causal gaps" in nature, that is, the lack of total determinism.[27] Rather than "intervening," God works in keeping with nature's indeterminacy. Finally, in order to avoid occasionalism (that is, the created order merely provides an occasion for God's works, without any true mediatory role), per our discussion above, one needs to speak also of the mediation of divine acts in cooperation with created agents.[28]

Not all scholars agree on quantum theory's compatibility with divine action.[29] Former quantum physicist Polkinghorne has rightly reminded us that, if not careful, the employ of indeterminacy may yield an episodic account of divine action by a "hole-and-corner deity."[30] Furthermore, he has wondered how out of lack of order ("chaos") would come something meaningful. More importantly, he also refers to the well-known "measurement problem" (a hugely complicated issue regarding its meaning and implications). For the sake of this discussion, let me (over)simplify what is the problem for him: when it comes to the "time development" of the wave function Ψ, it follows determinism (of Schrödinger's equation), whereas when it comes to interaction *between* quantum systems, "irreversible interaction" turns out to be indeterministic. Now, on this basis, Polkinghorne rejects the quantum principle as an aid for divine action because it would render it

---

24. Russell, *Cosmology*, 156 (emphasis original). See also Stoeger, "Epistemological and Ontological Issues Arising from Quantum Theory," 81–98.

25. See also Russell, *Cosmology*, 157, 159.

26. See also Russell, *Cosmology*, 155, 169–70.

27. Tracy, "Particular Providence and the God of the Gaps," 290.

28. Murphy, "Divine Action in the Natural Order," 340–42 particularly.

29. An outright "global" rejection of not only quantum-theology engagement but the whole NIODA project is Saunders, *Divine Action and Modern Science*; for a thoughtful responses and rebuttals, see Russell, *Cosmology*, 174–77; Wildman, "Divine Action Project, 1988–2003," 31–75.

30. Polkinghorne, *Science and Creation*, 58; more extensively and precisely in Polkinghorne, *Science and Providence*, 27–28 particularly.

episodic, applying only to the moments of "measurement" and their effects in the macroworld.[31] Is that so? Not necessarily. Russell has neatly argued that the "measurements" (irreversible interactions) include all kinds of phenomena ranging from "'micro-macro,' 'micro-meso,' and 'micro-micro' interactions" and "are not limited to interactions with the ordinary world around us." Therefore, only looking at those "episodic" moments when the effects of irreversible interactions cause effects at the macro-level is much too limited an outlook. A comprehensive, multilevel understanding alone may yield a "ubiquitous" and "pervasive" character of divine action.[32]

Chaos theory has brought to the popular consciousness the extremely intricate nature of natural processes, as discussed above. Particularly striking is the "extreme sensitivity to initial conditions displayed by some non-linear dissipative systems."[33] What is ironic about chaos theory is that while the behavior can be modeled by mathematical equations,[34] because of the sheer complexity it soon generates a process whose outcome is unpredictable. Minimally it can be said that chaos theory "illustrates the insurmountable epistemic limits of any finite intelligence."[35] But not only that: "it also suggests causal relationships where none were previously suspected."[36] So the term "chaos" has to be rightly handled; in scientific understanding it is deterministic and thus compatible with classical physics (otherwise, no equations would be possible of course). What makes it "chaotic" is that in light of our current knowledge, it relies on probabilities and statistical explanations. In that sense it represents a third alternative between classical and quantum physics, as it combines features of both.[37] Chaos theory has of course everything to do with science's better understanding of an unprecedented complexity of the universe.[38] What is also astonishing is that "chaos" is not merely a limitation to otherwise regular process of nature; nature (as open) employs "chaos" also for creative, novel, constructive purposes.[39]

Having registered above the grave doubts expressed by Polkinghorne towards quantum indeterminacy's relevance, not surprisingly he has turned

---

31. Polkinghorne, *Reason and Reality*, 40–41.

32. Russell, *Cosmology*, 164–67 (165), 171–73. Similarly, Murphy ("Divine Action and Natural Order," 340–42) supports the pervasive nature of divine actions in the quantum world.

33. Tracy, "Special Divine Action and the Laws of Nature," 266.

34. See Wildman and Russell, "Chaos," 49–90.

35. Tracy, "Special Divine Action," 266–67 (267).

36. Crutchfield et al., "Chaos," 35; that essay is an accessible primer to chaos theory.

37. Russell, *Cosmology*, 130.

38. See Küppers, "Understanding Complexity," 93–105.

39. Prigogine and Stengers, *Order Out of Chaos*.

to chaos theory in search of an asset. Somewhat similarly to Peacocke's "whole-part" influence, he surmises that because chaotic systems are extensively linked with other complex processes (and of course ultimately to the whole) God's influence can be understood in terms of "input of active information" as a way of selecting between alternative paths of development.[40] There are no compelling arguments against the claim that in an "open" world, including an "open" future (without compromising the basically deterministic nature of natural processes), "there is room for the operation of holistic organizing principles, . . . for human intentionality, and for divine providential interaction."[41] Similarly to other theological claims, this kind of holistic and multifaceted divine action is hidden to scientific exploration.[42]

Having now clarified the challenges to theological talk about divine action (and providence) vis-à-vis the contemporary scientific worldview and the promise of NIODA in combatting those challenges, let me turn to a theological assessment of that proposal. Following that sympathetic critical account, I wish to offer a constructive pneumatological proposal.

TOWARDS A PNEUMATOLOGICAL-TRINITARIAN THEOLOGY OF DIVINE ACTION AND PROVIDENCE

Revising and Reorienting the Non-Interventionist Divine Action Approach

Let me emphasize that the theologically driven critical remarks on the NIODA template should not be taken as undermining, let alone rejecting, its superb achievements. Critique arises out of the deep desire to refine it and so make it fit for a systematic/constructive theological work.

First, ironically, NIODA suffers from "dualistic" tendencies in its conception of divine action's conditions in creation. What I mean is this: when listing the scientific obstacles to divine action, the NIODA scholars tend to resort—against their better knowledge, I take it—to an outdated worldview in which "subject" (God) and "object" (world), physical and spiritual, divine and earthly are strictly taken as alternatives.

Coupled with that, second, is the tendency to make determinism (of natural processes) the default position, which has to be qualified at any cost "to make room" for God to act, instead of beginning from the current scientific understanding of the world's processes as regular and law like, but so utterly complex and probabilistic that openness is to be taken for granted

---

40. Polkinghorne, "Metaphysics of Divine Action," 153–54.
41. Polkinghorne, "Laws of Nature and the Laws of Physics," 442.
42. See Polkinghorne, "Laws of Nature and the Laws of Physics," 446.

(although, of course not openness for *divine* action). I fear at times the NIODA advocates take determinism more seriously than most scientists![43] On the other side, the whole concept of "indeterminacy," while certainly related to quantum and chaos theory, may be a wider and more complex concept, and (as a default position) calls for a robust analysis.[44] That is closely linked with a better philosophical-theological understanding of natural law: while respectful of the regularities of the world, there is no reason to consider God as prisoner to his own laws![45]

Related, third, is NIODA's almost pathological (or at least exaggerated) fear of "intervention." As N. T. Wright correctly notes, the continuous use of terms such as

> invasive, intrusive or . . . 'interventionist' . . . imply, or even presuppose, a latent Epicurean framework: the divinity is normally outside the process of the world, and occasionally reaches in, does something, and then goes away again. But in biblical thought heaven and earth—God's sphere and our sphere—are not thought of as detached or separate. They overlap and interlock.[46]

Fourth, NIODA is much more sophisticated in scientific-philosophical than (systematic-) theological argumentation and approach. Indeed, the whole effort so far has been motivated so much by apologetic concerns deriving from (at times somewhat noncritically) listening to natural scientists that the constructive theological work is yet to be done. Part of the weakness is its lack of an integral trinitarian conception of God's works in the world, its lack of trinitarian contours.[47]

Some critics of NIODA have wondered whether its use of various kinds of approaches to "make room" for divine action, namely, whole-part/top-down causation, quantum, and chaos theory, is a liability. I disagree with this criticism and wholeheartedly underline that multiplicity of tactics is rather a great asset.[48] This is far superior to "uniformitarianism," which reductionistically thinks that "God always and everywhere does the same

---

43. For a thoughtful reflection, see Stoeger, "Conceiving Divine Action in a Dynamic Universe," 240–44.

44. See further, Gregersen, "Three Types of Indeterminacy," 165–86; Ward, "Divine Action in an Emergent Cosmos," 288–89 (289).

45. See "Contingency and Natural Law," 72–122.

46. Wright, "Mind, Spirit, Soul and Body."

47. Russell (*Cosmology*, 192–93 and elsewhere), though, notes the need for that.

48. So also Gregersen, "Special Divine Action and the Quilt of Laws," 181–83.

job of creating-and-upholding an already established universe," after Schleiermacher and contemporary liberals.[49]

Finally, the foundational question that has to be asked in relation to the NIODA project is whether, contrary to all its claims otherwise, it still ends up being a new form of a God-of-the-Gaps theology. This has to do with its robust use of both quantum and chaos theory's alleged "openings." Although the approach avoids the old-time pitfall of the God-of-the-Gaps tactics in which God is needed whenever there are epistemological gaps (because NIODA speaks of permanent, ontological gaps in an indeterministic nature), it still is the case that the divine influence is pretty thin. Clayton expresses my doubts well: "A gap for divine action that cannot be closed may represent a breakthrough for the theologian, but inserting God into this space, even if it is a permanent opening rather than a gap, may well seem like a sleight of hand to one's scientific partners" and hardly convincing at all.[50] That said, it can be counterargued (and I think Clayton would agree with me) that the whole aim of the Divine Action project is minimalist, to provide the context for theologians to speak of divine acts in a meaningful way in the context of current scientific understanding of the world. As to how much that may or may not be convincing to nonbelieving scientists is a different matter.

A Pneumatological-Trinitarian Theology of Divine Action

Trinitarian theology is not only a distinctively Christian framework for conceiving the coming into existence of the created order but also for the Creator's continuous creation thereof. With the same love that the Father loves the Son, he loves the universe, his creation, by continuously providing for its life, meaning, and hope for the future. The Son as *Logos* and mediator of all creaturely work of God is the one in whom everything is held together. Through his Spirit the triune God is present in, under, above, and below, so to speak, all natural processes.[51] According to Gregory of Nyssa, "For all things depend on Him who is, nor can there be anything which has not its being in Him who is ... [A]ll things are in Him, and He in all things ... He Who holds together Nature in existence is transfused in *us*; while at that other time He was transfused throughout *our nature*."[52] Astonishingly—in

---

49. Gregersen, "Special Divine Action and the Quilt of Laws," 184.
50. Clayton, "Toward a Theory of Divine Action that Has Traction," 108.
51. For a full-scale trinitarian theology of creation, see ch. 4 in my *Creation and Humanity*.
52. Gregory of Nyssa, *The Great Catechism* 25.

light of the cosmologies of his times—Gregory's thinking is so thoroughly participatory and holistic that even heaven for him does not represent merely something transcendent but rather, "pervades all creation and . . . does not exist separated from being."[53] Many other theological witnesses to the same effect can be found in theological tradition.[54] The Australian Roman Catholic Denis Edwards succinctly summarizes the main thrust of a trinitarian theology of providence: "The trinitarian God works in and through the process of the universe, through laws and boundary conditions, through regularities and chance, through chaotic systems and the capacity for self-organization."[55]

Consequently, as already emphasized, theologically we must hold on to the widest and most diverse possible account of divine action in the world, rather than, say, debating whether due to quantum or chaos indeterminacy. Furthermore, very importantly, we should not seek to reveal the "'causal joint' between divine action and created causality," simply because we can't[56]—or else we could read God's mind! At the same time, we should of course consider scientific and theological explanations as complementary.

A key to a ubiquitous and comprehensive theology of divine action is the trinitarian doctrine of divine omnipresence—which also entails divine omniscience: "All things are present to him and are kept by him in his presence,"[57] as classically affirmed in Ps 139. Through his Spirit God is present everywhere and thus able to know everything. This is of course not to compromise but rather establish transcendence as well: "Precisely as the one who incommensurably transcends his creation, God is still present to even the least of his creatures. As in the case of his eternity, then, there are combined in his omnipresence elements of both immanence and transcendence in keeping with the criterion of the true Infinite."[58] In this sense, the establishment of divine action with the help of quantum theory (in its ubiquitous form) points in the right direction, "reemphasizing God's operational presence in the most basic processes of nature known to us,"[59] that is, even the subatomic. Here an analogical-metaphorical use of the scientific concept of field of force is appropriate: "the presence of God's Spirit in his

---

53. Gregory of Nyssa, "On What It Means to Call Oneself a Christian," 87; I am indebted to Zimmermann, *Incarnational Humanism*, 235.

54. Aquinas, *Summa Theologiae* 1.1.8; Luther, WA 23:133; LW 37:58.

55. Edwards, "Discovery of Chaos and the Retrieval of the Trinity," 157–75 (170).

56. Edwards, "Discovery of Chaos and the Retrieval of the Trinity," 172–73.

57. Pannenberg, *Systematic Theology*, 1:380.

58. Pannenberg, *Systematic Theology*, 1:412.

59. Gregersen, "Special Divine Action and the Quilt of Laws," 194.

creation can be described as a field of creative presence, a comprehensive field of force that releases event after event into finite existence."[60]

In keeping with the scriptural teaching (Ps 139; 104:29–30), the trinitarian presence in the world is funded by a robust pneumatological doctrine. Moltmann's striking term "immanent transcendence" well captures this dynamic. "Through his Spirit God himself is present in his creation. The whole creation is a fabric woven and shot through by the efficacies of the Spirit. Through his Spirit God is also present in the very structures of matter. Creation contains neither spirit-less matter nor non-material spirit; there is only *informed* matter."[61] In keeping with the complexity of the world—and infinity of the triune God—the presence of the Spirit is manifested in various forms in every being in the world.[62] Far from being subsumed in the natural processes or acting as yet another natural cause, the Spirit of God is transcendently immanent in all things.[63] Again, this is a theological claim and of course hidden to scientific experiments.

Gunton adds the important note that whatever problems may relate to the interpretation of Spirit of God in terms of "force-field," it has great value on the question of how to understand God's action: the idea of the Spirit's work "as interacting fields of force rather than billiard-ball-like entities bumping into one another, is of extreme importance in showing that the world is open to God's continuing interaction with it."[64]

A robust trinitarian panentheism ("Classical Panentheism"[65]) funds a dynamic, multifaceted divine action, providence, and causality. To be the Creator is far more than being the world's cause. While causality should not of course be eliminated from the theological thesaurus,[66] the main focus should be placed on the living, dynamic, creative presence of the Creator in the world:

> If the Creator is himself present in his creation by virtue of the Spirit, then his relationship to creation must rather be viewed as an intricate web of unilateral, reciprocal and many-sided relationships. In this network of relationships, "making,"

---

60. Pannenberg, *Introduction to Systematic Theology*, 49.
61. Moltmann, *God in Creation*, 212 (emphasis original).
62. Moltmann, *Spirit of Life*, 34.
63. Moltmann, *Spirit of Life*, 34, 35.
64. Gunton, *Triune Creator*, 175–76.
65. In chapter 10 of my *Trinity and Revelation*, I have developed a theological alternative to the impasse between Classical Theism and (forms of contemporary) Panentheism(s) which I call "Classical Panentheism."
66. Contra Moltmann, *God in Creation*, 14.

"preserving," "maintaining," and "perfecting" are certainly the great *one-sided* relationships; but "indwelling," "sympathizing," "participating," "accompanying," "enduring," "delighting," and "glorifying" are relationships of *mutuality* which describe a cosmic community of living between God the Spirit and all his created beings.[67]

Classical Panentheism also allows us to hold on tightly to both sides of the activity and relationship between God and the world: the "one-sided" creation and the "mutual" participation of creatures in preservation, perfecting, and final consummation.[68] The divinely given mandate (Gen 1:26–27) belongs to that invitation for collaboration and vice-regency.

Unlike we humans, the triune Creator is not in a hurry with the universe. Speaking of continuous creation and divine acts in the universe, we need to be reminded of the long timeline. If, as we think currently, the universe came into being about 14 billion years ago with extremely fine-tuned conditions, we have a lot of room, so to speak, to consider the breadth and depth of divine action throughout the universe's history. In that framework, talk about the multilevel (top-down/whole part and bottom-up, among others) causality and influence is both necessary and highly useful.[69]

In light of these theological reflections, we should also be reminded in this context that in keeping with the triune God's infinite nature, including omniscience, we should be open to recognizing "the profound metaphysical point that divine causality transcends any other category of causality."[70] This is not an effort to divorce God from the world, nor to make divine action more mysterious than it is. Rather, it is to cash out the implications of God's thoroughgoing, all-pervasive presence through the Spirit in the world created and sustained in and through the Son because of the Father's overflowing love.

An important step towards a comprehensive, ubiquitous theological account of the divine action is to affirm God's exceptional acts along with regular law-like events.

---

67. Moltmann, *God in Creation*, 14 (emphasis original).

68. I am aware that here I modify Moltmann's citation to serve my own "less" panentheistic and more classical account of the God-world relationship.

69. See also Russell, *Cosmology*, 160.

70. Carroll, "Aquinas on Creation and the Metaphysical Foundations of Science," 91; cited in Tracy, "Special Divine Action," 254.

Special Divine Action and "Miracles"

A proper way to test the theological suitability of a pneumatological-trinitarian account of NIODA is to consider what may be appropriately called the special divine action, namely instances when God seems to be executing a divine act which can be labelled miraculous or at least untypical. Not surprisingly these kinds of divine acts—say, a tangible answer to a specific prayer in terms of a healing of sickness, release from under a financial breakdown, or, say an instantaneous healing of a relationship—have come under a massive suspicion among the critics of divine acts. Not only among them but even for some advocates of NIODA such as Peacocke, the divine action does not include miraculous divine action.[71] Recall that the reason why theologians such as P. Tillich eschewed what he called the "supranaturalistic" is that he saw them as violations of nature's laws (although he rightly saw that if "miracles" were allowed, they should be called "sign-events" following Johannine terminology).[72]

Without being able to go into the important investigation of the ways the notions of the "miraculous" and "supernatural" have developed in the history of philosophy and theology, we can say safely that the Enlightenment-based rebuttal of the miraculous because of the alleged iron-clad determinism of the world hardly calls for a sustained theological-philosophical rebuttal. The reason is simply the openness of cosmos, discussed above. In that light, we can set aside the Humean claim for the miracle as the violation of natural laws. That claim is tied to the now-outdated Newtonian-Laplacean strict determinism and as such has lost much of its key appeal.

Against those who reject special divine action, K. Ward rightly wonders that while believing that "God, a supernatural being, has caused, and continues to cause, the whole universe to exist . . . [h]ow plausible it is, then, to say that such a God will refuse to operate in the world in particular ways?" Furthermore, he reminds us, because of the divine omnipresence, "no part of the physical universe is ever absent from God." If so, then the personal God truly interacts with the world, including being affected by world affairs. Now comes Ward's main challenge to those who deny special divine action: if God creates the world with an intentional act (as all theists believe), then it has to be said that "[s]ince the bringing of something into being is the strongest possible causal influence upon it, it may seem

---

71. See, e.g., Peacocke, "Prologue: Naturalism, Theism, and Religion," 9. Unfortunately, Peacocke mistakenly claims to find support for this anti-miraculous non-interventionist view in Eastern Orthodox theology by taking out of context a statement from Lossky (*Mystical Theology of the Eastern Church*, 70).

72. Tillich, *Systematic Theology*, 1:115.

unnecessary to espouse a theory that denies any particular influence of God upon the universe."[73]

I would add that in Peacocke's own deeply panentheistic, mutually conditioned theology, to suppose that something comes from "outside" to violate the natural laws seems like an odd fear. Only a deist could say so, but not a panentheist (nor even a Classical Theist). Furthermore, when personal beings are in mutual interaction and have causal effects, these influences are not external violations of other person's balance, so to speak. God similarly is believed to be (analogically speaking) a Person and hence intends to have a personal relationship.[74] Ward also makes the needed observation that unless one thinks of natural laws as reducible to a set of physical laws, the Humean fear of the violation thereof disappears. This is also supported by the simple notion that we no longer think that nature is totally deterministic (although it is "regular") and that therefore, the laws of nature "do not cover everything."[75]

Hence, the conclusion is that rather than denying the possibility of miracles, we just have to do away with the mistaken concept of miracles as "arbitrary interferences in an otherwise elegant and lawlike cosmos"—the violation of the laws of nature. Instead, we have to say that in the kind of created reality we live in, miracles have "their own form of intelligibility and rationality" as the personal God is affected by and responds to the needs, desires, and prayers of his creatures. Recall our conviction that "the divine Spirit interpenetrates the universe at every point." To call these divine "interventions" violations of laws is absurd. That natural sciences are neither able to predict nor fully investigate them, does not make miracles any less true.[76]

Ward rightly concludes that miracles are neither "immoral," that is, breaches of natural laws, nor "irrational," that is, "emergency-interventions" to fix what went wrong in nature. Rather, they are "law-transcending events, extraordinary events manifesting divine causality that modifies the normal regularities of nature with the purpose of manifesting the basis and goal of the physical world in a wider spiritual realm." One of the purposes of miracles is to "show the power of Spirit to relate matter to Spirit" in transcending the typical patterns of interaction.[77] The most profound Christian miracle, the resurrection of Christ, seems to point to freedom from decay

---

73. Ward, "Personhood, Spirit, and the Supernatural," 153–55 (155).
74. Wiles, "Religious Authority and Divine Action," 181–94.
75. Ward, "Personhood," 156–57 (157).
76. Ward, "Personhood," 160.
77. Ward, "Divine Action in an Emergent Cosmos," 297.

and dissolution, "showing the goal of the whole physical process to be the transformation of the physical into an incorruptible vehicle of divine life."[78] Significantly the miracles in the Gospel of John are called "signs" (*semeia*). Ultimately, miracles thus receive their meaning not from the past but from the future, new creation.

Christ's resurrection as the most profound divine action known to us reveals the ultimate meaning of the miracle. Rather than going against nature, it transcends and lifts up the natural. It points to the eschatological consummation when, according to the biblical promises, creation "will be set free from its bondage to decay" (Rom 8:21). In resurrection even death will be defeated (1 Cor 15:55).

In the final analysis, a theological perception of an event as miraculous is just that: *theological*. On the one hand, miracle can only be had through the eye of faith—and therefore, the "miracle does not replace faith by demonstrating the presence of God through sign language."[79] On the other hand, without faith, theological interpretation, even the strangest and most counterintuitive event can also be explained otherwise. Similarly, to the Book of Nature, a "miraculous act by itself is silent" and invites diverse interpretations.[80]

A BRIEF CONCLUDING REFLECTION

The task of this essay is simple and straightforward, namely to establish the possibility and nature of divine action vis-à-vis those opinions which (mistakenly) believe that the rebuttal follows more or less automatically from the contemporary scientific worldview. The basic aim is not primarily apologetic. It simply is the case that for a naturalist[81] nothing that happens in this cosmos is to be attributed to God. Rather, the main aim is to make meaningful the *theological* talk about providence and divine action—whether general or special. For that purpose, a careful scrutiny of the NIODA (non-interventionist objective divine action) was conducted. While taking that proposal as the point of departure, a robust pneumatological-trinitarian proposal was set forth as a way to correct the liabilities of that project and to

---

78. Ward, "Divine Action in an Emergent Cosmos," 297. On the importance of the resurrection of Christ in this regard, see also Polkinghorne, *Quarks, Chaos and Christianity*, ch. 6.

79. Schwarz, *Creation*, 221.

80. Schwarz, *Creation*, 225.

81. For a typology various forms of naturalisms and their theological implications, see ch. 2 in my *Creation and Humanity*.

advance a more coherent and comprehensive theological account of divine action.

Among the advocates of NIODA, there are differing opinions as to what might be the main avenue or platform for the establishment of the "openness" in nature to facilitate the divine action. The quantum indeterminacy and chaos theory are the main candidates. For a non-scientist such as myself, not capable of assessing the scientific ramifications, it is best not to be dogmatic. As long as leading believing scientists such as the late Peacocke (quantum theory) and Polkinghorne (chaos theory) make a compelling case for either one, the theologian hardly is able to resolve the issue. The theologian's contribution is to remind of the importance the Spirit: through the Spirit, the divine omnipresence and omniscience fund a comprehensive account of divine action.

CHAPTER 6

The Human Prototype
With Jesus, We See What We Were Created to Be

A FEW YEARS AGO, WIRED MAGAZINE reported on what it called "a star-studded panel of scientists" at the World Science Festival in New York City. The scientists had gathered to discuss what it means, from a scientific perspective, to be human.

Marvin Minsky, artificial intelligence pioneer, said the one thing we can do that other species can't is remember; we have cultures, ways of transmitting information. Cognitive scientist Daniel Dennett said we are the first species that can reason with one another. Physicist Jim Gates said we are blessed with the ability to know our mother; that is, we are conscious of more than ourselves, and that just as a child sees a mother, the species sees mother universe. Neuroscientist Antonio Damasio said that the critical factor was language. And on it went. Some were excited that science might be the key to unlock what it means to be human, while others doubted science's ability to do that.

The forum was typical of our age but unusual in the history of humankind. For most of history, philosophers and theologians, not scientists, have asked this question. But this question—What does it mean to be human?—does not puzzle only scientists and philosophers. It's one we all ask ourselves in one form or another.

Sometimes the question is couched in the language of the human potential movement: "How can I be all that I can be?" Sometimes it's a moral question: "How can I act like a decent human being in this situation?" Sometimes it centers on meaning: "What is life all about, and what is the place of a human being in it?" or, "Am I just a carbon-based biped, an evolutionary accident?" or, "What is the purpose of our short life on this planet?" These are old questions. The psalmist, centuries before the coming of Christ, framed the question like this, asking God: "What are human beings that you are mindful of them, mortals that you care for them?" (8:4 NRSV). With the coming of Jesus Christ, we might say, God finally gave an answer.

The great Swiss theologian Karl Barth, fittingly called the "church father" of the twentieth century, put it this way: "As the man Jesus is himself the revealing Word of God, he is the source of our knowledge of the nature of man as created by God."[1]

The logic of this simple statement is compelling: If men and women can know who they are only on the basis of the Word of God, then it is only by looking at the One who indeed *is* himself the Word of God, Jesus Christ, that we can know our identity and nature. Barth put it succinctly: All study and knowledge of human beings is "grounded in the fact that one man among all others is the man Jesus."[2]

In John 14:9, Jesus says, "Anyone who has seen me has seen the Father." We would not be doing any violence to the scriptural teaching should we add a parallel thought: "Anyone who has seen Jesus has seen the true human being."

When God speaks to us about himself and about us, he doesn't just utter words or leave a message. He speaks by becoming one of us.

Therefore—and only therefore—we know who we are because we have been created in his image, in the image of the one who became one of us and into whose image we ought to be conformed until the day when we see him face to face.

Growing up in my homeland, Finland, my dad would tell me enthusiastically about new engines, for either cars or airplanes, when they were in planning and initial construction. To describe them, he often used the word *prototype*: the original blueprint or model after which the engines would be made in the production process. He said the closer to the prototype, the better the engines.

Jesus, the revelation of God, is *the* prototype. He is the only one among us who faithfully and perfectly represents what God, the Creator, wished for the human person, created in his image, to be.

---

1. Barth, *Church Dogmatics*, Vol. III/2, 3.
2. Barth, *Church Dogmatics*, Vol. III/2, 132.

GOD BECAME MATTER

Unlike later creeds and theology, the New Testament does not speculate abstractly about the human nature of Jesus Christ. It speaks of Jesus's humanity in what theologians call "economic" terms—that is, in very concrete terms having to do with the actions of Christ.

Consider, for example, the Bible's astonishing claim that, as does every child, Jesus had to develop and grow (Luke 2:40). Even the more theological account of John's Gospel speaks of Jesus as weary and thirsty (4:6–7). Jesus showed human emotions such as sorrow (11:35) and anguish (12:27). Jesus struggled with accepting God's will (Matt 26:39; Heb 5:7–9). Jesus underwent temptations (Matt 4:1–11). While a host of other biblical testimonies could be added, we can summarize with the statement from Heb 4:15 that Jesus was tempted in every way as we are, yet never sinned.

The early Christian teacher Irenaeus helps us understand this dimension of Jesus's life with the concept of "recapitulation." Drawing on Eph 1:10, he wrote,

> Wherefore also he passed through every stage of life, restoring to all communion with God . . . This made it possible that God recapitulated in himself the ancient formation of man, that he might kill sin, deprive death of its power, and vivify man; and therefore his works are true.[3]

Irenaeus said that as incarnated man, Jesus exposed himself to the kinds of experiences typical of men and women. He did this with a view to our salvation and that we might have hope in this world. In the life and experiences of Jesus Christ, the Man from Nazareth, we discern that being a real human means having a life shaped by dependence, service, and ultimate self-offering to the Father—and all this in the face of the temptations and trials of life.

To probe deeper, we need to examine the phrase "the Word became flesh" (John 1:14). In some sense, this suggests that "flesh"—that is, man as a bodily, concrete, historical being—comes into the fullness of being when the Word (the *Logos*) becomes flesh. Man is God's self-utterance: God speaks out of himself into the empty nothingness of the creature and thus creates man.

Think about the implications of this. Whatever else we are as frail, failing, and sinful persons, we are also the product of God's speaking; our dear Lord, who was before us (John 8:58), became one of us.

---

3. Irenaeus, *Against Heresies* 3.18.

The idea of God assuming humanity is such a scandalous claim that even ancient Christian teachers struggled with it. The greatest teacher of medieval times, Thomas Aquinas, begins his discussion of the Incarnation in the *Summa Theologiae* by asking if it is a "fitting idea" for God to become human: "Since God from all eternity is the very essence of goodness, it was best for him to be as he had been from all eternity. But from all eternity he had been without flesh." To put it as a question: Why would God become flesh if he was already perfect goodness as spirit?

Aquinas listed other objections. For example, he highlighted the infinite difference between the divine and the human, including his observation that God, who fills the whole universe, can hardly be "contained" in a human life. In the end, however, on the basis of biblical teaching and the creeds, the Angelic Doctor happily concluded that indeed, it is most fitting for God to become human because God, the fountain of goodness and love, wished "to communicate itself in the highest manner to the creature" so that created nature could be joined to Creator.[4]

Other early Christians struggled to believe that human life, as such, is "fitting." Some said it was sinful to have a physical body or an emotional nature, especially passionate expressions. Spirituality and "care of the soul" were said to be the "core" of human existence. But the Incarnation tells us otherwise. If it is fitting for almighty God, Creator of heaven and earth, to become a human person who undergoes growth and development from infancy to youth to adulthood, to share the ordinary life of a working family, the betrayal of friends, the opposition of other people, and finally the anguish and fear of death—well, it is then fitting for us humans.

In assuming human life, almighty God affirmed the goodness of everything human, including embodiment, physical nature, weakness, and frailty. Hence, rightly understood, the German Catholic theologian Karl Rahner's daring statement is correct: "The fundamental assertion of Christology is precisely that God became *flesh*, became matter."[5] The Incarnation of the preexistent Logos is a most profound affirmation of the lasting value of men and women in all of their nature and existence.

LIFE WELL LIVED

There is a curious difference between the Gospels and later creedal traditions. Whereas the biblical authors were deeply interested in various aspects of the Savior's earthly life, in the creeds—as the Reformed theologian Jürgen

---

4. Aquinas, *Summa Theologiae III*, q. 1., a.1.
5. Rahner, *Foundations*, 196.

Moltmann observes—between the statements "born of the virgin Mary" and "suffered under Pontius Pilate," there is only a comma![6]

Why is Jesus's earthly life and ministry so important? Because it was a life lived in the way human life is supposed to be lived. It was a life of service, reaching out to others, helping others, finding one's fulfillment in voluntary submission to the Father's will.

The intent of nineteenth-century liberals to reduce Jesus to an ethical teacher is no reason to downplay the importance of Jesus's life. For the Bible-believing, faithful disciple, Jesus's reaching out to sinners, to people outside the covenant, to women, despised as the "weaker sex," and to children, considered inferior to adults, sets the blueprint for a life of inclusion.

Jesus's teaching about the kingdom—the righteous rule of the Father—is not a call to abandon the duties related to family, "tribe," and work, but rather a healthy reminder to put things in eternal perspective. The Savior's preaching about casting off all our sorrows in the confidence of the Father's care, which encompasses things both great and small, helps orient our lives in the stress of contemporary society.

But there is more. In Eph 2:14–15, Paul expands the meaning of Jesus by talking about him as the New Adam. The passage speaks of Jesus's creation "in himself" of "one new humanity" out of gentiles and Jews, the dividing line in that world between two kinds of people. This widening of Jesus's person beyond the contours of Jewish nationalistic faith is the key to the universal relevance of the gospel to all nations.

As human persons, we are part of something larger in the world. Current Western culture speaks in terms of isolated individualism, but the biblical message speaks for community and belonging. True, having been created in the image of God, each and every man and woman is a full image of God, and hence a person in the full sense of the word. But God's intention is not to create isolated individuals but rather communities in which each person can flourish. It is therefore significant that, as contemporary New Testament scholarship reminds us, the typical New Testament phrase "in Christ" is not only about my individual belonging to Christ but also about our belonging to Christ in the communion of believers of all ages.

LIFE WITHOUT END

The Resurrection not only confirms the finished nature of the Atonement, but it also seals the veracity of the earthly Jesus's claims to be a true man. A number of self-made messiahs appeared in the New Testament era; only

---

6. Moltmann, *Way of Jesus Christ*, 150.

one showed himself to be the true Messiah, the one sent by the Father. His identity was confirmed by God's raising him to new life.

The raising to new life of the crucified tells us it is possible for mortal human beings to enjoy life everlasting. As finite human beings, we are all subject to death and decay. The same is true of the earth we inhabit. Those who put their faith and hope in the eternal God can confidently rest in the assurance that beyond death there is life. As the first fruits, Christ has already been raised to life everlasting. The rest of the harvest follows him.

The coming-in-flesh of God, Jesus Christ, tells us we have hope in this life and the life to come. We can be assured that the One who has come to be one of us is not far from us either in life or in death. Martin Luther testified of Jesus Christ, the incarnate One, saying:

> [God] himself must be present in every single creature in its innermost and outermost being, on all sides, through and through, below and above, before and behind, so that nothing can be more truly present and within all creatures than God himself with his power. For it is he who makes the skin, and it is he who makes the bones; it is he who makes the hair on the skin, and it is he who makes the marrow in the bones; it is he who makes every bit of the hair, it is he who makes every bit of the marrow. Indeed, he must make everything, both the parts and the whole.[7]

---

7. Luther, *Luther's Works*, 37.58.

CHAPTER 7

Transformed, Freed, Empowered
The Spirit's Work in the Gifting and Vocation of All Believers

INTRODUCTION

For us Lutherans to consider the work and energies of the Holy Spirit as we dig deeper into our identity is an exciting task, for it is far more typical for us to refer such questions to Christ and the Trinity. The turn to the third person of the Trinity is a timely response to the call from our worldwide globalizing community, particularly from the Global South, where the majority of Lutherans can be found nowadays. Lutherans in Ethiopia, Tanzania, Indonesia, and elsewhere are reminding us to incorporate pneumatological resources and perspectives in our continuing identity search.

My task in this project is to reflect on the Spirit's work particularly from an anthropological perspective. I ask: What are some of the ways the Spirit of God is empowering, gifting, and inspiring the people of God in order for them to live out the central Reformation vision of the priesthood of all believers? What is the Spirit's role in our Christian missional vocation?

With those questions in mind, I wish to develop my theme in three interrelated steps:

- The Holy Spirit in Lutheranism—A Reminder
- The Holy Spirit and Gifting—A Challenge
- The Holy Spirit in the World—A Vision!

THE HOLY SPIRIT IN LUTHERANISM—A REMINDER

The Many Metaphors of the Spirit

What pneumatological resources do we have in our tradition? This question can also be framed in this way, twisting the classical dictum of Tertullian: What has Wittenberg to do with the Pentecost?

Some Lutheran theologians firmly believe that we do possess Spirit-resources and that the Pentecost belongs to Lutherans as much as to other Christian families. For example, in Danish theologian Reginald Prenter's classic *Spiritus Creator: Studies in Luther's Theology*, he insists that

> The concept of the Holy Spirit completely dominates Luther's theology. In every decisive matter, whether it be the study of Luther's doctrine of justification, of his doctrine of the sacraments, of his ethics, or of any other fundamental teaching, we are forced to take into consideration this concept of the Holy Spirit.[1]

Though undoubtedly an overstatement, his claims are still worth pondering. For while Lutheranism certainly is not known for a focus on the third member of the Trinity, and though Martin Luther never wrote a separate treatise on the Holy Spirit, the Reformer nevertheless had many valuable insights on the Spirit. Particularly important are more than twenty of his Pentecost-day sermons that were based on various texts supplied by the lectionary. And in his exposition of the third article of the Creed, he notably relates everything to the Spirit: the church, forgiveness of sins, resurrection of the body, and eternal life. Alternatively, we might consider Luther's pneumatology in the context of his trinitarian teaching, since the doctrine of the Trinity was so formative for Luther, so much so that Bernhard Lohse claims that "[w]ith this constant reference to Christ the Holy Spirit assumed an extraordinarily important place in Luther's theology."[2]

A gifted preacher, Luther often illustrated his sermons and writings with delightful pictures and metaphors. Taking a cue from Acts 17:28, he came up with the idea of calling the Father the "substance" of the Godhead, the Son the "motion" or "movement," having been sent by the Father, and the Spirit the "rest": "We live according to the Spirit, in whom the Father and the Son rest and live, as it were."[3] In explaining the meaning of the *Para-*

---

1. Prenter, *Spiritus Creator*, ix.

2. Lohse, *Martin Luther's Theology*, 235.

3. Martin Luther, *Galatians Commentary* (1519) on 4:6; Luther, *Luther's Works*, 27:290 [hereafter: *LW*].

clete in John 14–16, Luther compared the Spirit's role to that of the preacher who, like an excellent pastor, reminds the congregation of the dangers of false teachers and of those who boast in human merits. The Holy Spirit takes from Christ's own and shares that with us rather than delivering a "human dream and thought."[4] Particularly inventive is Luther's creative recasting of the creation narrative (Gen 1:2) into a poetic form with analogies drawn from nature:

> The Father creates heaven and earth out of nothing through the Son, whom Moses calls the Word. Over these the Holy Spirit broods. As a hen broods her eggs, keeping them warm in order to hatch her chicks, and, as it were, to bring them to life through heat, so Scripture says that the Holy Spirit brooded, as it were, on the waters to bring to life those substances which were to be quickened and adorned. For it is the office of the Holy Spirit to make alive.[5]

The Spirit's Work in Word, Salvation, and Church

Always a trinitarian theologian, standing firmly on the tradition of the church, Luther made every effort to establish an integral link between the Spirit and Christ. In his exposition of the Creed in the *Large Catechism*, he reminds us that:

> God ... created us ... to redeem and sanctify us. Moreover, having bestowed upon us everything in heaven and on earth, he has given us his Son and his Holy Spirit, through whom he brings us to himself ... [W]e could never come to recognize the Father's favor and grace were it not for the Lord Christ, who is a mirror of the Father's heart. Apart from him we see nothing but an angry and terrible Judge. But neither could we know anything of Christ, had it not been revealed by the Holy Spirit.[6]

As is well-known, the close and integral relationship between God's word and God's Spirit was a particular concern to him:

> No one can correctly understand God or His Word unless he has received such understanding immediately from the Holy

---

4. Luther, *Sermons on the Gospel of St. John* (1537), chs. 14–16; *LW* 24:363.

5. Luther, *Lectures on Genesis*, chs. 1–5, on 1:2; *LW* 1:9.

6. Luther, *Large Catechism*, Creed, art. 3, #64, 65; Tappert, *Book of Concord*, 419 [hereafter: *BC*].

Spirit. But no one can receive it from the Holy Spirit without experiencing, proving, and feeling it. In such experience the Holy Spirit instructs us as in His own school, outside of which nothing is learned but empty words and prattle.[7]

No wonder, then, that the gift of salvation wrought by the Triune God is communicated to us by the Spirit of God. Every confirmed Lutheran knows this passage from the *The Small Catechism*:

> I believe that by my own reason or strength I cannot believe in Jesus Christ, my Lord, or come to him. But the Holy Spirit has called me through the Gospel, enlightened me with his gifts, and sanctified and preserved me in true faith, just as he calls, gathers, enlightens, and sanctifies the whole Christian church on earth and preserves it in union with Jesus Christ in the one true faith.[8]

Similarly—and here we come to the center of Luther's pneumatological understanding—it is the work of sanctification or holiness that is distinctive of the ministry of the Spirit. Expressing this in an authentic trinitarian framework, Luther says: "As the Father is called Creator and the Son is called Redeemer, so on account of his work the Holy Spirit must be called Sanctifier, the One who makes holy."[9] Commenting on Rom 8:16 ("[I]t is the Spirit himself bearing witness with our spirit that we are children of God"[10]), the Reformer further reminds us of the testimony of the same Spirit in the heart of the believer.[11]

Yet the Spirit is at work not only in the individual believer's faith and life, but also in the Christian community. Another familiar passage from the *The Small Catechism* sums it up: "But the Holy Spirit has called me through the Gospel, enlightened me with his gifts, and sanctified and preserved me in true faith, just as he calls, gathers, enlightens, and sanctifies the whole Christian church on earth and preserves it in union with Jesus Christ in the one true faith."[12] In *The Large Catechism*, the Reformer elaborates on the various benefits the Spirit brings about in the church, including her calling "together [the church] by the Holy Spirit in one faith, mind, and

---

7. Luther, *The Magnificat*; LW 21:299. See further Silcock, "Luther on the Holy Spirit," 307.

8. Luther, *Small Catechism*, Creed, art. 3; BC, 345.

9. Luther, *Large Catechism*, Creed, art. 3, #36; BC, 415.

10. All biblical citations are from the Revised Standard Version unless otherwise noted.

11. Luther, *Lectures on Romans*; LW 25:359–60.

12. *Small Catechism*, Creed, art. 3, #6; BC, 345.

understanding" and the endowment with "a variety of gifts" in unity. Indeed, "Until the last day the Holy Spirit remains with the holy community or Christian people" and works out various ministries.[13]

Reflection: Anything Missing in Our Understanding of the Spirit's Work?

It is appropriate to pause for a moment and take stock of pneumatological resources and emphases in our tradition. I wish to make four brief comments and then further develop our theme in light of these observations.

First, against the common assumption or charge that Lutheranism has ignored the third person of the Trinity, this brief survey, supported by other essays in this collection, tells otherwise. Yes, there is a fairly rich repertoire of biblical and theological insights into the many roles of the Spirit in the life of the Christian and the church. Particularly important are the domains of Word, salvation, and the church. This is all good and certainly worth preserving.

But, second, it is clear that Lutheran pneumatology is almost exclusively focused on the "spiritual" and salvific aspects. It has fairly little to say of God's Spirit outside the personal and communal salvation and spirituality. That said, this is not only a Lutheran liability. Rather, the mainline doctrine of the Spirit, particularly in the Christian West, has concentrated on issues of spirituality, divine Word, salvation, sacraments, and some other ecclesial issues.

This has meant, third, that issues having to do with the "public"—or dare we call it "wordly"—work of the Spirit have received only scant and occasional treatment. Even though Luther himself invoked a few delightful metaphors from nature, issues related to the Spirit's role in creation have not played a significant role in our tradition. We Lutherans have similarly virtually neglected the Spirit's role in society, politics, economics, culture, entertainment, and the arts and sciences. And we have only very recently even acknowledged the whole issue of the potential role of the S/spirit(s) among religions, even among other Abrahamic faiths (Judaism and Islam).

Last but not least, we Lutherans have neglected, minimized, or outright resisted the ministry of the Holy Spirit in charismatic endowment, spiritual gifts, and dynamic spirituality—all profoundly important themes for the global Lutheran community of the third millennium. The charismatic freedom of the Spirit has been a contentious issue among Lutherans, and more often than not there have been attempts to "limit" the Spirit's work. Despite all this, the charismatic element is a key asset for cultivating and facilitating

---

13. *Large Catechism*, Creed, art. 3; BC, 416–17.

vocation among the whole people of God and we neglect it to the detriment of our ministry and spiritual health.

Let us now unpack these observations and relate our reflections and insights into the gifting, vocation, and the ministry of the whole people of God, for the sake of Triune God's mission in the world.

HOLY SPIRIT AND GIFTING—A CHALLENGE

Why Do We Struggle with the Charismatic Element?

Another way to title this subsection would be to ask of ourselves: "What Has the Wittenberg to do with Charisms!" Why are we Lutherans so often wary of speaking too much, or at all, of spiritual gifts and empowerment? There are a number of reasons. I begin with the most obvious ones.

The roots of our charismatic suspicion go far back in Christian history, at least to the second part of the second century, when a powerful Spirit-movement named Montanism emerged. It challenged the authority of the church and her hierarchy, particularly that of the bishops. Under the leadership of Montanus, this movement claimed to receive direct messages from the Spirit of God (meaning: unmediated by the church), and hence a divinely granted authority over existing ecclesiastical powers. In later history, even after the mainstream church defeated Montanism, charismatically endowed and usually prophetic movements arose over and over again, particularly during times of spiritual awakening and refreshment. For example, the medieval times know many such movement in the church catholic.

By the time the Protestant Reformation emerged, this ancient suspicion towards free-spirited groups and leaders had grown deep and wide. The mainstream church considered them a threat. Yet, this charismatic vitality did not die out.

Enter Martin Luther. The reformer had to fight simultaneously on two fronts. On the one hand, this former Augustinian monk had become critical of his own catholic church's reliance on the hierarchy and human leadership over the Spirit and Word. At the same time, counterintuitively, the Church of Rome, particularly among its numerous monastic orders, had developed a long and varied tradition of cultivating all kinds of mystical, spiritualistic, and charismatic phenomena, from healing and exorcism to prophetic word and other charisms. Luther thought that at times the Church of Rome gave these phenomena authority over the written Word.

On the other hand, he had to face the Reformation-era version of the Montanists, that is the Anabaptists (of various sorts) and other "Left-wing"

Reformers, whom he (mistakenly and pejoratively) called the "Enthusiasts." Rightly or wrongly, Luther assumed that they claimed a "direct," unmediated spiritual experience and so undermined the sacraments and the Word.[14]

This fear of the spiritualists resulted in what theology calls "cessationism." From the English word "to cease," it simply means the idea of coming to an end of the charismatic phenomena and miracles after the closing of the Christian canon in the fourth century. Why? The reason, so cessationists surmise, is that whereas before the biblical canon was in place divinely granted spiritual "signs" were needed to ascertain the authenticity of the ministry and teaching of a leader or a community, no such guarantees were required once the written Word was available to serve as the criterion. The Lutheran Reformation subscribed to this view. An example is Luther's distinction between two comings of the Spirit: first, "In the primitive church ... in a manifest and visible form ... with visible signs" including speaking in tongues and thereafter, including his own time, "without a visible form, namely ... through the spoken Word" into our hearts.[15]

I have suggested that there might be two categories of cessationism: first, what might be called "soft-core" cessationism, according to which there is no dogmatic denial of charisms even after the closing of the canon but rather a wondering of why they seem not to be happening now. In my understanding, Luther himself probably represented this interpretation as, even after having left his religious order, he for example testified and was open to what seemed to be miraculous healings. The second category could be dubbed "hard-core" cessationism, typical of some movements much later than Reformation, including the American Reformed fundamentalism of the turn of the twentieth century. Benjamin B. Warfield's *Counterfeit Miracles* (1918) showcases this interpretation: since spiritual gifts have ceased, should you encounter a claim to one, it must be counterfeit!

There are other reasons that have contributed to the Lutheran suspicion towards the charismatic element. These include a biased, careless interpretation of some doctrinal formulations and emphases which, rightly

---

14. In hindsight, and in fairness to the Anabaptists, with the exception of the extremes such as the followers of Münster, by and large left-wing Reformers did not want to get around the written Word. On the contrary, in current terminology they were fundamentalists who wished to take literally the biblical teaching, including pacifism. Similarly, even with regard to the sacraments, they did not necessarily want to undermine them, even if their theological understanding of them was radically different from the Catholics and Mainline Protestants. In their desire to go back to the believers' baptism, they appealed to the Bible and they were deeply concerned about widespread nominalism among the church folks who seemed to practice sacraments as a more or less automatic way of earning salvation.

15. Luther, *Galatians Commentary* (1535), LW 26:374–75.

used, are essential for the Lutheran understanding of faith. For example, a programmatic Lutheran insistence is that under normal circumstances the believer may encounter the Holy Spirit and the Spirit's work in the context of Scripture and the sacraments. While this does not have to mean an absolute rejection of the Spirit's freedom to move elsewhere, it is a pastoral-theological safeguard. A well-known prescription from *Smalcald Articles*, penned by Luther himself, states:

> In these matters, which concern the external, spoken Word, we must hold firmly to the conviction that God gives no one his Spirit or grace except through or with the external Word which comes before. Thus we shall be protected from the enthusiasts—that is, from the spiritualists who boast that they possess the Spirit without and before the Word and who therefore judge, interpret, and twist the Scriptures or spoken Word according to their pleasure . . . Accordingly, we should and must constantly maintain that God will not deal with us except through his external Word and sacrament.[16]

The same general rule is echoed in Luther's exposition of *Psalms* with regard to a pastoral situation in which a person needs the Spirit's touch for encouragement: "We must not, as the sectarians do, imagine that God comforts us immediately, without His Word. Comfort does not come to us without the Word, which the Holy Spirit effectively calls to mind and enkindles in our hearts."[17]

This tight linking of the Spirit and Word and sacraments can be a precious and comfortable Lutheran rule. But when its contextual and occasional nature is forgotten—namely that it was a polemic reaction against what the Reformers regarded as an extreme spiritualist bent among the Anabaptists—and when it is used carelessly against every claim for the reception of spiritual experiences, gifts, and manifestations, then the rule becomes counterproductive and even harmful. Our history knows too many such regretful instances. Furthermore, it may border on an attempt to curtail God's Spirit's freedom by human means, an effort doomed to failure!

Another significant obstacle to the embrace of the charismatic gifts and manifestations has to do with numerous and varied pastoral-theological problems among those who claim to be charismatics, whether in the Lutheran community or beyond it. They are so obvious and so well-known that it suffices to merely list a few of them:

---

16. Luther, *Smalcald Articles*, part 3, art. 8, #3, 10; *BC*, 312–13.
17. Luther, *Selected Psalms III*; *LW* 14:62.

- Abuse of gifts
- Pride and a sense of superiority
- Prosperity Gospel
- "Counterfeit" and false claims of the miraculous
- Divisions and splits in the community
- Strange and awkward claims, such as that (little) children serve as healers and exorcists

And finally, there is no denying the fact that Pentecostals of various stripes, people who often identify themselves as the custodians of the Spirit, have regrettably contributed to many prejudices against even authentic charismatic manifestations. Too many strange and unhelpful things have been done in the name of the Pentecost and the Spirit! On the other hand, Lutheran and other mainline constituencies are often envious of Pentecostals' success in gaining attention, drawing people, and expanding their ministries.

Now, having reflected on some of the main reasons for the Lutheran reservation against the charismatic element, let us attempt some constructive explorations into the significance and benefits of the Spirit's gifting and empowerment for the sake of the vocation of the whole people of God.

Charismatic Gifting and the Ministry of the Whole People of God in One Body

Let me begin with a somewhat provocative statement, namely that "the normal Christian life is charismatic!" To illustrate and deepen that claim, I lay out the following five short "theses" and further develop their meaning and significance for our topic:

- The charismatic is not an "exception," it is the norm
- The charismatic does not compete with Christ and Word
- The charismatic and the character belong together
- The charismatic is not (typically!) wild and uncontrolled
- The charismatic is for all believers—for vocations

So, what does charismatic gifting mean? What are we talking about when we speak of charisms? Since our confessional texts do not address this issue constructively, we go first to the New Testament teaching . . . Biblical texts are clear that charisms range from the more extraordinary (miraculous works, healing, exorcism, words of wisdom, prophetic words) to the more "mundane" (teaching, exhortation, giving generously). Just take a quick look at the following New Testament passages for evidence: 1 Cor 12:8–11, 28–31; Rom 12:6–8; 1 Pet 4:10. In other words, the domain of the charisms is broad. At the same time, charisms are manifold and diverse; there is no fixed "list" in the canon, as if only particular ones were normative.

According to the New Testament witness, all believers are given gifts. In that sense, all believers are charismatic: "To each is given the manifestation of the Spirit for the common good" (1 Cor 12:7). Each of us receives "gifts that differ according to the grace given to us" (Rom 12:6). These gifts are not assigned, let alone brought about, by human persons, not even by the leaders of the community. Rather, charisms, spiritual gifts, and endowments are distributed sovereignly by the "Spirit, who apportions to each one individually as he wills" (1 Cor 12:11). Yet this does not make void the Christian's active embrace and even pursuit of gifts. Paul instructs us that notwithstanding the divine sovereignty, the faithful are "earnestly [to] desire the higher gifts" (v. 31).

Importantly, the New Testament emphasizes that the gifts and endowments are not meant for boasting, to create sense of superiority, nor for selfish enjoyment. They are meant "for the common good" (v. 7), for the service and ministry, that is, for vocation. This central principle is brought home vividly and robustly in Paul's teaching in 1 Cor 12. The rough outline alone makes this clear. Drawing from the body-analogy (the church as the body of Christ), the chapter reveals three interrelated principles, at the center of which is the vocation or ministry of the whole people of God, through the empowerment and gifting of the Spirit:

- 12:1–3 The Lordship of Jesus Christ
- 12:4–11 The Diversity of Gifts, by One Spirit
- 12:12–27 The Unity of the Body in Service

Over against Lutheran fears that by opening ourselves up to the wide and rich charismatic energies of the Holy Spirit, our focus on Christ and Trinity might be thwarted, Paul reminds us first of the lordship of the Head of the Body. Pleasing to the Triune God is only such charismatic ministry that is based on an uncompromising lordship of Christ. There is no place for human pride and selfish motives; rather, charismatic gifting is about lifting up Christ and his name. Based on Christ's lordship, in an integral trinitarian logic, "there are varieties of gifts, but the same Spirit; and there are varieties of service, but the same Lord; and there are varieties of working, but it is the same God who inspires them all in everyone" (vv. 4–6). And all of that for the united, concerted ministry of the whole people of God, for the sake of the unity of the body in which everybody needs one another, and everybody may contribute to each other.

Knowing that the ultimate aim of the charismatic gifting and endowment is to facilitate our vocational capacity in ministry of the whole people of God, I turn now to consider in more detail the nature of the church's ministry.

Ministry as Charismatic-Diaconal Vocation of the Whole Community

Although the terms "ministry" and "minister" are commonplace in ecclesiastical English, it might come as a surprise that a single corresponding word is difficult to find in the New Testament. Instead, there are two terms that denote what we mean by the term ministry. The first one is *diakonia*, a word with several interrelated meanings and usages in the canon, but which for our purposes simply functions as the placeholder for our term *ministry*. An illustrative example is Paul's statement in 2 Cor 4:1 where he talks about his "ministry [*diakonia*] by the mercy of God" (so also 1 Pet 4:10). From the Greek word meaning "lowly service" (initially referring to the table service by the slaves), it communicates humble service for the benefit of others and a lowly status rather than a privilege.

Another term more or less synonymous with our English word *ministry* is the aforementioned *charisma*, meaning "graced" endowment or capacity from God. The root of the term *charism* lies in the Greek term *charis*, meaning grace. This reminds us that all gifts, endowments, and capacities are given to us with no consideration of our own merit. Such gifts stem from divine grace and benevolence. Hence, there is absolutely no place for pride or feelings of superiority. Therefore, charisms rightly understood have nothing to do with the "theology of glory": how can one who submits to the lordship of Christ (1 Cor 12:1–3), putting himself or herself willingly in a lowly place of serving others (*diakonia*), and receives charisms by the grace of God, boast?

Who, then, are the ministers—the charismatically gifted and endowed diaconal servants—of the church? The answer is simple and profound: the whole community is the "minister" of the church! Not a few select individuals or groups, but the whole church, every member of the body. This is the crux and essence of the Lutheran principle of the priesthood of all believers. There is not only one center or locus of ministry in the church, there are many, and they all contribute to the common good. In the words of the Episcopalian theologian Miroslav Volf, the Christian church is a "polycentric community" with the participation, gifting, and responsibility of all members instead of the traditional "bipolar" model in which those in office do the church's work and the laity observes.[18]

But what about the role and significance of the ordained ministers, pastors, bishops, and others? Yes, they do have indispensable work to do, but they are first and foremost a part of the community and serve alongside it. The ordained are there for the sake of the "order"[19] and diaconally-charismatically serve the community. The ordained are not above but rather in the community. One of their key tasks is to train others for the ministry (Eph 4:13). As with every member of the community, they are accountable to the community and to her Lord.[20]

A stunning description of the early church in the Book of Acts, in the aftermath of the Day of Pentecost, gives us an example in every age:

> They devoted themselves to the apostles' *teaching* and to *fellowship*, to the *breaking of bread* and to *prayer* . . . [And] many *wonders and signs* performed by the apostles. All the believers were together and *had everything in common*. They sold property and possessions to give to anyone who had need. They broke bread in their homes . . . praising God and enjoying the favor of all the people. And the Lord *added* to their number daily those who were being saved. (Acts 2:43–47)[21]

Just consider the amazing balance and richness of this particular community, gifted, freed, and empowered by the Pentecostal Spirit! United in fellowship, including both the regular teaching of the Word and the celebration of the sacraments, as well as the social-diaconal caring for each other's needs, they witnessed manifold charismatic phenomena and manifestations, and their outreach to people around them resulted in steady growth. What a pattern to imitate!

Having now inquired into Lutheran pneumatological resources with regard to the gifting and empowering of the ministry of the whole people of God, the third main section of the essay expands and enriches our vision of the work of the Spirit. Above, I noted the Lutheran lack of attention to the Spirit's role outside the church and personal salvation. This lacuna has to do with the "public" work of the Spirit in creation, the sciences, society, politics, economics, culture, entertainment, the arts, and other faith traditions.

---

18. Volf, *After Our Likeness*, 224–25.
19. Melanchthon, *Augsburg Confession*, 14; *BC*, 36.
20. See further Kärkkäinen, *Hope and Community*, ch. 18.
21. Emphases added.

THE HOLY SPIRIT IN THE WORLD—A VISION

The Spirit "Blows Where It Wills"

Jesus's statement in John 3:8 reminds us of the sovereignty and absolute freedom of the Spirit of God in the world that the Triune God has created. As we re-imagine our Lutheran identity at the beginning of the third millennium, it is well worth asking the following kinds of questions with regard to our conception of the freedom of the Spirit:

- What is the special ministry of the Spirit in creation? What kinds of resources can we find for discerning the Spirit in creation drawing on our tradition's robust creation theology, typically conceived of through the lens of the first article of the creed?

- What might the sovereign Spirit have to do in society, outside the church? Are there particular domains of human society in which the Spirit's role might be more prominent: perhaps in the arts and culture; in economics and work; in science and education; and so forth?

- Is there any connection between pneumatology and the secular-scientific framework in understanding the world and ourselves? Or are these two ways of explanation totally disconnected?

- What could we say about the reality and meaning of the "spirits," spiritual powers, power encounters, exorcism, and similar topics? While these questions are heard more frequently among Lutherans living in the Global South, in the Global North Lutherans routinely ignore or even blatantly deny them. Should we just leave these topics to Roman Catholics (who have recently reinstituted the ancient office of the exorcist, for example), to Pentecostal-Charismatics, and to some Evangelicals? Or should we instead help Lutheran communities to drink from our own spiritual-theological wells?

- What, if any, is the ministry and role of the Spirit of God among living faith traditions? How would pneumatology inform and guide Lutheran communities and believers living in diverse multireligious contexts?

- And what about secularism? Alongside religions, secularisms in various forms are growing and flourishing. Does pneumatology inform our understanding of what secularism might represent?

One way to inspire and construct a more truly global vision of the Spirit's work and domain is to speak of the "spheres" or "layers" of the Spirit. What if the Spirit of God is at work:

- in *creation*, as the Spirit of Life, bringing about, nourishing, and enlivening creation, with an invitation to a careful engagement with natural sciences as well as with green-environmental efforts?

- in *cosmos*, as the Divine Spirit among other S/spirit(s), spiritual powers, and spiritual energies, with a call for a faithful and wise discernment of the spirits?

- among *religions*, as the Spirit of the Triune God among the S/pirit(s) of other religions, with the invitation into a mutually enriching comparative theological work?

- in *society*, as the Public Spirit, in politics, economics, social structures, arts, and entertainment—leaving "not a square inch in the whole domain of our human existence" (A. Kuyper) untouched by the Triune God?

- in the *church*, as the Ecclesial Spirit, creating the Temple of the Spirit, a charismatically empowered, guided, sanctified, renewed, and unified community in the service of the world, including spiritual, diaconic, socio-political, and environmental tasks? And

- in personal *salvation*, as the Salvific Spirit, in all aspects of the *ordo salutis*, including not only the "spiritual" domain (election, new birth, sanctification, and so forth) but also mental-physical healing and charismatic endowment and gifting?[22]

A Final Challenge

This last section of the essay is by far the shortest—and intentionally so. At the moment, we have fairly little to report. For this is only the beginning of our exploration, a widening of our vision. Where this journey takes us we have yet to see.

In the meantime, let us be challenged and energized by the passionate words of Robert W. Cummings, a former generation's missionary to India, a Presbyterian turned Pentecostal. His call is to all Christian churches and communities, including to ours:

> Shameful neglect of the Holy Spirit is the great sin of the Christian Church, and it is the greatest sin of the average Christian. We forget that when the Church came into being at Pentecost *every* member, the *least* as well as the greatest, was supernaturally

---

22. For details, see Kärkkäinen, *Spirit and Salvation*, Part 1: Spirit.

filled with the Holy Spirit . . . We have told the men and women of our own day who have had great experiences to keep them in the background lest ordinary Christians . . . should get the idea that they, too, may have such wonderful experiences. We sum it all up when we piously sing, "I ask no dreams, no prophet ecstasies; no sudden rending of the veil of clay; no angel visitant, no opening skies." So we get none.[23]

---

23. Cummings, "Unto You Is the Promise," 1–2.

PART THREE

Ecumenical Theology

CHAPTER 8

Salvation as Justification and *Theosis*

The Contribution of the New Finnish Luther
Interpretation to Our Ecumenical Future[1]

> This life of the Christian in Christ is called in the Lutheran tradition participation in God, although it is often expressed in different terms. The sacramental word and sacraments and faith firstly bring it about that Christ joins himself in a real, but hidden way to the sinner. Participation in Christ and the divine nature means then that in the sinner there takes place a profound and fundamental renewal. From this wells forth true love of God and one's neighbour. In Lutheranism, this is called by the name, new birth, justification, adoption by God, deification of man.[2]

THIS STATEMENT BY THE Lutheran team in an Orthodox-Lutheran dialogue represents a New Perspective in the interpretation of the reformer's doctrine of justification.[3] Traditionally, it has been claimed that the main dividing issue between Roman Catholics and Lutherans is the differing interpretation

---

1. This essay is a slightly revised version of my presentation for the "Justification and Justice" Study Group of Faith and Order (USA) in Pasadena, California, October 2004.

2. Saarinen, *Faith and Holiness*, 74.

3. For this presentation I have kept bibliographical references to minimum. For my contributions on the various aspects of the topic with detailed bibliographical notes, see Kärkkäinen, *One With God*; Kärkkäinen, "Justification as Forgiveness of Sins and Making Righteous," 32–45; Kärkkäinen, "Ecumenical Potential of Theosis," 45–77; Kärkkäinen, "Holy Spirit and Justification," 26–39; Kärkkäinen, "Salvation as Justification and Deification," 59–76.

of the doctrine of justification by faith, and that the issue between Western churches (both Catholic and Lutheran) and Eastern churches is the irreconcilable breach between understanding salvation in terms of justification and *theosis,* respectively. With regard to the first conflict, it has become a mantra that for Lutherans, justification is a forensic action, God declaring the sinner righteous in God's sight, whereas for Catholics it is making the person righteous. With regard to the latter impasse, textbooks argue that for Lutherans the concept of *theosis* is almost blasphemous for several reasons: first, it approaches the idea of a "theology of glory"; second, it entertains the problematic view of human-divine synergy, and, finally, it champions the idea of freedom of the will. For Catholics, traditionally, the concept of *theosis* has been more acceptable for the simple reason that their understanding of salvation includes becoming righteous (sanctification), and they have never eschewed talk about good works as an integral part of salvation.

Recently, a new paradigm has emerged in ecumenical Luther studies that could become a major influence on the future of the Christian ecumenical movement. The New Interpretation of Luther's theology, as advanced by the so-called Mannermaa School at the University of Helsinki, has challenged the prevailing German Old School approach, as it were. Beginning in the late 1970s, under the leadership of Tuomo Mannermaa, now emeritus professor of ecumenics at the University of Helsinki, the Mannermaa School has offered an alternative reading of Luther's theology.[4] Significantly enough, the impetus for this new reading of Luther's theology came as a result of the dialogue between the Lutheran and Eastern Orthodox churches,[5] to be more precise, between the Russian Orthodox Church and Lutheran Church of Finland. This new paradigm has also been influential in the longstanding Roman Catholic-Lutheran conversations on justification.

As early as 1977, the Finnish-Lutheran and Russian Orthodox dialogue produced a highly influential soteriological document titled "Salvation as Justification and Deification." The preamble to the theses claims that

---

4. The publications of the Mannermaa School are written mainly in German (and Scandinavian languages). Not until 1998, was the first English monograph, a collection of essays by Finnish Luther scholars edited by two leading American Lutheran experts, offered to the English-speaking world entitled, *Union with Christ* (Braaten and Jenson). This year saw the publication of the English translation of the groundbreaking work by Mannermaa, *Christ Present in Faith.* A succinct introduction to the methodological orientations and the main results of the Mannermaa School can be found in Mannermaa's essay, "Why is Luther so Fascinating?," 1–20. For a synopsis, see also Kärkkäinen, *One with God,* ch. 4.

5. A meticulous study on the ecumenical dialogues between Lutherans and Orthodox is offered by Saarinen, *Faith and Holiness.*

Until recently, there has been a predominant opinion that the Lutheran and Orthodox doctrines of salvation greatly differ from each other. In the conversations, however, it has become evident that both these important aspects of salvation discussed in the conversations have a strong New Testament basis and there is great unanimity with regard to them both.[6]

It was found that the doctrine of deification covers the idea of a Christian's life as righteous and sinful at the same time, as the Lutheran theology has always emphasized.

The basic theses and claims of the New Interpretation can be summarized as follows:

1. Luther's understanding of salvation can be expressed not only in terms of the doctrine of justification, but also—occasionally—in terms of *theosis*. Thus, while there are differences between the Eastern and Lutheran understandings of soteriology, over questions such as free will and understandings of the effects of the Fall, Luther's own theology cannot be set in opposition to the ancient Eastern idea of deification.

2. For Luther, the main idea of justification is Christ present in faith (*in ipsa fide Christus adest*). Justification for Luther means a "real-ontic" (a somewhat controversial term we will discuss below) participation in God through the indwelling of Christ in the heart of the believer through the Spirit.

3. In contrast to the theology of the Lutheran Confessions, Luther does not make a distinction between forensic and effective justification, but rather, argues that justification includes both.[7] In other words, in line with Catholic theology, justification means both declaring righteous and making righteous.

4. Therefore, justification means not only sanctification, but also good works, since Christ present in faith makes the Christian a "Christ" to the neighbor.

---

6. Kamppuri, *Dialogue between Neighbours*, 73.

7. For the Mannermaa School, the distinction between "Luther's theology" (denoting the theology of the Reformer himself) and "Lutheran theology" (the subsequent theology of the Confessional Documents of the Lutheran Church, as drafted under the leadership of Philip Melanchthon) is vital. Finnish scholars argue that one of the weaknesses of the older Luther research, as conducted mainly in the German academy, is the neglect of this vital distinction. Indeed, one of the main motifs of the New Perspective is to dig into core themes of Martin Luther's own theology and not hasten to read Luther in light of his later interpreters or *vice versa*.

In this essay, I will approach the question of the compatibility of justification and *theosis* through the lenses of this New Paradigm of Luther studies and draw out its implications for the future of ecumenism.[8] I will first present further insights from the Mannermaa School and second, a number of critical questions and challenges in order to further ecumenical conversation. My aim is neither to convince my audience of the supremacy of the New Paradigm, nor naively believe that the Christian West and East (or even the Western Churches, Protestant and Catholic) could too easily move beyond the centuries-long doctrinal and cultural differences in terms of understanding salvation. In a questioning and learning spirit, I would rather remind my colleagues of the need to maintain an open mind to new ways of viewing ancient questions as well as of the complexity of the issues under consideration. This open mind regarding essential Christian teachings could ready us for new ecumenical breakthroughs.

JUSTIFICATION AS PARTICIPATION IN GOD[9]

In the new interpretation of Luther's theology, justification can be described in at least three interrelated ways, namely, participation in God, the presence of Christ, or *theosis*. Luther also occasionally uses other images such as "union with God," *perichoresis*, the famous Eastern term, and others.

Christ's real presence in a believer is the leading motif in Luther's soteriology. A classic formulation can be found, for example, in his *Lectures on Galatians* (1535). Speaking about "true faith," Luther says, "it takes hold of Christ in such a way that Christ is the object of faith, or rather not the object, but so to speak, the One who is present in the faith itself. . . . Therefore faith justifies because it takes hold of and possesses this treasure, the present Christ."[10] For the Mannermaa School, thus, the leading idea in Luther's theology of salvation and justification is the insistence on "Christ present in faith" *(in ipsa fide Christus adest)*. In other words, Christ in both his person and his work is present in faith and is through this presence identical with the righteousness of faith.

---

8. For a somewhat skeptical view, see Vandervelde, "Justification and Deification—Problematic Synthesis," 73–78.

9. For documentation and details, see Kärkkäinen, *One With God*, ch. 4 especially.

10. Luther, *Luther's Works*, 26:129–30. Ted Peters ("Heart of the Reformation Faith," 6–14) offers a helpful comparison between three models of faith, namely faith as believing, faith as trusting, and faith as the real presence of Christ. When discussing the third model (10–12), he dialogues with the Finnish Interpretation and its emphasis on Christ's presence as the heart of the Reformer's understanding of justification.

Justification for Luther means primarily participation in God through the indwelling of Christ in the heart through the Spirit. Through faith, a human being also participates in the characteristics of God, or as Luther often says, of the word of God. On the one hand, this participation means putting down those human traits that are contrary to the righteousness of God, and on the other hand, participating in the goodness, wisdom, truthfulness, and other characteristics of God. Luther also expresses this truth by saying that God in fact becomes truthful, good, and just in the person when God himself makes the person truthful, good, and just. Never is there reason to boast, though, since even the presence of Christ and its consequences are always hidden in the Christian.

Luther's view of justification can also be called *theosis*, according to the ancient doctrine of the Fathers with whom Luther agreed. Justification and deification, then, mean the "participation" of the believer in Christ which, because Christ is God, is also a participation in God himself. This participation is the result of God's love,[11] human beings cannot participate in God on the basis of their own love; rather God's love effects their deification. Christian participation in Christ thus is the result of the divine presence in the believer as love. This participation, following Athanasius and others, is a participation in the very *ousia* of God. Luther, unlike the Orthodox tradition, does not know the distinction between God's energies and God's essence; yet the distinction between God and the human being is not negated. God still remains God and the human being the human.

There is, then, what the Mannermaa School calls a "real-ontic" unity between Christ and the Christian though the substances themselves do not change into something else. What makes the claim of this new paradigm unique—and controversial, especially with regard to the established canons of German Luther interpretation—is that the idea of Christ's presence is "real-ontic," not just a subjective experience or God's "effect" on the believer, as the neo-Protestant school has exclusively held. I will come back to this key concept at the end of the essay.

---

11. Mannermaa argues that for Luther the structuring principle of theology is not justification as is routinely assumed but rather a creative juxtaposition between the theology of the cross and love. This comes to culmination in the 1518 Heidelberg Disputation, the last thesis of which (# 28) contrasts the love of God and human love. See further, Kärkkäinen, "'Evil, Love and the Left Hand of God,'" 215-34.

THEOSIS IN LUTHER'S THEOLOGY

The Finnish scholar Simo Peura, who has written a full-scale monograph on *theosis* in Luther, shows that the idea of deification is an integral motif of Luther's theology. The most explicit passage comes from Luther's *Sermon on the Day of St. Peter and St. Paul* (1519): "For it is true that a man helped by grace is more than a man; indeed, the grace of God gives him the form of God and deifies him, so that even the Scriptures call him 'God' and 'God's son.'"[12] Another example comes from Luther's Christmas sermon of 1514: "Just as the Word of God became flesh, so it is certainly also necessary that the flesh become Word. For the Word becomes flesh precisely so that the flesh may become Word. In other words: God becomes man so that man may become God. Thus power becomes powerless so that weakness may become powerful. The Logos puts on our form and manner."[13]

Another way to look at the doctrine of justification in Luther and its parallels with the Eastern doctrine of *theosis* is to focus on Luther's doctrine of God. What is highly significant here is the fact that for Luther the divinity of the triune God consists in that "God gives" himself. The essence of God, then, is identical with the essential divine properties in which he gives of himself, called the "names" of God: Word, justice, truth, wisdom, love, goodness, eternal life, and so forth. "The *theosis* of the believer is initiated when God bestows on the believer God's essential properties; that is, what God gives of himself to humans is nothing separate from God himself."[14] A Christian is saved when the "spiritual goods" or the names of God are given to her or him. God is, as Luther says, the whole beatitude of his saints; the name of God donates God's goodness, God himself, to the Christian; the spiritual goods are God's gifts in the Christian. Not only is the human being saved when God gives himself to the Christian; in that very same act, God proves to be the real God when he donates his own being to humanity. "Thus, God realizes himself and his own nature when he gives his wisdom, goodness, virtue, beatitude, and all of his riches to the Christian, and when a Christian receives all that he gives."[15]

In light of the interpretation of Luther's own theology as presented above, it will not come as a surprise that the Mannermaa School posits a radical difference between Luther's own theology and the theology of subsequent Lutheranism; their thesis is that Luther's own theology has the

---

12. Luther, *Luther's Works* 51, 58.
13. Quoted in Mannermaa, "Theosis as a Subject of Finnish Lutheran Research," 43.
14. Mannermaa, "Why is Luther So Fascinating?," 10.
15. Peura, "Christ as Favor and Gift," 50.

potential of creating a common foundation in relation to both Catholicism and Eastern Orthodoxy. The conclusion of the Mannermaa School with regard to the differences between Luther's theology and the theology of the Lutheran confessions and subsequent Lutheranism is well worth hearing because of its profound ecumenical implications. According to Peura, for Luther,

> Justification is not a change of self-understanding, a new relation to God, or a new ethos of love. God changes the sinner ontologically in the sense that he or she participates in God and in his divine nature, being made righteous and "a god."[16]

The relationship between effective and forensic justification comes to light also in Luther's theology in his usage of two classic concepts, namely, "grace" (*gratia,* favor) and "gift" *(donum).* The former denotes that the sinner is declared righteous (the forensic aspect) and the latter that the person is made righteous (the effective aspect). As early as the beginning of his career, in his Lectures on Romans (1515/1516) (following the terminology of Augustine and the medieval tradition, on the basis of Rom 5:15) Luther expresses an opinion that is totally in line with the mainline Catholic teaching, but that later Lutheranism has lost sight of: "But 'the grace of God' and the 'gift' are the same thing, namely, the very righteousness which is freely given to us through Christ."[17] In other words, Luther found it most important already in those early years to relate grace and gift closely to each other, and to understand them both as given to the Christian through Christ. Thus we can see that grace and gift together constitute the donated righteousness of a Christian.

For Luther, then, a distinction between effective and forensic righteousness is not an issue as it has been in subsequent Lutheran doctrine. What is crucial to Luther's own doctrine of justification is the distinction between two kinds of righteousness, namely, the righteousness of Christ and the righteousness of the human being. The first type Luther defines as the alien righteousness that is being infused to us from outside; it is that kind of righteousness that Christ is in himself and is the righteousness of faith. It is this righteousness of Christ that makes the human being just. Furthermore, Luther states that this first type of righteousness is given without our own works solely on the basis of grace. This is the famous *sola gratia.* Human activity is totally excluded in this process. The infusion of this first

---

16. Peura, "Christ as Favor and Gift," 48.
17. Luther, *Luther's Works* 25, 306.

kind of righteousness is more than mere forensic imputation, though; it also means the realization of the righteousness of Christ in the believer.

The other kind of righteousness is given righteousness, in this sense human righteousness. Luther calls it "our" righteousness. It is a result of the first kind of righteousness and makes it effective, "perfects" it. Even though it is called "our" righteousness, its origin and source is outside the human being, in the righteousness of Christ. Christ's righteousness is the foundation, cause, and origin of human righteousness. Christ present in faith "absorbs all sin in a moment," since the righteousness of Christ infused into the human heart is "infinite"; at the same time, the power of sin and death is deteriorating day by day but is not fully deteriorated until death. The infusion of Christ's righteousness into the heart of the believer marks the beginning of the process of nullifying the power of sin and transforming the fallen nature. The emerging good deeds have nothing to do with salvation because the believer is already justified and the only purpose of the good deeds now is the good of fellow people.

JUSTIFICATION AND GOOD WORKS

What then, if any, is the role of good works in Luther? This has been, again, a major dispute between not only Lutherans and Catholics, but also Lutherans and Orthodox. In line with *sola gratia*, Luther insists we can certainly do nothing for our salvation. On the contrary, God makes the sinner *nihil*, "nothing" to help him or her to open up to the righteousness of God. Yet good works spring from the union—*theosis*, if you may—between Christ and the believer and thus, from Christ's real presence in the believer.

A Christian becomes a "work of Christ," and even more a "christ" to the neighbor; the Christian does what Christ does.[18] The Christian identifies with the suffering of his or her neighbor. Christ is the subject of good works. This is what Christ present in faith effects in the believer.

The presence of Christ for Luther is not only "spiritual" or *extra nos* (outside of us) but rather *in nobis* ([with]in us), in the language of the Mannermaa school, in a "real-ontic" way. According to Luther, "since Christ lives in us through faith . . . he arouses us to do good works through that living faith in his work, for the works which he does are the fulfillment of the commands of God given us through faith."[19] As *donum* (gift) Christ gives himself in a real way to the Christian to make him or her participate in the divine nature.

---

18. See further, Kärkkäinen, "Christian as Christ to the Neighbor," 101–17.
19. Luther, Heidelberg Disputation #27; *Luther's Works* 31, 57.

CRITICAL REMARKS AND TASKS FOR THE FUTURE

My first major query about the New Interpretation of Luther has to do with methodological considerations. As already mentioned, the idea of a "real-ontic" union between God and the human being is the key affirmation. In order to understand the significance of this concept one has to take into consideration the views against which this is presented as an alternative. The Mannermaa School is critical of the neo-Protestant, neo-Kantian views according to which we do not have any means of knowing anything about God, we can only know God's effects in our lives. This so-called transcendental-effect orientation has blurred the meaning of the real presence of Christ in Luther research, they claim. This older paradigm has argued that Luther was moving beyond the old scholastic metaphysics with its idea of "essence" toward a more relational view of knowledge. So, based on neo-Kantian philosophy, this view believes that theology cannot know anything about the "essence" (ontology) of God, but only recognize his "effects" in us. The Mannermaa School argues that this kind of reasoning does not reflect Luther's "realistic" ontology, but rather is a later philosophical construction. The Mannermaa School is also critical of later interpretative frameworks—mainly among German scholars—of Luther such as the Existentially oriented approach according to which Christ's presence is only a subjective experience in the believer. Against this modern approach, the Mannermaa School wants to honor Luther's allegedly "medieval" ontology and philosophy as is appropriate in its historical context.

    I have several observations to make here: I believe the New Interpretation is quite right in questioning the prevailing neo-Kantian and neo-Protestant approaches. Yet at the same time I think that what the Mannermaa School offers as an alternative is not very viable either. On the one hand, the exact meaning of the term "real-ontic" is left open. Some friendly critics, especially the American Dennis Bielfeldt,[20] have made the obvious observation that there are number of ways to understand this elusive concept; he speaks of various "ontic/ontological" models that could explain what the Mannermaa School here argues.[21] On the other hand, even if we could argue that Luther's theology is based on the typical medieval ontology, one cannot on that basis alone argue that the union between God and human being is "real-ontic." To me this sounds almost tantamount to the

    20. See further, Bielfedlt, "Ontology of Deification," 90–113

    21. The issues gets even more complicated when we take into consideration the fact that Helsinki scholars—quite right in my opinion—"think of this indwelling in terms of mystical presence," even though they do not consider Luther to be a "mystic"; here the term mystic means same as "ineffable." Saarinen, "Third Demension of Faith," 15.

old charge—mistaken I believe—against the "physicalist" understanding of *theosis* in the Christian East; even if it is not, the view is subject to misunderstanding. My point here is that while the Mannermaa School has been quite successful in offering a critical response to the canons of the German research, the constructive task still lies ahead.

My second query has to do with the quite liberal use of the concepts of *theosis* and union among the Helsinki scholars in explaining Luther's doctrine of salvation. Simo Peura himself notes that the term *theosis* itself only occurs little more than thirty times in the whole extensive Luther corpus. That is not much indeed. Yet, in fairness—and this is of course a major point in the Mannermaa School's line of argumentation—it has to be acknowledged that the idea of deification may be much more extensive than the term itself. The occasional use of the term *unio* is then invoked by the New Interpretation supporters as another key here. Basically that is a correct observation. Yet they fail to deal with the obvious question, how close does Luther's idea of *unio* come to the Eastern understanding of union? The term *union* is quite widely used in Christian theology—say, for example, in the theology of John Calvin and in theologies as far removed from Lutheranism and Eastern Orthodoxy as Anabaptism or Methodism.[22] It is quite another thing to say that all traditions intent the same meaning with the common word.

This takes me to the third—and I believe—a major critical question to the New Interpretation, an issue the Mannermaa School has almost completely neglected as obvious as it is. It has to do with theological, especially theologico-anthropological ramifications of the doctrine of salvation in Luther and the Christian East.[23] No amount of passages in Luther showing a similarity between his understanding of salvation and the concept of *theosis* can hide the importance of looking at Luther's anthropology, doctrine of sin and the Fall, and understanding of grace, especially when it comes to the role of human will with regard to God's gracious offer of salvation. Theological anthropology is of course integrally related to the question of nature *versus* grace relationship. In what ways is Luther's understanding different from the Thomistic view which emphasizes continuity. A corollary issue, closely related to all of this, has to do with the notion of faith, and how that effects soteriological categories. In this essay, of course, I cannot even begin to tackle this complicated set of issues. My only point here is that unless the Mannermaa School is able to offer a theological analysis of

22. See further, Kärkkäinen, *Union with God*, ch. 5.
23. Some helpful insights are offered in Hinlicky, "Theological Anthropology," 44–47.

these key anthropological and theological conditions of Luther's theology, the insistence on the convergence between justification and deification cannot be conclusively established. The Roman Catholic-Lutheran dialogue process devoted considerable time to this issue, yet the issue could hardly be resolved. However, the New Interpretation has been curiously silent about these issues and has not highlighted their significance properly.

A fourth major task for ecumenical Luther scholarship is to critically dialogue with and glean from the developments in New Testament studies on justification, law, Judaism of the time, and related issues as advanced by the New Interpretation of Paul under the tutelage of E. P. Sanders, James D. G. Dunn, and a host of others (as well as their critics). My hunch is that much of what the Mannermaa School is saying is in line with the new understanding of Paul.[24] Nevertheless, the fact that Luther built much of his theology on the distinction between the Law and the Gospel, perhaps differently from what the recent NT scholarship understands, may also lead to refinement of some of the findings of the Mannermaa School.

Other tasks await ecumenical reflection such as the relationship between the passivity of faith in Lutheranism and the Eastern Orthodox idea of *synergia*. While I believe Luther's own theology—especially the idea of Christian as "christ" by virtue of the "real presence" of Christ in the believer—may have resources to tackle this thorny issue, I also acknowledge that curiously little has this question occupied scholars.

IN LIEU OF CONCLUSIONS: PROSPECTS FOR THE FUTURE

We need to ask again what, then, is the relationship between justification and deification? The suggestion by the Orthodox Lucian Turcescu according to which it is a matter of two-stages of salvation (justification initial, *theosis* final) is hardly convincing either biblically or theologically.[25] Rightly this proposal has been critiqued by George Vandervelde among others.[26] I agree with this rebuttal of Turcescu's view; yet, I find Vandervelde's

---

24. See further, Kärkkäinen, *Union with God*, ch. 2. I find the comment by Turcescu ("Soteriological Issues in the 1999 Lutheran-Catholic Joint Declaration on Justification," 64–65) that according to "[c]ontemporary biblical scholarship . . . Paul's most frequently used image to refer to the salvation in Christ [is] "justification" (*dikaiosune*)" quite odd. In my reading of contemporary biblical scholarship "justification" is one of the many complementary images by Paul; furthermore, the meaning of this term in the New Testament is more debated than Turcescu implies.

25. Turcescu, "Soteriological Issues," 67.

26. Vandervelde, "Justification and Deification," 73

argumentation less than convincing because of his tendency to separate the two discourses—that of justification and of *theosis*—rather than viewing them complementary. Of course it is true that these two discourses come from two different theological and anthropological environments; yet, in my understanding this rather reflects the legitimate plurality in the biblical canon. There is a host of soteriological metaphors of salvation each speaking to a particular context and need. Therefore, I believe, it is more fruitful biblically, theologically, and ecumenically to see these two discourses as complementary rather than conflicting or exclusive of each other. At least, I would like to challenge my colleagues to re-consider the issue.

In my reading, the Joint Declaration between Catholics and Lutherans[27] is going into the right direction by highlighting the diverse nature of even the concept of justification (let alone the constellation of other metaphors):

> Justification is the forgiveness of sins (cf. Rom 3:23–25; Acts 13:39; Luke 18:14), liberation from the dominating power of sin and death (Rom 5:12–21) and from the curse of the law (Gal 3:10-14). It is acceptance into communion with God: already now, but then fully in God's coming kingdom (Rom 5:1–2). It unites with Christ and with his death and resurrection (Rom 6:5).[28]

Under the subheading 4.2, "Justification as Forgiveness of Sins and Making Righteous," the document says: "These two aspects of God's gracious action are not to be separated, for persons are by faith united with Christ, who in his person is our righteousness (1 Cor 1:30): both the forgiveness of sin and the saving presence of God himself."[29]

To clarify my approach here, I am not saying that Catholic, Lutheran, and Orthodox soteriologies have given up—or should give up—their distinctive features. What I am saying is that much of the problematics attached to traditional positions, mostly going back to the time of the Reformation and Counter-Reformation, are historically conditioned and no longer form an irreconcilable obstacle to dialogue and joint ventures. I am not naïve about what ecumenism is. Ecumenical thinking does not mean collecting pieces from here and there and putting them together to make a more appealing mixture. Sometimes ecumenical work may lead to a more precise

---

27. Lutheran World Federation and Roman Catholic Church, *Joint Declaration*. For a detailed discussion, see Kärkkäinen, *One With God*, 99–108.

28. See Lutheran World Federation and Roman Catholic Church, *Joint Declaration*, #11.

29. Lutheran World Federation and Roman Catholic Church, *Joint Declaration*, #22.

and explicit acknowledgment of differences between various Christian traditions or to acknowledgment of convergence despite legitimate differing emphases. The approach taken by the Joint Declaration is to be commended: "[The] Joint Declaration has this intention: namely, to show that on the basis of their dialogue the subscribing Lutheran churches and the Roman Catholic Church are now able to articulate a common understanding of our justification by God's grace through faith in Christ." Then it adds that this "does not cover all that either church teaches about justification; it does encompass a consensus on basic truths of the doctrine of justification and shows that the remaining differences in its explication are no longer the occasion for doctrinal condemnations."[30] This is a fruitful way to proceed, I suggest, toward a bright future in the ecumenical discussions between Eastern Orthodox and Lutheran theologies as well.

As a footnote, let me suggest that the ecumenical discussion of the doctrine of salvation is not only urgent for the sake of Christian unity, but also in light of the relation of Christian faith to other religions. The theology-of-religions question may open up new vistas for reconsidering ancient Christian doctrines and help us move beyond the ecumenical impasse. What if the doctrine of divinization were a viable candidate for all Christians to talk about salvation in relation to other religions such as Hinduism and Buddhism and, say, African spiritualities?[31] In addition to other religions, the relevance and accuracy of soteriological discourse should also be studied in relation to other cultures where the questions of "salvation" come yet from another angle.[32] Little work, if any, has been done in these areas specifically—this is a call for all of us, regardless of our respective traditions.

---

30. Lutheran World Federation and Roman Catholic Church, *Joint Declaration*, #5.
31. See Kärkkäinen, *One With God*, 1-4, 133-37.
32. See further, Grieve, *Justification in the World's Context*.

CHAPTER 9

Sacraments and (Dis-)Unity
A Constructive Ecumenical Proposal towards Healing the Divisions and Facilitating Mutual Recognition

INTRODUCTION: A VISION FOR RESPONDING TO THE SCANDAL OF DISUNITY

It "STRANGELY WARMS MY heart" to see that the Wheaton Conference has chosen the question of the unity of the church as its topic for this year. This is an important and urgent issue for all Christians but particularly so for evangelicals. I agree with late Lutheran systematician Wolfhart Pannenberg that "[f]or the first time . . . the scandal of divided Christendom has reached such a head that it has become intolerable for the faith consciousness of countless modern Christians." Rightly, Pannenberg raises this important question: "How can we recognize and treat one another as Christian brothers and sisters united by faith in the one Lord and its trinitarian exposition in the church, yet at the same time say nothing about full communion with one another?"[1]

Indeed, so much is at stake with the issue of divisions and unity that, to further cite Pannenberg, only "[if] Christians succeed in solving the problems of their own pluralism, they may be able to produce a model combining pluralism and the widest moral unity which will also be valid for political life."[2] This is a badly needed call for the religiously pluralistic and

---

1. Pannenberg, *Systematic Theology*, 3:411.
2. Pannenberg, "Christian Morality and Political Issues," 38.

secular world of ours. Indeed, if we Christians are not able to constructively deal with the plurality and diversity among us, how can we ever fulfill our mission to the world?

In this essay, I propose the possibility in the current theological milieu—building on a half century of ecumenical work and reflection—of tackling the scandal of disunity in a new constructive manner. Indeed, in a manner that would allow major Christian families to recognize the full ecclesiality (the full "churchliness") of other Christian communities even with regard to the most contentious issues related to sacraments and ministry. I believe that this does not require us to compromise our distinctive identities but that it would require us to imagine the sacramental and ministerial markers and borderlines in a new, constructive manner.

Boldly and simply stated, my vision is no less than this: that the Catholic traditions (both Eastern Orthodox and Roman Catholic), the Anglican and Protestant traditions, as well as the Free Churches and Independents could come to a place of mutual recognition as churches of the one and same Church of Christ, a communion of communions. If this sounds like a grand and bold vision, it is! And I know that, while touching on many complicated theological-ecumenical issues, this brief presentation does not allow me to tackle many details and debates; readers interested in technical details and references can get them in my *Hope and Community: A Constructive Christian Theology for the Pluralistic World*, vol. 5 (Eerdmans, 2017) which also engages the "wider ecumenical" issue of religious pluralism and visions of community among four living faiths.

Since no ecumenical proposal comes from nowhere, let me locate my own position and the perspective it comes from. I take the mainline Protestant rule, to be more precise, the Lutheran "rule of ecclesiality" (as expressed in the Augsburg Confession [*Confessio Augustana*] #7) as the defining guideline and seek to find commonalities with both older and younger ecclesial traditions. An ordained Lutheran minister (Evangelical Lutheran Church in America [ELCA]), I also have deep affinities with Pentecostal-Charismatics and other Independents and wish to engage them in a way that has not happened much in the past. This means that although my approach is particular and perspectival, it does not have to be exclusively so. The ecumenist may also build on one's tradition self-critically and attempt to transcend it for the sake of inclusivity and unity-in-diversity of the whole church. If I have learned anything during more than two decades of intense ecumenical work at regional, national, and international forums, it is this: Only proposals that are specific and particular further the effort to resolve ecumenical problems, but those proposals have to be specific and particular with a view toward inclusivity rather than cementing already existing hard walls.

Having now briefly laid out my ultimate goal and having reminded us of the grave scandal of disunity, the rest of the presentation follows in this way: First, I will outline more specifically what the ecumenical impasse of lack of mutual ecclesiastical recognition is all about. I do so by outlining three main positions and how deeply differing understandings of the role and meaning of sacraments and ministry lie behind them. Second, I will take a critical look at a debate at the center of this dispute about ecclesiality, namely, how do we discern the presence of Christ in a Christian community? While all churches agree that the presence of Christ (and indeed, the whole Trinity) is church-constitutive, they differ on how that can be decided in a definitive manner. The third major section takes me to the constructive proposal itself: taking a lead from CA #7, I lay out as clearly and transparently as possible my tentative ecumenical vision for mutual recognition. Fourth—and in this last section I have to paint with very broad strokes—I recommend some new and fresh resources and tools to continue this ecumenical work. Some of these resources are emerging and in the process of development in international ecumenical theology, even as I write.

THE BASIC ECCLESIOLOGICAL-ECUMENICAL DILEMMA: THREE DEFINING POSITIONS

The most basic ecumenical dilemma and scandal facing the Church of Christ has to do with the deeply and radically differing positions concerning the ecclesiality of the church—that is, what makes the church, church. The underlying problem is simply this: the continuing impossibility of mutual recognition of the ecclesiality (the "churchliness") of other Christian communities. In other words, some churches do not consider others as churches but as something "less" or "defective," such as "Christian communities." This wound is particularly deep between the "older" (Roman Catholic and Orthodox) and "younger" churches (free churches and various types of independent churches), but it also relates to Protestant and Anglican communities. My own Lutheran Church is not considered a "full church" in the theological sense of the word by some important ecclesiastical counterparts; hence, Lutheran sacraments are not fully valid; neither is our ministry.[3]

The problem of ecclesiality has to do with the radically different ways of conceiving what makes the church, church. The key debate relates to the

---

3. According to the Vatican (*Lumen Gentium*, #15 and 26), Protestants, Anglicans, and free churches are not "churches" but rather ecclesial communities.

role of sacraments, episcopacy, and personal confession of faith. For the sake of clarity and pedagogical usefulness, let us name three main positions.

First, for Orthodox and Catholic ecclesiology, not only does the church carry out the sacraments, but the sacraments first and foremost make the church. This means that only where there is the celebration of the sacrament of the Eucharist (whose attendance requires water baptism), there is the Christian church. And for that celebration to be ecclesiologically valid, there needs to be a bishop whose standing is considered to be linked with the first apostles (somewhat differently defined in those two traditions, a topic into whose details there is no need to delve here). In sum: this is the "sacramental" and "episcopal" (lowercase) rule of ecclesiality.[4]

Second, for the youngest Christian family, the free churches, decisive is the presence of personal confession of faith of men and women who then gather together as the church. Faith is mediated directly through the preaching of the Word, as it were, and does not necessarily require mediation by the sacraments or office. The celebration of the sacraments of water baptism and the Lord's Supper is an important part of the church's life, but they are not considered ecclesiologically constitutive and, where personal faith is missing, might even be taken as something formal and useless. Furthermore, among those free churches that have an ecclesiastical office by the name of "bishop,"[5] it does not have any ecclesiologically determinative function.

Third, there is the Protestant mainline definition of the church's "foundation" in terms of the preaching of the gospel and administration of the sacraments (baptism and Eucharist). Although for Anglicans and many Protestants (all Lutherans and some Reformed) the theology (of salvation) is sacramental in the sense that one comes to the faith and is sustained in it by the sacraments (when integrally linked with the Word), neither sacraments nor ministerial patterns are considered ecclesiologically constitutive after the manner of Orthodox and Catholic theology. As a result, even if they have a bishop (as a large number of Lutherans do), that office is not constitutive for the being of the church and can also be otherwise.[6]

---

4. Hence, in what follows, the word "episcopal" (as distinct from the proper name of the Episcopal, i.e., Anglican, Church) is used in that technical theological sense.

5. This is common among most African American churches in the United States, as well as in a large number of Pentecostal and other free churches all over the world, particularly in Africa but also in the former Soviet Union and elsewhere.

6. A materially similar presentation (limited to Orthodox/Catholics and free churches) can be found in Miroslav Volf, *After Our Likeness*, 130–35. For details, see my "Unity, Diversity, and Apostolicity," 487–506.

Now, the ecumenical and ecclesiastical implications are simply these: for Orthodox and Catholics, neither Protestant/Anglican communities, regardless of their sacramentality, nor free churches qualify as churches. That is because they lack episcopal and sacramental validity for the reasons explained above. Even the Anglican and Protestant celebration of the sacraments (particularly the Eucharist) is invalid because of the episcopal deficit. On the other hand, for free churches, particularly in the beginning years of the movements, no amount of appeal to episcopacy or sacraments had any church-constitutive meaning; indeed, putting them in the forefront often elicited a response against mere formal religion. The mainline Protestants (and Anglicans, I suppose) come closest to not having binding reasons for nonrecognition of either free churches, as long as they also honor the sacraments (and they do appreciate the preaching of the Word, after all), or Orthodox and Catholics (without endorsing their exclusive appeal to episcopal succession).

This impasse over mutual recognition is an open wound for ecclesiology and ecumenism. If we were not so used to it, it would seem unbearable, excruciating. And it is! Neither theologically nor in terms of common sense—let alone Christian love!—can it be tolerated anymore. By it Christian churches who claim the presence of one and the same Lord continue refuse to grant the same to other Christian communities with similar claims![7] Taken seriously, the implications of nonrecognition lead to conclusions and implications that are simply absurd and bizarre. We gather around the Table of the Lord and the Baptismal Font with full assurance of the presence of the Triune God among us—while at the same time denying the same for other Christian churches.

After this outline of the main positions, let me now advance to a critical scrutiny of the "art of the ecclesiality discourse" and assess the conditions and promises of a constructive proposal.

HOW DO WE DISCERN THE PRESENCE OF CHRIST IN THE CHURCH?

There is an ecumenical consensus about the presence of Christ (and therefore, of the Spirit and the triune God) as ecclesiologically constitutive. This rule goes back to the church fathers and is solidly based in the New Testament witness. The theologically pregnant Matthean passage affirms: "For where two or three are gathered in my name, there am I in the midst of them" (18:20). Ignatius taught that "wherever Jesus Christ is, there is the

---

7. Similarly, Volf, *After Our Likeness*, 133–34 and passim.

Catholic Church," and Irenaeus expressed the same with reference to the Spirit's presence.[8] Tertullian's oft-cited maxim states: "But where three are, [there] a church is."[9] This issue is not contested. What is debated has to do with the way Christ's (and the Spirit's) presence can be determined, as it is hardly self-evident.[10] It is widely agreed that whatever instruments one may employ to determine Christ's ecclesiologically constitutive presence, they cannot be so external to the task that they fail to disclose something essential about the church. In other words, they cannot be arbitrary—and yet, obviously, they also have to be externally perceivable.[11]

It is here that the Anglican (formerly Pentecostal) Miroslav Volf takes up the task in an important ecclesiological proposal searching for a minimalist, yet significant principle of ecclesiality. He does so by seeking to develop a theology of the church based on the best and "redeemable" elements of congregationalist-free church traditions, in dialogue with Catholic and Orthodox ecclesiologies.[12] Building on the above-mentioned programmatic passage from Matt 18:20, Volf puts forth his tentative description of what makes the church, church: "Where two or three are gathered in Christ's name, not only is Christ present among them, but a Christian church is there as well, perhaps bad church, a church that may well transgress against love and truth, but a church nonetheless." Volf claims that this definition expresses what Ignatius, Irenaeus, Tertullian, and others argued, and that it is also in keeping with the rule of ecclesiality propounded by the seventeenth-century English founder of the Baptist movement, John Smyth:[13] "A visible communion of Saincts is of two, three, or more Saincts joyned together by covenant with God & themselves, freely to use al the holy things of God, according to the word, for their mutual edification, & Gods glory. Mat. 18 20 Deut. 29, 12. &c Psal. 147, 19 & 149, 6–9. Rev. 1. 6."[14]

Volf takes several steps toward a promising ecumenically fruitful position by suggesting that even the free church traditions join the ecumenical consensus according to which the two sacraments, water baptism and Eucharist, serve the task of identifying Christ's presence. That is a tentative but also important response to the question of how to discern Christ's (and the

---

8. Ignatius, *To the Smyrnaeans* 8; Irenaeus, *Against Heresies* 3.24.1.

9. Tertullian, *On Exhortation to Chastity* 7.

10. So also, Volf, *After Our Likeness*, 129.

11. Volf, *After Our Likeness*, 129–30.

12. For an exposition and useful comments, see Graham Hill, *Salt, Light, and a City*, ch. 12.

13. Volf, *After Our Likeness*, 135–37 and passim (136; emphasis removed).

14. Smyth, *Principles and Inferences Concerning the Visible Church*, 252.

Spirit's) church-constitutive presence. Furthermore, important particularly to the mainline Reformation churches, the sacraments are tightly integrated with the Word of God, the gospel, as the sacraments left alone can hardly mediate Christ's presence.[15] As much as the Baptist Smyth underscored the unmediated presence of Christ in the church, even he considered necessary the use of "the holy things of God," namely, "the meanes of salvation . . . : the word, Sacraments, prayers."[16]

So far, all churches are most likely to follow my argumentation, even if for Orthodox and Catholics this is not yet enough. Indeed, where Volf's free church-driven (but mainline Protestant church-sympathetic) proposal differs strongly from the Roman Catholic and Orthodox ecclesiologies is that it does not accept their claims for the necessity of a specific kind of office, namely, episcopacy, for the validity of the sacraments.[17] As a Protestant theologian, I agree with Volf's refusal to make a bishop the absolute requirement for the sacraments' validity.[18] But instead of leaving the issue there and so living with the impasse, I wish to bring to the discussion table the ecumenically pregnant definition of ecclesiality from the mainline Protestant traditions, particularly from Lutheran ecclesiology, with the hope that several important steps toward rapprochement could be had in relation to Orthodox and Catholics.

TOWARD A MUTUAL RECOGNITION OF THE ECCLESIALITY OF THE CHURCH: A CONSTRUCTIVE PROPOSAL

Locating the Proposal

I will take as a starting point the description of the ecclesiality of the church from the "middle" of the ecclesiality debate spectrum, namely, mainstream Protestantism. According to the Lutheran Augsburg Confession (article 7), the church

---

15. Volf, *After Our Likeness*, 152–54.

16. Smyth, *Principles and Inferences*, 254. For a highly useful discussion, see, Haight, *Christian Community in History*, 251–53 particularly.

17. Volf, *After Our Likeness*, 133–34, 152. I will not go into the details of differences as to how Orthodox ecclesiology distinctively expresses this condition; see Volf, *After Our Likeness*, 130–31.

18. Let me hasten to mention that Volf's position is not historically convincing because he overlooks the fact that for Ignatius (at least), the rule of ecclesiality as the presence of Christ is conditioned on the presence of the bishop as the presider at the Eucharist; Ignatius, *To the Smyrnaeans* 8.

is the assembly of all believers among whom the gospel is preached in its purity and the holy sacraments are administered according to the gospel. For it is sufficient for the true unity of the Christian church that the gospel be preached in conformity with a pure understanding of it and that the sacraments be administered in accordance with the divine Word.

In other words, as long as the gospel and sacraments are there, it "is not necessary for the true unity of the Christian church that ceremonies, instituted by men, should be observed uniformly in all places."[19] Clearly, the theological and ecumenical cash value of CA 7 lies in that as long as the gospel and sacraments are there, most everything else can be named a matter of *adiaphora*, including church structures and ministerial patterns.[20]

Hence, the ecumenical potential of CA 7 runs wide and deep. Before reaching out to Roman Catholics and Orthodox with this position, though, let me register some additions to the two conditions (Word and sacraments) among some Protestants and free church advocates. They have to do with the "discipline" (ethical and "behavioral" criterion) and the question of whether some particular structures (like offices) might be divinely sanctioned or not (i.e., governance). This is the case with the Reformed counterpart: in Calvin's ecclesiology, "discipline," that is, obedience, is listed as a necessary condition[21] and there is also a claim for divinely sanctioned structures and offices.[22] The same applies to the first and formative free church tradition, the Baptist movement. While materially agreeing with the Lutheran definition, it added, similarly to the Reformed, fixed structures and obedience as conditions.[23] When it comes to the Radical Reformation, the additional elements are even more numerous. While the 1527 Swiss Brethren's Schleitheim collection of Seven Articles contains, importantly, baptism and the Lord's Supper, it also listed the ban, separation from the world, pacifism, and refusal to take an oath.[24]

19. *Confessio Augustana* (Augsburg Confession [henceforth: CA]), 32.

20. For useful comments, see Saarinen, "Lutheran Ecclesiology," 171–73.

21. Calvin, *Institutes*, 4.1.9. Note that even the current Presbyterian Church of the USA's *Book of Order* devotes the largest section to discipline (rather than, say, to worship or government).

22. Calvin (*Institutes*, 4.3.1) begins his consideration of offices: "We are now to speak of the order in which the Lord has been pleased that his Church should be governed." For Reformed orthodoxy's fixation on a certain order, following the fourfold office based on Eph 4:11, namely, pastors, teachers, presbyters, and deacons, see Pannenberg, *Systematic Theology*, 3:385.

23. Smyth, *Principles and Inferences*, 252, 253, respectively.

24. The articles (also called the Schleitheim Confession) can be found, e.g., at the

Now, what to do with these Protestant and free church additions? On what basis is it not self-contradictory on my part to reject the Catholic and Orthodox requirement of episcopacy for ecclesiality while overlooking the other kinds of additions by the Reformed, Baptists, and Anabaptists? My response is that the additional requirements by the Reformed and the free churches are merely that—*additions*—and are not meant to necessarily discredit or reject the foundational claim for ecclesiality by the Lutherans; if they were forced, I assume, not only the Reformed but also (at least, most of) the free churches would be willing to negotiate the additions and live with the CA 7 definition. That is markedly different from the categorical rejection of the ecclesiality of all other churches (but the Orthodox) by Roman Catholics.

The Ecumenical Promise of the Gospel and Sacraments as Ecclesial Rule

Ecumenically, it is of utmost importance that, notwithstanding serious challenges to the acknowledgment of full ecclesiality to Protestant (and Anglican) communities, the Catholic Hans Küng notes this:

> Catholic theology has never had any positive objection to raise against the two classic Protestant signs: without the preaching of the gospel in accordance with Scripture and the administering of the sacraments as divinely ordained there can be no true Church according to the Catholic view either; both are absolute prerequisites for the Catholic Church too.[25]

This robust statement is definitively endorsed by Vatican II's *Lumen Gentium*: "This Church of Christ is truly present in all legitimate local congregations . . . [in] which the faithful are gathered together by the preaching of the Gospel of Christ, and the mystery of the Lord's Supper is celebrated." So, what is the problem from the Roman side? It has to do with placing the preaching and sacraments in the context of a certain kind of episcopal ministry, as only a "bishop [is] marked with the fullness of the sacrament of Orders," and therefore, "[e]very legitimate celebration of the Eucharist is regulated by the bishop."[26] As long as that claim is taken as a final statement

---

Anabaptists website. Menno Simmons's marks of the true church include pure doctrine, baptism, the Lord's Supper, obedience to the Word, love, confession of Christ, and suffering for God; Simons, *Reply to Gellius Faber (1552)*, 752; for similar kinds of descriptions, see also 744, 755.

25. Küng, *Church*, 346; materially similarly Moltmann, *Church in the Power of the Spirit*, 341.

26. Second Vatican Council, *Lumen Gentium*, #26.

from the Catholics, I see little hope for rapprochement. But what if it could be placed in a slightly different context?

I find useful Küng's note that at the core of the Catholic objection to the sufficiency of the CA 7 principle of ecclesiality lies the fear that "these two characteristics of the true Church are not truly distinguishing features" and hence do not fulfill the required task of identifying where the true church really is.[27] If that is the case, I think there is some hope of bringing the divergent viewpoints closer together if we consider the issue in light of the marks of the church, classically taken as the identifying distinctives of or pointers to the true church. I think it is an ecumenical consensus that the two defining features of the ecclesiality of CA 7 are integrally and irreconcilably linked with the four marks: unity, holiness, catholicity, and apostolicity. Indeed, Küng himself, as a Catholic theologian, contends that the marks "do not mean anything if they are not based on the pure Gospel message, valid baptism, and the proper celebration of the Lord's Supper. Always and in every case the Church must be certain it is in essential agreement with the original New Testament message."[28] Isn't there some kind of real mutuality between the two "marks" of CA 7 and the four "marks" of the creed? Neither set of requirements alone is specific and concrete enough to help us discern where the presence of the triune God may lie in an ecclesiologically constitutive manner. When linked together, however, they help us be more confident. Rather than a vicious circle of trying to prove what one presupposes, this linking can be seen as a *mutuality* of enrichment, information, and specification.

The legitimate fear among the Catholics and Orthodox concerning the challenge of being able to discern Christ's community-forming presence may also be eased by the following observation concerning Protestant Reformers. As much as the Reformers emphasized the immediacy of believers to Christ (to defeat what they saw as the destructive human-made hierarchy-related and institutional obstacles), in no way could CA 7 be made a matter of a "community of believers" merely coming together as individuals to be the church. That would of course make the claim for ecclesiality random and release it from all traditional safeguards. Indeed, that liability should be carefully minded by free churches, as they at times tend to emphasize problematically the mere unmediated access to Christ by all.

The community's ecclesiality depends on the preaching and sacraments, which both represent apostolicity as they go back to Jesus and the institution by the apostles. Recall the *Large Catechism* (on the third article

---

27. Küng, *Church*, 346.
28. Küng, *Church*, 347.

of the creed): "It is the mother that begets and bears every Christian through the Word of God."[29] Referring to sacraments in this regard, Pannenberg rightly notes that the idea of the church as a "mother" begetting and nurturing believers alone would defeat the mistaken interpretation of Christian gathering as arbitrary. I think this is a highly important criterion for the Orthodox and Catholics.

Furthermore, it seems to me that sticking with the two foundational standards, *pure* gospel and *right* administration of sacraments—as much as it is true that the Protestant Reformation failed to provide any specific criteria for their ascertainment—also leads toward unity in faith and love for all communities committed to them. Whatever else purity and correctness may mean, they must stand in continuity with the apostolic Scriptures and creeds (again, as much room as there may be for differences in details of formulations). Rather than pushing toward exclusivity, isn't their embrace instead compelling the Christian community to consider as true church any community bound by and committed to the same ecclesiastical criteria? Pannenberg succinctly argues, on that basis, that

> the universal unity of the church across the ages finds manifestation in the worship of the local congregation that exists in virtue of its apostolic basis, having fellowship with past saints and martyrs. For the pure teaching of the apostolic gospel and administration of the sacraments that is faithful to their institution constitute the church's unity across the centuries and at the same time characterize each local congregation of believers as the church of Christ.[30]

And, as Küng helpfully reminds us, believing the church to be one, holy, catholic, and apostolic for ourselves, we "want to believe and hope for others too."[31]

Having now considered the criteria for the "observable" ecclesiologically constitutive forms of Christ's presence—with hope for an ecumenical rapprochement—we note that Christ's presence is not of course limited to that function alone. Moltmann importantly reminds us that on the basis of the New Testament texts we should expect Christ's presence in many forms and places. "Christ is present in the apostolate, in the sacraments, and in the

---

29. Luther, *Large Catechism* 2; Calvin, *Institutes*, 4.1.4; see Pannenberg, *Systematic Theology*, 3:100–101. For the rediscovery of the idea in contemporary evangelical ecclesiology, see Harper and Metzger, *Exploring Ecclesiology*, 11–12.

30. Pannenberg, *Systematic Theology*, 3:101.

31. Küng, *Church*, 53–59 (53); so also Moltmann, *Church in the Power of the Spirit*, 337–38.

fellowship of the brethren." The term "apostolate" here denotes "the medium of the proclamation through word and sacrament, as well as the persons and community of the proclaimers." There are a number of New Testament assurances, such as "he who hears you hears me" (Luke 10:16) and "I am with you always, to the close of the age," to those going out to share the gospel by preaching and baptizing. Similar promises of Christ's presence are attached to the celebration of the Eucharist (1 Cor 11:23–27). The baptized will be sharing death and life with Christ (Rom 6:1–12). Second, Christ has pledged his presence in the children, the poor, and other "little ones." Matt 25:31–36 is an extended exposition of that theme. And so forth.[32]

If this proposal set forth here briefly in skeleton form has any value in itself, it calls all ecumenically minded to work together towards the common goal. What kind of resources and tools might be available for such a work? This last section briefly taps into a set of new and emerging ecumenical paradigms and developments.

New Resources, Tools, and Perspectives

Let me first list the kinds of resources and tools I have in mind and then briefly introduce them. Clearly this is nothing close to a comprehensive listing. Rather, it is suggestive and also related to the projects and enterprises I myself am involved with.

- "Ecumenical Recognition"
- "Receptive Ecumenism"
- "Partial Communion" and "Provisionality"
- "Ethnography as Ecumenism"
- "Ecumenism as Comparative Theology"

"Recognition" in Philosophical, Interdisciplinary, and Ecumenical Perspective

Those of you among us who are philosophically trained know that the concept of "recognition" (*die Anerkennung* in German) is a long-lived and long-debated concept. Behind it is this simple and profound question: On what basis would it be possible for the human person or group to fully recognize the Other and her identity in the midst of differences, divergences, and even

32. Moltmann, *Church in the Power of the Spirit*, 121–32.

potential conflicts? The current pluralistic and multicultural and multireligious world has brought those questions back to the center of attention. Issues related to negotiating between the "one" and "many," "we" and "they," or "unity" and "diversity" have been on the menu of thinkers from the ancient Greek philosophers all the way up to leading modern thinkers.

Among the modern philosophers, no thinker scrutinized the problematic of recognition with greater influence than Hegel.[33] His sustained reflections on the intersubjective concept of recognition, particularly through the lens of the master-slave analogy, have continued to inspire generations of thinkers.[34] At the heart of Hegel's conception are reciprocal recognition and the idea that in a real sense, one receives one's own personhood from the other—and commensurately, helps the other to have the same.[35] The space of the other, so to speak, is not so foreign a territory that one could not inhabit it in some sense, and that is likewise true from the other's perspective.

In contemporary philosophy, a programmatic recognition scholar is the Canadian philosopher Charles Taylor. He rightly argues that "[n]onrecognition or misrecognition can inflict harm, can be a form of oppression, imprisoning someone in a false, distorted, and reduced mode of being."[36] In political science, the most noted recognition theorist is the German Axel Honneth. His theory of recognition consists basically of three parts: love, respect, and esteem. What can be called "emotional recognition" emerges in the early years of one's life at home in an intimate relationship of love and worth. "Rights-based" recognition is related to learning to respect and receive respect in the legal structures of society. Esteem is related to a "community of values," in a society that values one's accomplishments. Honneth's conviction is that only through recognition from the most important social groups and communities can our personal being emerge and develop. This puts the obligation to love, respect, and show esteem—or solidarity, as he also calls it—to others in relevant contexts in the society, or else denial of

---

33. The main locus for Hegel's philosophy of recognition is in his *Phenomenology of Spirit* (1807), also known as the *Jena Lectures on the Philosophy of Spirit* (available in English in various versions, alternatively titled as *The Phenomenology of Mind*. The master-slave analogy is in B.IV; "The True Nature of Self-Certainty" ("Self-consciousness" in other translations). Of course, Descartes and Kant (especially) contributed to what became a full-scale philosophy of recognition in Hegel; see Lim, "Ecclesial Recognition", 46–53.

34. Anderson, *Hegel's Theory of Recognition*; from a theological perspective, see De Nys, *Hegel and Theology*, chs. 1 and 2 particularly.

35. Hegel, *Phenomenology of Mind*, #126.

36. Taylor, "Politics of Recognition," 25.

recognition or misrecognition takes place.[37] Honneth's conviction is that only through recognition from the most important social groups and communities can our personal being emerge and develop.

Now, based on these and related contributions, ecumenical recognition "focuses on the possibility of recognizing the other [church] as a true church," and as such it is a key "part of a conscious process of changing the identification of the other [church]."[38] This is exactly what *The Church: Towards a Common Vision* (2013) does: "Visible unity requires that churches be able to recognize in one another the authentic presence of what the Creed of Nicea-Constantinople (381) calls the 'one, holy, catholic, apostolic Church.'"[39] In other words, ecumenical recognition "examines whether churches may accept the legitimacy and authenticity of other churches as the Church in the dialogical process towards fuller communion."[40] It includes recognition of each other's baptism, ministry, worship/liturgy, and so forth.

Recognition has nothing to do with cancelling out particular identities. Take a lesson again from Küng:

> As long as these Churches recognize one another as legitimate, as long as they see one another as part of one and the same Church, as long as they are in fellowship as Churches with one another and hold common services, and especially celebrate the Eucharist together, and as long as they are helping one another, working together and standing together in times of difficulty and persecution, there can be no objection to their diversity. All the differences, however profound, between the individual Churches are then swallowed up by the certainty that all are one in the unity of the Church of Christ.[41]

---

37. Honneth, *Struggle for Recognition*; Honneth, *I in We*; see also Honneth, *Disrespect*.

38. Hietamäki, "Recognition and Ecumenical Recognition," 458. The term "recognition" had also been employed in ecumenism earlier; for this see Meyer, "Anerkennung," 25–41. For the current state of the discussion, see Saarinen, "Anerkennungstheorien und Ökumenische Theologie," 237–61.

39. World Council of Churches, *Church*, 9.

40. Lim, "Ecclesial Recognition," 7.

41. Küng, *Church*, 356–57.

PART THREE: Ecumenical Theology

The Promise of "Receptive Ecumenism"

The new paradigm of "receptive ecumenism" is related to the standard ecumenical term "reception," although it also goes beyond it. By "reception" is meant "the process by which the churches make their own the results of all their encounters with one another, and in a particular way the convergences and agreements reached on issues over which they have historically been divided."[42] Reception is already present in the New Testament—just think of the Pauline words of institution of the Eucharist (1 Cor 11:23). Reception was also a key issue in the early centuries, particularly with regard to the ways the churches embraced and understood the pronouncements of ecumenical councils.[43] No wonder the question of reception has received a lot of attention in the modern ecumenical movement.[44] Not only doctrinal reception but also "the broader process by which churches can receive elements such as liturgy, spirituality and forms of witness from one another's traditions" relates to this task.[45] Reception, if it really is true and genuine, does not leave the church the same; it may lead to renewal and change.[46] This is exactly what happened in the historic agreement on justification between the Vatican and Lutherans in 1999 as both parties' self-understanding and way of embracing a formative doctrinal stance were impacted.[47]

Now, the leading idea behind the new approach named "receptive ecumenism" stems from the collaborative work of the British Catholic theologian Paul D. Murray of Durham University. Its main premise is simple and profound, stating that "the primary ecumenical responsibility is to ask not 'What do the other traditions first need to learn from us?' but 'What do we need to learn from them?'"[48] The impetus behind receptive ecumenism is

> to take seriously both the reality of the contemporary ecumenical moment—wherein the hope for structural unification in the

---

42. Joint Working Group, *Nature and Purpose of Ecumenical Dialogue*, #59 (appendix D; 82–83); for background, see Rusch, *Reception*.

43. See Kelly, "New Ecumenical Wave."

44. The most recent ecumenical document is *Reception*, Joint Working Group between the Roman Catholic Church and the World Council of Churches.

45. Joint Working Group, *Reception*, #2.

46. Joint Working Group, *Reception*, #13.

47. See Lutheran World Federation, *Joint Declaration on the Doctrine of Justification*, #7 (in the preamble).

48. This definition can be found, e.g., in "About Receptive Ecumenism," on the webpage of the Durham University Department of Theology and Religion, Centre for Catholic Studies, Projects & Research Interests; https://www.dur.ac.uk/theology.religion/ccs/projects/receptiveecumenism/about/.

short to medium term is, in general, now widely recognized as being unrealistic—and the abiding need for the Christian churches precisely in this situation to find an appropriate means of continuing to walk the way of conversion towards more visible structures and sacramental unity.[49]

For that to happen, receptive ecumenism recommends the following kinds of attitudes and postures: willingness to change oneself rather than the other; "[t]o learn *from* and *across* our denominational differences in a mutually enriching way that fosters growth *within* traditions by finding the beauty of another tradition's focus"; and openness to continuing growth and change of tradition.[50]

"Partial Communion" and "Provisionality": Modest and Humble Goals

A differently formulated goal of ecumenical work—"partial" rather than full communion—can be linked with the tactics of recognition and mutual reception explained above. It also sticks with the concept of "provisionality" of ecclesiastical traditions and communities on this side of the eschaton. In the spirit of receptive ecumenism, in that kind of approach one would be willing to have one's own identity and self-understanding be transformed rather than working from an assumption that only fully arriving according to one's ready-made plan would qualify as a result.

The partial communion paradigm starts with this obvious question: What if full communion were unattainable as a goal? Without cynicism or an attempt to "lower standards," most all ecumenists agree that full communion[51] seems to be too ambitious a goal of unity—at least for the time being. If so, why not seek a partial communion? That is a more modest and realistic standard to begin with. Partial communion "means mutual recognition despite substantial or significant differences or disagreements."[52]

This notion of communion admits many degrees. Consider the principle of partial communion in relation to one of the defining aspects of ecclesiality, apostolicity, which is also the foundation for the church's missionary nature. According to the American Jesuit R. Haight, "The apostolic character of common ecclesial existence provides the grounds for partial

---

49. Murray, "Introducing Receptive Ecumenism," 1; see further Murray, *Receptive Ecumenism and the Call to Catholic Learning*; for an assessment, see Barrett, *Unity in Process*.

50. "About Receptive Ecumenism," emphasis in original.

51. See Edwards, "Meanings of Full Communion," 11.

52. Haight, *Ecclesial Existence*, 277.

communion. . . . [A]s a common apostolic dimension in all the churches, this ecclesial existence contains the possibility to serve as a basis for partial communion among the churches. Indeed, it urges such communion and even demands it."[53]

In keeping with the modest call of partial communion, ecumenism could envision flexible, creative, and diverse processes and structures in the service of seeking unity. That kind of imagination, rather than rigid structures, better fits the mosaic of the Christian church at both local and global levels. That would allow for new kinds of ecumenical players, such as the Global Christian Forum,[54] to be engaged as a full partner. It would also allow free churches, emerging communities, Christian coalitions, and similar groups to have a stronger voice. Flexible structures and processes with partial communion as the goal would much better fit the diverse and globalized church than rigid and fixed agendas. Partial communion as the goal is based on the conviction that diversity in itself is not the problem; exclusivity is.

Partial communion goes alongside the concept of the "provisionality" of Christian traditions and denominations. Indeed, all denominational identities and claims for the ecclesiality of any particular church (family) are by definition provisional. This is the case for two reasons. First of all, on this side of the eschatological consummation, each communion is but an anticipation of the final gathering of all people and churches in eschatological consummation. As an *anticipation*, each church is provisional. Second, each local community, each local church, while a full church, is always partial, provisional, in relation to other local churches. Under one Head (Christ), there cannot be "bodies" so independent that they are not members of the body of Christ. This same provisionality also characterizes the ecclesial category of "denomination," which in itself is an intermediary concept, denoting something between the local church and the final eschatological gathering of all people under one God.

On top of theological reasons, provisionality is also called for by the complexity and diversity of the contemporary global church. No doubt that as inevitable as it may be that denominational markers will be with us "until the end," there is also a widespread and increasing loosening or fluidity of those markers, particularly due to the constant emergence of new ecclesial structures and experiments. Regrettably, the contemporary ecumenical movement at large is still blind and deaf to these trends. Modern (and contemporary) ecumenism is still focused on negotiating merely between solid identities; it is blind to the emerging hybrid identities of local communions,

---

53. Haight, *Christian Community in History: Ecclesial Existence*, 285–86.
54. See their official website: http://www.globalchristianforum.org/.

networks of communions, and even more recent denominations.⁵⁵ Even worse, contemporary ecumenism also operates as if "denominations" were composed only of established mainline communities and provides little room for the significance of many free churches, Pentecostal/charismatic groups, emerging churches, and other newcomers.⁵⁶

"Ethnography as Ecumenism"

Too often ecclesiological and ecumenical discourse loses touch with the realities of church life and becomes speculative and abstract. Instead of merely theoretically reflecting on ecclesiology and church life, an ethnographic approach seeks to find some empirical, grassroots-level information and observations concerning the church. Such sociological, psychological, phenomenological, and other empirical studies were first named "Ethnography as Ecumenism," and it is currently a transatlantic research program. I have tweaked it to "Ethnography as Ecumenism." Somewhat similarly to congregational studies, it believes that ecclesiology needs "supplementation by judicious narratives" as correctives to an overly formal ecclesiology that stays away from "real" church life.

"Ecumenism as Comparative Theology"

The term "ecumenism as comparative theology" obviously builds on the wider concept of comparative theology, an emerging theological subdiscipline that engages other faith traditions with regard to specific, detailed themes and topics. Building on but also going farther than the more abstract and general theology of religions, it seeks to engage in an interfaith comparative work that is specific and deep. With regard to ecclesiology and ecumenism, it focuses on religious communities, whether the church, ummah, synagogue, sangha, or similar. It looks at the being and nature of the community, its "liturgy" and rites, its mission, and so forth—and does so by delving deeply into specific scriptural, historical, and contemporary authoritative and defining texts.

Ecumenism as comparative theology focuses on the questions of divisions and unity within one faith tradition and in relation to others. To give an obvious example: why, how, and for what reasons is the Islamic *ummah* divided into two major—and innumerable smaller—denominations and

---

55. See further Volf, *After Our Likeness*, 19–20.
56. So also, Volf, *After Our Likeness*, 20–21.

groups and why are they not able to recognize each other? Put that in a comparative Christian perspective and you are doing ecumenism as comparative theology.

It is amazing how this kind of exercise can help clarify, put in perspective, and foster reconsideration of internal Christian divisions and reasons for them. It may resource and empower the search for mutual recognition for the sake of the pluralistic world in a way that getting stuck with intra-Christian resources may not allow. My *Hope and Community* takes many steps towards that direction, and I hope it can serve as a call for many such enterprises.

CHAPTER 10

Is the Spirit Still the Divine Line Between the Christian East and West?

Revisiting an Ancient Problem of *Filoque* with a Hope for an Ecumenical Rapprochement

DO EAST AND WEST CONFESS THE SAME TRINITARIAN FAITH?

ACCORDING TO CONVENTIONAL THEOLOGICAL wisdom, "in general, Greek theology—of the Christian East—emphasizes the divine hypostases (persons), whereas Latin theology—of the Christian West—emphasizes the divine nature."[1] In other words, it is claimed that the East begins with the threeness of the Trinity, the West with the oneness or unity.[2] While not without grounds, this kind of description is also a caricature.[3] A related issue, of course, has to do with the later *filioque*-clause and its ecumenically dividing results.

---

1. LaCugna, "Trinitarian Mystery of God," 170. LaCugna calls the Eastern view emanationist in terms of descending order from Father to Son to Spirit and finally to the world, whereas the Western can be depicted as a circle enclosing all Trinitarian members in which the whole Trinity relates to the world.

2. The classic work contrasting Eastern and Western views is Régnon, *Études de théologie positive sur la sainte Trinité*, 3 vols.; see also Congar, *I Believe in the Holy Spirit*, vol. 3: xv–xxi.

3. O'Collins, *Tripersonal God*, 140.

In order to address the question put forth in the title of the essay, I will first take a closer look at key postpatristic developments in the West. The reason for this choice is the common understanding that from St. Augustine, theological work in general and Trinitarian reflection in particular has its center in the Latin-speaking church. Furthermore, early Eastern contributions have been registered above quite extensively. Second, based on that discussion, I seek to focus on the question of the derivation of the Spirit. Finally, I attempt to offer some helpful ecumenical viewpoints toward a reconciliation and mutual acknowledgment.

So, what is the legacy of Augustine's Trinitarian thinking?[4] And how does it relate to the question in the subheading: Do East and West confess the same Trinitarian faith? At the moment it is quite challenging to discern scholarly consensus in the interpretation of Augustine's view of the Trinity.[5] The older consensus is that because of his neo-Platonic leanings, Augustine put stress on the unity of the divine essence and had a hard time in accounting for distinctions. That would of course mean that his approach would be diametrically opposed to the Eastern view.[6] One of the most vocal contemporary critics of Augustine along this line, Colin Gunton, has argued Augustine did not correctly understand the tradition, certainly not the teaching of the Cappadocians, and ended up viewing the divine substance "behind" relations. For the Cappadocians, so this critic says, on the contrary, relations are "ontological" whereas for the Bishop of Hippo only "logical."[7] Thomas Marsh joins in and accuses Augustine of replacing the earlier Latin emphasis on the divine monarchy of the Father with "divine substance or nature which *then* is verified in Father, Son and Holy Spirit."[8] All of this has even caused some to speak of the "Theological Crisis of the West!"[9]

---

4. "It is impossible to do contemporary Trinitarian theology and not have a judgment on Augustine." Barnes, "Rereading Augustine's Theology of the Trinity," 145.

5. Rightly, Barnes laments that too much of Augustine's interpretation goes without actually reading Augustine! Barnes proposes to offer a new reading of the Bishop of Hippo based on reading everything he wrote on the topic of the Trinity; however, while fresh, Barnes' reading is also somewhat idiosyncratic since he focuses so much on the earlier writings. See Barnes, "Rereading Augustine's Theology of the Trinity," 145–46.

6. E.g., Prestige, *God in Patristic Thought*, 237; de Margerie, *Christian Trinity in History*, 110–121.

7. Gunton, *Promise of Trinitarian Theology*, 38–43 especially.

8. Marsh, *Triune God*, 132.

9. Gunton, "Augustine, the Trinity, and the Theological Crisis of the West," 33–58.

Not all are convinced that this is a fair reading of Augustine.[10] Two foundational problems are found in the older interpretation of Augustine, the correction of which may change our picture of the view of the Trinity held by this most influential early Western theologian. First, it is doubtful whether the Cappadocians had as developed a social doctrine of the Trinity as is assumed, and second, whether Augustine really started with the unity of the divine essence rather than with the distinctiveness of persons. Rather, it has been suggested, Augustine could have built on the Cappadocians' view: "Augustine begins where the Cappadocians leave off: accepting their answer to the question 'why not three gods?' he proceeds to ask 'three what?'"[11] The best way to look at this debate is to discern key ideas in Augustine's Trinitarian teaching.[12]

Augustine of course affirms the tradition concerning consubstantiality as well as distinctions of the Son and Spirit.[13] Furthermore, somewhat similarly to Eastern theologians, Augustine depicts the Father as the *principium,* primary or beginning of the deity.[14] Well-known are the reflections of Augustine on the Spirit in the Trinity. He conceives the Spirit as communion (of the Father and the Son),[15] their shared love,[16] and a gift.[17] In book 8 of *De Trinitate,* he develops his thought on the Trinity with the help of the idea

---

10. The most vocal critic of the alleged neo-Platonic influence on Augustine is Barnes, "Rereading Augustine's Theology of the Trinity." A careful, cautious interpretation, quite critical of the old consensus, is offered by Studer, *Trinity and Incarnation,* 167–85.

11. Cary, "Historical Perspectives on Trinitarian Doctrine," 9. A helpful summary of views pro and con can be found in Olson and Hall, *Trinity,* 44–45.

12. Main sources for Augustine's Trinitarian teaching besides the 15-volume "On the Trinity," written between 400 and 420 are "The City of God," "Confessions," "Tractates on the Gospel of John," "Letter 169 to Bishop Evodius," "Letter 11 to Nebridius," "On the Spirit and the Letter," "On the Soul and Its Origins," and "Sermons on Selected Lessons of the New Testament." Olson and Hall contains a comprehensive listing of Augustine's writings on the Trinity ("Trinity," 46n97).

13. E.g., Augustine, "Letters 169," 540: "The Son is not the Father, the Father is not the Son, and neither the Father nor the Son is the Holy Spirit . . . [T]hese are equal and co-eternal, and absolutely of one nature . . . an inseparable trinity." For the consubstantiality of the Son with the Father, see e.g., Augustine, "On the Trinity," 1.6.9:21–22; and for the Spirit with the Father and Son, see e.g., Augustine, "On the Trinity," 1.6.13:23–24; 7.3.6:108–9.

14. Augustine, "On the Trinity," 4.20.28–29: 84–85. See further, Studer, *The Grace of Christ and the Grace of God in Augustine of Hippo,* 104–5.

15. Augustine, "On the Trinity," 5.11.12: 93; 15.27.50: 226–27. See further, Ratzinger, "Holy Spirit as *Communio,* 325–39.

16. Augustine, "On the Trinity," 15.17.27: 215; Augustine, "Homilies, Tractates on the Gospel of St. John," 105.7.3:396.

17. Augustine, "On the Trinity" 5.12.13:93–94; 5.15.16:95.

of interpersonal love in terms of filiation and paternity. The Father is Lover, the Son the Beloved, and the Spirit the mutual Love that connects the two. Here of course the obvious question arises whether this depersonalizes the Spirit: shared love can hardly be a "person."[18]

For Augustine, incarnation is a major Trinitarian event, and it shapes his view of the Trinity more fully than is often acknowledged by his interpreters.[19] He takes pains in convincing his readers that incarnation is a unique event. For example, in expositing the gospel story about Jesus's baptism, Augustine argues that while the manifestation of the Spirit in the form of a dove and the Father's voice from above were temporary and symbolic, the incarnation is a permanent assumption of humanity in a real union of two natures.[20]

Pannenberg, who otherwise is somewhat critical of the Augustinian legacy,[21] has shown convincingly that "Augustine took over the relational definition of the Trinitarian distinctions which the Cappadocians, following Athanasius, had developed. He made the point that the distinctions of the persons are conditioned by their mutual relations."[22] For Augustine the relations are eternal.[23] The Eastern idea of *perichoresis*, mutual interpenetration, is no stranger to his views.[24] At the same time, Augustine was also building on the Cappadocians' idea mentioned above of the unity of the three persons in their outward works, the consequence of which is that from the creaturely works we may know the divine unity.[25]

18. Hilberath, "Pneumatologie," 446–47.

19. See further, Barnes, "Rereading," 154–68; Studer, *Trinity and Incarnation*, 168–185 especially.

20. Augustine, "Letters," 169.2.5—9:540–41.

21. Pannenberg is critical of the entire Western tradition up until Barth which employs a mental or psychological analogy of the Trinity, which in Pannenberg's view leads to the primacy of a divine single mind rather than the idea of divine unity in terms of relationality. Pannenberg calls this approach a "pre-trinitarian, theistic idea of God." Pannenberg, "Father, Son, Spirit," 251.

22. Pannenberg here refers to Augustine, "On the Trinity," 8.1; Pannenberg, *Systematic Theology*, 284. In his "Sermon on Matthew 3:13," Augustine speaks of a distinction of persons, and an inseparableness of operation. Augustine, "Sermon on New Testament Lessons. Matthew 3:13," 2.1–23, especially 2.15:259–266 (262). See also Augustine, "On the Trinity," 5.11.12:93 for an important statement about relationality in Trinity.

23. Pannenberg, *Systematic Theology*, 1:284.

24. Augustine in "On the Trinity" says it strongly: "in that highest Trinity one is as much as the three together, nor are two anything more than one. And They are infinite in themselves. So, both each are in each, and all in each, and each in all, and all in all, and all are one." Augustine, "On the Trinity," 6.10.12:103.

25. Augustine, "On the Trinity," 1.4.7:20; 4.21.30:85; see further, Pannenberg, *Systematic Theology*, 1:283–84.

It is often claimed that the psychological analogies are key to the Trinitarian teaching in Augustine. It is true that the latter part of his *On the Trinity*[26] employs images such as *mens/noti- tia/amor*—mind, mind's knowledge of itself, and the mind's love for itself—an illustration of Father as Being, Son as Consciousness, and Spirit as Love.[27] His logic is compelling: if the human mind knows love in itself, it knows God since God is love. These illustrations are of course biblically sustainable based on the idea of humanity as *imago Dei* (Gen 1:26–27). However, it is important to note that Augustine did not try to derive the Trinitarian distinctions from the divine unity. The psychological analogies that he suggested and developed in his work on the Trinity were simply meant to offer a very general way of linking the unity and trinity and thus creating some plausibility for trinitarian statements.[28]

Furthermore, the bishop of Hippo was aware of the limitation of the images.[29] The potential weakness of this analogy of self-presence, self-knowledge, and self-love—widely used in subsequent tradition—is that it leans toward a "monopersonal, modalistic view of God."[30] This is interesting in that in principle Augustine's analogies grow out of an interpersonal, thus communal and relational context, especially when it comes to love. Richard of St. Victor in the Medieval era picks up the relational aspect of Augustine's emphasis on love and develops it into a communion theology.

He considers the origin of the Spirit in a nuanced way. The Spirit proceeds "originally" from the Father and also in common from both the Father and Son, as something given by the Father.[31] In other words, Augustine is careful in safeguarding the Father as the primary source of the Spirit.[32] And even when the Son is included in the act of procession of the Spirit, it

---

26. In addition to "On the Trinity" 8–15:166–228, analogies are also discussed in "Homilies. Tractates on the Gospel of St. John" 23:150–57, as well as in "Letters" 11:228–30 and 169:539–543, among others.

27. Augustine, "On the Trinity" 8.10.14:124; 9.2.2:126–27. The idea of Mind, of course, has its legacy in early Christian theology beginning from the Apologists, who taught that as the Word the Son is the Father's thought/idea. Augustine also developed further the idea of the "vestiges of the Trinity" with the help of the tripartite constitution of the human soul, *memoria/intelligentia/voluntas*: memory, intelligence, and willing. Augustine, "On the Trinity," 9.8:131; 10.10.14–16: 141–42; 11.10—11.17–18: 153–54.

28. Pannenberg, *Systematic Theology*, 1:284; see also 287: "Augustine's psychological analogies should not be used to derive the trinity from the unity but to simply illustrate the Trinity in whom one already believes."

29. Augustine, "On the Trinity," 15.23.43:222.

30. O'Collins, *Tripersonal God*, 137.

31. Augustine, "On the Trinity," 15.26.47:225.

32. See Augustine, "On the Trinity," 4.20.29:84–85.

is not from two sources but rather from a single source in order to protect divine unity.[33] I think it is important to notice here that again Augustine's legacy is somewhat ambiguous. On the one hand, there is no denying that Augustine's idea of the Spirit as the shared love between Father and Son and his teaching about the double-procession of the Spirit helped the Christian West to ratify the *filioque* clause. On the other hand, had the West been more sensitive to the shared tradition and to the sensibilities of the East, Augustine's idea of the procession of the Spirit from the Father through the Son and thus in a secondary way, possibly could have helped avoid the conflict between East and West. Eastern theologians are not necessarily against the idea of the Spirit proceeding from the Father (who is the source after all) through the Son. And for Augustine, unlike so much of later Western tradition, the Spirit's derivation also from the Son did not necessarily mean inferiority in status any more than the Son's generation from the Father does (this was of course the affirmation against the Arians).[34]

Now, in light of key ideas of Augustinian teaching, we are in a place to try to address at least tentatively the question of the subheading, namely, do East and West confess the same Trinitarian faith? I think it very important to make the distinction between Augustine's own ideas and his legacy as carried on by later (Western) tradition.[35] Looking at Augustine's own writings, it "hardly appears that Augustine had little interest in the distinctions of the persons, or that he was averse to the full import of the Incarnation."[36] Nor is it true that Augustine developed his Trinitarian theology abstractly based on analogies; he did not. He is thoroughly biblical as a quick look, for example, in the first half of the *De Trinitate* clearly shows, let alone his biblical expositions. Nor is it right to say that—in contrast to the Cappadocians and Athanasius—Augustine neglected spirituality and salvation.[37] His focus on incarnation alone would counter-argue this charge.

In light of these considerations, a more nuanced and sophisticated way of looking at the differences between the Christian East and West is in order.[38] I think it is best done by trying to discern the key characteristics

33. Augustine, "On the Trinity," 5.14:94–96.

34. See further, O'Collins, *Tripersonal God*, 139.

35. For a balanced judgment, see Letham, *Holy Trinity in Scripture, History, Theology, and Worship*, 198–200.

36. Letham, *Holy Trinity in Scripture, History, Theology, and Worship*, 195. So also Gerald O'Collins, *Tripersonal God*, 135.

37. This is one of the theses of LaCugna's *God for Us*, 81–104.

38. Overstatements abound and those need to be corrected: "We must acknowledge that the doctrine of the trinity in the East is an integral part of its total theological understanding. The same cannot be said for the Western formulation stemming chiefly

and unique features in each without trying to artificially reconcile those nor make them more dramatic than they are.[39] Almost everyone agrees that for Eastern theologians the significance of the *hypostatic* distinctions among Father, Son, and Spirit has often been a key concern. The East has wanted to speak of the "concrete particularity of Father, Son, and Spirit."[40] Furthermore, as noted several times, they have emphasized the Father as the source of the deity. Son and Spirit proceed from the Father from eternity. In the West, there has often been more emphasis on the divine being/substance/essence from which the personal distinctions derive. Consequently, there has been emphasis on the joint working of the three in the world.[41] Whatever the difference between the Christian East and West, each of them has faced its own challenges: for the East, it was the danger of tritheism because of the emphasis on three different *hypostaseis* and subordinationism because of the idea of the Father as the source of divinity. Westerners have tended to be more modalistic. Moreover, Eastern theological traditions in general and Trinitarian ones in particular have been more pneumatologically oriented, whereas in the West, Christology has often played the key role. This, again, brings us to the question of the *filioque* to be discussed in what follows.

Having said all this, one also has to acknowledge that there are several aspects of the Augustinian tradition that were picked up by later Western tradition that led to the eclipse of the Trinitarian doctrine so evident in the judgment of contemporary theologians. First, with all his stress on relationality, there is no denying that Augustine also emphasizes the divine unity and substance.[42] Therefore, there is some truth in the insistence that whereas for the Christian East distinctions of persons (*hypostaseis*) are the key to Trinity; for Augustine substance is, though not to the neglect of relations. Second, Augustine's idea of the Spirit as shared love between Father and Son is problematic ecumenically and biblically. In the Bible, God is love rather than Spirit. Furthermore, Augustine's idea feeds the idea of *filioque*.

---

from Augustine. Here, the doctrine is an unneeded appendage to theology." Cobb, "Relativization of the Trinity," 5.

39. Letham's *Holy Trinity* includes a quite helpful chart of the key features of both East and West even when it tends to be quite categorical (250–51).

40. Grenz, *Rediscovering the Triune God*, 8. See also Gunton, *Promise of Trinitarian Theology*, 39.

41. This is the so-called "Augustinian rule": the works of the Trinity *ad extra* are indivisible.

42. LaCugna's comment is an overstatement yet contains a kernel of truth: "[Augustine's] focus on the individual apart from its personal and social relations flows directly from the ontology that begins from substance rather than person." LaCugna, *God for Us*, 102. LaCugna, however, qualifies this by saying that was not Augustine's intention, yet it was picked up by his followers.

And last but not least, this analogy can hardly argue for any distinct personality of the Spirit. Third, while Augustine seemed to handle analogies of the Trinity with care and was aware of their limitations, many of his followers elevated them to a role that easily leads away from the concrete biblical salvation history into abstract speculations. While valid in itself—based on the idea that humanity is created in the image of the Triune God—it can end up being a Trinitarian theology "from below." There are not only similarities but also differences between the Trinity and humanity.[43]

IS THE ORIGIN OF THE SPIRIT STILL A THEOLOGICAL IMPASSE?

As is well known, the Bible does not clarify the interrelations of Father, Son, and Spirit. A classic example, with reverberations still felt, is the question of the procession of the Spirit. On the one hand, Jesus says that he himself will send the Spirit (John 16:7) or that he will send the Spirit (called *Parakletos* here) who proceeds from the Father (John 15:26). On the other hand, Jesus prays to the Father for him to send the Spirit (John 14:16), and the Father will send the Spirit in Jesus's name (John 14:26).[44] Because of the lack of clarity in the biblical record as well as the rise to prominence of the Augustinian idea of the Spirit as shared love (another idea which of course has its basis in the biblical idea of the Spirit as *koinonia*), the Christian West added the Spirit's dual procession, *filioque* (from Latin: "and from the Son") to the Niceno-Constantinopolitan Creed that originally said that the Holy Spirit "proceeds from the Father." While some of the historical details are somewhat debated,[45] it is clear that in the first major breach of the Christian church in 1054 the *filioque* clause played a major role with political, ecclesiastical, and cultural issues. The Christian East objected vigorously to this addition claiming that it was a one-sided addition without ecumenical consultation,[46] that it compromises the monarchy of the Father as the source

---

43. See further, Volf, "'Trinity Is Our Social Program,'" 403–23.

44. In terms of biblical scholarship, speculation into the "immanent" and "economic" sendings is quite problematic. See e.g., Letham, *Holy Trinity*, 203. Those distinctions have to do with postbiblical historical and systematic constructions.

45. The standard view is that this addition was first accepted by the Council of Toledo in 589 and ratified by the 809 Aachen Synod. It was incorporated in later creeds such as that of the Fourth Lateran in 1215 and Council of Lyons in 1274. See, e.g., Gonzales, *Story of Christianity*, 1:264–265; Latourett, *History of Christianity*, 304, 360. A standard full-scale study on the theology and history of *Filioque* is Oberdorfer, *Filioque*.

46. "Can a clause deriving from one theological tradition simply be inserted in a creed deriving from another theological tradition without council?" Stylianopoulos

of divinity,⁴⁷ and that it subordinates the Spirit to Jesus with theological corollaries in ecclesiology, the doctrine of salvation, and so on.⁴⁸ While the details of the origin of the *filioque* addition in the West are not fully known, besides the Augustinian idea of the Spirit as the mutual love, it is believed that the addition also served a function in opposing Arianism. Mentioning the Son alongside the Father as the origin of the Spirit was seen as a way to defend consubstantiality.⁴⁹

With all its exaggerations,⁵⁰ the Eastern critique of the *filioque* is important both ecumenically and theologically and should not be dismissed.⁵¹ The West did not have the right to unilaterally add *filioque*.⁵²

In my judgment, *filioque* is not heretical even though ecumenically and theologically it is unacceptable and therefore should be removed.⁵³

and Heim, *Spirit of Truth*, 32.

47. Ware, *Orthodox Church*, 210–14, defends the Father's monarchy as the reason for opposing *Filioque*. Ware critiques the Western idea of Father and Son as two independent sources of the Spirit. Ware, however, does not take into consideration the quite nuanced view of Augustine according to which the Father is the principal source while the Son is the source of the Spirit in a derivative sense, Augustine, "On the Trinity," 15.17.27.

48. Vladimir Lossky has most dramatically articulated the charge of "Christomonism" against Western theology. According to him, Christianity in the West is seen as unilaterally referring to Christ, the Spirit being an addition to the church, to its ministries and sacraments. Lossky, "Procession of the Holy Spirit in Orthodox Trinitarian Doctrine," ch. 4. See also Nissiotis, "Main Ecclesiological Problem of the Second Vatican Council and Position of the Non-Roman Churches Facing It," 31–62. All of these three objections, namely, that it was a unilateral act, it subordinates the Son to the Spirit, and that it compromises the Father's monarchy were already presented by the most vocal critic in history, the ninth-century patriarch of Constantinople, Photius in his *On the Mystagogy of the Holy Spirit*, 51–52, 71–72 especially.

49. Against the standard view, Richard Haugh surmises that the addition happened just by way of transposition with any conscious theological reason. Haugh, *Photius and the Carolingians*, 160–61.

50. Photius insisted that the Holy Spirit proceeds from the Father *alone*, the Son having no part to play. The intention of this polemical statement was not of course to argue the total exclusion of the Son from the Spirit but to defend vigorously the monarchy of the Father as the source of the deity of both Spirit and Son. See further, Letham, *Holy Trinity*, 205.

51. For an important Orthodox statement, see Needham, "Filioque Clause," 142–62.

52. Peters puts it bluntly: "The insertion of *filioque* in the Western version of the Nicene Creed was an act of unwarranted authority and certainly not done in the interest of church unity." Peters, *God as Trinity*, 65.

53. Pannenberg, *Systematic Theology*, 1:319 concurs. Peters makes the brilliant point that in principle there is nothing against adding to the creeds as long as it is done in concert. Theology is an ongoing reflection, elaboration, and processing of tradition. No creed as such has to be the final word. See Peters, *God as Trinity*, 66.

Ecumenically and theologically it would be important for the East to be able to acknowledge the nonheretical nature of the addition. Furthermore, the Christian East should keep in mind the fact that with all its problems, at first *filioque*, as mentioned above, was used in the West in support of consubstantiality, an idea shared by both traditions.[54]

IN LIEU OF CONCLUSIONS, SOME HOPE FOR THE FUTURE

While there are those who for some reason or another support the *filioque* clause,[55] there is a growing consensus among Western theologians, both Roman Catholic and Protestant, about the need to delete the addition and thus return to the original form of the creed.[56] J. Moltmann for years has appealed for the removal of the addition and has suggested a more conciliar way of putting it, namely, that the Spirit proceeds "from the Father of the Son." He wants to emphasize the biblical idea of reciprocity of Spirit and Son.[57] An alternative to *Filioque* "from the Father through the Son" would be also acceptable to the Christian East. It would defend the monarchy of the Father (and in that sense, some kind of subordination of the Son to Father, an idea not foreign to the East) and still be ambiguous enough.[58]

---

54. See further, Letham, *Holy Trinity*, 213.

55. Well-known is the defense of *Filioque* by Karl Barth, who feared that dismissing it would mean ignoring the biblical insistence on the Spirit being the Spirit of the Son. See Barth, *Church Dogmatics*, I/1:480. Gerald Bray defends the addition with reference to the doctrine of salvation. In his opinion, the Eastern doctrine of *theosis* with its focus on pneumatology severs the relationship between Son (atonement) and Spirit. Bray, "*Filioque* Clause in History and Theology," 142–43. While I disagree with Bray, I also commend his relating the question of the *Filioque* to the Spirit, which is indeed at the heart of Eastern theology. For this, see further the comment by Theodore Stylianopoulos ("Biblical Background of the Article on the Holy Spirit in the Constantinopolitan Creed," 171): "At stake was not an abstract question but the truth of Christian salvation." For this quotation, I am indebted to Letham, *Holy Trinity*, 203.

56. For a helpful discussion, see Vischer, *Spirit of God, Spirit of Christ*. For Roman Catholic support of the removal of the *filioque* clause, see Congar, *I Believe in the Holy Spirit*, 3:72ff. In addition to Moltmann and Pannenberg, to be discussed in what follows, a strong defender of the Eastern view has been the Reformed Thomas F. Torrance, who was instrumental in the Reformed-Orthodox dialogue. For the dialogue, see Torrance, *Theological Dialogue between Orthodox and Reformed Churches*, 2:219–32. For his own views in this respect, see Torrance, *Trinitarian Perspectives*, 110–43. For these references to Torrance, I am indebted to Letham, *Holy Trinity*, 218n66.

57. Moltmann, *Trinity and the Kingdom of God*, 178–79, 185–87.

58. Bobrinskoy, *Mystery of the Trinity*, 302–3. Again, my appreciation for bringing this source to my attention goes to Letham, *Holy Trinity*, 217n64. For incisive

I agree with Pannenberg that beyond *Filioque* there is a weakness that plagues both traditions, namely, the understanding of relations mainly in terms of origins. Both East and West share that view both in their own distinctive way, the East by insisting on the role of the Father as the source and the West by making the Father primary in the deity with their idea of the proceeding of the Son from the Father and then the Spirit from both.[59] This blurs the key idea of Athanasius—the importance of which he himself hardly noticed—that relations are based on mutuality rather than origin.

The Lutheran Ted Peters, who supports the removal of the *filioque* clause, however, remarks that the idea of the Spirit proceeding both from the Son as well as the Father also points to something valuable. It highlights relationality and communality, the Spirit being the shared love between Father and Son (and by extension, between the Triune God and the world). Furthermore, on this side of Pentecost, it reminds us of the importance of resurrection and ascension: the risen Christ in Spirit is the presence of Christ. "In this work of transcending and applying the historical event of Jesus Christ to our personal lives, we must think of the Spirit as proceeding from Jesus Christ."[60] Finally, Peters notes, within the divine life the Spirit indeed is the principle of relationship and unity. "The separation that takes place between Father and Son—the separation that defines Father as Father and the Son as Son—is healed by the Spirit. It is the Spirit that maintains unity in difference."[61]

comments, see also O'Collins, *Tripersonal God*, 139.
59. Pannenberg, *Systematic Theology*, 1:319.
60. Peters, *God as Trinity*, 66.
61. Peters, *God as Trinity*, 66.

PART FOUR

Interreligious Theology

CHAPTER 11

The Re-Turn of Religion in the Third Millennium

Pentecostalisms and Postmodernities

INTRODUCTION: IN SEARCH OF AN "EXPERIENTIALIST" RELIGION FOR THE NEW WORLD

THE HARVARD THEOLOGIAN HARVEY COX, once (in)famous for his failed prophecy of the diminishing role of religion in the *Secular City*, suggests a re-turn of religion in the beginning of the new millennium, a religion which has to do with *Fire from Heaven*:

> As the first days of the new millennium draw closer, the prospects for the human spirit seem both promising and chilling. For the past three centuries, two principal contenders—scientific modernity and traditional religion—have clashed over the privilege of being the ultimate source of meaning and value. Now, like tired boxers who have slugged away too long, the two have reached an exhausted stalemate ... People are still willing to rely on science for the limited things it has proven it can do, but they no longer believe it will answer their deepest questions. They remain vaguely intrigued with the traditional religions, but not with conventional churches ... Increasing numbers of people appear ready to move on, and are on the lookout for a more promising map of the life-world ... As both scientific modernity and conventional religion progressively lose their ability to provide a source of spiritual meaning, two new contenders

are stepping forward—"fundamentalism" and, for lack of a more precise word, "experientialism." Both present themselves as authentic links to the sacred past. Both embody efforts to reclaim what is valuable from previous ages in order to apply it to the present and future. Which of these two rivals eventually prevails will be decided in large measure by which one grasps the nature of the change we are living through . . . Most agree that we are entering a period in which we will see the world and selves less cerebrally and more intuitively, less analytically and more immediately, less literally and more analogically . . . Perhaps it has taken the very recent and unprecedented meeting of east and west to produce this new stage of consciousness. In any case, these thinkers find evidence for a new phase of history in virtually every field of human endeavor—in atonal and improvisational music, in the environmental movement, in new styles of painting and sculpture, in experimental architecture, and especially in poetry. I think one can also fit in pentecostalism.[1]

While observers of postmodernities—as well as life in the beginning of the new millennium—would probably be shouting "Amen" to Cox's litany, the last sentence sounds heretical at its best and incredible at its worst. Pentecostalism and postmodernities? What possibly would these two have to do with each other?

While it is of course possible that a prophet like Cox may turn out to be wrong again, before inquisition, it is only fair to hear more about his reasoning. Having established first that fundamentalisms—whether those of a Christian sort or a Muslim or Hindu or other religious type—are but "recent reactions to different forms of modernity" and yet ironically "claim to have a firm grip on absolute truth" in matters of religion (and at times of politics), what he calls "experientialism," is "more disparate and inchoate, harder to describe than fundamentalism." As an example of the latter, Cox mentions liberation theologies and feminist theologies. What is common to both fundamentalisms and experientialisms is that they can appear in more than one religion—and indeed, are doing so in the beginning of a new millennium.[2]

So, "experience" matters in the new religiosity: "Pentecostals talk about *experience* a lot. The old tent-meeting adage that 'a man with a doctrine doesn't stand a chance against a man with an experience' is still frequently quoted [among Pentecostals]."[3] What are some other features of

---

1. Cox, *Fire from Heaven*, 299–301.
2. Cox, *Fire from Heaven*, 300–305 (citations in 303 and 304 respectively).
3. Cox, *Fire from Heaven*, 312.

this new emerging "experientialism" that in Cox's view bespeaks the rise of Pentecostalism? In his *Fire from Heaven*, he discusses features such as a new appreciation of affections and the mysterious/mystical, healings and deliverances, nonhierarchical structures and involvement of all (rather than those educated formally), and grassroots spirituality. Cox also mentions similar kinds of things emerging in the renewal of other religions such as documented and ably discussed in Seyed Hossein Nasr's *Islamic Spirituality: Manifestations,* which defines spirituality as the something that "is open to the transcendent dimension" and where the person "experiences ultimate reality." While focusing on the most likely candidate in Islam, Sufism, the principle has a wider application as well.[4]

Before taking a closer look at potential similarities and dissimilarities between Pentecostalisms and postmodernities, a few clarifying thoughts are in order to make sure we are all using the two terms in the same way. Following that, the rest of the essay seeks some common features between Pentecostalisms and postmodernities as well as differences and differing orientations.

The Challenge of Defining Pentecostal Identity

The main title of this essay is to be taken literally: it speaks of both Pentecostalisms and postmodernities in plural (the symposium organizers had already met me halfway, having suggested the topic in the form "Pentecostalism and *postmodernities*"!). While nothing like a uniform definition of Pentecostalisms exists, a helpful orientation to the myriads of movements known by that umbrella name is the terminology adopted by *The New International Dictionary of Pentecostal and Charismatic Movements*.[5] That typology lists, first, (Classical) Pentecostal denominations such as Assemblies of God or Foursquare Gospel, owing their existence to the famous Azusa Revival; second, Charismatic movements, Pentecostal-type spiritual movements within the established churches (the largest of which is the Roman Catholic Charismatic Renewal); and third, neo-Charismatic movements, some of the most notable of which are the Vineyard Fellowship in the USA, African Initiated Churches, and the China House Church movement, as well as an innumerable number of independent churches and groups all over the world. Numberwise, the Charismatic movements (about 200 million) and neo-Charismatics (200–300 million) well outnumber Classical Pentecostals

---

4. Cited in Cox, *Fire from Heaven*, 309.

5. While canons are still in the making, this is the typology adopted in Burgess and van der Maas, *New International Dictionary of Pentecostal and Charismatic Movements*.

(75–125 million). Diversity is the hallmark of Pentecostalisms. The diversity arises in two dimensions: the cultural and the theologico-ecumenical. Pentecostalism, unlike any other contemporary religious movement, Christian or non-Christian, is spread across most cultures, linguistic barriers, and social locations.[6] Related to this is the theological and ecumenical diversity, which simply means that there are several more-or-less distinct Pentecostalisms. When I use the term "pentecostalisms" in what follows, I am mainly speaking of the first category, namely, Pentecostal churches, under whatever name they are known all over the world, and thus leave aside Charismatic movements within established churches and all independent Pentecostal-type movements. Still, speaking of Pentecostalisms in the plural is a valid and needed choice in light of the great diversity even within that oldest subgroup. How different in ethos, manifestation, and to some extent in theology are, for example, Yoido Full Gospel Church in Seoul, Korea—the world's largest church with more than one million adherents—from the African-American (Black) Pentecostal churches of the US South from the small Pentecostal congregations in any European country, and so on.

The question of what makes Pentecostalisms—in other words, what is its identity?—is a notoriously difficult one. Unlike, say, Lutheranism or Roman Catholicism, Pentecostal identity is not based on creeds or shared history. Nor can Pentecostal identity be based on ecclesiastical structures since you can find the whole repertoire of them from most local-church autonomous models (Scandinavia) to Congregationalist (Continental Europe and England) to Presbyterian (white Pentecostals in the USA) to episcopal (Black Pentecostals in the USA and elsewhere) to other types.

If there is a common denominator, not only among (Classical) Pentecostals but also between them and, say Roman Catholic Charismatics and African Instituted Churches, it has to do with a unique spirituality. While it can be named in more than one way, it has everything to do with a Christ-centered charismatic spirituality with a passionate desire to "meet" with Jesus Christ as he is being perceived of as the Bearer of the "Full Gospel," i.e., Jesus as Savior, Sanctifier, Healer, Baptizer with the Spirit, and the Soon-returning King.[7] Spirituality, rather than theology/creeds or sociol-

---

6. The diversity is well documented. For an up-to-date account, see e.g., the annual statistic lists in the January issue of *International Bulletin of Missionary Research* compiled by David B. Barrett and Todd M. Johnson.

7. A definitive study of the main motifs of "Full Gospel" is Dayton, *Theological Roots of Pentecostalism*. For a fine account of key themes and orientations in Pentecostal spirituality, see Spittler, "Spirituality, Pentecostal and Charismatic," 1096–102.

ogy of religion[8] is the key to understanding Pentecostalism.[9] No one else has argued so forcefully and convincingly for the primacy of spirituality as the way to define Pentecostalisms as Walter J. Hollenweger, the most noted theological observer of the movements. Hollenweger for decades has insisted that it was the early years of the emerging Pentecostal movement that gave the movement its *prodigium*. The first decade of the movement, says Hollenweger, forms the heart, not the infancy, of Pentecostal spirituality.[10] Features such as orality of liturgy, narrativity of theology and witness, maximum participation at the level of reflection, prayer, and decision-making in a community characterized by inclusion and reconciliation, inclusion of dreams and visions into personal and public forms of worship, and a holistic understanding of the body-mind relationship reflected in the ministry of healing by prayer, were formative at the movement's inception.[11] For Hol-

---

8. In the past, a typical way of dismissing Pentecostals in terms of deprivation theory was the norm among the sociologists of religion, often with little or no firsthand knowledge of the movement itself. For a balanced critical discussion, see Miller, "Pentecostalism as a Social Movement," 97–144.

9. Here I cannot engage the complicated question of the theological and spiritual origins of Pentecostalism, a debated issue among specialists. Four main proposals have been set forth. (1) Some connect the origins of the modern Pentecostal movement with the work of Charles F. Parham and his students at Topeka, Kansas. (2) Non-white historians and theologians of the movement often emphasize the primary role of the Black Holiness preacher William Joseph Seymour and the Apostolic Faith Mission that arose in Los Angeles, California, in April 1906. (3) Others, who note that some of their leaders or members spoke in tongues prior to either Parham or Seymour, see themselves as constituting the earliest Pentecostal denominations, thereby claiming to be the original Pentecostals. (4) Finally, some view the origins of Pentecostalism as a sovereign work of God that can be traced to no single leader or group, but rather to a spontaneous and simultaneous outpouring of the Holy Spirit around the world. For starters, see Robeck, "Pentecostal Origins from a Global Perspective," 166–80; Cerillo, "Interpretive Approaches to the History of American Pentecostal Origins," 29–52. Despite some differing terminology, they agree on the basic outline of the history.

10. Hollenweger, *Pentecostals*, 551. See also Land, *Pentecostal Spirituality*, 14, 47.

11. Hollenweger, "After Twenty Years' Research on Pentecostalism," 6. More recently, Hollenweger has summarized the "roots" of Pentecostalism in these terms: (1) the Black oral root; (2) the Catholic root, (3) the evangelical root, (4) the critical root, (5) the ecumenical root. Hollenweger, "From Azusa Street to Toronto Phenomenon," 3–14.

Hollenweger, "Verheissung und Verhangnis der Pfingstbewegung," 265–88. Similarly, e.g., J. Kwabena Asamoah-Gyadu, an African Pentecostalist, defines the movement as "Christian tradition that emphasize salvation in Christ as a transformative experience wrought by the Holy Spirit. Consequently, pneumatic phenomena such as 'speaking in tongues,' prophecies, visions, healing and miracles in general, perceived as standing in historic continuity with the experiences of the early church, are sought, accepted, valued, and consciously encouraged among members as signifying the presence of God and experiences of his Spirit." Asamoah-Gyadu, "Christian Education in the Modem African Church," 228.

lenweger, thus, Pentecostalism represents a religious movement *sui generis*, *"eine neue Konfession*," which cannot be reduced to either Fundamentalism, Evangelicalism, or even to Protestantism as such.[12]

Pentecostalisms Flirting with Postmodernities?

What about Pentecostalisms' relation to postmodernities? It would be of course useless to even to begin to define postmodernities.[13] I believe we can work with a very minimal characterization of that phenomenon, such as lack of metanarratives; rediscovery of the aesthetic, nonrational, mystical, and similar "soft values"; lack of trust in institutions; search for holism in life—negatively put, eschewal of dualistic explanations—new communication patterns; and dynamic, somewhat confused understanding of the relationship between individual and communal, local and global, and so on. As good as any description of postmodernity in general is offered by Os Guinness:

> Postmodernism announces itself as a break with modernism, just as modernism did earlier with tradition. Where modernism was a manifesto of human self-confidence and self-congratulation, postmodernism is a confession of modesty, if not despair. There is not truth, only truths. There are no principles, only preferences. There is no grand reason, only reasons. There is no privileged civilization (or culture, belief, norms, and styles), only a multiplicity of cultures, beliefs, periods, and styles . . . There is no grand narrative of human progress, only countless stories of where people and their cultures are now. There is no simple reality or any grand objectivity of universal, detached knowledge, only a ceaseless representation of everything in terms of everything else.[14]

In general, religion and religiosity matters to postmodern people, it's just often a different kind of religion from, say, *Kulturprotestantismus*. In the English-speaking world, a new expression of Christian spirituality and ecclesiology is emerging under the name the *Emerging Churches*, an

---

12. Asamoah-Gyadu, "Christian Education in the Modem African Church," 265.

13. Personally, I find extremely helpful the way Graham Ward, who is of course also known as a major theological advocate of Radical Orthodoxy, outlines the complex and fluid relationships between contemporary theologies and postmodernities in his *Theology and Contemporary Critical Theory* as in his other main guide to the topic which he edited: *The Postmodern God*.

14. Guinness, *Fit Bodies, Fat Minds*, 103–5.

authentically postmodern phenomenon—or perhaps, one should say: phenomena (in the plural).

Some Pentecostal theologians—and theological observers such as Cox and Hollenweger—have flirted with postmodernities. Beginning from the mid 1990s, there have been a number of experiments in hermeneutics to that effect[15] and later the discussion has expanded to other areas that Pentecostalisms and postmodernities may have in common such as the principle of embodiment and the search for holism, the importance of narrative, and so on.[16]

James K. A. Smith has recently tried to match two candidates as unlikely as ours, namely, Pentecostalism and Radical Orthodoxy! An odd courtship, indeed! Smith argues that while, on the one hand, in Pentecostalism one can discern certain parallels to Radical Orthodoxy, there are also, on the other hand, defined differences, and highlighting those differences is important as well.[17] Let me do something similar and attempt a correlation of postmodernities and Pentecostalisms by suggesting—the word *suggest* has to be taken at face value here, meaning that at the moment I am asking as many questions as I am arguing for anything—some parallels and some differences. I am discerning similarities between postmodernities and Pentecostalisms with regard to the following themes: rediscovery of "primal spirituality," emphasis on "the materiality of salvation" and search for holism, as well as the cherishing of communitarianism and empowerment of all. Having discussed these and related features, in the final part of the essay, I turn my critical eyes on counter-forces and orientations in Pentecostalisms that make any correlating with postmodernities suspect and inchoate.

If there is any thesis for my discussion, it would be something like this: while undoubtedly there are similarities and shared orientations between postmodernities and Pentecostalisms, there are also number of things that differentiate them from each other not only because Pentecostalisms shares

---

15. See, e.g., Cargal, "Beyond the Fundamentalist-Modernity Controversy," 163–87; Byrd, "Paul Ricoeur's Hermeneutical Theory and Pentecostal Proclamation," 203–14; Arche, "Pentecostal Hermeneutics," 63–81. For a much less enthusiastic appraisal and with some criticism, see also Kärkkäinen, "Pentecostal Hermeneutics in the Making," 76–115.

16. An important contribution here is Johns, "Pentecostalism and the Postmodern Worldview," 73–96. Lately, however, more modest and self-critical remarks have emerged such as those found in Poirier and Lewis, "Pentecostal and Postmodernist Hermeneutics, 3–21. For a helpful theological reflection by a Roman Catholic theologian, well versed in Pentecostalism, see Del Colle, "Postmodernism and Pentecostal-Charismatic Experience," 97–116.

17. Smith, "What Hath Cambridge to Do with Azusa Street?," 97–114.

a different "foundation"[18] from postmodernities, but also because Pentecostalisms as an emerging and developing spirit-movement is loaded with dynamic tensions, even potential contradistinctions. At the moment, it is too early—after the first centennial—to know what Pentecostalisms as a phenomenon is in the final analysis.

DISCERNMENT: IN SEARCH OF PARALLELS BETWEEN POSTMODERNITIES AND PENTECOSTALISMS

"Primal Spirituality"

If Pentecostalisms' identity could—and should—be defined in terms of spirituality rather than, say, texts or traditions, then that may be the main clue to seeking for connections with postmodernities. Indeed, that is the thrust of what has been attempted recently. According to Cox, Pentecostalism

> has succeeded because it has spoken to the spiritual emptiness of our time by reaching beyond the levels of creed and ceremony into the core of human religiousness, into what might be called 'primal spirituality,' that largely unprocessed nucleus of the psyche in which the unending struggle for a sense of purpose and significance goes on. Classical theologians have called it the 'imago dei,' the image of God in every person. Maybe the Pentecostals are referring to the same thing with different words . . . My own conviction is that Pentecostals have touched so many people because they have indeed restored something.[19]

I welcome the way Cox approaches the core motif of Pentecostalism, namely, its "experientialist" spirituality, by employing the concept of "primal spirituality" widely employed in English-speaking religious studies. "Experience," as we all know, is a notoriously difficult and many-faceted concept. Any "turn to experience" in modern theology adds as much fog as it does clarity to discussion. Speaking of Pentecostalism's "turn to experience"—the movement which he regards as the "most" postmodern of all Christian

---

18. Teaching on the other side of the Atlantic, I am of course well aware of the raging "foundationalism" debate among postmodernists and therefore using this checkered term, I am putting it in quotes. With all postmodern attempts to exclude "foundations" from contemporary *thesaurus*, my own understanding is that while the term should be handled with care, it still has a legitimate place in the discourse.

19. Cox, *Fire from Heaven*, 81.

expressions in the contemporary world[20]—in terms of primal spirituality includes three interrelated components: "primal speech," "primal piety," and "primal hope." "Primal speech" highlights the spiritual importance of "ecstatic utterance," *glossolalia*, speaking in tongues—an activity known throughout Christian history as well as among other religions. "In an age of bombast, hype, and doublespeak, when ultraspecialized terminologies and contrived rhetoric seem to have emptied and pulverized language, the first pentecostals learned to speak—and their successors still speak—with another voice, a language of the heart," Cox argues. "Primal piety" speaks of the spiritual importance of vision, healing, dreams, dance, and other archetypal religious expressions. What is important here is that "the reemergence of this primal spirituality came—perhaps not surprisingly—at just the point in history when both the rationalistic assumptions of modernity and the strategies religions had used to oppose them (or to accommodate to them) were all coming unraveled." "Primal hope" points to "pentecostalism's millennial outlook—its insistent that a radically new world age is about to dawn."[21]

Postmodernists, of course, gladly welcome the rediscovery of what is here called "primal spirituality." What strikes one visiting for example typical Emerging Churches worship services is the interesting mixture of old and new, in terms of the latest high-tech audio-visual aids combined with ancient mystical, semi-sacramental or then, highly emotional, exuberant movements, sounds, and the like. At the same time, it has to be said that of course "For many thoughtful people, all three of these qualities of the pentecostal phenomenonon—glossolalia, dreams and trances and millennialism—appear at best merely bizarre and at worst downright scary."[22]

Alongside this emphasis on experience and primal spirituality, Pentecostalisms share with postmodernities the new appreciation of the affectivity of religious experience and knowledge—a feature J. K. A. Smith also finds in common between Pentecostalism and Radical Orthodoxy.[23] For any observer of Pentecostal worship services, the presence of an affective element is visible in music, dance, drama, movements, tears and laughter, and so on. Smith even argues that the adoption by Pentecostals of these kinds of features also speaks of what he calls "affective epistemology," which does not privilege only and times not even primarily discursive, analytic

---

20. See also Cox, Review of *Pentecostal Spirituality*, 3–12. Steven Land's book from 1992 is a landmark work by a Pentecostal theologian on the importance of eschatologically loaded, charismatic, Christ-centered spirituality as the "core" of Pentecostalism.

21. Cox, *Fire from Heaven*, 81–82.

22. Cox, *Fire from Heaven*, 83.

23. Smith, "What Hath Cambridge to Do with Azusa Street?," 111.

argumentation but gives a fair place to intuition, emotions, and other non-rational aspects of the human being.[24]

The philosopher Smith further contends that because of an emphasis on the role of experience and its rootage in affective epistemology, Pentecostal theology—differently from Evangelical theology—resists the kinds of dualisms that postmodernists as well as Radical Orthodox advocates are also resisting.[25] This takes me to the second feature in Pentecostalism with parallels in postmodernity: the search for wholeness of salvation, embodiment, and what I call here "the materiality of salvation."

The Materiality of Salvation

In an important article titled "Materiality of Salvation: An Investigation in the Soteriologies of Liberation and Pentecostal Theologies,"[26] Miroslav Volf has argued that with all their differences, these two Christian movements share a vision of salvation in this-worldly, physical, material, embodied terms. While neither of the movements, of course, leaves behind the eschatological, future-oriented hope, relegating salvation merely to the future will not do either. True, liberationists focus their efforts on socio-political (including gender) liberation, while for Pentecostals it is more about the individual's release from sicknesses and ailments, physical or emotional. All the same, there is resistance to excluding the bodily this-worldly reality from the vision of salvation. Smith reminds us of the fact that, contrary to common assumptions about the "otherworld-liness" of Pentecostalisms, the movement is also characterized by a commitment to social justice, empowerment of the powerless and a "preferential option for the marginalized" tracing back to its roots at Azusa Street as a kind of paradigm of marginalization—a revival in an abandoned stable, led by an African-American preacher.[27]

While Volf takes Luther as his main example of what he calls traditional theologies' "spiritualist" orientation, I would like to point to the contemporary Lutheran theologian W. Pannenberg, the greatest living

24. Smith, "What Hath Cambridge to Do with Azusa Street?," 111.
25. Smith, "What Hath Cambridge to Do with Azusa Street?," 111.
26. Volf, "Materiality of Salvation," 447–67.
27. Smith, "What Hath Cambridge to Do with Azusa Street?", 110. Smith makes here a reference to the Hispanic Pentecostal Liberationist Eldín Villafañe who makes an interesting connection between sacramentality and helping the poor and marginalized: "Hispanic Pentecostalism must reappropriate from its Catholic sacramental past the understanding and challenge that worshipping Jesus is also accomplished through its ministry and service to and with the poor" (112). See Villafañe, *Liberating Spirit*, 218.

systematician. What amazes me in the Munich systematician's pneumatology which—alongside that of the Reformed J. Moltmann—represents a holistic, world-embracing vision, in keeping with currents in the doctrine of the Spirit, is that it completely misses the topic of healing and exorcisms as well as empowerment in terms of spiritual gifts. All good talk about the continuity between the first creation and the coming new creation is oblivious to its implications for our lives here and now as embodied creatures, in need of restoration, healing, and release.[28]

Smith sees this central feature of Pentecostalisms deriving from its "positioning of radical openness to God, and in particular, God doing something *differently* or *new*," of which for him one of the biblical examples is the narrative of Acts 2, namely:

> Peter's courage and willingness to recognize in these "strange" phenomena the operation of the Spirit and declare it to be a work of God . . . In postmodern terms, we might describe this as an openness to alterity or otherness . . . Because of this, Pentecostal communities emphasize the continued ministry of the Spirit, including continuing revelation, prophecy, and the centrality of charismatic giftings in the ecclesial community . . . Included in this ministry of the Spirit is a distinctive belief in the healing of the body as a central aspect of the work of the Atonement. This central belief is an indication of a Pentecostal deconstruction of fundamentalist dualisms . . . The centrality of belief in physical healing is an indicator of this: it is a fundamental assertion of the value of embodiment and should constitute a radical critique of all dualisms, as does RO's [Radical Orthodoxy] "incarnational" ontology. By affirming that God is concerned with the health of the body, we affirm materiality, embodiment, and the sensible world.[29]

Embodiment of course stands at the heart of postmodernities and thus is a high value in postmodern Christian theologies as well.[30]

---

28. See further, Kärkkäinen, "Working of the Spirit of God in Creation and in the People of God," 17–35. In contrast to Pannenberg, Moltmann, *Spirit of Life*, ch. 9, discusses widely these topics; even more broadly, Moltmann's constructive theology appears to me postmodern in many ways even though Moltmann never engages the postmodern discourse!

29. Smith, "What Hath Cambridge to Do with Azusa Street?," 109–10, 112.

30. For a brief discussion, see, e.g., Cunningham, "Trinity," 186–201 (186 esp.). American Process theology similarly—even though as far as I can tell, independently from and at least beginning much earlier than postmodernities—insists on the importance of the principle of embodiment for a sound Christian theology: "Panentheism maintains that God is not defined as pure spirit in contrast to the physical world that

Related to the principle of the materiality of salvation is the Pentecostal insistence on the deliverance and freedom from evil, not only in the future but here already. This is of course a feature that finds resonance especially in cultures of the Global South. In the words of the Ghanaian theologian Ogbu Kalu:

> Going through life is like a spiritual warfare and religious ardor may appear very materialistic as people strive to preserve their material sustenance in the midst of the machinations of pervasive evil forces. Behind it is a strong sense of the moral and spiritual moorings of life. It is an organic worldview in which the three dimensions of space are bound together; the visible and the invisible worlds interweave. Nothing happens in the visible world that has not been predetermined in the invisible realm. The challenge for Christianity is how to witness the gospel in a highly spiritualized environment in which the recognition of the powers has not been banished in a Cartesian flight to objectivity and enlightenment . . . The argument here is that Pentecostalism in Africa derived her coloring from the texture of the African soil and from the interior of her idiom, nurture, and growth; her fruits serve the challenges and problems of the African ecosystem more adequately than did the earlier missionary fruits.[31]

Communitarianism

One of the many things that amazes—and confuses—me about postmodernities is its checkered and in many ways confusing way of negotiating the relationship between persons and communities. On the one hand, postmodern mindsets are a rebuttal of modernity's "turn to individuality," if that is being understood in terms of atomistic, separated individuals as is the case in the lifestyles of contemporary urban villages. Not only have postmodern philosophies unmasked and torn apart the whole concept of "self" and thus the individual in modernity's sense, but the likeminded psychologists, sociologists, and others have also re-constructed "self" in terms of "person," which is all about relationality,[32] connections, belonging, and sharing. Cer-

---

s/he created; God is in some sense incarnate in this world." Clayton, "God and the World," 209. Similarly, many Feminist theologians, such as Sally McFague, have already for long time called theologians' attention to this.

31. Kalu, "Preserving a Worldview," 122.

32. For a fine theological account of all of this, see Grenz, *Social God and Relational*

tainly no man (or woman) is an island after the advent of postmodernity. That said, on the other hand, no movement is so careful to preserve, cherish, and cultivate some kind of "individuality" and uniqueness. Call it alterity, difference, or some other term. It is all about the same. Even in postmodern ghettos individuals do not want to be subsumed under any kind of collectivity that washes off differences. Be that as it may, my point in relation to the discussion at hand is simply this: postmodernity celebrates communities, communalism, belonging. Observing Pentecostalisms, especially their mission, I discern a definite cultivation and building up of communalism. Should we thus speak of a distinctive Pentecostal *koinonia*?[33]

For postmodern people and Pentecostals, communities are shaped and brought about by a shared narrative, a story that is unfolding in the life of the community. Under the apt title, "Pentecostal Story as a Hermeneutical Narrative Tradition," the Pentecostal theologian Kenneth J. Archer speaks to this effect:

> The Pentecostal community is a distinct coherent narrative tradition within Christianity. Pentecostal communities are bound together by their charismatic experiences and common story. The Pentecostal narrative tradition is one embodiment of the Christian metanarrative. Yet, because the Pentecostal community understands itself to be a restorational movement, it has argued that it is the best representation or embodiment of Christianity in the world today. This may sound triumphalist; yet, Pentecostals, like all restorational narrative traditions of Christianity, desire to be both an authentic continuation of New Testament Christianity and a faithful representation of New Testament Christianity in the present societies in which they exist. Of course, the understanding of what was and should be New Testament Christianity is based upon a Pentecostal understanding. Moral reasoning, which includes biblical-theological interpretation, is contextualized in the narrative tradition of the Pentecostal community. Pentecostals will engage Scripture, do theology, and reflect upon reality from their own contextualized communities and narrative tradition.[34]

Self; for a brief, helpful discussion see also Cunningham, "Trinity," 186–202.

33. See further Kärkkäinen, "Church as the Fellowship of Persons," 1–15.

34. Archer, "Pentecostal Story," 40–42. This sounds very postmodern—McIntyrean, and, indeed it is. Interestingly enough, a key resource for Archer's construal of Pentecostalism is A. McIntyre's insights into the importance of narrative and tradition(s) for community formation.

This is, indeed, what is happening all over among Pentecostal communities, whether in the "homelands" or "mission fields." It is significant that in the beginning of the third phase of International Dialogue between Pentecostals and Roman Catholics focusing on communion ecclesiology, Miroslav Volf and Peter Kuzmic of (then) Yugoslavia made the programmatic statement that Pentecostal soteriology and pneumatology point . . . unmistakably in the direction of an *ecclesiology of the fellowship of persons*.[35]

> In the life of the community, Pentecostals have found a new sense of dignity and purpose in life. Their solidarity creates affective ties, giving them a sense of equality. These communities have functioned as social alternatives that protest against the oppressive structures of the society at large. Along with some social critics, Pentecostals have discovered that effective social change often takes place at the communal and micro-structural level, not at the macro-structural level.[36]

According to Kuzmic and Volf, the dynamic of the fellowship is concretely lived out through the *charismata*. "As fellowship should be the unalienable modus of the Church's existence, so the *charismata* should be a permanent feature of its life."[37] Consequently, worship experience with the deep desire to "meet with the Lord" stands at the heart of Pentecostal church life. Even when spiritual manifestations such as speaking in tongues, words of wisdom, or healings are missing, there is both openness to and expectation of those tangible signs of the presence of God in the communion of the saints.[38]

---

35. Kuzmic and Volf, "Communio Sanctorum," 2. See further, Kärkkäinen, "Church as Charismatic Fellowship," 100–121.

36. Pontifical Council for Promoting Christian Unity, "Evangelization, Proselytism and Common Witness: Final Report of the Dialogue (1990–1997)," #43. One is reminded of the important statement by the Reformed theologian Brunner, *Misunderstanding of the Church*, 10–11: "The Body of Christ is nothing other than a fellowship of persons. It is 'the fellowship of Jesus Christ' or 'fellowship of the Holy Ghost' where fellowship or *koinonia* signifies a common participation, a togetherness, a community life. The faithful are bound to each other through their common sharing in Christ and in the Holy Ghost, but that which they have in common is precisely no 'thing,' no 'it,' but a 'he,' Christ and His Holy Spirit."

37. Kuzmic and Volf, "Communio Sanctorum," 16.

38. There is obviously a connection here with the sacramental principle of traditional churches: whereas sacramental churches consider sacraments as the preferred way of securing the divine presence, along with the preached word, for Pentecostals the emphasis is on the gifts of the Spirit. There have been attempts by some Pentecostal theologians to find commonalities between Pentecostal spirituality, especially its emphasis on *glossolalia*, speaking in tongues, as a way of "securing" the divine presence and sacraments as "signs" of the divine presence. While there are some connecting

What is significant about the Pentecostal *koinonia* was well captured earlier in the Catholic-Pentecostal dialogue in the Pentecostal position paper: "It may hardly be gainsaid, that the Pentecostal revivals of the present century have taken the *koinonia* of/with the Holy Spirit out of the cloistered mystical tradition of the Church, and made it the common experience of the whole people of God."[39] Pentecostal *koinonia* at its best represents a principle of democratization and reconciliation: not only is there access to God and "holy things" for all men and women, but also the access to ministry and leadership. It is not about education, status, or wealth but about the empowerment of the Holy Spirit. Coupled with the belief in and claim of empowerment of all Christians, men and women, young and old, rich and poor by the same Holy Spirit, Pentecostal communities have launched massive mission projects all over the world.[40] Consequently, this has led to the enthusiastic application of the "voluntary principle" which may be *the* key to the massive growth and explosion of the Pentecostal mission enterprise. As Andrew M. Lord summarizes it,

1. Mission is primarily motivated without reference to church organizations, i.e., mission is primarily a 'bottom-up' not a 'top-down' activity;

2. Mission is the domain of every believer, i.e., not limited to a particular class of person, e.g. clergy, religious;

3. Mission arises out of an experience of God, i.e., out of more than just human concern or cultural context.[41]

Especially during the birth years of the Pentecostal movement in the United States, Pentecostal *koinonia* acted as a powerful social, political, and ecumenical critic. Men and women, white and black, Methodists and Catholics—they all worshiped together, shared leadership, claimed the "power from on high." No wonder that not only the religious establishment but also the then liberal secular establishment, with the *Los Angeles Times* in the forefront, ridiculed and ostracized the fledgling movement as scandalous

---

points, I also think the differences are so dramatic that at the most one can only point to some common underlying motifs behind *glossolalia* and, say, the Eucharist. See further, Macchia, "Tongues as a Sign," 61–76.

39. Ervin, "Koinonia, Church and Sacraments," 8–9.

40. For discussion of Pentecostal missiology and the Spirit's role therein, see Hollenweger, *Pentecostals*, 288–306; Kärkkäinen, "'Truth on Fire,'" 33–60; Kärkkäinen, "Mission, Spirit, and Eschatology"; Kärkkäinen, "Pentecostal Missiology in Ecumenical Perspective," 207–25; Kärkkäinen, "Missiology, Pentecostal and Charismatic," 877–85.

41. Lord, "Voluntary Principle in Pentecostal Missiology," 83.

and heretical.[42] The Pentecostal belief that "the color line was washed away in the Blood of the Lamb" was such a blow against the turn-of-the-twentieth-century racist, gender-exclusive, and socio-politically conservative mindset.[43]

Talk about postmodern soundings! Talk about democratic ideals! Against institutions, against established norms, against hierarchies, against exclusions. For inclusivity, for empowerment of all, for opportunities for all.

CRITICAL REFLECTIONS: IN SEARCH OF DYNAMIC TENSIONS AND BUILT-IN CONTRADISTINCTIONS

The Question of "Foundations"

While some other connecting points between postmodernities and Pentecostalisms could be found and further discussed, such as the place of the aesthetic in the worship service, enough has been said of that. In this final part of the essay, I would like to turn my eye on features, orientations, and developments in Pentecostalisms and their mission work that speak against or differently from postmodernities. Since this is not a student essay written in hopes of good grades—and thus having the burden of "proving" the thesis—I would rather like to confuse the waters, already mudded enough, and attempt to set the discussion in a broader perspective.

To begin with, any parallels between Pentecostalisms and postmodernities have to be counterbalanced by a careful look at real differences. As hinted above, the differences arise out of two sets of factors: first, from the simple fact that in my understanding Pentecostalisms as a Christian movement is based on a particular "foundation," and secondly, because Pentecostalisms as a phenomenon appears as an emerging, developing reality with built-in tensions, even potential contradistinctions.

While both Pentecostalisms and postmodernities are formed by and bring about their own particular narratives, behind Pentecostalisms there is also a Big Story, the story of the Gospel. While the gospel story can be read, interpreted, and lived out in many ways and in many "colors"—as Bishop Lesslie Newbigin used to remind us and as Pentecostal mission practice is illustrating so vividly all around the world—it still is that same story. Briefly put: all similarities between postmodernities and Pentecostalisms have to be checked against this radical difference of "foundation."

---

42. This is well documented in the new study by the leading Pentecostal historian and ecumenist Cecil M. Robeck, *Azusa Street Mission and Revival*.

43. See further Hollenweger, "Critical Tradition of Pentecostalism," 7–17.

Pentecostalisms as They Appear

More complicated and complex is the reflection on the implications of Pentecostalisms' built-in tensions to our topic. Let me put it bluntly and then attempt to unpack: it seems to me that against every feature of Pentecostalisms that seems to connect it with postmodernities, there is another side of Pentecostal spirituality and manifestation, just as authentic and genuine, that seems to either compromise or right down destroy the connection. Let me take one topic at a time.

While spirituality is the legitimate and appropriate way of defining Pentecostalism, it also is the fact that very soon after their birth, Pentecostal movements made a determined effort to define themselves along the lines of written texts, ecclesiastical formulae, and so forth—in other words, to make themselves look more like their respected Protestant and Evangelical counterparts. The U.S. Assemblies of God, the largest white Pentecostal denomination in North America and the biggest international Pentecostal family of churches, defined its identity already in terms of sixteen Statements of Faith. While highlighting Pentecostal distinctives such as speaking in tongues, divine healing, and urgent eschatological expectation, the Statements also tie the Pentecostal movement into a conservative, quite literalist Bible hermeneutics, dispensational eschatology, and so on. At first the doctrinal contours, however, were looser and more fluid. Then came the need for institutional solidification and especially wider Evangelical acceptance for a movement that came out of margins. Consequently, in 1948 the U.S. Assemblies of God redefined some of the doctrinal statements to get in line with strictly defined Fundamentalistically oriented (then) Evangelical formulations such as the "inerrancy" of Scripture.[44] In general, the location of Pentecostalism in the camp of conservative Christians, especially in the United States and many parts of Europe and as a result of aggressive missionary work also in many former mission lands, is the historical and social background for Pentecostalism's current manifestation. The alliance with Fundamentalism, however, is a complicated and in a way self-contradictory development. Among all Christians, it is the Fundamentalists who have most vocally opposed the Pentecostal claim for the continuing miraculous work of the Spirit. Similarly, the rather Fundamentalistic understanding of revelation and inspiration they inherited may be at odds with a Pentecostal worldview.[45]

---

44. All of this is documented and ably discussed in Robeck, "National Association of Evangelicals," 922–25.

45. For an important discussion, see Sheppard, "Pentecostalism and the Hermeneutics of Dispensationalism," 5–34.

The alliance with the conservative, at times even fundamentalistic, Christianity also helps explain another built-in tension in Pentecostal theology and missiology: the principle of the freedom of the Spirit—or lack thereof—in relation to other religions. The Evangelical theologian Clark Pinnock, himself inclusivist, states the obvious: "One might expect the Pentecostals to develop a Spirit-oriented theology of mission and world religions, because of their openness to religious experience, their sensitivity to the oppressed of the Third World where they have experienced much of their growth, and their awareness of the ways of the Spirit as well as dogma."[46] This has not, however, been the case for the most part.[47] While Pentecostals have excelled in missionary activities with impressive results by any standards, their thinking about the ministry of the Spirit in the world lags behind. Not only that, but—aligning with the more conservative wing of the church—they have also been the first to raise doubts about any kind of saving role of the Spirit apart from the proclamation of the gospel. Most often Pentecostals have succumbed to the standard conservative/fundamentalist view of limiting the Spirit's saving work to the church (except for the work of the Spirit preparing one to receive the gospel). A case in point is the recent warning from an official of the Assemblies of God. According to this statement, a pluralistic approach to theology of religions poses a three-fold problem: (1) it is contrary to Scripture; (2) it replaces the obligation for world evangelism; and (3) those who fail to fulfill the Great Commission are ultimately not living under the Lordship of Christ.[48] This is of course not to say that Pentecostals do not believe in the work of the Spirit among religions.[49] It is just to say that their reservations about work of the Spirit in

---

46. Pinnock, *Flame of Love*, 274.

47. For a helpful history of Pentecostal views of religions, see Yong, *Discerning the Spirit(s)*, 185–97, on Charismatic Christians' views, see 107–206; see also Kärkkäinen, "Toward a Pneumatological Theology of Religion," 187–98.

48. Carpenter, "Tolerance or Irresponsibility," 19.

49. An exciting study task for Pentecostals—and others—would be to inquire into potential connections, if any, between the Pentecostal "primal spirituality" and spiritualities of religions, especially those of Asian cultures. It seems to me that Pentecostal pneumatology—even when its potential to pursue that question seems to be trapped in a particular fundamentalistic-conservative milieu—has striking similarities with living religions such as Hinduism and Buddhism in their resistance to modernity's reductionistic, over-rationalistic, and at times dualistic worldview. The movement towards a post-/late-modern dynamic worldview with its willingness to reassess the canons of modernity has certainly opened up mainline Christian pneumatologies to a more holistic, dynamic reflection on the Spirit. Pentecostalism has that kind of undergirding primal spirituality as a wonderful asset. It is yet to be seen if suggestions such as those by Yong will elicit a wide-ranging resurgence of Pentecostal reflection or if that task will be left only for Charismatic and neo-Charismatic movements. See further, Kärkkäinen,

the world emerge from their marriage with the conservative segment of the church rather than from their own spiritual and pneumatic heritage.[50]

When it comes to the materiality of salvation, Pentecostal spirituality, church life, and mission work gives an inchoate picture. Having aligned themselves with Fundamentalists and their dispensationalist eschatology, as well as socio-politically conservative Christians, many Pentecostals, especially white Pentecostals, have also had serious doubts about the value of investing in the world which is to disappear.[51] Fortunately, Pentecostals have not been consistent with their eschatological faith and thus over time have invested huge amounts of energy and resources in social programs, both at the individual and structural level. Yet this mixed feeling has always been there speaking against the idea of the materiality of salvation.

At the same time, the idea of the materiality of salvation in the hands of too many Pentecostals and Charismatics has also turned into gross materialistic search for financial and other benefits. The misdeeds of many Pentecostal leaders in their greedy search of money and prestige are too well documented to deserve much reflection. Any visit to many Pentecostal churches not only in the USA but also all over in the Global South from Africa to Asia to Latin America paints a picture with serious questions to any theologian and missiologist. Health and wealth are made the prime indicator of God's blessings, and spiritual techniques for reaching them are fine-tuned by ever new itinerant charismatic preachers. Through satellite broadcasting, Prosperity Gospel shows are being brought into our living rooms. On the other hand, Pentecostalisms also suffer from the same kind of "spiritualist" reductionism Volf sees indicative of many traditional theologies, namely, prioritizing the salvation of the "souls" to the point where the wholeness of the human being as an embodied *imago Dei* is being missed. In Pentecostal preaching and witnessing, you can hear simultaneously both voices: seeking for wholeness of salvation and emphasis on the salvation of the soul.

Finally, when it comes to the communitarian nature of Pentecostalism, a mixed picture also emerges. Pentecostalisms are no less prone to embrace the "religion of individualism" so rampant not only in the Global North but also to a growing degree in the Global South as CNN, McDonalds, and the global entertainment industry spread the good news of Western Culture even to the ends of the earth. Nor are Pentecostal communities necessarily more inclusive or welcoming. Rightly, then, does the Pentecostal theologian

---

Spirit in the World.

50. Some individual Pentecostal theologians serve as trail-blazers in the new understanding of this complicated issue. For starters, see Yong, *Beyond the Impasse*; Yong, *Spirit Poured Out on All Flesh.*

51. See Kärkkäinen, "Are Pentecostals Oblivious to Social Justice?," 387–404.

from Singapore, Simon Chan, lament that Pentecostalism suffers from individualism: "My relationship with God is primary, while my relationship with others is secondary."[52] Consequently, he suggests that Pentecostals need an ecclesiological pneumatology as a corrective.[53] Pentecostals also need to listen carefully to their contemporary theologians to help them rediscover the communal nature of the Holy Spirit in charisms, spiritual gifts, and empowerment. In his *Baptized in the Spirit*, with a telling subtitle, *A Global Pentecostal Theology*, Frank Macchia, having confessed that "with their individualistic understanding of Spirit baptism . . . [Pentecostals] have lacked the conceptual framework in which to understand its connection to the church's communally gifted life,"[54] he issues this important call: "The Spirit is the Spirit of communion. Spirit baptism implies communion. That's why it leads to a shared love, a shared meal, a shared mission, and the proliferation/enhancement of an interactive charismatic life."[55] Even speaking in tongues, the most distinctive gift for many Pentecostals, is not unrelated to the *sanctorum communio*. Since no believer compasses the wholeness of *charismata*, the fullness of God can only be experienced in solidarity, *koinonia* with others in the church body.[56]

Indeed, again, having aligned themselves with religiously and socially conservative forces, many Pentecostals faithfully stick with color-line, status-line, and other markers of exclusion. Certainly, white Pentecostals have become anti-ecumenical against their original vision of the unity of all Christians as a result of the pouring out of the Spirit. And even a cursory look at many Pentecostal churches betrays highly hierarchic, institutionalized, and rigid church structures.

Implications for Missions

My point in telling about all of these counter-forces is neither to blame Pentecostals—other churches are certainly in no better place—nor to try to please everybody, both those in favor and those suspicious of Pentecostals; nor am I trying to redeem my own argument by telling my audience that I am well aware of the pros and cons when it comes to comparing postmodernities and Pentecostalisms. My point is simply twofold: First, undoubtedly, there are some parallels between postmodernities and Pentecostalisms as

52. Chan, "Mother Church," 180.
53. Chan, "Mother Church," 196–208.
54. Macchia, *Baptized in the Spirit*, 203.
55. Macchia, *Baptized in the Spirit*, 205.
56. Macchia, *Baptized in the Spirit*, 65.

my discussion revealed (and which I am not repeating here). Those parallels are significant missiologically and theologically in that they point to some new developments in the cultures and religiosities of the new millennium. While it takes careful and sustained theological—and hopefully also ecclesiological—reflection to decide what should we then do in Christian mission under these changed circumstances, discerning and analyzing those trends is of urgent importance. Postmodernities and Pentecostalisms are helpful pointers to something new happening in the world. Second, granted parallels, there are "foundational" differences, as my discussion again highlighted. Therefore, the main question, as to what the relationship between postmodernities is and Pentecostalisms, cannot be answered in the confines of this essay. At best, what can be done at this stage is to underline the tension-filled, inchoate picture.

Going back to the larger question, namely, the implications for Christian mission for the new millennium—whatever the precise relationship between postmodernities and Pentecostalisms may be—perhaps we should take the essay title literally and speak not only in terms of "return," i.e., coming back, but more importantly also in terms of "re-turn," i.e., turning around or making another turn. When religion has re-turned into the life of the third millennium at the global level, it is not only re-appropriating old realities such as experience, mysticism, communion, healing, and so on, but also re-configuring them in a new postmodern context.

The "turn" to the *spirit* is part of postmodernity's religiosity. For the Christian church, the turn to the *Spirit*—both "return" and "re-turn"—opens new vistas and new horizons. In the words of J. Moltmann, this is "A Pentecostal Theology of Life":

> The gift and presence of the Holy Spirit constitutes the greatest and most wonderful reality that we—the human community, all living beings, and the entire earth—can experience. For present in the Holy Spirit is not just one spirit of the many good and evil spirits that exist, but the very God who creates, gives life, blesses, and redeems . . .
>   . . . *The Mission of Life*
>   Mission is in the original and eternal sense the *Missio Dei*. Only if our Christian mission follows and corresponds to the divine sending is it a mission with trust in God and sound faith. Only if we as people correspond to the divine mission to other people do we respect their worth and divine image and repudiate the temptation to dominate them religiously. The *Missio Dei* is nothing less than the sending of the Holy Spirit from the Father through the Son into the world in order that the world

can escape ruin and live. Simply put, what is brought by God through Christ into the world is life. 'I live, and you should live also' (John 14.19). For the Holy Spirit is the 'source of life' and brings life into the world: life in its entirety, life in its fullness—unhindered, indestructible, eternal life. The creative and life-inspiring Spirit of God brings eternal life here now, before death—not only after death—for the Spirit brings Christ into the world, and Christ is the 'resurrection and the life' in person . . . According to the synoptic Evangelists, wherever Jesus is, life is, for there the sick are healed, the weary are comforted, the outcasts are accepted, and the demons of death are cast out. According to the book of Acts and the apostolic epistles, wherever the Holy Spirit is present, there is life, for there one finds joy for the victory of life over death and there the power of eternal life is experienced. Mission, in this divine sense, is nothing else than a movement of life and healing which spreads comfort and courage for life and uplifts those who want to die. Jesus did not bring a new religion in the world, but a new life.[57]

---

57. Moltmann, "Pentecostal Theology of Life," 3, 10–11.

CHAPTER 12

How to Speak of the Spirit among Religions

Trinitarian *Prolegomena* for a Pneumatological Theology of Religions

INTRODUCTION

> To me, mindfulness is very much like the Holy Spirit. Both are agents of healing. When you have mindfulness, you have love and understanding, you see more deeply, you can heal the wounds in your own mind ... Mindfulness helps us touch nirvana, and the Holy Spirit offers us a door to the Trinity.
>
> —Thich Nhat Hanh[1]

> ... provisionally, at least, the Holy Spirit could be discerned to be present and active even in Buddhist rituals opposing world's forces of destruction insofar as the biblical fruits of the Spirit, for example, could be detected.
>
> —Amos Yong[2]

To speak of the presence of the Spirit in the world and among religions is a notoriously challenging task. While most everybody agrees that the

1. Hanh, *Living Buddha, Living Christ*, 14, 20.
2. Yong, *Does the Wind Blow the Middle Way?*, 266.

presence of the Holy Spirit is not limited to the sphere of the Christian church, nothing like unanimity exists concerning the nature and efficacy, if any, of the activity of the Spirit. Take the examples above. How do we know whether the claims of the Vietnamese-American Buddhist Thich Nhat Hanh and Malaysian-American Christian Amos Yong can be substantiated in the grammar of these respective faiths? And if for a moment we agree their statements are valid, what then are the implications for faith and interfaith dialogue?

The purpose of the present paper is to make a contribution to the continuing discussion of the role of the Spirit in the world, especially among religions, by setting forth some trinitarian "rules"—better to say guidelines—for speaking about the Spirit. In other words, I argue that the proper context for advancing a pneumatological theology of religions is a healthy trinitarian framework. Having recently finished the monograph *Trinity and Religious Pluralism*, I have felt the need to continue the theology of religions reflection from a pneumatological perspective. It seems to me too often pneumatological approaches to religions suffer from an inadequate Trinitarian framework which results in a disconnection between the Spirit and Christ and/or the Spirit and God; these disconnections, in turn, lead to the separation between the Spirit and the church and the Spirit and the kingdom. A healthy Trinitarian theology, my essay argues, is the best safeguard against lacuna such as those.

Before engaging the task, one needs however to stop and ask the obvious question: Can one—or: in what sense can one—speak of the presence of the Spirit among religions? Not only that, but one also needs to ask the even more foundational question: How can we speak of the Spirit in the world in the first place? In other words: Not only it is highly challenging to address the topic of the Spirit in relation to other religions; the whole task of speaking of the Spirit in the world seems to encounter numerous problems as the current symposium illustrates. Should we focus on the "hidden" or "veiled" presence of the Spirit in the world, or, as John Polkinghorne puts it,[3] on the Spirit's "exuberance often exhibited in contemporary charismatic experience"? Or, to use Kathryn Tanner's terminology: Should we speak of the "immediate," direct and instantaneous or the "gradual," "human and fully fallible" mediated presence of the Spirit?[4] The New Testament theologian James D. G. Dunn adds many more challenges such as the pneumatological discourse either cosmically or anthropologically conceived, pneumatology stressing either the continuity or discontinuity between the divine and

---

3. Polkinghorne, "Hidden Spirit and the Cosmos," 1.
4. Tanner, "Workings of the Spirit," 1.

human spirit, and so on.[5] With reference to Vladimir Lossky of the Christian East, Polkinghorne reminds us: "The Holy Spirit, as person, remains unmanifested, hidden, concealing Himself in His very appearing."[6] This prompts the obvious question: How can we even begin to give any kinds of "guidelines" for discerning the presence of the Spirit in the world? In the symposium discussion we came to the conclusion that while any talk about the Spirit—of God—needs to be approached with great care and humility, it is still the task of the theologians to try to set forth some guidelines to make our human speech about the divine more appropriate. While never exhausting the divine reality, we still need to say something.[7]

In the first part of my presentation, I will set the stage for a trinitarian approach to the question of Christianity's relation to other religions. This orientation calls for remarks on three interrelated topics: Where are we in the theology of religions discourse? Where are we in the talk about the Trinity? And, in what ways, if any, have these two coalesced? In the second part, I will map out key tasks and challenges that lie before us on the way to reflecting theologically on the role of the Spirit among religions. My approach is thus more methodological, a kind of prolegomenon, the implications of which need to be taken up and tested in an actual interreligious dialogue. Yet, going beyond the mere prolegomenon—and in order to make my discussion more concrete and specific—in the second part I will also reflect on the meaning of these Trinitarian rules for Islam-Christian encounter based on a long-term dialogue between the Roman Catholic Church (in France) and Muslims.[8] Significantly enough, that dialogue took a Trinitarian ap-

---

5. Dunn, "Towards the Spirit of Christ," 1–2 especially.

6. Lossky, *Mystical Theology of the Eastern Church*, 160. Quoted in Polkinghorne, "Hidden Spirit and Cosmos," 2.

7. D. Lyle Dabney makes the remark that in the contemporary postmodern context, talk about God takes place through the lenses of pneumatology in that it addresses first the question of human identity. If I correctly understand Dabney's approach, this does not mean a return to the old idea of Classical Liberalism, so aptly caricatured by K. Barth, that to speak of God one needs to speak loudly of the human person. Dabney's program has to do with his desire to qualify and supplement (but of course not to leave behind) the older theological methods in either Catholicism, which begins with the first article (of the creed, i.e., with God and creation), or Protestantism, with the second article (Christ and redemption), in favor of a turn to the third article, thus the Spirit. See Dabney, "Who Do You Say I am?", 1.

8. For details, see my *Trinity and Religious Pluralism*, ch. 10. Since the late 1970s, there has been a theological and pastoral dialogue in France between the Roman Catholic Church and a significantly large Islamic community. Full documentation (in French) of the dialogue facilitated by the Secretariat for Relations with Islam (*Secrétariat pour les Relations avec l'Islam*; hereafter S.R.I.) can be found in Jukko, *Trinitarian Theology in Christian-Muslim Encounters*.

proach and also addressed the role of the Spirit in relation to the Islamic faith.[9] Tentatively, therefore, it provides an opportunity to test the trinitarian guidelines presented here.

PART I

Major Turns in the Theology of Religions

Christian theology of religions has taken several significant turns despite its relatively short history.[10] Here I am concerned only about one particular turn in its history. Let me call it a movement from Christocentric to Theocentric to Pneumatocentric approaches, and finally towards Trinitarian approaches. As long as Christian theology was based on a more or less exclusivist standpoint, the point of departure for the theology of religions discourse was the finality of Christ.[11] A turn to Theocentrism seemed to give more space for opening up to other religions; in that phase, Trinity was nothing more than an obstacle for the dialogue, especially with monotheistic faiths such as Judaism and Islam. Soon, among theologians from across the ecumenical spectrum (from Eastern Orthodoxy to Roman Catholicism to Protestantism of various sorts), a turn to the "Spirit" was enthusiastically initiated.[12] The turn to pneumatology seemed to promise a lot. After all, doesn't the Spirit speak for universality while Christ speaks for particularity? Pneumatology also seemed to connect with the strongly pneumatological and spiritualistic orientations of other religions, especially in the East.

---

9. To my task here I bring in the typical weakness of theologians of religions, namely, inadequate knowledge of other religions. The few years that I have lived and taught in Buddhist Thailand hardly make me anything more than an amateurish observer of an Asian religion. So, I leave it to specialists in religions to take the next step.

10. I am not, of course, suggesting that the *question* of the theology of religions—Christianity's relation to other religions—is a new one. It is not (for a detailed biblical and historical review, see further my book *An Introduction to the Theology of Religions*, parts II–III). My remark here refers to the fact that as a *separate* theological discipline, theology of religions is a fairly new development, stemming from somewhere in the 1950s or so.

11. I am making vast generalizations here. Christocentrism (or, to be more precise, Christocentrisms) is in itself a diverse approach, from a traditional Protestant exclusivistic stance to a post-conciliar official Catholic inclusivism to the moderate pluralism of some Catholic thinkers, such as the early Paul Knitter.

12. See, e.g., Yong, "Turn to Pneumatology in Christian Theology of Religions," 437–54. This turn to the Spirit reflects the wider pneumatological renaissance in theology. See further my *Pneumatology*, ch. 1.

The latest phase of the theology of religions discourse is the turn to the Trinity.[13] Before looking at this latest phase, a few summary comments concerning the current stage of Trinitarian discourse are in order.

Trinitarian Discourse in Contemporary Theology

Schematically, one may outline the emerging theological consensus about the Trinity in the following way: First, the doctrine of the Trinity is the structuring principle of Christian theology rather than an appendix to Christian talk about God. Thus, to identify the God of the Bible one needs to refer to the triune God: Father, Son, and Spirit.

Second, making Trinity the beginning and structuring principle of Christian theology and the doctrine of God means that to speak of God means to speak of Jesus Christ who reveals the Father in the power of the Spirit. Third, the knowledge of the Christian God—Father, Son, and Spirit—can only be possible through God's self-revelation in the Son. Rather than being an exercise in speculative theology, Trinity is a datum of revelation.[14] Therefore, fourth, history matters! The biblical God—Father, Son, and Spirit—cannot be understood as an abstraction apart from the events of history. The coming of Jesus, incarnation, and resurrection from the dead by the Father through the Spirit are historical claims. Fifth, while not all contemporary theologians are "Social Trinitarians," a strong consensus understands the Christian God as a divine communion.[15] This is the theological conclusion from the biblical idea that God is love.

One might assume these perspectives would be enthusiastically applied to the question of Christianity's relation to other religions. In general, this has not been case until very recently.

---

13. See my *Trinity and Religious Pluralism*, 1–12.

14. This much has to be said even though the consensus among students of the Bible recognizes that there is no doctrine of the Trinity in the Bible, not even in the New Testament. However, there is a trinitarian structure to the biblical salvation history, to the coming of God's kingdom, inaugurated by Jesus Christ in the power of the Spirit. Dunn's essay ("Towards the Spirit of Christ") carefully traces the beginnings of the Trinitarianism in the NT with reference to the Spirit-Christ relationship.

15. Oberdorfer, "Holy Spirit—a Person?" speaks here of the personhood as constituted socially; thus "*person* does not simply mean *individuality with self-consciousness*" (1). On page 9, he says: "Persons only exist in relations, and their personality is not independent of these relations."

Trinity and Religions at a Meeting Place: A History of Research

The pioneer in the field was the Catholic, Asian-American scholar of religion Raimundo Panikkar. In his small, yet highly significant book, *The Trinity and the Religious Experience of Man* (1973), Panikkar argued for the viability of a Trinitarian approach based on the groundbreaking idea that not only do all religions reflect a trinitarian substructure, but that there is a Trinitarian structure to reality.[16] While taking departure from his Christian faith, he ends up constructing a highly idiosyncratic view of the Trinity.[17] What bothers me in Panikkar's proposal, among other things, is the divorce on the one hand between Christ and history, and consequently, between Spirit and Christ.[18]

The next major study on the topic did not come until 2000, titled *The Meeting of Religions and the Trinity*, by the Catholic Gavin D'Costa[19] from England. For my program, D'Costa's contribution is threefold. Having first shown the fallacy of pluralistic approaches, both Christian as well as among other religions, D'Costa, secondly, works hard to argue that because of the presence in the world of the Spirit of God, "there too is the ambiguous presence of the triune God, the church, and the kingdom."[20] In other words, the Spirit's presence in the world is not only integrally Trinitarian but also ecclesiological, which in turn is related to the coming of the kingdom. This means that D'Costa wants to keep together Spirit, Trinity, church, and kingdom in a way only few contemporary theologians are willing to do outside exclusivistic approaches to religions. Third, D'Costa argues that while religions as such are not salvific,[21] we Christians can—and should—learn a lot through "the Holy Spirit's invitation to relational engagement." My sympathies in general go with D'Costa's approach even though, ironically,

---

16. The choice term for Panikkar to describe this is *cosmotheandrism*.

17. For Panikkar, the Father is the kenotic "Nothing," the Absolute Nameless; the Son is God; and the Spirit is "immanence" and mediator who, like Hinduism's Divine *Sakti*, penetrates everything and manifests the divine.

18. See further my *Trinity and Religious Pluralism*, 128–33 especially.

19. For an exposition and critical assessment, see my *Trinity and Religious Pluralism*, ch. 4.

20. D'Costa, *Meeting of Religions and the Trinity*, 11. Further, it would be an interesting topic to consider how D'Costa's view of the "ambiguous" presence of God through the Spirit in the world is related to either Polkinghorne's idea of the "veiled" presence of the Spirit or Tanner's "mediated" presence.

21. There is a heavy debate among Catholic theologians as to the right reading of Vatican II concerning this question. Knitter argues for a pluralistic reading of Vatican II, while D'Costa argues, alongside the current magisterial opinion, for an inclusivist interpretation.

I find the grounds for his proposal less than convincing and not winning ecumenical support.[22]

Another Catholic theologian, the veteran theologian of religions Jacques Dupuis, in his magnum opus *Toward a Christian Theology of Religious Pluralism* (1997),[23] had already made a lasting contribution to the topic of the Trinity and religions. Echoing the typical recent turn in this field, in his later work, Dupuis shifted emphasis from Christ to the Spirit and the Trinity.[24] What makes me somewhat critical of Dupuis's approach is his tendency to downplay the integral relation of the Spirit to the church and consequently, the relation of the kingdom to the church.

The most significant trinitarian theology of religions outside Catholic theology comes from the hand of S. Mark Heim, who originally comes from Evangelicalism. His book *The Depths of the Riches: A Trinitarian Theology of Religious Ends* (2001)[25] is perhaps the "most pluralistic" theology of religions yet to appear: on the basis of the diversity in the triune God, Heim advances the thesis that not only are religions different, but they also have different, God-willed "ends" in terms of salvation goals. While I applaud Heim's sincere effort to construct a new way of looking at other religions through the lens of the Christian doctrine of the Trinity, I find both the methodology and main results of his proposal wanting.[26] Furthermore, curiously enough, Heim is almost silent about the role of the Spirit in his theological construction.

The most recent contribution to a distinctively pneumatological theology of religions with a view to the importance of the Trinity is offered by Amos Yong, a Pentecostal, in his *Beyond the Impasse: Toward a*

22. D'Costa bases his proposal on the one hand on a selective reading of the biblical data, especially on the Paraclete passages of John 14 and 16, and on the other hand, on Vatican II and subsequent papal pronouncements on religions. I think much better biblical grounds can be found to support the integral relationship between Spirit and church. In addition, to non-Catholics, reference to a particular church's teaching documents hardly wins much hearing. See further my *Trinity and Religious Pluralism*, 76–79.

23. For an exposition and critical assessment, see my *Trinity and Religious Pluralism*, ch. 3.

24. It is noteworthy that the first major contribution by Dupuis was Christocentric: See Dupuis, *Jesus Christ at the Encounter of World Religions*.

25. For an exposition and critical assessment, see my *Trinity and Religious Pluralism*, ch. 9. Even with all the criticism against his proposal, I also think that Heim has significantly advanced the discussion. He avoids the typical fallacy of a "rough parity" pluralism by insisting on real differences among religions and being bold about setting forth a proposal of his own. Panikkar is another pluralist whose proposal genuinely values difference even though he envisions a future "convergence" of religions.

26. For the critique, see my *Trinity and Religious Pluralism*, 143–51 especially.

Pneumatological Theology of Religions.[27] He sets forth three "axioms" for the development of a pneumatological theology of religions in a Trinitarian framework: first, God is universally present and active in the Spirit; second, God's Spirit is the life-breath of the *imago Dei* in every human being and the presupposition of all human relationships and communities; and third, the religions of the world, like all else that exists, are providentially sustained by the Spirit of God for divine purposes. Now these axioms are hardly debatable. Yet they beg for further elucidation and clarification. It is not self-evident how "Trinitarian" they are; what is distinctively Trinitarian about these claims? Other proposals exist,[28] yet for the purposes of this presentation the ones I have mentioned seem to be the most pregnant theologically.

In the second part of the presentation—in a critical dialogue with theologians mentioned so far, yet also going beyond their work—I will reflect on the topic of speaking about the Spirit among religions in a Trinitarian context. I will also reflect on the implications for Christian-Muslim encounter.

PART II

Trinity as the Way to Distinguish the Christian God Among Gods

It was no less a theological giant than Karl Barth who made this programmatic statement:

> The doctrine of the Trinity is what basically distinguishes the Christian doctrine of God as Christian, and therefore what already distinguishes the Christian concept of revelation as Christian, in contrast to all other possible doctrines of God or concepts of revelation.[29]

---

27. For the contribution of Karl Rahner, Wolfhart Pannenberg, and the Evangelical-Charismatic theologian Clark Pinnock, see my *Trinity and Religious Pluralism*.

28. Still another study that deals in a significant way with our topic should be mentioned, idiosyncratic as it is in its approach and bordering on a "universal theology": namely, the book by the senior religious scholar Ninian Smart (in collaboration with his student, the Eastern Orthodox Stephen Konstantine) titled *Christian Systematic Theology in a World Context*. My reading of that book leaves me wondering if it goes beyond the contours of a specifically *Christian* theology of religions in that Smart and Konstantine build their "trinitarian" doctrine on a mixture of religious traditions which does not easily commend itself to more typical trinitarian approaches.

29. Barth, *Church Dogmatics*, I/1, 301. Materially the same is argued in Jenson, *The Triune Identity*, ix: "The doctrine of the Trinity comprises . . . the Christian faith's repertoire of ways of *identifying* its God, to say *which* of the many candidates for godhead we mean when we say, for example, 'God is loving'" (italics in the original).

In other words, Trinity is not an appendix to the notion of "One God"; rather, the "name"[30] of the biblical God is Father, Son, and Spirit. It is not possible to speak of Father as "God" as if Son and Spirit were not needed to consider God. The Father's relation to Son and Spirit is foundational for the identity of the Father.[31] This also means that the understanding of God becomes relational, indeed "the triune identities are *relations*" and therefore, to quote Robert W. Jenson:

> What there is to being God the Father is being addressed as "Father" by the Son, Jesus; what there is to being God the Spirit is being the spirit of this communication. *In that* Jesus cries, "Father, into your hands . . ." and *in that* he who says this will be the final event, *there is* the Father. *In that* Jesus gives his spirit, and *in that* this gift will constitute the final community, *there is* the Spirit.[32]

Consequently, Trinity introduces not only relationality (communion) into the life of God, a topic I will take up in what follows, but also history and time. God's relation—reaching out—to the world in incarnation, salvation, and consummation is not something external to the divine life. "Rather, God's involvement in the course of the world affairs is so intimate that the character of divinity itself is shaped by it."[33]

While there is of course no reason to limit the knowledge of God to the particularity of Jesus of Nazareth, it also is true, to quote Heim, that ". . .

---

30. When saying this, I am not necessarily convinced that Jensen's idea of Father, Son, and Spirit as "proper name" in the New Testament as Yahweh was in the Old Testament is the best way to put it.

31. See further, Jenson, *Triune Identity*, 51, 73. When insisting on the necessity of holding on to the Trinitarian identification of the Christian God, I am not at the same time denying the importance of establishing some commonality between the Christian God and the gods of other religions or, as it has been put in classical theology, the God of the Philosophers. Pannenberg has seen this clearly. While he insists on the uniqueness of the triune God, based on the biblical revelation as it interprets salvation history, he also insists on the correlation between general god-talk and talk about the distinctively Christian trinitarian God. Taking his cue from the fact that in the Bible the term *god* not only serves as a proper name *(Yahweh)* but also as a general designation *(Elohim)*, he argues that specifically Christian god-talk only makes sense in connection with terms for species. Therefore, to make God-talk intelligible, both in Christian theology and in relation to especially the Jewish faith but also other (theistic) faiths, Christian theology should not cut off ties to philosophical and religious discourse. This also guards Christian trinitarian talk from "involuntarily regressing to a situation of a plurality of gods in which Christian talk about God has reference to the specific biblical God as one God among others." Pannenberg, *Systematic Theology*, 1:69.

32. Jenson, *Triune Identity*, 175 (italics in the original).

33. Peters, *God—The World's Future*, 108.

the Trinity is unavoidably Christocentric."[34] It is one of the tendencies of (pneumatological) theologies of religions to seek release from the contours of history, and (as they believe) of particularity.[35] It is an understandable, yet theologically highly problematic road.[36] In terms of interfaith dialogue it means that to bracket out Trinity for the sake of dialogue when talking to, say, Muslims, is a strategy which creates more problems than it solves.

Regarding the Islamic faith, the most obvious question is of course whether Yahweh, the Father of Jesus Christ, is the same God as Allah, as the Qur'an claims (Sura 29:46). Things get complicated when Trinity is introduced to the picture. For Muslims, the Christian doctrine of the Trinity is a distortion (Sura 5:73 among others), a form of tritheism, making Christians not true monotheists but rather "associators" (those who have committed the sin of *shirk*, associating other deities with God.[37] In my reading, the Muslim-Catholic dialogue in France left the question of the identity open—wisely so. However, they were quick to affirm that dialogue between Muslims and Christians "takes place between believers, between religious men and women who seek God in their own tradition," and that they "both Christians and Muslims are believers in the creator God, and they speak to this one God and seek him."[38]

Coming back to the Spirit, one could ask in light of this: Does this mean diminishing the role of the Spirit—or trying to limit the cosmic sphere of the Spirit? On the contrary, to quote the Catholic pneumatologist Kilian McDonnell, OSB: "To do pneumatology is to insist that the Spirit is equal to the Father and to the Son."[39] According to the New Testament

---

34. Heim, *Depth of the Riches*, 135.

35. I understand thinkers such as Panikkar as advocating a Christology "from above" rather than "from below" since he first constructs a "Christic" principle apart from historical contours and only then reads it back, if at all, into the person of Christ. This is materially what he is saying in his often-quoted dictum: "Jesus is Christ but Christ is not Jesus." Methodologically, it is of course ironic that a contemporary theologian and scholar of *religions* such as Panikkar could be found guilty of championing a "from above" approach.

36. Smart and Konstantine (*Christian Systematic Theology*, 177) seem to insist on the importance of not ignoring history since ". . . the Divine occurs as transcendent in the midst of history," yet they do it in a way that eschews the particularity of Christian theology (with its claim to Jesus's incarnation).

37. See further my *Trinity and Religious Pluralism*, 156–58.

38. Jukko, *Trinitarian Theology in Muslim-Christian Encounters*, 84, 89. I have critiqued the Catholic Dupuis—in his explicitly Trinitarian theology of religions!—for too easily establishing the identity between the Muslim and Christian God (*Trinity and Religious Pluralism*, 63–64; see also 53).

39. McDonnell, "Pneumatology Overview," 189. For a more accessible source, see McDonnell, "Theological Presuppositions in Our Preaching about the Spirit," 219–35.

testimony, "the Spirit is not less important for understanding who God is and what God does than the saving work of Christ."[40] Let me take a closer look at the implications of the way we speak of the presence and ministry of the Spirit in the world.

The Trinitarian Presence of the Spirit in the World

There is an ancient rule—pejoratively labeled the "Augustinian rule of thumb"[41]—according to which the inner works of the Trinity are separable and the outward works inseparable. Notwithstanding the contemporary critique of the rule,[42] it still serves as a guiding principle when speaking about the role of the Spirit in the world, even among religions. In order to refer to the presence of the Spirit, whether as the life-principle, the divine breath of all living creatures, a (soteriological) "gift," or as the agent of eschatological transformation,[43] one needs to speak of the Spirit of Yahweh, the Spirit of the God of Jesus Christ. Pneumatological discourse unrelated to the Father and Son may seem to promise more, yet it begins to loose its contours and

---

40. McDonnell, "Pneumatology," 189. It is of course ironic that while in Christian theology in general, pneumatology has suffered from a secondary place in relation to Christology, in the *theology of religions* the opposite has been the case lately. For an interesting way to discuss this relationship in a trinitarian framework, see further McDonnell, "Pneumatology," 190–92; and "Theological Presuppositions," 221–23, especially. McDonnell calls Christ the "what" (content of the gospel and thus of Christian preaching) and the Spirit the "how," the total horizon within which theological reflection and preaching takes place. In other words, after Pentecost, the apostles where not sent out to preach about the Spirit but rather about Christ—in the power of the Spirit.

41. The rule was in effect well before Augustine; what Augustine did was to highlight the second part of the rule (the indivisibility of the outward works of the Trinity); by doing so, he echoed also the teaching of the Cappadocians in the East.

42. Among others, Rahner, Jenson, and the late Catholic Catherine Mowry LaCugna have expressed severe critique towards the rule. E.g., Jenson's main reason for the critique is that the idea of the indivisibility of outer works is being understood in terms of the creative and saving works being *indifferently* the work of each person rather than in terms of being the joint work of Father, Son, and Spirit. This critique, however, is hardly convincing. Why should one understand (the second part of) Augustine's role in this way; ironically, it was used by the Cappadocians to establish the unity of the godhead in terms of the unity of operation.

43. An urgent task for contemporary pneumatology with significant implications for the theology of religions is to establish the continuity of the work of the Spirit from creation to new creation. Pannenberg has done some important groundwork here. See further my "The Working of the Spirit of God in Creation and in the People of God, 17–35. See also Yong, *Beyond the Impasse*, 36–42. This seems to be the goal of the project by Dabney ("Who Do You Say I Am?", 12) as well: "Such a theology encompasses both creation and redemption from a perspective of creation and new creation."

often ends up being nothing other than another way to affirm a typically modernist idea of a "rough parity" of all religions.

Trinity serves here as elsewhere in a criteriological function. As Dupuis notes, Trinity helps us avoid three typical, interrelated errors. The first error puts Christ and God in opposition as if one could choose *either* a "theocentric" *or* "Christocentric" option. The second error that Trinity helps us avoid is either "regnocentrism" (the idea of the kingdom of God at the center) or "soteriocentrism" (salvation, rather than a Savior, at the center) as the focus at the expense of Christology, as for example Knitter seems to be doing.

The third error is to champion that kind of pneumatological approach that tends to diminish the role of Jesus Christ as more limited than that of the Spirit. Indeed, the basic fallacy of the first wave of pneumatological approaches to the theology of religions was the desire to make the Spirit an itinerant preacher who only occasionally joined forces with the other Trinitarian members. The Augustinian rule is not good news to that kind of a pneumatological theology of religions that seeks release for the Spirit from the confines of the Father-Spirit and Son-Spirit relationship. It is of course true that while Jesus Christ[44] represents particularity, the Spirit represents universality,[45] yet this is only in a healthy Trinitarian context. The freedom of the Spirit cannot be set in opposition to the person and ministry of Jesus Christ, any more than that of the Son to the Father.[46]

All of this requires some answer to the all-important question for our purposes: how do we establish the Spirit-Christ/Christ-Spirit relationship? This, in turn, will affect how we conceive of the relationship between the

---

44. For pluralists such as Panikkar, only "Jesus" (of Nazareth) denotes particularity; "Christ" for Panikkar means a "Christic" principle, freed from the confines of historical contours, thus making it possible to identify more than one C/christ. "Jesus is Christ, but Christ is not [merely or not even primarily] Jesus." Here the Christic principle basically serves the same kind of "freeing" function that for some other theologians the Spirit does in relation to Jesus/Father.

45. In what follows, I will come back to take another look at the widely used concepts of "universal" and "particular" in the sphere of the theology of religions.

46. One way, popular in both patristic theology (Irenaeus, *Adv. Haer.*, 4.4) and current theology (e.g., Yong, *Beyond the Impasse*, 43–44) is to speak of Son and Spirit as "two hands" of God. While it makes the point, it also supports the kind of subordinationism which contemporary trinitarian theology wants to avoid (LaCugna, *God for Us*, 24–29, named this tendency "orthodox subordinationism"!). I find the approach of Pannenberg healthier—and more biblical—in that there are mutually dependent relationships among Father, Son, and Spirit. E.g., Father cannot be Father without the Son, who humbly differentiates himself from the Father, thus acknowledging the lordship of the Father of the kingdom.

church and Spirit, and consequently, church and kingdom. Let's take one topic at a time.

Pneumatology and Christology as One Divine Economy

In the New Testament, Son and Spirit presuppose each other.[47] The role of the Spirit comes to focus in that Jesus was related to the Spirit,[48] and the Spirit is the Spirit of Christ.[49] A trinitarian "Spirit-Christology"[50] "shows the influence of the Holy Spirit throughout the earthly life of Jesus, from his conception through the power of the Spirit (see Luke 1:35) to his resurrection at the hands of God by the power of the same Spirit (see Rom 8:11)."[51] In other words, Jesus is both the giver[52] and receiver of the Spirit. The Spirit's role, on the other hand, is to help us turn to Christ and by doing so to the Father.[53]

47. One of the reasons why the approach of writers such as Smart and Konstantine to *Christian* theology of religions does not commend itself to me is the superficial handling of biblical materials concerning the historical Jesus and its relation to the question of the relation of Jesus/Christ to Spirit. They just simply ignore historical questions and, somewhat like Panikkar, feel free to propose a new construal of Spirit and Christ without much support from anywhere. Consequently, it seems to me the authors too easily find parallels between Christian Trinity and, say, *sat-cit-ānanda* (being, consciousness, and bliss) of Advaita Vedanta tradition or the Hindu vision of three deities, *Brahma, Shiva, Vishnu*. I don't of course find the search for these parallels problematic in any way; what I am saying here is that one cannot too easily assume them.

48. Well aware of the fact that a strand of "historical Jesus scholarship" (e.g., J. D. Crossan) has been reluctant to make much of the connection of the (eschatological) Spirit to Jesus of Nazareth, I can safely go with the majority of contemporary biblical scholars who argue that it is absolutely integral to the identity and mission of Jesus to be conscious of the presence of God's Spirit in his life (N. T. Wright, J. D. G. Dunn, et al.).

49. For details, see Dunn "Towards the Spirit of Christ," 9–13 especially. I am of course aware of the diversity of New Testament theologies of the Spirit. This diversity, in my understanding, however, does not in any way negate my basic argumentation here. See further my *Pneumatology*, 28–36.

50. My quotation marks indicate that what I am saying here does not necessarily entail subscription to any particular kind of Spirit-Christology or to a Spirit-Christology at all (understood in the technical sense of the word).

51. Dupuis, *Toward a Christian Theology*, 206. See also, Pannenberg, *Systematic Theology*, 3:16–17: "The christological constitution and the pneumatological constitution do not exclude one another but belong together because the Spirit and the Son mutually indwell one another as Trinitarian persons."

52. Dunn ("Towards the Spirit of Christ," 6–8) shows convincingly that in the earliest Christian pneumatology it was the Exalted Christ who was the giver of the Spirit.

53. As Michael Welker ("Spirit in Philosophical and Theological Perspectives", 5) argues, differently from philosophical traditions, the biblical teaching (e.g., John 16:13) conceives not of the Spirit as "a self-referential personality" but as the one who will bear

Wherever the Spirit inspires the knowledge of God, be it within the sphere of the church or outside, salvation brought about by the Spirit is referred to the saving work of Christ, his incarnation, death, and resurrection. As Dupuis says, there are not "two distinct channels [that of the Son and the Spirit] through which God's saving presence reaches out to people in distinct economies of salvation,"[54] but one. Making the relationship between the Christ and the Spirit mutually presupposing does not in any way deny the universal, cosmic sphere of the ministry of the Spirit. Rather, it is a question of being able to recognize which Spirit, whose Spirit.

The integral relationship between Jesus Christ and the Spirit also introduces the cross into the equation, another topic routinely eschewed in the theology of religions for the sake of not blocking dialogue, as many believe.[55] With reference to Moltmann's theology of the cross, my former student at Fuller Eugen Matei puts is succinctly: "The cross, therefore, where God *himself* was in Christ (2 Cor 5:19), is the place where God represents and reveals himself, and even more than that, it is the place where he identifies and defines himself."[56] In other words, the cross is not something external to the divine life of the Trinity but an identifying element.[57] Yes, the cross is a scandalous event, but it also is an everlasting testimony to the willingness of the triune God to not only share in the suffering of the world but also to let suffering and pain become part of the divine life. The Spirit, at work in the world after the cross, is the Spirit of the crucified and risen Christ. In a very helpful way, Michael Welker emphasizes that the biblical view of the Spirit "is not a self-referential personality but an utterly empathetic personality with a multicontextual presence."[58]

In asking the tough question concerning how Christ's presence and grace reach out to Muslims, the Catholics referred to the universal presence and ministry of the Holy Spirit as integrated with—rather than separate from—the cross, based on the groundbreaking statement of Vatican II's *Gaudium et Spes* (#22):[59]

---

witness to Christ.

54. Dupuis, *Toward a Christian Theology*, 196.

55. For an important article, see Wells, "Holy Spirit and Theology of the Cross," 476–78.

56. Matei, "Practice of Community in Social Trinitarianism," 186.

57. For Moltmann, this means that the cross is an event between God and God, an inner-divine event (as well as, of course, in relation to the world). One does not need to affirm Moltmannian interpretation, however, to make my point.

58. Welker, "Spirit in Philosophical and Theological Perspective," 5.

59. See further, Jukko, *Trinitarian Theology in Christian-Muslim Encounters*, 157.

> All this [the union with the dead and risen Christ] holds true not only for Christians, but for all men of good will in whose hearts grace works in an unseen way. For, since Christ died for all men, and since the ultimate vocation of man is in fact one, and divine, we ought to believe that the Holy Spirit in a manner known only to God offers to every man the possibility of being associated with this paschal mystery.

Does this mean, then, that Islam is a way of salvation? Catholics affirmed that Islam is a way "towards" God and that, on the level of religion, the Muslims are believers who come to God via another way than Christians. Islam is seen as a way to God and as a place of the Spirit. Yet the salvific structure per se of the Islamic faith was not affirmed.[60]

Speaking of the universal presence of the Spirit integrally related to the particularity of Jesus and his cross[61] helps us qualify and critique the mantra according to which the Spirit represents universality whereas the Son particularity. This is correct to a point, not as an absolute rule. Consider biblical passages such as the Prologue to the Gospel of John, which paints a picture of the Word in no less universal terms.[62] If Christology is depicted in both particular and universal terms, what can be said about the Spirit in this respect? Spirit not only speaks to universality but also of particularity; any talk about the Spirit in a Trinitarian context is always specific even if universal in its scope. Otherwise, we loose all contours to distinguish, Whose Spirit? Furthermore, as Welker has strongly argued elsewhere, all talk about the Spirit need be particular in order to be "concrete" and specific.[63] One also needs to be careful about using the term "universality" in this context, not only because it smacks too much of modernity and its preference for the kind of "generic" pneumatologies so evident in much of Christian theology of religions, but also because, when going back to the beginnings of Christian theology, any kind of universal claims by a small group of religious enthusiasts seemed to be quite a scandalous (and thus particular!) claim.[64]

---

60. See further, Kärkkäinen, *Trinity and Religious Pluralism*, 159.

61. Dabney ("Who Do You Say I Am?", 16) makes the claim that the Gospel of Mark (which serves as the main biblical basis for his pneumatological approach to theology) ". . . places the story of the life, death, and resurrection of Jesus Christ in a Pneumatological context." In the symposium discussion, questions were raised about whether Mark really is the Gospel that makes this case most vocally.

62. See further, Dupuis, *Toward a Christian Theology*, 188–90.

63. Welker, *God the Spirit*.

64. See further, Wells, "Holy Spirit," 476–78.

Now, to add one more dimension to the Spirit-Christ relation, that of the church: How should we speak of this triad?[65] On the basis of that discussion, we will expand the discussion to concern the kingdom's relation too.

Spirit, Church, and Kingdom

One of the reasons that I find the proposal of the Catholic Dupuis somewhat truncated (as much as I affirm, for instance, its genuinely Trinitarian pneumatology as indicated in the discussion above) is that he tends to undermine the integral relationship between God and God's kingdom as if the latter would make Christian theology more exclusive. He also tends to resist the integral relationship between God and the church in the world.[66] Different from Dupuis and many others (such as Knitter), another Catholic, Gavin D'Costa, insists on the integral relationship between the presence of the Spirit and the Father and Son, which then translates into an integral relationship between the triune God and the church.

D'Costa contends that the Holy Spirit's presence within other religions is both intrinsically trinitarian and ecclesiological. It is trinitarian in referring the Holy Spirit's activity to the paschal mystery of Christ, and ecclesial in referring the paschal event to the Spirit's constitutive community-creating force under the guidance of the Spirit.[67] The gift of the Spirit is not just for individual believers, but aims at the building up of the fellowship of believers. The Spirit unites believers with Christ and into fellowship with others. The story of Pentecost (Acts 2) expresses the fact that the Spirit does not simply assure each believer individually of his or her fellowship with Jesus Christ, but that he thereby, at the same time, founds the fellowship of believers.[68] In the New Testament, this is expressed in terms of the church being the people of God, body of Christ, temple of the Spirit.

The renewal of communion theology has helped us revive the understanding of the Christian God as relational, as Love.[69] Salvation is not "individualistic" (even though it is personal). To be saved means to be in

---

65. See the important contribution by Miroslav Volf and Maurice Lee, "Spirit and Church," 20–45.

66. For details, see my *Trinity and Religious Pluralism*, 59–66.

67. For details and bibliographical references, see my *Trinity and Religious Pluralism*, 69–72. D'Costa finds the biblical support for this mainly in the Johannine Paraclete passages (John 14–16). In my view, those Johannine passages are only one instance of a larger and more convincing New Testament approach; see *Trinity and Religious Pluralism*, 77–78.

68. Pannenberg, *Systematic Theology*, 3:12, 13.

69. Here the definitive work is Zizioulas, *Being as Communion*.

communion. In the words of the Orthodox Zizioulas, becoming Christian means a move from "biological" individuality to "ecclesial" communion. This reflects the way of being of God: God exists as communion. The church is the image of the triune God and as such is inviting and inclusive. The Holy Spirit is the Spirit of communion (2 Cor 12:13). Establishing the close connection between the triune God and the church does not, however, lead to a kind of "ecclesiocentrism" that is blind to either the Spirit's presence everywhere in the world and in creation as the principle of all life or to the Spirit's activity in society and history, peoples, cultures, and religions.

What then is the role of the kingdom of God? Kingdom is of course a much larger entity than the church. The church is the sign of the coming of the kingdom of God and is being drawn to the eschatological movement through which God fulfills his purposes in the world. Having created the world, God cannot be God without his kingdom, as Pannenberg has most vocally argued.[70] As noted, Trinity rules out these kind of "kingdom-centered" approaches in which the advancement of the kingdom is set in opposition to or divorced from the Father, Son, and Spirit. Trinity also rules out that kind of "pneumato-centered" approaches in which the "universal" ministry of the Spirit is divorced from christological contours.

The kingdom of God is the kingdom of the Father, and in its coming the Son serves as a humble Son in the power of the Spirit. Again, it is negotiable how much "wider" is the sphere of the kingdom than the church. But however that relationship is defined, I see it mistaken to separate the two so much that the church becomes an obstacle to rather than a God-willed agent that participates in the kingdom's coming.

This prompts the question concerning Islam's relation to the church and the kingdom. The French dialogue contended that Muslims can be regarded as co-members in the kingdom of God. This insight brings the task of spiritual discernment to the surface. The mission of the church and the work of the Holy Spirit are given new dimensions when the children of the kingdom are to be recognized in the world. If so, the dialogue continued, both Christians and Muslims should participate in the building of the kingdom until it comes at the eschaton. Yet an important distinction was made: Muslims are not building the church, which is the task for Christians, but the kingdom, which is a wider concept. Here there is a close relationship between the kingdom and the Spirit; the building of the kingdom is seen as

---

70. Pannenberg, *Systematic Theology*, 1:311–13 especially. This is not limiting God's freedom since it is in his sovereign freedom that God has created the world.

a sign of the work of the Spirit who acts and makes the messianic kingdom come.[71]

Going back to the notion of the triune God as communion and the Spirit as the principle of relationality, let us reflect on the implications for the encounter with the Other.[72]

"The Holy Spirit's Invitation to Relational Engagement"[73]

The triune God as a perichoretic communion is a helpful way to negotiate the dynamic and tension between one and many. The Trinity as communion allows room for both genuine diversity (otherwise we could not talk about the Trinity) and unity (otherwise we could not talk about one God). Trinity "unites transcendence and immanence, creation and redemption in such a way that from the Christian standpoint dialogue [with Muslims in this case] becomes possible and meaningful," affirmed the Catholics engaged in the dialogue with Muslims.[74] Communion serves as the paradigm for relating to the Other among human beings too. It is not about denying differences nor eliminating distinctives as is typical of various sorts of "rough parity"–type pluralisms; rather, communion is about encountering the Other in a mutually learning, yet challenging atmosphere.

The Christian, coming from a particular perspective, is both encouraged and entitled to witness to the triune God of the Bible and his saving will, yet at the same time prepared to learn from the Other. This helps the Christian to get to know the Other and may also lead to the deepening of one's own faith. "The other is always interesting in their difference and may be the possible face of God, or the face of violence, greed, and death. Furthermore, the other may teach Christians to know and worship their own trinitarian God more truthfully and richly." Thus, D'Costa believes that trinitarian theology provides the "context for a critical, reverent, and open engagement with otherness, without any predictable outcome."[75]

I further agree with D'Costa that other religions are not salvific as such, but other religions are important for the Christian church in that they

---

71. Jukko, *Trinitarian Theology in Muslim-Christian Encounters*, 193–97.

72. "God's radical relativity *ad extra* is a mirror image of the same radicality *ad intra*: that is to say, the whole universe, as image or 'vestige' of the Trinity, is endowed with the character of radical relativity . . . Things are but reciprocal constitutive relationships." Panikkar and Barr, *The Silence of God*, 142.

73. Section title in D'Costa, *Meeting of Religions*, 109.

74. Jukko, *Trinitarian Theology in Muslim-Christian Encounters*, 221.

75. D'Costa, *Meeting of Religions*, 9.

help the church to penetrate more deeply into the divine mystery. This is the essence of what D'Costa calls the Spirit's call to "relational engagement." The acknowledgment of the gifts of God in other religions by virtue of the presence of the Spirit—as well as the critical discernment of these gifts by the power of the same Spirit—means a real trinitarian basis to Christianity's openness toward other religions. It also ties the church to the dialogue with the Other: wherever the presence of the Spirit—and thus the presence of God—is to be found it bears some relation to the church. Thus, the discernment of the activity of the Holy Spirit within other religions must also bring the church more truthfully into the presence of the triune God. Again, citing D'Costa, "if the Spirit is at work in the religions, then the gifts of the Spirit need to be discovered, fostered, and received into the church. If the church fails to be receptive, it may be unwittingly practicing cultural and religious idolatry."[76] The church better be ready for surprises since there is no knowing a priori what beauty, truth, holiness, and other "gifts" may be waiting for the church.[77] Catholics affirmed that it is the Holy Spirit who urges Christians to dialogue and makes Christians discover aspects of their own faith that they have not known or recognized in Christ. Even more, ". . . the Christian-Muslim encounter can help, among Christians, to receive the revelation of God in Jesus Christ."[78]

Both Welker and Polkinghorne[79] speak of the "context-sensitivity" and "encounter-sensitivity" of the Holy Spirit. This means that the Holy Spirit is not "a power which acts and operates in each and every context in 'the same way'" and that "[a]ll associations of uniformity and homogeneity" must be balanced by statements that speak of diversity. The Spirit's presence and ministry is both multicontextual and polyphonic. Not only that, but "[t]he context-sensitivity and encounter-sensitivity of the Spirit is also correlated with His vulnerability."[80] Spirit-inspired and Spirit-guided dialogue with followers of other faiths is always particular and specific. The challenges to and riches from the Muslim faith are not necessarily the same as those with other faiths.

---

76. D'Costa, *Meeting of Religions*, 115.
77. D'Costa, *Meeting of Religions*, 133.
78. Jukko, *Trinitarian Theology in Muslim-Christian Encounters*, 161, quotation 219.
79. Welker gives a reference to Polkinghorne, *Faith in the Living God*, 71.
80. Welker, "Spirit in Philosophical and Theological Perspective," 5–7; see also 8–9.

Concluding Reflections and Tasks for the Future

In the symposium the idea of a "truth-seeking community" arose. The church is a community in search of truth. Interfaith dialogue reflects—as the Catholic-Muslim dialogue affirmed—the dialogical nature of God who in the Son enters the world he has created and through the active presence of the Holy Spirit seeks every person created in God's image.[81] The church is drawn to the movement of the coming of the kingdom in its service, humbly and boldly giving its testimony to the Lordship of Christ and grace of God available to all.[82] As a truth-seeking community, the church is also called to receive new insights in its dialogue with religions.

The present essay has ventured to offer a few tentative guidelines as to how to speak of the presence and ministry of the Holy Spirit among religions. Nothing more than a beginning of a prolegomenon to a pneumatological theology of religions in a Trinitarian framework can be done in the confines of a short essay. Many critical tasks arise out of this reflection such as the following:

First, how do we establish the principle of continuity in pneumatology so that salvation communicated by the Spirit is not foreign to the created order? Here the work of Dabney with its idea of the theology of the third article—pneumatology—seems promising.

Second, related to this is the question of the role of the Spirit in relation to the general religious nature of humanity.[83] Amos Yong's desire to develop a distinctively Pentecostal pneumatological theology of creation and anthropology raises hopes.[84] Dabney's work also bears on this question in that for him anthropology serves as the springboard for doing theology in the postmodern context.

Third, the need to establish criteria for spiritual discernment is a continuing task for the theology of religions. Strangely enough, none of the symposium presentations tackled this issue even though persons such as Yong elsewhere have offered important insights into the topic.[85] The task of spiritual discernment, however, is wider and more comprehensive than often perceived. In addition to developing criteria for discerning evil/demonic

---

81. See further my *Trinity and Religious Pluralism*, 160–61.
82. See further, Jukko, *Trinitarian Theology in Muslim-Christian Encounters*, 213–14.
83. Here we could learn a lot from theological anthropologies of both Pannenberg and Rahner.
84. Yong, "Spirit(s), the Heaven Above and the Earth Beneath."
85. See Yong, *Beyond the Impasse*, ch. 6.

spirits, discernment also has much to do with the capacity and resources to identify the work of God's/divine Spirit vis-à-vis other spirits.[86]

Fourth, it would be highly interesting to consider in more detail What is the significance of the "syncretistic" nature of the Christian faith to our topic?[87] How is this related to the Spirit's call for engagement?

Fifth, it would be also important to continue reflections on the epistemological contours of a pneumatological theology of religions.[88] Of course, this essay in itself is already a step in that process. What I have in my mind, in addition, is the recent debate on this side of the Atlantic concerning the topic of "foundationalism" in a postmodern context. This prompts the question of whether building a theology of religions with a Trinitarian "foundation" implies a foundationalist epistemology. I don't think so, but in this essay I cannot deal with the issue.[89]

Yet the most important task has to do with continuing a careful and painstaking dialogue with a particular religion. Prolegomena by definition are abstract and general; dialogue is particular and specific.[90] Regarding the Muslim-Christian dialogue I tend to agree with the ironic conclusion of the French dialogue:[91]

> In sum, it can be said—paradoxical as it may sound—that even though the proper theological foundation for the interfaith dialogue with Muslims is the Christian doctrine of the Trinity, . . .

---

86. The scientist Donald G. York's attempt to develop the biblical idea of Wisdom as the work of the Spirit of God especially in relation to decision making may offer some seed thought to this task. See York, "Spirit in Evidence," 18–21 especially. Recently, several Catholic theologians have reflected on the role of the Spirit in ethics and moral theology; this work may offer some resources for the task of the discerning of the Spirit as well.

87. Pannenberg, among others, has argued that one of the distinctive features of the Christian faith is its capacity to incorporate elements from various religions more successfully than other faiths.

88. Yong's proposal is that of a "foundational pneumatology" (see ch. 3 in *Beyond the Impasse*).

89. I have touched on this in my *Trinity and Religious Pluralism*, 168n5.

90. Some of my doctoral students at Fuller Theological Seminary have utilized a Trinitarian framework in an interfaith dialogue, for example, Lewis Winkler, whose PhD thesis has to do with a dialogue between Pannenberg's Trinitarian doctrine and Islamic monotheism as the latter is expressed in some leading contemporary Islamic theologies. Another doctoral student of mine, Linh Doan of Vietnam, has looked at the more recent theology of the Thich Nhat Hanh (referred to in the beginning of the essay) and its claim for bridges between the Buddhist notion of mindfulness and the Christian view of the Holy Spirit.

91. As summarized and developed by myself in my *Trinity and Religious Pluralism*, 162 (with sources to original documentation in Jukko's book).

the doctrine itself cannot be used in actual encounters with Muslims, since the Islamic faith denies it at the outset. . . . How this translates to the Trinitarian conviction, shared by all Christians . . . is one among the crucial theological questions to be pondered. Trinity pushes Christians to dialogue with other religions, especially with monotheistic "cousins," yet at the same time it also sets rules for Christian talk about God.

In terms of an epilogue, let me add a final word of warning and qualification to my "trinitarian rules." While I believe it is urgent theologically to reflect on the Spirit's life in the world and among religions through a rigorous Trinitarian framework, we also have to remind ourselves of the fact that "knowing" the ways of the Spirit is only possible by doxology. Indeed, Trinitarian doctrine is essentially doxological in its origins and character.[92] To use the poetic expression of yet another Catholic pneumatologist, Hans Urs von Balthasar, the Spirit is "the Unknown beyond the Word." Therefore, Balthasar reminds us that even without in any way wanting to divorce itself from the Trinitarian contours, faith is also a "venture of transcending the Word into the Spirit." This means that

> The Word no longer leads us by the hand, equipping us with recipes and traveling plans that one need only consult: rather, we are exposed in the dimension of creative invention, sharing in the breath of the Creator Spirit and even . . . breathing him out ourselves together with God. It in only in faith that we can let go of the handrail of the Word, so that we can walk without vertigo in the sphere of freedom; only in believing hope dare we join Peter in leaving the ship to venture out into the billowing infinity of the divine Spirit.[93]

---

92. See further, McDonnell, "Pneumatology," 197–98.

93. von Balthasar, "Unknown Lying Beyond the Word," 110–11. For applications to dialogue, see Imbelli, "Unknown Beyond the Word," 326–35.

CHAPTER 13

Dukkha and *Passio*

A Christian Theology of Suffering in the (*Theravada*) Buddhist Context

FIRST WORDS: APPROACH AND GOAL

THIS ESSAY ARGUES THAT a key common concern between Buddhist and Christian religions is the topic of suffering.[1] This is because of the prominence of the theme of suffering in both the Buddhist and Christian vision of liberation and "salvation." Consequently, my contention is that a successful missionary encounter in any Buddhist environment requires a lot of careful attention to the meaning of suffering and the means of release from under its power.

I will significantly limit the scope of my investigation. From the Buddhist side, I will concentrate not only on the *Theravada* branch but also on its manifestation in one of the main locations of *Theravada* in the contemporary world, Thailand.[2] From the Christian side, I will focus on the

---

1. I would like to acknowledge my indebtedness to the work of my Thai student Satanun Boonyakiat, who recently finished an excellent doctoral dissertation titled, "A Christian Theology of Suffering in the Context of Theravada Buddhism in Thailand." During the process of mentoring (with Professor Bill Dyrness), I had an opportunity to revisit many experiences and ideas springing from the years that I spent in Thailand in firsthand contact with *Theravada* Buddhism.

2. Among the many divisions in Buddhism in Cambodia, Laos, Myanmar, Sri Lanka, and Thailand, the two main ones (besides *Vajrayana*, *Zen*, and Pure Land) are *Theravada* and *Mahayana*. About 95 percent of Thais consider themselves Buddhists,

resources of the Renewal Theology and Missiology through the lens of Pentecostal tradition. While I know well that the Renewal tradition is larger than that of Pentecostalism, I am also convinced that Pentecostal theology and missiology may serve as *a* representative.

During the course of discussion I will further explain the rationale for other limitations, including the omission of the traditional theodicy question as well as that of socio-political suffering/liberation. The essay consists of two parts: in the first part I will attempt to discern and discuss the understanding of suffering in each religious tradition. In the second part, I will compare and contrast the Buddhist and Christian visions of liberation with a view to proposing theological guidelines for a missionary encounter. I will finish with some tasks and themes for further reflection.

PART I: TWO PERSPECTIVES ON SUFFERING: DUKKHA AND PASSIO

The Buddhist Insight into Suffering

> The Noble Truth of *dukkha*, monks, is this: Birth is *dukkha*, aging is *dukkha*, sickness is *dukkha*, death is *dukkha*, association with the unpleasant is *dukkha*, dissociation from the pleasant is *dukkha*, not to receive what one desires is *dukkha*—in brief the five aggregates subject to grasping are *dukkha*.[3]

In his first sermon after the Enlightenment, "Setting the Wheel of Dhamma in Motion," Gautama Buddha set forth *dukkha* as the basic principle of Buddhist teaching and worldview (the first "Noble Truth"). With all their differences, all Buddhist schools consider *dukkha* ("suffering") to be the main challenge and, consequently, extinction of *dukkha* to be the main goal. Suffering is inescapable as long as one is in the circle of life and death, *samsara*. To be more precise, it is the craving (the second "Noble Truth") which is the real root and cause.[4] Behind the (misplaced) craving,

---

and the remaining minorities consists of Muslims (by far the largest one) and Christians (as well Hindus, mainly immigrants from India). For a succinct introduction to Thai Buddhism, see, Kusalasaya, *Buddhism in Thailand*.

3. *Dhammacakkappavattana Sutta* 11 (*Samyutta Nikāya* 56.11 in Access to Insight [ATI], http://www.accesstoinsight.org/tipitaka/index.html; I also add the standard Pali Text Society [PTS] reference: S v 420. I have replaced the English translation "suffering" (in other renderings "pain" or "stress" or similar) with *dukkha*.

4. Similarly to the notion of *dukkha*, the term *tanhā* ("craving" or "desire") used by Buddha is a multifaceted concept. It is customary to divide it into three meanings:

according to the Buddha, is ignorance.⁵ The logic of the emergence and continuation of suffering rooted in craving due to ignorance is indebted to the law of *kamma*.⁶

Buddhist scholars consider *dukkha* and the rest of the "Noble Truths" (the origin and way of extinction) as the *summa* of everything in Buddhism and its Scriptures.⁷ While most of the Buddhists in Thailand are fairly ill-versed in the doctrinal heritage of their religion—which is understandable in light of a deep and pervasive "animistic"⁸ orientation of everyday religiosity and spirituality with its focus on spirits—one can hardly find a Thai who couldn't recite the essence of Buddha's first sermon at the Deer Park. "Consequently, the Buddhist concept of suffering certainly governs the understanding of Thai Buddhists, and, at the same time, it inevitably influences the responses of Thai Christians to the reality of human suffering."⁹

The term *dukkha* is notoriously difficult to translate, as even a quick look at different English renderings of the Pali original reveals: terms such as "suffering," "pain," "stress," and "unsatisfactoriness" are used. None of them, however, can capture the ambiguity of the original term—and most of them, taken in isolation from the Buddhist worldview, can easily lead us astray.

---

craving for sensual pleasures, craving for existence, and craving for non-existence (which means the longing to avoid unpleasant conditions or situations such as when an old person does not want to grow old).

5. See *Paticca-samuppada-vibhanga Sutta: Analysis of Dependent Co-arising* (*Samuyttanikāya Nikaya* 12.2, ATI; PTS: S ii 2) for the famous analysis of Gautama concerning the idea of "Dependent Origination" which names ignorance as the genesis of the cycle of actions and dispositions which ultimately lead to suffering, and identifies "complete abandoning of ignorance" as the way out of it.

6. *Kamma* ("the law of reaping and sowing") has two sides in the Buddhist analysis: on the one hand the "bad" *kamma*, which consists of "unskillful" actions and attitudes such as greed or hatred and on the other hand, the "good" *kamma*, which consists of "skillful" actions and attitudes such as non-greed, non-hatred, and non-delusion. Good *kamma* produces good while bad *kamma* bad effects and results. Venerable Phra Dhammapitaka, *Dictionary of Buddhism*, 60.

7. Chandngarm, *Arriyasatsee*, 9–14. According to this leading Thai Buddhist scholar, even other cardinal beliefs such as Dependent Origination and Threefold Training (in morality, mentality, and wisdom) are dependent on the core (39–40).

8. I am well aware of the fact that current anthropological discourse doesn't endorse the use of the term "animism." Yet, I can hardly find a more suitable term to describe the religious phenomenology of, say, Thailand. It is of course one of the great ironies of the folk religious transformation that all living faiths, not excluding parts of Christianity, tend to shift focus on "animistic" practices, rituals, and rites. This orientation is all the more astonishing with regard to *Theravada*, a form of Buddhism, the most "orthodox" and most non-theistic doctrinally!

9. Boonyakiat, "Christian Theology of Suffering," 3.

The world-renowned Buddhist teacher Walpola Rahula chooses not to even attempt a translation of *dukkha* to avoid obvious misunderstanding.[10]

The common suspicion that according to Buddha life is nothing but suffering and pain, while containing a seed of truth, is also in many ways misleading.[11] First of all, the term *dukkha* means much more than—and in many ways something much different from—"suffering": along with suffering, pain, and sorrow, the term denotes imperfection, impermanence, emptiness, insubstantiality, and so forth.[12] Second, the focus on *dukkha* does not imply that for Buddhism life is pessimistic (any more than optimistic for that matter). The Buddhist vision of life is rather realistic. As is well-known, Gautama gave a long litany of things in life that are enjoyable and should be enjoyed, from economic security to enjoyment of wealth to happiness on account of living a good life.[13]

Gautama's observation according to which "the five groups of existence connected with clinging are *dukkha*" reminds us of the five aggregates that make up a human being, namely, the physical (or material), feeling, perception, mental formations, and consciousness. Besides and beyond these five aggregates there is no permanent "self" or "individual" in the Western sense of the word. Even these aggregates, of course, are nothing permanent! This is the essence of the Buddhist notion of *anattatā*, no-self. Coupled with the idea of no-self and *dukkha*, is the third "characteristic of existence," namely impermanence.[14] Of course, human beings cannot fathom this reality, and thus craving emerges, which helps explain *dukkha*! Sentient beings are instead fooled by the idea of continuity, movement, and wholeness.[15] A most ironic thing about the Buddhist worldview is that while the "self" is impermanent—in other words, a fleeting reality—*dukkha* is something "essential," "permanent." *Dukkha* simply describes how life is! The same can be said of *kamma*; in the world characterized by non-being and impermanence, those two "laws" seem to be in place whatever happens.

In the Buddhist vision, suffering is both a built-in and inevitable reality; on top of that, sentient beings also encounter various types of sufferings

10. Rahula, *What the Buddha Taught*, 16n2.

11. Here there is an interesting parallel between *dukkha* and the idea of "vanity" in Ecclesiastes. It would be an interesting line of investigation to pursue that comparison. For starters, see Polish, "Buddha as a Lens for Reading *Koheleth*/Ecclesiastes," 370–82; Vasanthakumar, "Exploration of the Book of Ecclesiastes," 147–77; Lorgunpai, "Books of Ecclesiastes," 155–62.

12. See further, Rahula, *What the Buddha Taught*, ch. 2.

13. See, e.g., *Anana Sutta: Debtless* (Anguttara Nikāya 4.62, ATI; PTS: A ii 69).

14. See further, *Samyutta Nikāya* 22.59, ATI (PTS S iii 66).

15. Venerable Phra Dhammapitaka, *Tri-Luk*, 23–24.

such as those outlined above.¹⁶ For the Buddha, *dukkha* has three interrelated meanings:¹⁷ First, *Dukkha-dukkhatā*: the state of suffering in terms of feeling and sensation; this meaning comes closest to the English "suffering." Second, *Viparināma-dukkhatā*: the state of suffering inherent "in the change or the state of suffering which [is] concealed within the infidelity of happiness." This is the "post-enjoyment" realization of the ending of the pleasure. Third, *Sankhāra dukkhatā*: the state of suffering due to formations, related to the "three characteristics of existence"—teaching.¹⁸

Satanun Boonyakiat summarizes succinctly the Buddhist notion of *dukkha* in its various dimensions and forms:

> In summary, the term "suffering" in the Buddhism has a complex meaning. On the one hand, it simply means physical and emotional pain. On the other hand, it refers to the state of suffering that is inherent in the change and conflictual state result[ing] from impermanence. The Buddha points out that human beings must encounter various kinds of suffering. Physical and emotional suffering associated with birth, old age, and death is unavoidable because it is the true basis of human nature. The feeling of suffering is the result of craving or clinging to someone or something. Moreover, the Buddha teaches that suffering is the stressful and conflictual nature of all things caused by their impermanence. Therefore, nothing can provide complete fulfillment to those who attach to it. The Buddha proclaims this truth not to add a burden to human misery, but to help people recognize it and to start the process of suffering solving.¹⁹

The Christian Theology of Suffering

In light of the prevalence in the Thai mind of the idea of suffering, Satanun Boonyakiat laments the fact that Christian "theological approaches to suffering, driven by the agenda of the people in the west, often focus on the problem of evil and theodicy rather than addressing the reality of human

---

16. An insightful illustration of these two types of suffering is the following: built-in suffering is like a family member whereas the miscellaneous suffering is like a visiting guest. See Muthukan, *Buddha-Sart*, 16–17.

17. See also the helpful and clear exposition of *dukkha* in Ingram [Christian] and Loy [Buddhist], "Self and Suffering," 99–100.

18. Boonyakiat, "Christian Theology of Suffering," 70.

19. Boonyakiat, "Christian Theology of Suffering," 77.

suffering per se."[20] As a result, he surmises, those responses make little sense to the Thais. Key questions for Christian missionary responses then are—rather than the classical theodicy question as to how to reconcile the idea of a good, loving God with the problem of evil—the following ones: Do Christians and Buddhists refer to the same reality when speaking of "suffering"?[21] Is craving behind the Buddhist explanation of the root of suffering similar to the Christian notion of sin? What is the way of liberation? In other words, in this dialogical investigation, rather than focusing on the question of *Why* suffering? (which, of course, is a crucial *theological* dilemma), I will place the emphasis on *How* to deal with suffering? and *What* is suffering in light of the gospel?

This orientation helps us focus and limit this part of the investigation to prepare us for a comparison and contrast with a view to implications for mission. Rather than attempting any kind of traditional inquiry into the "whence evil" theodicy question, I will just offer a brief statement about the issue of suffering in Christian tradition and then attempt to highlight the Pentecostal approach.

While Christian theology does not speak about suffering in one voice, all Christian traditions agree that suffering—however it may be related to the Fall and sin—only came into existence in the second movement following God's good creation.[22] In that sense, Christian tradition considers suffer-

---

20. Boonyakiat, "Christian Theology of Suffering," 3–4. Well-known in Buddhist tradition is Gautama's refusal to tackle the metaphysical questions of the ultimate origins of evil; instead, the Buddha wanted to turn attention to the "practical" task of dealing with suffering in order to be released from it. For the classic story of the man wounded with an arrow thickly smeared with poison which makes this point, see *Cula-Malunkyovada Sutta: The Shorter Instructions to Malunkya* (*Majjhima Nikāya* 63, ATI; PTS: M i 426).

21. Jay McDaniel makes the important observation that even though it is often assumed "that the appropriate aim of dialogue is an identification of similar concerns . . . Contrary to expectations talk between Buddhists and Christians may also lead in different directions." In other words, what each religion means with the alleged shared concern or theme may not be the same. McDaniel, "God of the Oppressed," 689. Whereas in contemporary interfaith encounters there is often a felt need to both minimize the differences and also highlight the alleged convergences between religions—in order to boost the dialogue—some informed observers make the healthy remark that an honest acknowledgment of the differences may be the key to a fruitful exchange. Malcom David Eckel speaks of the encounter of the world's religions in terms of "the maxim that opposites attract" and remarks that "nowhere does this simple truism seem more readily confirmed than in the encounter between Buddhism and Christianity. . . . In some ways it is hard to imagine two more unlikely candidates for the deep sense of communication and communion conveyed by the term 'dialogue.'" Eckel, "Perspectives on the Buddhist-Christian Dialogue," 43.

22. As said, this presentation does not give an opportunity to even begin to tackle

ing and evil in some sense parasitic to goodness.[23] The mainline Christian tradition has denied the idea of an ontological primacy of evil and thus of suffering, even when suffering is related via the Fall and sin to Satan, God's chief opponent. Furthermore, while there is a strong theological tradition in Classical Theism resisting the idea of linking suffering too closely with God, contemporary theology, having rediscovered the biblical teaching[24] and formative contributions of Martin Luther's "theology of the cross,"[25] speaks robustly of suffering in God, in other words, divine suffering.[26] In the words of J. Moltmann, Christian theology has no choice but to replace the *apathy axiom* (idea of an impassible) God for the notion of *theopathy*.[27] The main reason is the biblical idea that God is love.[28] Love that is not engaged and subject to sharing pain is not worth its salt. God's passion can be called "active passion," since it is voluntary identification with the suffering of the world and is based on love.[29]

There is yet another formative Christian idea about suffering: the redemptive suffering of Christ. While, again, Christian tradition does not speak in one voice about *how* redemption happened (and will happen) in the event of Jesus Christ,[30] there is a shared conviction that without the

---

the profound and utterly complicated theological questions about the origins of suffering, such as what exactly is the relation of suffering (and which kinds of suffering) to the Fall and sin; whether life before the Fall was "perfect" in the sense that suffering at least in the negative sense was not yet there (as traditional theology has tended to believe); whether there is any kind of Christian answer to the question of the ultimate origins of suffering (say, in relation to the tragic events in the angelic world as traditional theologies have speculated), and so forth.

23. This is not necessarily a statement in support of Augustine's traditional view of evil as the *privatio boni* (privation of goodness) but rather a more general statement based on creation theology.

24. Including the important contributions by Jewish scholarship such as the groundbreaking work of Abraham Heschel on prophets.

25. See further, Veli-Matti Kärkkäinen, "Evil, Love and the Left Hand of God," 215–34.

26. Again, the whole question of what is the appropriate and theologically consistent way of speaking of a suffering God or God in suffering, will not be tackled here.

27. Moltmann, *Trinity and the Kingdom*, 22–25.

28. Again, in the words of Moltmann: "A God who cannot suffer is poorer than any man. For a God who is incapable of suffering is a being who cannot be involved. Suffering and injustice do not affect him. . . . But the one who cannot suffer cannot love either. So he is also a loveless being." Moltmann, *Crucified God*, 222.

29. Moltmann, *Trinity and the Kingdom*, 23.

30. Another heavy-weight theological debate would engage questions such as what happened on the cross in terms of its salvific effects (so-called atonement theories) and in what ways the cross is related to the whole history of Jesus Christ.

suffering of the Son of Man salvation would not be available.[31] Finally, to sum up in few strokes of pen the vast area of the theology of suffering with regards to its many forms and motifs, Christian tradition also agrees that there are experiences and forms of suffering that just belong to human life in general and to the Christian experience in particular. In a cautious way, Christian tradition is even saying that suffering in that sense may be conducive to one's growth in faith. This is not to say that suffering is necessarily a "good" thing, but it is to say—differently from Buddhism—that suffering may also play some role in the hands of the loving and caring Father who allows his creatures to undergo moments of suffering.[32]

Now, enter Pentecostals (as representatives of Renewal Theology and Missiology); what is Pentecostalism's take on the topic of suffering? In many ways, Pentecostal-Charismatic spirituality has tended to be on the other side of the question:

> Pentecostal/charismatic Christianity has (re)introduced to Christian spirituality an ideal of victorious Christian living, an intensive faith expectation, and emphasis on spiritual power to overcome problems in one's life. The attitude of 'overcoming' is characteristic to Pentecostal and charismatic preaching. Often there is a heightened expectation of divine intervention, even in situations that seem impossible.[33]

Indeed, rather than suffering and pain, Pentecostals have highlighted themes such as victory and healing. As a general observation, one has to admit that there is precious little talk about suffering in much of Pentecostal literature.[34] One may thus wonder, to cite the title of my earlier writing, if "'Theology of the Cross' [is] a Stumbling Block to Pentecostal/Charismatic

---

31. See the helpful discussion in Ingram and Loy, "Self and Suffering," 100–102.

32. "[T]here are, in fact, forms of suffering which belong, in God's intention, to the human condition. Not all of what we experience as suffering is totally absurd, a mistake, an oversight, or the consequence of sin. There is something about a significant portion of suffering through which we pass that belongs to the very foundations of beings—something without which our human being would not and could not be what is meant to be." Hall, *God and Human Suffering*, 57. This said, one should be very careful of not sanctioning suffering in a way that would thwart attempts to help deliver people from it. An insightful Pentecostal-Charismatic discussion of mistaken notions of suffering (particularly with regard to illness and healing) is Blue, *Authority to Heal*, chs. 1 and 2 particularly.

33. Kärkkäinen, "Theology of the Cross," 150.

34. It is illustrative of this tendency that neither the recent major missiological treatise on Pentecostalism (Anderson, *Spreading Fires*) nor the most important Pentecostal systematic theological presentation (Yong, *Spirit Poured Out on All Flesh*) have the term "suffering" in their index or any discussion of the theme.

Spirituality"?[35] This is all the more astonishing when one takes into consideration the fact that even in the midst of victories and deliverances:

> The first Pentecostal churches suffered at the hands of mainline Christian denominations. Their people comprised the poor, the uneducated, those from the margins of society, and the oppressed—in contrast to the rich, the influential and the powerful who occupied the pews of mainline churches. The hostility these Pentecostal churches faced from established Christendom and the outside world made them look up with even greater earnestness; thereby enhancing their own spirituality, their spiritual equipment for service, their zeal to suffer for God and their hope in an imminent future with God.[36]

This pointed remark by the Indian Pentecostal theologian Gabriel Reuben Louis, in his response to a presentation, "Toward an Asian Pentecostal Theology," by Korean Pentecostal missiologist-theologian Wonsuk Ma, is a healthy reminder of the important *lacuna* in Pentecostal spirituality. Louis further laments that while today's Pentecostalism has embraced the early vision of the "Latter Rain," it is looking for its benefits mainly for the sake of this-worldly goods and enjoyment. While the theme of suffering, he continues, "may not be that relevant for a Pentecostal theology in a rich and prosperous West . . . [it is] in a poor and miserable Asia. . . ." Rather than assigning all or even most suffering to the spirit world, Louis contends, contemporary Pentecostalism should rediscover the important lesson from their forebears: "It is human to suffer; it is human to experience pain; it is human to be despised, forsaken and oppressed. This was what our own fore-fathers in the Pentecostal faith went through, and this is what most of the people of Asia go through even today."[37] The omission or downplaying of the theme of suffering among Pentecostals is of course not limited to the Asian or Western contexts; similar kinds of charges have been leveled for example against African Pentecostalism.[38]

On the other hand, there are significant efforts underway by Pentecostal theologians and missiologists to address more intentionally the theme of suffering in human life and Christian experience. While acknowledging and

---

35. Kärkkäinen, "Theology of the Cross," 150.

36. Louis, "Response to Wonsuk Ma." This is a response to Wonsuk Ma, "Toward an Asian Pentecostal Theology."

37. Louis, "Response to Wonsuk Ma."

38. See, e.g., Asamoah-Gyadu, *African Charismatics,* 218, 228–32; Gifford, *Ghana's New Christianity,* 50. For an important discussion, see Burgess, "Nigerian Pentecostal Theology," 29–63.

strongly endorsing the Pentecostal mentality of overcoming, the Pentecostal biblical scholar and missiologist William W. Menzies, with wide experience from the Asian context, admits that healings are mysteries and "Good people are not always healed." As a consequence, he suggests a biblical theology of suffering for Pentecostals.[39] This task has been taken up by another Assemblies of God biblical scholar, Martin William Mittelstadt, who has written on *The Spirit and Suffering in Luke-Acts*,[40] focusing his study on the topic seldom discussed by Pentecostals who otherwise have launched major investigations on this most treasured part of the New Testament. The Pentecostal theologian-missionary of Puerto Rico, Samuel Solivan, has contributed a significant theological treatise titled *The Spirit, Pathos and Liberation* in which he attempts an outline of Hispanic Pentecostal theology through the lens of suffering and liberation,[41] and the Sudanese Pentecostal Isaiah Majok Dau has reflected on *Suffering and God* in the context of the tragic civil war in his homeland.[42] What is noteworthy about these two theological treatises is that while Pentecostal in orientation, they engage widely Christian tradition and diverse theological views. I will take up these contributions in my constructive part of the essay.

PART II: TWO VISIONS OF LIBERATION: ORTHO-DOXY AND ORTHO-PATHOS

Liberation through Right Knowledge: The Way of *Ortho-doxy*

While suffering is inevitable, "The Buddha believes that suffering is resolvable. He pointed out that overcoming suffering does not accomplish by avoiding problems or neglecting suffering, but by confronting the reality of suffering and learning how to respond to it correctly. Therefore, the essence of the first truth is rightly accepting the reality of suffering as it is, and perceiving life and the world as they are."[43] How, then, would the Buddhist and Christian notions of suffering compare with each other? While both religions agree on the reality and multifaceted nature of suffering, the main differences have to do with three underlying issues. These differences of

---

39. Menzies, "Reflections on Suffering," 141. See also the important essay by the British Pentecostal biblical scholar who has written extensively on healing, Warrington, "Healing and Suffering in the Bible," 154–64.

40. Mittelstadt, *Spirit and Suffering in Luke-Acts*.

41. Solivan, *Spirit, Pathos and Liberation*.

42. Dau, *Suffering and God*.

43. Boonyakiat, "Christian Theology of Suffering," 77–78.

orientation should be kept in mind and reflected upon when constructing a missionary approach.

For Buddhism, suffering is an unavoidable structure of reality,[44] whereas for Christian faith, suffering is in some sense parasitic on goodness. In other words, Christian tradition, in light of creation, does not consider suffering as ontologically primary or necessary.[45]

When it comes to the "cause" or "reason" behind the suffering, Buddhist and Christian visions differ sharply. As mentioned above, for Buddhism the cause behind suffering is craving because of ignorance in the framework of *kamma*. In other words, the "something" behind the human dilemma is impersonal. When it comes to the Christian explanation of the cause of suffering, ultimately it is to be found in the personal God rather than in a formal principle of reality.

To sharpen and clarify the Christian view, I follow the helpful typology suggested by Boonyakiat who speaks of three ways of looking for the causes behind suffering; these are all interrelated and, as said, finally to be referred to the Almighty and Loving God.[46] First, according to the message of "retribution theology," suffering is the result of sin. This explanation comes closest to the Buddhist notion of retribution in the framework of *kamma* but is also different because the Buddhist explanation is based on an alleged "natural law of action and effect" rather than the actions of a personal God. It is highly significant that the Christian idea of "reaping and sowing" is placed in a theo-logical framework: "Do not be deceived: God cannot be mocked. A man reaps what he sows" (Gal 6:7 NIV). Another major difference has to do with the Buddhist notion of attributing the consequences to the next lives rather than to this life.[47] Retribution theology appeals to Thai

---

44. In order to understand properly the "necessary" nature of suffering in the Buddhist vision, one must keep in mind the fact that whereas "other religions might ask why there is suffering—as though it should not be there—... the Buddhist simply acknowledges the fact that there is suffering." Indeed, even "karma and samsara do not explain suffering; they are suffering." Lai, "Tillich on Death and Suffering," 574.

45. This is not to argue against the existence of some kind of suffering from the beginning of creation such as loneliness, limitations, temptation, and anxiety as Hall, *God and Human Suffering* (ch. 1) argues. Even those kinds of potential for suffering is not ontologically primary in the Buddhist sense. See also the important work by Farley, *Tragic Vision and Divine Compassion*.

46. Boonyakiat, "Christian Theology of Suffering," ch. 3. See the helpful comparison between Buddhist and Christian notions in Rahula, *What the Buddha Taught*, 32.

47. It is of course true that the Christian idea of reaping and sowing also has next-life implications in terms of choices and actions done in this life having consequences for the afterlife. Yet the radical difference is that in the Christian vision, one only has this one life to make choices and that, according to the Bible, the reaping begins already in this life.

Christians since in contrast to the Buddhist *kamma*, sin can be dealt with in terms of repentance and faith.[48]

Second, according to the message of liberation theology, part of suffering in the Christian vision is the result of oppression, which of course is not unrelated to the Fall and sinfulness of humanity. This is to say that unlike the Buddhist analysis which assigns one's suffering to one's own acts and dispositions, in the Christian view much suffering comes to the innocent because of the wrongdoings of others, including structural sin. Beginning from the Exodus, there is the biblical promise of God acting on behalf of and empowering those who suffer under oppression, injustice, neglect, and other similar situations. The existence of massive injustice, poverty, oppression (particularly of minorities such as the Mountain Peoples), and corruption both confuse and burden Thais when they realize that so much of that suffering cannot be attributed to the innocent sufferers. In the final analysis, in Christian theology even this suffering must be referred to God in one way or another (depending on one's theodicy) rather than to a nonpersonal, formal principle governing reality.

Third, there is also the biblical and theological tradition that simply makes suffering the function of mystery. There is suffering in the world and in Christian experience that simply evades explanation. Just consult the Book of Job—or many Psalms. In comparison with the Buddhist vision, it is highly significant that both Job and Psalms are part of the Wisdom literature. They are meant to heal our ignorance by telling us there is also suffering without any immediate cause or reason—other than the mystery of God, the Personal God. Again, it is comfortable for Thai Christians to receive the message that there simply are sufferings which cannot be attributed to any cause conceived by humans, not even sin in the individual life or in the structures but that even that kind of suffering is taken up by the Loving and Just God.

Yet another radical difference between the Buddhist and Christian vision is that "Savior has no place in the Buddhist worldview. An individual must control and be responsible for his or her own destiny."[49] One is one's own refuge, and no one else, not even Buddha,[50] can save one from the law

---

48. Boonyakiat, "Christian Theology of Suffering," 127–28, issues a call for his fellow Thai Christians to see clearly the importance of this point.

49. Boonyakiat, "Christian Theology of Suffering," 114.

50. In *Mahayana* Buddhism, the *Boddhisattva*—differently from the *Theravada Arahat* (*ariya-puggala*)—is willing to postpone his own entrance into the *nibbana* to help others reach the goal. Even that, however, is not the function of a "savior" but rather of a "good neighbor" even when the Boddhisattva may grant his own merit to help the other. Only in Pure Land Buddhism is there a notion of "mercy" and perhaps

of *kamma*. In other words, Buddhism, particularly in its original "orthodox" version is "an atheistic and humanistic system that locates human beings at the center of their existence and believes that humankind can overcome the problem of human suffering by their own endeavors. It also implies the denial of . . . Savior who delivers humankind from suffering."[51]

So, what then is the Buddhist vision of liberation? It is the removal of ignorance, in other words, right understanding and right thought—to name the first two aspects of the "Noble Eightfold Path."[52] I therefore have named it *ortho-doxy*, following the Christian vocabulary.[53] Of course, the Middle Way or the Noble Path also includes other things such as right action and right effort, but still it is true that everything focuses on the right insight, right knowledge, right understanding. Behind suffering is the wrong understanding; healing therefore comes in the form of enlightened knowledge that removes ignorance.[54] And as said, it is each human person's own responsibility to reach the goal. Over against the *Theravada* Buddhist human-centered idea of *ortho-doxy*, I will suggest a Christian idea of *ortho-pathos*.

"salvation" somewhat similar to that in Christianity. For differences between *Mahayana* and *Theravada* in this respect, see Davis, *Poles Apart*, 98–104.

51. Boonyakiat, "Christian Theology of Suffering," 115. Calling Buddhism "atheistic" is not to say that in Buddhism there is no place for divine beings and gods. Yes, there is—even in its original form. The Buddhist worldview locates angels, divinities, divine beings on top of the hierarchy of reality, and Gautama himself—as any of his followers—knew of divine beings; the point in calling Buddhism atheistic is the marginal, in some sense, "counterproductive," role of gods and divinities. Turning to gods in the Buddhist vision means turning away from one's own responsibility to redeem one's self from the predicament of *dukkha*.

52. The Middle Way or The Noble Eightfold Path consists of "right" understanding, thought, speech, action, livelihood, effort, mindfulness, and meditation. This is not a sequence but rather they are simultaneous acts. The various aspects are all interrelated and mutually supportive. For a brief, accurate description, see Rahula, *What the Buddha Taught*, ch. 5.

53. I acknowledge the fact that the term *orthodoxy* is only partially fitting to describe the Buddhist vision based on knowledge and understanding. In its commonsense Christian usage, orthodoxy is of course that: right knowledge and grasping of basic teachings of religion. In its etymology, however, the term of course means something like "right glory," in other words "right worship." While that aspect is foreign to Buddhism (except for the everyday "animistic" form), it accurately describes the ancient Christian vision in which the knowledge of God is both a function of and the result of right prayer and worship as much as a rational act.

54. I have intentionally left out of the consideration the ultimate state of the Buddhist vision of "salvation," namely *nibbana* (*nirvana*) in order to make the discussion more manageable. A reliable, helpful Buddhist reflection can be found in Masao, "Suffering in the Light of Our Time," 1–13.

Liberation through Right Suffering: The Way of *Ortho-pathos*

If the Buddhist strategy of seeking for release from suffering is knowledge-based, for Christians, the problem of suffering demands not only—or even primarily—a rational explanation or even right knowledge but rather, faith-based proper response: patience, trust, and hope. This is the way of *ortho-pathos*, "right suffering" to use constructively the terminology of Solivan.[55] Whereas for him the term is a shorthand for a Pentecostal Hispanic liberation theology, helping complement the weaknesses of mere *orthodoxy* with little focus on concrete action and *orthopraxis* with its distant and disengaged relation to a particular sufferer's life-situation, I make the term *orthopathos* a function of embracing in faith, hope, and love the biblical idea of suffering, both divine and human. Focusing now on a constructive missiological response from a Renewal Perspective through the lens of Pentecostalism, I will suggest four interrelated tasks for such an endeavor. I argue that for Pentecostals to facilitate a proper missionary interfaith encounter, these four interrelated aspects of a "suffering theology" of *orthopathos* should play a role:

- "Divine Suffering": embracing of the biblical God of love who shares in the *passio* and *pathos* of the world and makes it his own;

- "Redemptive Suffering": clinging to the "theology of the cross" that facilitates not only forgiveness of sins but also a concrete hope based on Christ;

- "Integrative Suffering": accepting suffering and pain as part of a victorious Spirit-filled life and ministry;

- "Healing Suffering": engaging in mature faith and hope the ministry of healing and compassion to help those who suffer.[56]

Divine Suffering. In order for Pentecostals to embrace the biblical idea of divine suffering, the implications of the belief in "an apathetic God" need

---

55. For this Latino theologian, the term *orthopathos* is the third "leg" of the theological "table" alongside *orthodoxy*, right belief and *orthopraxis*, proper action or ethics. Building solely on orthodoxy has often led to Christian passivity about the issues of oppression and injustice, whereas focusing on praxis alone "as a critical reflection on action . . . remains distant from the very persons it seeks to serve or represent." Consequently, *orthopathos* then positively means, "the type of critical, theological and personal first-hand engagement with the biblical, theological and social reality of suffering and marginalized communities." Solivan, *Spirit, Pathos, and Liberation*, 11.

56. That my list here does not include more intentionally the kind of socio-political aspects typical of Liberation theologies is not because I don't consider them important. I just want to keep this discussion more focused and limited.

to be exposed and corrected. This is what Solivan is doing in a most helpful way in a critical dialogue with the whole of Christian tradition. As he constructs a liberating theology of *orthopathos*, he sees it necessary to revisit the whole Christian tradition beginning from the Fathers with their engagement with the Greek Hellenistic notion of a passionless deity all the way to Luther's theology of the cross and contemporary revival of the theme of the *Crucified God*.[57] Old Testament study would be a good place for Pentecostals to rediscover the idea of a passionate, engaged, loving God who is in pains for his people and the peoples.[58] The New Testament speaks of the suffering of the Son in submitting his life onto the hands of the Father and of the suffering of the Father in handing over his Son to death, as well as the passionate Spirit sharing—as the bond of love, as tradition says—in this divine suffering.

Consequently, Pentecostals have a need to rediscover the biblical teaching about the relationship between the Spirit and suffering, not only the Spirit and empowerment. Having scrutinized a number of Pentecostal biblical investigations into the Lucan pneumatology, the most precious section in the Pentecostal "canon within the canon," Mittelstadt concludes that there is "a failure to integrate the intersecting of the Spirit with suffering."[59]

With all their emphasis on the power of God in healings, exorcisms, and other kinds of "power encounters" as well as the vibrant expectations of God's desire to intervene miraculously, Pentecostal theology needs to embrace the view of the loving, *passio*nate and *com*passionate God who weeps and anguishes over the suffering of his children and whose fatherly heart is broken because of the brokenness of life. As foreign as that view of God is for both the Hellenistic philosophical tradition and the "atheistic" Buddhist religious tradition, it is compelling as well. And even when it is perceived as scandalous, it cannot be abandoned for the sake of "relevance." Embracing the idea of a passionate God makes Pentecostal ministers and missionaries compassionate toward their neighbors and the religious Other.

Redemptive Suffering. While the generic idea of redemptive or "vicarious" suffering on behalf of others is not unknown in Buddhism—think of, for example, the commonly known story of the sixteenth-century Queen Srisuriyothai's self-sacrifice to save her people under the threat from the King of Burma or the annual ritual of *loikrathong*, which seeks to embody

57. Solivan, *Spirit, Pathos, and Liberation*, ch. 2.

58. A formative work with which Solivan also dialogues widely is that of the Jewish scholar Heschel, *Prophets*.

59. Mittelstadt, *Spirit and Suffering*, vii. The "Pentecostal neglect" included the standard works on Lucan pneumatology by R. Stronstadt, H. Ervin, J. Shelton, and R. Menzies (20–28 in Mittelstadt).

the sending away of the sins of the past year exploiting candles and miniature rafts—any notion of somebody suffering (death) to atone for sins or even taking up the other person's suffering onto himself is utterly foreign to the *Theravada* tradition.[60] A resort to such a vicarious act done by another person, even a divinity would mean shrinking from one's own responsibility to deal with one's *kamma*.

I leave out of my discussion here the complicated and complex question of how to deal with the problem of atonement vis-à-vis Thai culture[61] and focus rather on the more general idea of the Christian "theology of the cross," the redemptive suffering of Christ, and the call to Christians to follow the suffering Christ on the way to Golgotha. As mentioned above, a foundational difference between Buddhist and Christian views of salvation/liberation is the emphasis in the former on human initiative and capacity and in the latter on the benefits of the Savior. I just leave it here and move on to the corollary part.

In the Christian vision those who follow the suffering Christ are called to identify with and share in his sufferings. Pentecostals would do well in listening to the call of the late Pope John Paul II who began his encyclical "On the Meaning of Christian Suffering" with the quote from St. Paul: "Declaring the power of salvific suffering, the Apostle Paul says: 'In my flesh I complete what is lacking in Christ's afflictions for the sake of his body, that is, the Church.'"[62] The Holy Father reminded Christians of the fact that while redemption was accomplished by Christ's suffering on the cross, every Christian is called to suffer for the sake of the church and other people.[63] He quotes several times the familiar biblical verse from Rom 5:5 which speaks of the pouring out in our hearts of God's love through the Holy Spirit as

---

60. See further Simmer-Brown, "Buddhist Response to the Gospel of Luke," 107–9 particularly.

61. One of my students at Fuller Seminary (School of Intercultural Studies), an American missionary to Thailand, recently finished a groundbreaking PhD dissertation on the themes of "face and shame" in Thai culture and its religious, theological, and sociological implications. See Flanders, "About Face." Part of that discussion is a multidisciplinary theological reflection on how to best speak of atonement in an Asian culture not plagued with the consciousness of guilt and condemnation (as in post-Reformation cultures of the Global North) but rather with shame and the avoidance of not "losing one's face" as the all-embracing cultural norm and motif. For a brief discussion (in anticipation of a published monograph), see Flanders, "Face" and "Shame," in *Global Dictionary of Theology*.

62. Pope John Paul II, "Letter On the Meaning of Christian Suffering," #1. See also the thoughtful reflections on Christian and Buddhist views of suffering and its meaning in Ryan, "Gethsemani II," 249–51.

63. Pope John Paul II, "Letter On the Meaning of Christian Suffering," #3.

the power for a hopeful suffering, suffering which sees meaning beyond suffering.⁶⁴

This is what the Sudanese Pentecostal theologian Isaiah Majok Dau calls "suffering as a direct result of being followers of Christ."⁶⁵ Living in that war-stricken land, he rejoices over the fact that in the contemporary situation the Pentecostal church has become "a community capable of absorbing suffering"⁶⁶ and thus embodying the sufferings of Christ for the benefit of others.

Integrative Suffering. As a result of having missed the integral relationship in the biblical materials between the Spirit and suffering, "While Pentecostal leadership continues the call for the same empowering of the Holy Spirit and commissioning to gospel proclamation, often lacking is Luke's emphasis on the persistent tension between persecution and Spirit-inspired mission." An important theological and spiritual lesson for Pentecostals thus is to learn that "upon reception of the Spirit, recipients are not all powerful." Indeed, "Luke offers a vivid reminder of the limitations of Spirit-enablement."⁶⁷

This all means that Pentecostals need to learn and embrace as an integral part of Christian experience the moments of failure, weakness, despair, sickness, and other forms of suffering. Not only contemporary Pentecostalism but also the first audience of the Lucan message had to tackle with this same challenge. Having experienced the empowering, healing, and delivering power of the Holy Spirit in their midst, the first Christians had to come to grips with opposition, harassment, betrayals, and other kinds of struggles. According to Mittelstadt, nothing less is at stake here than the principle that "Opposition is rooted within the plan of God."⁶⁸ With a life story filled with tragedies such as epidemic disease in childhood, having one of his eyes

---

64. Pope John Paul II, "Letter On the Meaning of Christian Suffering," #23, among others.

65. In a most helpful and theologically grounded analysis of forms of suffering, Dau distinguishes the following types of sufferings which he sees presented in the biblical narrative: suffering as a consequence of sin, suffering as a corrective and disciplinary measure, suffering as a test of faith or faithfulness, suffering as a direct result of being followers of Christ, and innocent suffering. Dau, *Suffering and God*, ch. 5.

66. Dau, *Suffering and God*, 59–61. He says that was not always the case. Indeed, in the past suffering people not only did not look at the church as the community for suffering people but rather as something different and foreign. Nowadays, happily enough, "the church . . . has become the centre for social solidarity, ritual and healing" (60).

67. Mittelstadt, *Spirit and Suffering*, vii.

68. Mittelstadt, *Spirit and Suffering*, 8.

permanently impaired, long-time civil war, and his wife's life-threatening diseases, Dau calls "suffering as a test of faith and faithfulness."[69]

The Thai theologian Satanun Boonyakiat rightly argues that the term "integrative suffering" "enables Christians to see that some sort of suffering can belong to the human nature from the beginning. It also reveals that suffering is not always wrong because it can serve life and enrich our relationship with God."[70] He continues, saying that the idea that certain kinds of suffering "can belong to and have a positive role in God's good creation also makes Christian faith flourish" as well as relieves Christians from a naïve, unrealistic view of life—so much mocked by the realistic Buddhist vision.[71]

The presence—and hope-filled and patient embrace—of suffering in the Christian life and ministry is wonderfully embodied in Paul Yonggi Cho's experience. A Korean pastor, he comes from and reflects Buddhist (and Confucian) themes. In a collection of sermons titled *When I Am Weak, Then I Am Strong*, the lead sermon reflects on the presence of sufferings—in the form of the "thorn in the flesh" (2 Cor 12:7-10)—in the life of St. Paul, who also claimed divine revelations, abundance of mercy, and extraordinary victories. Pastor Cho urges "that we should be motivated in our lives of faith in God to let all the thorns of difficulties and trials become opportunities through which we can receive His blessings."[72] Knowing that these sufferings in the life of the Christian minister may turn out to be God's blessings, Cho advises us not to resist them with our own strength.[73] "Pastor Cho's Pentecostal theology of hope is an interesting mixture of bold faith-expectation, the kind of 'stubborn' faith of the woman in the Gospel of Luke (18:1-8) approved by Jesus, and obedient submission to endure suffering and pain as coming from the hand of a good God."[74]

Healing Suffering. In Christian faith the follower of Jesus Christ is called to alleviate the suffering of other men and women. While not denying the role of personal responsibility over the consequences of one's choices, there is the calling for all Christians to follow in the footsteps of their Master who devoted his life to healing, exorcism, hospitality, and reconciliation—at times even at the expense of one's own well-being and safety. Let me highlight here the importance of healing for its obvious importance to

---

69. Dau, *Suffering and God*, 185–90.

70. Boonyakiat, "Christian Theology of Suffering," 92. The concept of "integrative suffering" is from Hall, *God and Human Suffering*, 54–62.

71. Boonyakiat, "Christian Theology of Suffering," 101.

72. Cho, *When I am Weak*, 72.

73. Cho, *When I am Weak*, 72.

74. Kärkkäinen, "March Forward to Hope," 258.

Pentecostal spirituality and mission. In the mainline, Buddhism, particularly the *Theravada* tradition, teaches that one should not be too active in intervening in another person's suffering in order to avoid interrupting the *kamma* and *samsara*-nature of reality.[75]

Let me offer a personal testimony here to illustrate my point. When I lived with my family in Bangkok, my then young daughters often challenged and questioned my neglect of beggars on the street corners. Every visitor to the capital of Thailand or any other city knows that there is a huge number of beggars, many of them handicapped or otherwise health-impaired, including mothers with small children on their laps. While my own reason for not responding to the needs of many of these desperate people had more to do with—in addition to the obvious incapacity of being able to help the huge number of people because of the financial limitations of a missionary—the justified suspicion of being exploited for the benefit of the greedy "mafia," my Thai Buddhist interlocutors argued that an act of benevolence might be an exercise in intervening with another person's *kamma*.[76]

While I am a bit concerned about the concept of exploiting a "power encounter" as a means of persuading the followers of other religions—because it may easily turn into a "battle" between religions in terms of who represents the most "powerful" form of religion, hardly consonant with the Christian teaching focused on the suffering and crucified Messiah—I also

---

75. This general principle holds even when one takes into consideration the Buddhist tradition of the extraordinary compassion of Gautama towards not only all sentient beings but also all other beings and the fact that in *Mahayana* history, Gautama is known not only as the teacher of wisdom but also as magical healer and miracle worker, including passing through walls, flying, and walking on water. The Mahayna tradition also knows of self-sacrificial acts of healing and alleviation of other people's pain such as the story of Vimalakīrti. A virtuous *Boddhisattava*, he made himself sick and in the presence of Sākyamuni (Gautama) and his disciples explained that the reason why there is sickness is because of ignorance and thirst for existence. In order to help fellow men and women realize it, he tied his own healing to the healing of the others. The story can be found in *Vimalakīrti Nirdeśa Sutra* 5.6–7.

76. Again, I am informed enough of the complicated and complex state of affairs in the Buddhist capacity—or lack thereof—to respond to social concern both generally and in terms of the *Theravada* tradition. Any informed observer knows that while Western, particularly American-based (*Mahayana*) Buddhism, is anxious to highlight the capacity of that religion to elicit a proper response to social needs, it also is the case that in most *Theravada* lands (and in many *Mahayana* regions) there simply is not much record of acts of "redemptive suffering." Many personal conversations with (Thai *Theravada*) Buddhists, including monks and other informed mentors, have simply strengthened in my mind the conviction that in the mainline, that religious tradition is by and large focused on one's own capacities to facilitate liberation. (Ironically, a few blocks from my house in Temple City—a predominantly Asian populated area of the greater Los Angeles area—there is the headquarters of a non-profit [*Mahayana*] Buddhist organization of social concern!)

affirm wholeheartedly the biblical idea of healings as a way to affirm God's compassion, love, and care. In the highly "animistic" Buddhist environments, the presence of healings has the potential of alleviating men's and women's suffering in a way that may also open them to the gospel.

When engaging in the ministry of healing, whether in miraculous or more "natural" ways, Christian ministers also have to negotiate the dynamic wisely described in W. M. Menzies's Pentecostal "Reflections on Suffering":

> Prudence requires that we neither capitulate prematurely to the problem of human suffering, nor are we to demand of God that he intervene, as if he were a 'cosmic bellhop' governed solely by urgent calls from his children. A better option seems to be to engage in Apostolic ministry, to reach out to God on behalf of the suffering, and to intercede for human need until the Lord whispers to us that he has another purpose in hand. This, I believe, is an appropriate Pentecostal understanding of our responsibility regarding the engagement with human suffering.[77]

LAST WORDS: TASKS FOR FURTHER REFLECTION

This essay builds on the assumption that suffering—however diversely it is understood in these two traditions—may be a viable candidate for a proper interfaith and missionary encounter with (*Theravada*) Buddhism. Having outlined the two respective views of suffering and causes behind it, I have attempted to contrast the visions of liberation and suggest several tasks for Renewal Theology to facilitate a proper missionary response.

I have several topics for further reflection in my mind; some of them are such that intentionally I had to leave out to make the discussion more manageable; others are offshoots from this reflection. Let me just list them in no order of importance and thus issue an invitation for continuing mutual reflection grouped under two subheadings, first Christian and then Buddhist. From the Christian Renewal side I would be interested in knowing more about these issues, among others:

- What would it mean to Renewal Theology as a whole and the Pentecostal version thereof if the topic of suffering were included in the substructure of that tradition in a more integral and robust way? Would that move affect the stress on faith-based optimism and the mentality of overcoming?

---

77. Menzies, "Reflections on Suffering," 149.

- What might be some of the aspects of the wider Renewal Theology framework that were not present in the Pentecostal form of that tradition? Are there any significant areas or themes missing?

- What are some of the ways the Renewal/Pentecostal approach to an interfaith missionary encounter with Buddhism differ from that of other Christian traditions?

- Would the inclusion of the Liberationist task affect significantly this interfaith encounter in the framework of how suffering and liberation might play their roles?

- What are some of the lessons we (as outsiders to the Thai *Theravada* milieu) would learn from Thai Christians in terms of our own tackling with the problem of suffering?

From the Buddhist perspective, I wish to gain more insights into these topics, among others:

- How would reflection on and interfaith encounter take place in other Buddhist contexts, particularly with regard to *Mahayana* traditions? Would some of the themes be differently interpreted, particularly those having to do with the possibility of "redemptive suffering" and "healing suffering"?

- Consequently, would a Pure Land context move the two traditions, Christian and Buddhist, even closer to each other—if there is, as is often assumed, a notion of "grace" available in that version of Buddhism?

- Are there valuable lessons that *Theravada* Buddhists may teach Christians when it comes to suffering and liberation?

CHAPTER 14

Calvin and Religions

FIRST WORDS: CALVIN'S VIEW OF RELIGIONS IN HIS CONTEXT

THE UNCOMPROMISING STATEMENT FROM Luther's *Large Catechism* illustrates the generally shared mindset toward religions by Protestant Reformers: "For all outside of Christianity, whether heathen, Turks, Jews, or false Christians and hypocrites . . . abide in eternal wrath and damnation. For they have not the Lord Christ, and, besides, are not illumined and favored by any gifts of the Holy Ghost."[1] Luther's right hand, Philipp Melanchthon, similarly contended: "It is certainly true that outside the Church . . . there is no forgiveness of sins, grace, or salvation, as among the Turks, Jews, and heathen."[2] John Calvin in the mainline concurred with his Lutheran colleagues and with them shared serious doubts about his Reformed colleague Ulrich Zwingli's allegedly more open-minded attitude as presented in his *Exposition of the Christian Faith to the Christian King* (1531, Francis I of France). Luther accused Zwingli of becoming a "full-blown heathen." What really annoyed Luther was the teaching in that book that in heaven

> You will see in the same fellowship all holy, godly, wise, brave, honorable people, the redeemed and the Redeemer, Adam, Abel, Enoch, Noah, Abraham, Isaac, Jacob, Judah, Moses, Joshua . . .

---

1. Martin Luther, *Large Catechism*, Part First: Ten Commandments, First Commandment. For a brief consideration of the views of religions and the theology of religions among the Protestant Reformers, including Calvin, see Veli-Matti Kärkkäinen, *Introduction to the Theology of Religions*, 71–77, 85–87.

2. Melanchthon, *On Christian Doctrine*, 212.

also Isaiah and the Virgin Mother of God of whom he prophesied, David . . . and Paul; Hercules, Thesus, Socrates, Aristides, Antigonus, Numa, Camillus, the Catos and Scipios and all your ancestors who have departed in the faith . . .[3]

What is also similar between Luther and Calvin is that neither one of them had any meaningful experience of, or contact with, other living religions. As Samuel Zwemer puts it, "Calvin's knowledge of the pagan nations was taken from the Bible and classical literature. There is no proof that he had ever come in touch with the newly discovered world of Asian and African paganism."[4]

It goes without saying that Calvin, in common with other Protestant Reformers, did not present any systematic consideration of Christianity's relation to other religions. To Calvin's—and Luther's—credit we have to grant, however, that he "lived in the sixteenth century, not in the nineteenth. We cannot expect of him a world-view and world vision like that of William Carey. But he was not blind or deaf to the heathen world and its needs."[5]

Because of the dearth of any formal theology of religions in the teaching of the Geneva Reformer, the current attempt to reconstruct his views of religions needs to be acknowledged as just that, a reconstruction. The issue of the theology of religions is a question Calvin himself never had to face, and as such his "answer" is open to more than one interpretation. Let me state openly and clearly how I attempt to do this after-the-fact theological construal. First, I will assess as carefully as I can Calvin's views of religion or religiosity and how they may help us better reconstruct his judgment of living religions that he knew about. Second, I will attempt to discern main ideas in Calvin's understanding of the "knowledge of God the Creator," with regard to its universality and limits. Third, I will turn my attention to the uncompromising judgment of religions and gods in the Geneva Reformer's thought. Thereafter, fourth, I am ready to explain the necessity of the Mediator, the Christ. Fifth, before my conclusions, I will offer a brief case study by zooming in on the question of Calvin's assessment of Islam as a religion. While Calvin probably never had much contact with Muslims, his writings—especially those of an exegetical nature—make reference to Islam and its religious views. I will end my essay with reflections on Calvin's legacy to contemporary evangelicalism.

---

3. Martin Luther, *Word and Sacrament IV*, 290.

4. Zwemer, "Calvinism and the Missionary Enterprise," 208. Similarly, Slomp, "Calvin and the Turks," 138.

5. Zwemer, "Calvinism and the Missionary Enterprise," 207.

THE VALUE OF RELIGION(S)

While the most natural way of beginning the inquiry into Calvin's theology of religions might appear to be his well-known insistence on the existence of the sense of the divine among all men and women, having been created in the image of God, I will turn first to his view of religion(s) and religiosity, which in my assessment plays a foundational role in his embedded theology of religions. The famous opening lines of Calvin's *Institutes*[6] may have much to do with the reconstrual of his theology of religions in that the Reformer understands the knowledge of God and the knowledge of human beings to be mutually conditioned—of course, not equal since the former precedes and informs the latter—but nevertheless mutual:

> Our wisdom, in so far as it ought to be deemed and solid Wisdom, consists almost entirely of two parts: the knowledge of God and of ourselves. But as these are connected together by many ties, it is not easy to determine which of the two precedes and gives birth to the other. For, in the first place, no man can survey himself without forthwith turning his thoughts towards the God in whom he lives and moves; because it is perfectly obvious, that the endowments which we possess cannot possibly be from ourselves; nay, that our very being is nothing else than subsistence in God alone. (I.1.1)

The significance of this statement lies in the observation that if the knowledge of the human person is a constitutive part of the knowledge of God, then religiosity as part of human nature and life cannot be ignored. In other words, if Calvin claims, as he does, that in order to know God one must turn to the human being, then the role of religiosity as a constitutive part of humanity has to be taken into consideration when speaking of God.[7]

This indeed is something Calvin categorically states: "For, properly speaking, we cannot say that God is known where there is no religion or piety" (I.2.1).[8] Therefore, it is no wonder that religion is everywhere in

---

6. References to John Calvin, *Institutes of the Christian Religions*, will be given in the main text (e.g. I.1.1.).

7. Building on the long history of tradition, in contemporary theology the Roman Catholic K. Rahner and Protestant W. Pannenberg have argued forcefully for the theological significance of religiosity as constitutive of humanity.

8. Interpreting Calvin's use of the term "piety" along the lines of Schleiermacher's Liberal theology and his turn to the subjectivistic "feelings of absolute dependence" (as some historical theologians have done) is in my understanding a mistaken road. That discussion, however, falls outside my key concerns in this essay and thus I do not

the world because *sensus divinitatis* (the sense of the divine)—which for Calvin is a matter without dispute (I.3.1)—has been implanted so deeply in the hearts of men and women and manifests itself and is being mediated by religions.

> Certainly, if there is any quarter where it may be supposed that God is unknown, the most likely for such an instance to exist is among the dullest tribes farthest removed from civilisation. But, as a heathen tells us, there is no nation so barbarous, no race so brutish, as not to be imbued with the conviction that there is a God. Even those who, in other respects, seem to differ least from the lower animals, constantly retain some sense of religion; so thoroughly has this common conviction possessed the mind, so firmly is it stamped on the breasts of all men. Since, then, there never has been, from the very first, any quarter of the globe, any city, any household even, without religion, this amounts to a tacit confession, that a sense of Deity is inscribed on every heart. (I.3.1)

It seems to me the sense of the divine among religions and religious ideas is but part of the wonderful providence of the good God celebrated by Calvin in the opening lines of his *Institutes* when he speaks of "those blessings which unceasingly distil to us from heaven, [and] are like streams conducting us to the fountain" (I.1.1). Somewhat ironically, for Calvin even the existence of idolatry is a tribute to the necessity and power of religion as the mediator of the sense of the divine:

> Nay, even idolatry is ample evidence of this fact. For we know how reluctant man is to lower himself, in order to set other creatures above him. Therefore, when he chooses to worship wood and stone rather than be thought to have no God, it is evident how very strong this impression of a Deity must be; since it is more difficult to obliterate it from the mind of man, than to break down the feelings of his nature,—these certainly being broken down, when, in opposition to his natural haughtiness, he spontaneously humbles himself before the meanest object as an act of reverence to God. (I.3.1)

Commenting on Acts 8:27, which speaks of the Ethiopian Eunuch who came to worship in Jerusalem, Calvin grants that "the name of the true God was spread far abroad" and that there were seemingly "some worshippers in far countries," whether in the East or among Romans and beyond.

---

engage it.

There were places with "some smell of the knowledge of the true God," as he puts it.[9]

Lest some may draw from the existence of false ideas among religions the conclusion that therefore religions per se are evil, Calvin states the opposite: "It is most absurd, therefore, to maintain, as some do, that religion was devised by the cunning and craft of a few individuals, as a means of keeping the body of the people in due subjection, while there was nothing which those very individuals, while teaching others to worship God, less believed than the existence of a God" (I.3.2). So convinced is the Reformer of the role of the religions in God's world that he boldly argues this as a self-evident fact even among non-Christian writers such as Plato:

> For it is the very thing which Plato meant (in *Phœd. et Theact.*) when he taught, as he often does, that the chief good of the soul consists in resemblance to God; i.e., when, by means of knowing him, she is wholly transformed into him. Thus Gryllus, also, in Plutarch (*lib. guod bruta anim. ratione utantur*), reasons most skilfully, when he affirms that, if once religion is banished from the lives of men, they not only in no respect excel, but are, in many respects, much more wretched than the brutes, since, being exposed to so many forms of evil, they continually drag on a troubled and restless existence: that the only thing, therefore, which makes them superior is the worship of God, through which alone they aspire to immortality. (I.3.3)

This is, of course, not to say that therefore the sense of the divine is generally well cultivated and properly discerned; indeed, the contrary is the case.[10] Yet the corruption of the knowledge of God in religions does not make void the role of religions. The "seed of religion" is implanted in all human beings even in their corrupted nature.[11] Richard Plantinga accurately summarizes Calvin's assessment of religions:

---

9. Calvin, *Commentary on the Acts*, vol. 1, on Acts 8:27.

10. See, for example, *Institutes*, I.4.1., among many other similar passages (this one with reference to Rom 1:22): "But though experience testifies that a seed of religion is divinely sown in all, scarcely one in a hundred is found who cherishes it in his heart, and not one in whom it grows to maturity so far is it from yielding fruit in its season. Moreover, while some lose themselves in superstitious observances, and others, of set purpose, wickedly revolt from God, the result is that, in regard to the true knowledge of him, all are so degenerate, that in no part of the world can genuine godliness be found."

11. Calvin, *Commentary on the Gospel of John*, on 1:5: "The light which still dwells in corrupt nature consists chiefly of two parts; for, first, all men naturally possess some seed of religion; and, secondly, the distinction between good and evil is engraven on their consciences." (Hereafter all references to Calvin's commentaries will be from this edition.)

What are the implications of Calvin's position? First of all, religion is no arbitrary invention or construction; even those who deny God feel an inkling of divine fear or terror. Second, atheism is not really possible because the sense of divinity cannot be destroyed; it lies deep within us in the marrow of our bones. This is a doctrine we learn, Calvin says, not in school but in the womb.[12]

Having established the role of religion as the mediator of the sense of the Divine, which points to the potential of reaching to the saving knowledge of God that can only come from the self-revelation in Christ, let me now highlight the importance of Calvin's idea of the knowledge of God as the Creator.

THE KNOWLEDGE OF GOD THE CREATOR: ITS UNIVERSALITY AND LIMITS[13]

As routinely mentioned—following Calvin's way of titling the first two books of his *Institutes*—the knowledge of God has two facets, namely, the knowledge of God as Creator and as Redeemer. In this section, I will establish the presence of the former in Calvin's theology based on the creative and providential works of God. However one may theologically connect this with the traditional notions of "natural knowledge of God" and "general revelation,"[14] it is axiomatic for Calvin that some kind of "preliminary" knowledge of God exists, deeply embedded in the structure of the human being.

> My meaning is: we must be persuaded not only that as he once formed the world, so he sustains it by his boundless power, governs it by his wisdom, preserves it by his goodness, in particular, rules the human race with justice and Judgment, bears with them in mercy, shields them by his protection; but also that not a particle of light, or wisdom, or justice, or power, or rectitude,

12. Plantinga, "God So Loved the World," 284.

13. The question of the knowledge of God in Calvin's theology is a huge topic. I will not attempt any kind of comprehensive treatment of that. I solely focus on those aspects of the topic that have direct bearing on Calvin's theology of religions. The standard source is Dowey, *Knowledge of God in Calvin's Theology*.

14. As is well known among students of Calvin's theology, the distinction between the two types of the knowledge of God in his thinking does not follow neatly the standard theological divide between general and special revelation. The knowledge of God the Creator goes beyond the limits of the traditional understanding of general revelation. For a reliable discussion, see Dowey, *Knowledge of God*, especially ch. 2.

or genuine truth, will anywhere be found, which does not flow from him, and of which he is not the cause; in this way we must learn to expect and ask all things from him, and thankfully ascribe to him whatever we receive. (I.2.1)[15]

So evident is this knowledge of God that Calvin agrees with some philosophers of old who had called the human person "a *microcosm (miniature world)* . . . [and] the human race . . . a bright mirror of the Creator's works." Indeed, adds Calvin, "infants hanging on their mothers' breasts have tongues eloquent enough to proclaim his glory without the aid of other orators" (I.5.3). Commenting on Acts 14:17, Calvin even goes so far as to say that "God hath, indeed, revealed himself to all mankind by his word since [from] the beginning."[16] While this kind of general knowledge of God does not suffice for salvific knowledge of God per se, it surely is the fountain of "piety, out of which religion springs." Piety for Calvin is nothing less than "that union of reverence and love to God which the knowledge of his benefits inspires" (I.2.1).

Parallel to his argument concerning religions, Calvin ironically argues for the certainty of the general knowledge of God on the basis of the miserable condition of humanity: "For as there exists in man something like a world of misery, and ever since we were stript of the divine attire our naked shame discloses an immense series of disgraceful properties[,] every man, being stung by the consciousness of his own unhappiness, in this way necessarily obtains at least some knowledge of God" (I.1.1).

In fairness to Calvin, we have to set the record straight: having first established the value of religions as the mediators of the sense of the divine and the existence of a general knowledge of God on the basis of the fact that God is the Creator and Preserver of the world, we may not imagine that that is enough for humanity to know about God. It is one thing for Calvin to establish firmly the universal knowledge of God the Creator and another thing to ascertain the proper usage of that kind of knowledge of God. Here Calvin gives an uncompromising judgment:

---

15. Similarly, for example, *Institutes*, I.5.1: "Since the perfection of blessedness consists in the knowledge of God, he has been pleased, in order that none might be excluded from the means of obtaining felicity, not only to deposit in our minds that seed of religion of which we have already spoken, but so to manifest his perfections in the whole structure of the universe, and daily place himself in our view, that we cannot open our eyes without being compelled to behold him. His essence, indeed, is incomprehensible, utterly transcending all human thought; but on each of his works his glory is engraven in characters so bright, so distinct, and so illustrious, that none, however dull and illiterate, can plead ignorance as their excuse."

16. Calvin, *Commentary on the Acts*, vol. 2, on 14:17.

> Those, therefore, who, in considering this question, propose to inquire what the essence of God is, only delude us with frigid speculations,—it being much more our interest to know what kind of being God is, and what things are agreeable to his nature. For, of what use is it to join Epicures in acknowledging some God who has cast off the care of the world, and only delights himself in ease? What avails it, in short, to know a God with whom we have nothing to do? The effect of our knowledge rather ought to be, *first*, to teach us reverence and fear; and, *secondly*, to induce us, under its guidance and teaching, to ask every good thing from him, and, when it is received, ascribe it to him. For how can the idea of God enter your mind without instantly giving rise to the thought, that since you are his workmanship, you are bound, by the very law of creation, to submit to his authority? (I.2.2)

A similar kind of uncompromising statement can be found in the beginning of the discussion on the need for Scripture, special revelation, to complement and correct what is lacking in the knowledge of God as Creator:

> Therefore, though the effulgence which is presented to every eye, both in the heavens and on the earth, leaves the ingratitude of man without excuse, since God, in order to bring the whole human race under the same condemnation, holds forth to all, without exception, a mirror of his Deity in his works, another and better help must be given to guide us properly to God as a Creator. (I.6.1)

A number of other passages can be easily found to the same effect.[17]

To underline his point, Calvin makes a distinction between the mere "knowing" of God and "fearing" God. Commenting on Josh 4:24, he says that the difference between the Israelites and the other nations was that "the nations may know [Yahweh] but that Israel alone may 'fear thy God.'" Only this "special knowledge," as Calvin puts it, makes the difference.[18] At the same time—while judging quite harshly the inadequacy of the general knowledge of God among the pagans—Calvin is pastorally mindful of the need of evangelists to try to find a common point between the audience and the "full gospel" presentation. He finds a biblical precedent in Paul's and Barnabas' missionary experience in Lystra as recorded in Acts 14.

> There is no express mention made indeed of the Word, because they spake to the Gentiles . . . We know that the order of teaching

---

17. See further the rest of *Institutes*, I.6.1; and also I.4.2; I.5.1; I.5.12–15.
18. Calvin, *Commentary on Joshua*, on 4:24.

doth require that we begin with things which are better known. Seeing that Paul and Barnabas spake to the Gentiles, they should have in vain essayed to bring them unto Christ. Therefore, it was expedient for them to begin with some other point, which was not so far separate from common sense, [perception,] that after that was confessed they might afterward pass over unto Christ. The minds of the men of Lystra were possessed with that error, that there be more gods than one. Paul and Barnabas show, on the contrary, that there is but one Creator of the world.[19]

THE JUDGMENT ON RELIGIONS AND THEIR GODS

Since the purpose of this essay is to give a preliminary assessment of Calvin's implicit and unthematic theology of religions, it will do no good to mount evidence on one side of the issue, whether a negative or positive attitude to other religions, but rather it is preferable to make an effort to take stock of the whole evidence. If the acknowledgment of the value of religion as the mediator of the knowledge of God, the universality of the *sensus divinitatis*, as well as the knowledge of God as the Creator—albeit truncated and limited—embedded in the structure of the human being having been created in the image of God and provided for by the same Creator, all point to a more tolerant and accepting spirit with regard to religions, there are also several key orientations in Calvin's theology that bespeak judgment on religions. The first has to do with what Calvin saw as the mainstream biblical way, namely, an uncompromising judgment of the gods of the nations vis-à-vis the acknowledgment of and humble submission to the one and only true God. The following lengthier summary statement offers a testimony to this judgment.

> First, then, let the reader observe that the Scripture, in order to direct us to the true God, distinctly excludes and rejects all the gods of the heathen, because religion was universally adulterated in almost every age. It is true, indeed, that the name of one God was everywhere known and celebrated. For those who worshipped a multitude of gods, whenever they spoke the genuine language of nature, simply used the name god, as if they had thought one god sufficient. And this is shrewdly noticed by Justin Martyr, who, to the same effect, wrote a treatise, entitled, *On the Monarchy of God*, in which he shows, by a great variety of

---

19. Calvin, *Commentary on the Acts*, vol. 2, on 14:15. A similar strategy was followed by Paul in his speech in Athens.

evidence, that the unity of God is engraven on the hearts of all. Tertullian also proves the same thing from the common forms of speech. But as all, without exception, have in the vanity of their minds rushed or been dragged into lying fictions, these impressions, as to the unity of God, whatever they may have naturally been, have had no further effect than to render men inexcusable. The wisest plainly discover the vague wanderings of their minds when they express a wish for any kind of Deity, and thus offer up their prayers to unknown gods. And then, in imagining a manifold nature in God, though their ideas concerning Jupiter, Mercury, Venus, Minerva, and others, were not so absurd as those of the rude vulgar, they were by no means free from the delusions of the devil. We have elsewhere observed, that however subtle the evasions devised by philosophers, they cannot do away with the charge of rebellion, in that all of them have corrupted the truth of God. For this reason, Habakkuk (2:20), after condemning all idols, orders men to seek God in his temple, that the faithful may acknowledge none but Him, who has manifested himself in his word. (I.10.3)

Calvin states categorically that the Bible's "exclusive definition . . . annihilates every deity" created by men and women for their own purposes whether that god be the sun worshiped by the Persians or the stars venerated by many nations or even the wisdom loved by the Greeks (I.11.1).[20] The biblical God is a jealous God who does not tolerate other deities (I.12.1). What makes the idol an idol is that it is a human invention rather than something appointed by God.[21]

THE NECESSITY OF THE MEDIATOR

Along with judgment of religions and their gods, Calvin also balances his otherwise affirmative standpoint toward religiosity by arguing forcefully for the need of Christ, the Mediator of true knowledge of God and salvation.

---

20. *Institutes*, I.11.2–3 lists a number of familiar biblical passages to support this claim. Commenting on Josh 2:11, Calvin commends to the reader Rahab's decisive shift from serving idols to serving the God of the Bible: "For it is perfectly clear that when heaven and earth are declared subject to the God of Israel, there is a repudiation of all the pagan fictions by which the majesty, and power, and glory of God are portioned out among different deities." Calvin, *Commentary on Joshua*, on 2:11. In *Institutes*, I.11.8. Calvin offers interesting speculations into the origins of idols, for example, entertaining the possibility of relation to the custom of honoring the dead among many nations.

21. Calvin, *Commentary on the Acts*, vol. 1, on 7:41.

> The whole human race having been undone in the person of Adam ... is so far from availing us, that it rather turns to our greater disgrace, until God, who does not acknowledge man when defiled and corrupted by sin as his own work, appears as a Redeemer in the person of his only begotten Son. Since our fall from life unto death, all that knowledge of God the Creator ... would be useless, were it not followed up by faith, holding forth God to us as a Father in Christ ... Wherefore, we must conclude with Paul, "After that in the wisdom of God the world by wisdom knew not God, it pleased God by the foolishness of preaching to save them that believe," (1 Cor. 1:21) ... Therefore, although the preaching of the cross is not in accordance with human wisdom, we must, however, humbly embrace it if we would return to God our Maker, from whom we are estranged, that he may again become our Father. It is certain that after the fall of our first parent, no knowledge of God without a Mediator was effectual to salvation. Christ speaks not of his own age merely, but embraces all ages, when he says "This is life eternal that they might know thee the only true God, and Jesus Christ, whom thou hast sent," (John 17:3). (II.6.1)

Even the chosen people of God in the Old Testament could not be saved without the Mediator (II.6.2), and, therefore, the ultimate purpose of prophecies in the old covenant is to turn the eyes of the Jews to Christ (II.6.4). Whether Jews or gentiles, the way of salvation is the same,

> For though in old time there were many who boasted that they worshipped the Supreme Deity, the Maker of heaven and earth, yet as they had no Mediator, it was impossible for them truly to enjoy the mercy of God, so as to feel persuaded that he was their Father. Not holding the head, that is, Christ, their knowledge of God was evanescent; and hence they at length fell away to gross and foul superstitions betraying their ignorance, just as the Turks in the present day, who, though proclaiming, with full throat, that the Creator of heaven and earth is their God, yet by their rejection of Christ, substitute an idol in his place. (II.6.4)

Calvin's view of double predestination[22] undoubtedly plays into his theology of religions. According to the Catholic Francis Sullivan:

> It is clear that for Calvin the mere fact that the newly discovered peoples had not, until now, had a chance to hear the gospel preached is a manifest sign that all their ancestors were among

---

22. For a definition of double predestination, see III.21.5.

the reprobate, for if God had willed their salvation, he would have made it possible for them to come to the knowledge of the truth, and thus to faith in Christ, without which there was no possibility of their salvation. Even now, when they have a chance to hear the gospel, it is God's intention, with regard to those whom he has predestined to damnation, that it should blind them and make them all the more guilty.[23]

Calvin did not acknowledge the possibility of the second chance, as his comments on the disputed passage of 1 Pet 3:19 reveal: "Moreover, the strange notion of those who think that unbelievers as to the coming of Christ, were after his death freed from their sin, needs no long refutation; for it is an indubitable doctrine of Scripture, that we obtain not salvation in Christ except by faith; then there is no hope left for those who continue to death unbelieving."[24]

At the same time, Calvin was not totally dogmatic about how much knowledge of Christ the person needs to be saved. Commenting on Acts 10:5, he grants that Cornelius did not seem to have any knowledge of the Savior, yet as a recipient of the gifts of the Spirit, this gentile can be compared to the Old Testament saints who were exercising faith in Christ whom they did not yet know.[25]

In order to make my discussion more focused, I will next offer a brief consideration of Calvin's views of a particular religion, Islam. While both he and Luther probably had no firsthand contact with Muslims, he offered scattered remarks on that religion.

CALVIN ON ISLAM

While there are several studies on Luther's views of Muslims[26]—whom he most often calls, similarly to Calvin, the "Turks"—there is little research on Calvin in this respect.[27] Both Calvin and Luther often lump Muslims together with the "Papists" (Catholics of the time), and sometimes even with

---

23. Sullivan, *Salvation Outside the Church*, 78.
24. John Calvin, *Commentaries on Catholic Epistles*, on 1 Pet 3:19.
25. Calvin, *Commentary on the Acts*, vol. 1, on 10:5.
26. For a brief overview, see Grislis, "Luther and the Turks," 275–91.
27. The main critical study is that offered by Slomp, "Calvin and the Turks," 126–42. A massive study (which unfortunately is not accessible to most English-speaking readers) about the attitudes of the Reformers of Zurich is Victor Segesvary, *L'Islam et la Réforme*.

others who in their outlook were heretical, such as the Anabaptists.[28] It is thus not often easy to make a distinction between Calvin's more general pejorative remarks on various kinds of opponents and Muslims in particular.

As mentioned above, Calvin most probably had very little, if any, firsthand contact with Muslims. His writings do not contain any direct citations from the Qur'an.[29] However, historically, his times were of course influenced by the Turkish Empire. The Turkish emperor Sulayman I, sometimes called "The Magnificent," was Calvin's contemporary. Calvin's keen interest in political developments (to which there is also testimony in his introductory letter to the King of France in the *Institutes*), made him well aware of the affairs of the Muslim world. From Calvin's "footnote" remarks on Daniel 3:21, it has been gleaned that he might have met members of the Turkish delegation that disembarked in Marseilles in 1534 on the way to meet the king.[30]

There is no doubt that Calvin was concerned about the Turks' military and religious power over Europe. In his commentary on Jeremiah 13:21, which speaks of the threat of Assyrians and Babylonians, Calvin makes this pointed remark,

> The case was similar to that of the Turks at this day, were they to pass over to these parts and exercise their authority; for it might be asked the French kings and their counsellors, "Whose fault it is that the Turks come to us so easily? It is because ye have prepared for them the way by sea, because ye have bribed them, and your ports have been opened to them; and yet they have wilfully exercised the greatest cruelty towards your subjects. All these things have proceeded from yourselves; ye are therefore the authors of all these evils."[31]

28. In some cases, even Jews are included: "This delusion of Satan is equally common among Papists, Turks, Jews, and other nations" (Calvin, *Commentary on Psalms*, vol. 1, on 32:1).

29. Slomp, "Calvin and the Turks," 135. Slomp lists three references to the term "Qur'an" (for which Calvin uses the French translation "Alcuran") in Calvin's writings. One example is in his commentary on John 16:14 to be cited below; the other two are in the sermons on Job 33 and 2 Tim 1:6-8.

30. So Slomp, "Calvin and the Turks," 127. Dan 3:21 (RSV) speaks of men who "were bound in their mantles, their tunics, their hats and their other garments." Calvin adds this remark: "We know that the Orientals then wore turbans as they do now, for they wrap up the head; and though we do not see many of them, yet we know the Turkish dress; then the general name is added" (*Commentary on Daniel*, vol. 1, on 3:21).

31. Calvin, *Commentary on Jeremiah-Lamentations*, vol. 2, on Jer 13:21. It is instructive to note that in his *Commentary on Isaiah* (vol. 3), on 36:20 Calvin surmises that God has indeed raised "the Turk ... haughtily against us," and that whatever prosperity there is among them, that is also not something the Turks could have produced

Similarly, Calvin was greatly distressed by the threat of Muslim forces to the safety of the church: "My readers now understand, that all the sects by which the Church has been lessened from the beginning, have been so many streams of revolt which began to draw away the water from the right course, but that the sect of Mahomet was like a violent bursting forth of water, that took away about the half of the Church by its violence."[32]

Calvin's has harsh comments on the Muslim faith concerning their rejection of and replacement of Christ for idols (II.6.4).[33] His exposition of the Paraclete passage of John 14:25 lumps together Mohammed, the Pope, Anabaptists, and Libertines and condemns their interpretations of "new revelations" after the coming of Christ and the Holy Spirit.[34] In his commentary on Acts 22:14, he even accuses Muslims (and Papists!) of inventing "a new God."[35] John 16:14 names both Mohammed and the pope as Anti-Christ.[36] In the same context, Calvin juxtaposes Islam and Christianity, one being built on the foundation of the Qur'an, the other on the Word of God.[37]

In the light of these and similar fears of Islamic threat, and judgments of Islamic faith by Calvin, it is interesting that commonalities between the two religions have been suggested. According to Zwemer:

---

on their own. Calvin sees here a parallel between what happened in Israelite history when the Lord raised opponents to the People of God and his own times with regard to the church. Similarly to biblical times, the same Lord is also going to destroy those whom he has used against his own people.

32. Calvin, *Commentaries on the Philippians, Colossians and Thessalonians*, on 2 Thess 2:3.

33. Similarly, for example, Calvin, *Catholic Epistles*, on 1 Pet 1:3: "Hence they who form their ideas of God in his naked majesty apart from Christ, have an idol instead of the true God, as the case is with the Jews and the Turks." So also his comments on 1 Pet 1:21. Yet another example can be found in Calvin, *Catholic Epistles*, on 1 John 2:22: "It hence follows, that Turks, Jews, and such as are like them, have a mere idol and not the true God. For by whatever titles they may honor the God whom they worship, still, as they reject him without whom they cannot come to God, and in whom God has really manifested himself to us, what have they but some creature or fiction of their own?"

34. Calvin, *Commentary on the Gospel of John*, vol. 2, on 14:25.

35. Calvin, *Commentary on the Acts*, vol. 2, on 22:14. Interestingly enough, he uses in this passage the term Muhametistae instead of Turks.

36. Calvin, *Commentary on the Gospel of John*, vol. 2, on 16:14.

37. Calvin, *Commentary on the Gospel of John*, vol. 2, on 16:14: "Mahomet asserts that, without his Alcoran, men always remain children. Thus, by a false pretense of the Spirit, the world was bewitched to depart from the simple purity of Christ; for, as soon as the Spirit is separated from the word of Christ, the door is open to all kinds of delusions and impostures. A similar method of deceiving has been attempted, in the present age, by many fanatics. The written doctrine appeared to them to be literal, and, therefore, they chose to contrive a new theology that would consist of revelations."

> Islam indeed ... is the Calvinism of the Orient. It, too, was a call to acknowledge the sovereignty of God's will. 'There is no god but Allah.' ... Calvinism and Islam had much in common. Both are opposed to compromise and all half-measures. Both were a trumpet-call in hard times for hard men, for intellects that could pierce to the roots of things where truth and lies part company. Intolerance is sometimes a virtue. The very essence and life of all great religious movements is the sense of authority; of an external, supernatural framework or pattern to which all must be made comfortable.[38]

Zwemer is not alone in his opinion. Jan Slomp likewise argues that there are similarities between the teachings of Calvinism and the Qur'anic message, similarities such as the teaching on the sovereignty and glory of God. Too bad, Slomp laments, that Calvin never took time to study the Qur'an, which was available to him through his friend Oporinus.[39] What about evangelizing Muslims? "Were a Turk to offer himself for baptism, we would not at once perform the rite without receiving a confession which was satisfactory to the Church" (IV.16.24).

LAST WORDS: CALVIN'S LEGACY AND PROSPECTS

There is a tendency in contemporary reflection on the theology of religions to try to find positive and affirming elements in every theologian's and theological movement's heritage. Often this leads to a somewhat uncritical and unbalanced reading of the evidence in favor of a more tolerant attitude toward other religions. While this kind of "twisting the evidence" may need to be tolerated for the time being as a way of balancing the overly negative assessments of the past, in a longer perspective it hardly is able to redeem its promises.

Our discussion has revealed that on religions and religiosity, there are two kinds of material in Calvin's writings. On the one hand, he affirms the significance and necessity of religion(s) as the mediator of the sense of the divine (which may or may not lead to the true knowledge and fear of God). This is a path that contemporary evangelicals would do well to follow.[40] On the other hand, religions as they now appear, apart from the revelation of

---

38. Zwemer, "Calvinism and the Missionary Enterprise," 212–13.

39. Slomp, "Calvin and the Turks," 138.

40. For an overview and assessment of the state of evangelical reflections on religions and the theology of religions, see Kärkkäinen, "Evangelical Theology and the Religions," 199–212.

God, have distorted the knowledge of God and are under God's judgment.[41] Thus, there is a need for divine intervention. Contemporary evangelicalism by and large agrees.[42]

Bluntly put: neither Calvin nor Luther—nor even the somewhat more open-minded Zwingli—ever endorsed other religions as in any way salvific, or their scriptures as divine revelations. In keeping with the mindset of the times, as well as the tradition of the church, other religions were held to be vastly inferior to the Christian faith and by any account were incapable of mediating saving knowledge of God. Furthermore, Calvin's remarks about persons and beliefs in other religions (in his case, remarks limited to the Muslim faith) were often pejorative and harsh—but no different from the opinions of other Reformers.

It is understandable, therefore, that Calvin never saw a need to construct any kind of biblical or systematic theology of religions. He commented on other religions and their relation to Christianity only occasionally and without any conscious effort to put them in a perspective. That said, it is significant that with hindsight one can see indications of an embedded, unthematic contribution to what we nowadays call the theology of religions. While Calvin did not develop these ideas with the theology of religions in mind, their potential should be investigated and reflected upon by contemporary evangelicals. Let me mention the most important tasks in this regard, gleaning from and summarizing the main insights from Calvin:

1. What is an evangelical assessment of the value of religions as mediators of the knowledge of God?[43]

2. What is an evangelical assessment of the value and limits of the existence of the sense of the divine in the human being? As this has everything to do with theological anthropology, that should occupy the minds of contemporary evangelicals.

3. How could evangelicals think of the role of the universal nature of the knowledge of God as Creator and Provider and of its relation to the knowledge of God as Savior? As is well known, evangelical theology

---

41. One of the few reflections on the pros and cons among religions from a theological perspective among evangelicals is Pinnock, *Wideness in God's Mercy*, chs. 3 and 4 respectively.

42. For a representative discussion, see Geivett and Phillips, "Particularist View," 211–45, 259–70.

43. Some contemporary evangelicals have engaged living religions and the religiosity of the world and offered theological reflections based on those observations: McDermott, *Can Evangelicals Learn from World Religions?*; Corduan, *Tapestry of Faiths*; Tennent, *Christianity at the Religious Roundtable*.

of religions to date has majored on the question of the possibility of salvation and left the theological reflection on the knowledge of God as Creator to others.

PART FIVE

Interdisciplinary Theology

CHAPTER 15

Multidimensional Monism
A Constructive Theological Proposal for the Nature of Human Nature

FIRST WORDS

LET ME STATE AS a way of introduction something which certainly is obvious but still is worth mentioning: there is currently a bewildering confusion about the nature of human nature not only among philosophers of mind and (those) neuroscientists (who think philosophically!) but also among Christian philosophers and theologians. On the one hand, common intuitions, universal religious teachings, and mainstream of classical philosophy envision some kind of dualistic[1] account of humanity in which an important distinction is made between the physical and mental. On the other hand, among neuroscientists, philosophers of mind, and large number of other scientists a monist-physicalist account has gained the upper hand.

When it comes to my own academic field, systematic (or constructive or doctrinal) theology, a couple of general observations are noteworthy. First, beginning from the mid-twentieth century or so, a definite shift has taken place away from traditional dualism towards a highly integrated, mutually conditioned-account of the human person as a physical-mental totality. Second, unlike some Christian philosophers and biblical scholars, systematicians, however, have not yet engaged in any significant measure the dynamic interdisciplinary conversation among philosophers of mind, neuroscientists, and others. Indeed, at the moment of this writing I cannot

1. As is rightly noticed, a concept such as dualism has to be handled with great care and hence we should rather speak of dualisms (in plural).

think one single major presentation of Christian doctrine of humanity written by a systematician which would contain a truly interdisciplinary dialogue.[2] What is most astonishing to me is the total omission of this kind of engagement in the recent massive two-volume theological anthropology by David Kelsey of Yale; in a theological discussion of more than one thousand pages, most everything else is investigated but not the contributions of philosophy of mind and brain sciences![3]

So, it is about time to have systematic-constructive theologians to provide accounts of the nature of human nature. The plan of this essay is the following: I will first explain what kinds of underlying intuitions and assumptions lie behind my constructive proposal. Thereafter, I will engage in some detail the major contender to dualism(s) and physicalist monism in contemporary philosophy and theology, namely nonreductive physicalism. Although my own proposal owes to its insights, I also find it wanting in the final analysis. The rest of the essay following these two topics will be devoted to explaining and defending the program of "multidimensional monism."

UNDERLYING ASSUMPTIONS AND CONVICTIONS

The constructive theological proposal of human nature developed and defended in this essay is funded by number of convictions which I briefly mention here but do not have space to argue in much detail.[4]

First, I take it for granted that any contemporary theological account of human nature should acknowledge and endorse the current common knowledge of the integral connection between brain events and mental life. Intelligence, emotions, sociality, as well as behavioral patterns such as criminality or altruism can be linked very tightly to the neuronal basis. Notwithstanding complicated philosophical interpretations of neuroscientific results, there is no denying the tight link between the functioning of the

---

2. This is of course not to deny the contributions of some systematicians, say Michael Welker of Heidelberg University, Germany and Niels Henrik Gregersen of Copenhagen University, Denmark who have discussed human nature in a widely interdisciplinary manner. What I am saying is that these contributions have not yet found their way to "normal" systematic theological presentations. In this regard, it is interesting that the two leading international constructive theologians who have published theological "summas," namely Wolfhart Pannenberg and Jürgen Moltmann have completely missed the interdisciplinary conversation about human nature although both of them for decades have interacted in the doctrine of creation with natural sciences from cosmology to physics to quantum theory to evolutionary biology.

3. Kelsey, *Eccentric Existence*.

4. Detailed argumentation can be found in Kärkkäinen, *Creation and Humanity*, chs. 12 and 13 particularly.

brain and human behavior. Perhaps as a surprise to many comes the linkage between observed neural activity and exercise of spiritual and religious activities.[5]

Second, I claim that while the traditional body-soul dualism finds support in biblical terminology and theological tradition, it has been a great gain for theology to come to a new appreciation of the tight mutual relationship between the physical and mental. As Pannenberg notes, in light of current knowledge "we know conscious and self-conscious life only as bodily life . . . bodily functions condition all psychological experience. This is true even of self-consciousness."[6] I do not believe that this shift towards a unified, monistic, and holistic view is a result of an accommodation of theology into the demands of secular philosophy and sciences but rather the move is in alignment with early theological intuitions.

Important early patristic thinkers defended the psychosomatic unity even when they of course continued distinguishing between body and soul (spirit). It can be argued that the rise in patristic and later Christian theology of body-soul–dualism happened because theology capitulated before secular philosophy. Pannenberg goes so far as to claim that "[t]his process illustrates the acceptance by early Christian thinking of ideas that the Hellenistic culture of the age took for granted" and hence "is not an interpretation that has any essential place in Christian anthropology."[7] Consider that Pannenberg himself is not a monist or physicalist but rather represents an integral holistic property-dualist type of view. (For fairness' sake, it has to be added that even with the accommodation, early theologians also critiqued some key aspects of pagan anthropology, including the immortality and preexistence of soul, as well as its divinity.)

Third, I believe that even the mainstream biblical vision of human nature is not necessarily dualistic but advocates a holistic and integral view in which physicality plays a bigger role than tradition has claimed. By the

---

5. Groundbreaking interdisciplinary work is being done at the Institute for the Bio-Cultural Study of Religion founded by the neuroscientist Patrick McNamara and philosopher of religion Wesley J. Wildman; see the website for research and resources: http://www.ibcsr.org/. A massive collection of essays on evolutionary and neurological bases of religion, including neurotheology, as well as related issues, is the three-volume McNamara, *Where God and Science Meet*. For an insightful critique of neuro-theology and neurology of religion, see Brown, "The Brain, Religion, and Baseball: Comments on the Potential for a Neurology of Religious Experience," in McNamara, *Where God and Science Meet*, 2:229–44.

6. Pannenberg, *Systematic Theology*, 2:181–82 (hereafter, *ST*); see also Green, *Body, Soul, and Human Life*, 16.

7. Pannenberg, *ST* 2:182; for "The Triumph of Dualism" in early theology, see Martin and Barresi, *Rise and Fall of Soul and Self*, 61–74.

middle of the twentieth century, or even before, both the Old Testament and New Testament scholars had rediscovered the deeply holistic and integral, account of humanity in the biblical canon.[8] Understandably this shift towards (more) monistic conception was resisted by Conservatives,[9] if not for other reasons then because it was first advocated by "Liberals" (particularly R. Bultmann).

Even Paul's view of human nature, once it had been saved of the overly Hellenistic with the acknowledgment of deep Hebrew influences, helped rediscover the category of the physical.[10] As a result, "a number of more recent, extensive studies have led to verdicts similarly supportive of Paul's essential wholism" and "emphasis on embodied life in this world and the next, while combating body-soul dualism."[11] The philosopher Nancey Murphy summarizes accurately the situation in the biblical scholarship on human nature:

> A survey of the literature of theology and biblical studies throughout the twentieth century, then, shows a gradual displacement of a dualistic account of the person, with its correlative emphasis on the afterlife conceived in terms of the immortality of the soul. First, there was the recognition of the holistic character of biblical conceptions of the person, often while still presupposing temporarily separable "parts." Later there developed a holistic *but also physicalist* account of the person, combined with an emphasis on bodily resurrection.[12]

To that summary statement, I would like to add an important observation from the pen of the prominent British biblical scholar James D.G. Dunn: "[W]hile Greek thought tended to regard the human being as made up of distinct parts, Hebraic thought saw the human more as a whole person existing on different dimensions. As we might say, it was more characteristically

---

8. Importantly, the Hebrew term *nephes* refers to the whole person rather than to mere "soul." The term occurs no less than about 800 times in the OT and has as its etymology the meaning of "throat" or "gullet"; hence, they denote human need (as a thirsty throat) and physicality; see further, Green, *Body, Soul, and Human Life*, 57. That said, the monist orientation of the OT does not rule out duality or plurality in its presentation of the human being, as even a casual reader notes.

9. An influential advocate of dualism has been the biblical study by the philosopher, John Cooper in *Body, Soul, and Life Everlasting*, followed by other philosopher-theologians and even some conservative biblical scholars.

10. See Robinson, *Body*, 11.

11. Green, *Body, Soul, and Human Life*, 7–8.

12. Murphy, *Bodies and Souls, or Spirited Bodies?*, 10.

Greek to conceive of the human person 'partitively,' whereas it was more characteristically Hebrew to conceive of the human person 'aspectively.'"[13]

Fourth, it is clear to me that the neither can the mental be reduced to the physical base nor can the causal power of the mental on physical be denied. Briefly put: I am against both reductionism and causal closure. It is absolutely fundamental to our concept of actions performed intentionally (as opposed to involuntarily) to assume mental causation.[14] A crucial issue for theologians is to defeat what the British neuropsychologist Donald McKay used to call "nothing-buttery,"[15] namely, the identity theory according to which all mental phenomena, whether intellectual, emotional, or moral, are but brain/neural states. Along with identity-theory, I also reject other related theories of the mind-body–relationship which eliminate mental causation, including psychophysical parallelism and epiphenomenalism.

Fifth, I believe that while behind traditional dualism(s) there are absolutely important intuitions and convictions which no authentic Christian theology cannot afford to leave behind, those intuitions can be maintained in certain type of monistic views as well. The key intuitions I have in mind include the following: that there is "more" to human life than just the material;[16] that there is something "more" than merely material processes that explain the uniqueness and dignity of human life; that affirming morality and an ethical base calls for "more" than material explanation;[17] and that there is hope for life eternal and therefore, even at the moment of my personal death, I am not forgotten by God.

An appealing route to some prominent Christian philosophers, psychologists, and neuroscientists to negotiate between traditional dualism(s) and current move towards physicalist monism is nonreductive physicalism. Would that be the way to go in light of the underlying convictions mentioned above? Let us take a closer look at nonreductive physicalism before proceeding onto the constructive proposal.

---

13. Dunn, *Theology of Paul the Apostle*, 54 quoted in Murphy, *Bodies and Souls*, 21.

14. My claim is not to deny that at the moment the causal interaction between the bodily and mental is one of the unresolved problems. We simply don't know currently as to "how reasons—our beliefs, desires, purposes, and plans—operate in a world of causes, and to exhibit the role of reasons in the *causal* explanation of human behavior." Dretske, *Explaining Behavior*, x.

15. MacKay, *Clock Work Image*, 21. See the now-classic argument in Armstrong, *A Materialist Theory of Mind* for the view that mental states are nothing but brain states.

16. Ward, *More Than Matter?*

17. E.g., Rickabaugh, "Responding to NT Wright's Rejection of the Soul"; so also Moreland and Rae, *Body and Soul*.

NONREDUCTIVE PHYSICALISM: PROMISES AND LIABILITIES

The Agenda of Nonreductive Physicalism

Whereas among neuroscientists, the reductionist identity theory still seems to be the prominent view;[18] in Anglo-American philosophy of mind, nonreductive physicalism/materialism in its various versions seems to hold the dominant position.[19] The minimalist description of nonreductive physicalism simply is that in its attack on reductionism it considers the mental as an emergent novel property (or capacity or event) that "supervenes," that is, is dependent on the subvenient base, but that cannot be reduced to its base.[20]

How to defeat reductionism[21] is obviously the main agenda of nonreductive physicalists. Terminologically, an important distinction has to be made between "methodological reductionism," that is, "a research strategy of analyzing the thing to be studied into its parts" and "causal reductionism," "the view that the behavior of the parts of a system . . . is determinative of the behavior of all higher-level entities (also called "parts on whole" and "bottom up"), as well as "ontological reductionism," which claims that "higher-level entities are 'nothing but the sum of their parts.'" The last two are of course related, but regarding the latter, one needs to make yet another distinction. Whereas ontological reductionism claims that "as one goes up the hierarchy of levels, no new kinds of metaphysical 'ingredients' need to be added to produce higher-level entities from lower," for "reductive materialism," the higher-level processes are not only the function of the lower but they are not even "real." That is accurately called "reductive materialism." That is the target of all nonreductivists.

A key resource for nonreductive physicalism is the use of the theory of emergence.[22] Emergence is the view that new structures, capacities, and processes will come to existence, that these cannot be reduced to the

---

18. For an important current defense of type identity, see Gozzano and Hill, *New Perspectives on Type Identity*.

19. Bickle, "Multiple Realizability."

20. Many other more-or-less synonymous nomenclatures are used, including "[pluralistic] emergent monism," "constitutional monism," "open-system emergence" or "deep physicalism," "dual aspect monism," and "emergent dualism.") Most (but not all) of them are monist in a particular way, namely, *physically/materialistically* (while not denying the reality of the mental, including, in most cases, even religiosity).

21. An important current statement and defense of reductionism is Kim, *Physicalism, or Something Near Enough*, ch. 4.

22. For a now classic essay, see Popper, "Natural Selection and the Emergence of Mind," 339–55.

lower level, and that they can exercise a causal influence downwards. This means that the mental, most prominently, consciousness, is derived from the biological/physical basis but is not to be reduced to it and that it may have causal influence on the subvenient base.[23] The concept of "emergence," however, is a complicated matter. As a result, not any form of supervenience necessarily helps defeat the identity theory, as there are also reductionist interpretations thereof.[24] The one needed for an antireductionist program is one with the claim that there are a number of ways a particular supervenient property may be instantiated and that it is context specific (the principle of multiple realizability[25]). In other words, it has to be the case that mental properties (against the co-variation thesis) could change without the change in the base property due to contextual factors.[26] For example, a rich lady giving money to help a poor man on the street corner can be a genuine token of generosity, while the same kind of gift by this married lady to her secret lover would not be. In other words, supervenient properties can be multiply realizable and therefore are not identity relations.[27]

If mental causation is to be affirmed, as nonreductive physicalists robustly do, then it means that there needs to be the possibility of the top-down (and whole-part) mental causation. That is not of course to deny bottom-up causation but to claim that that is not the only form. The most persistent critic of nonreductive physicalism, Jaegwon Kim, ironically makes the valid point as he claims that

> the emergentist and nonreductive physicalist are mental realists, and Mental Realism, via Alexander's dictum,[28] entails causal powers for mental properties . . . [as] mental properties, on both positions are irreducible net additions to the world. And this must mean . . . that mental properties bring with them *new causal powers, powers that no underlying physical-biological properties can deliver.* . . . To be real, Alexander has said, is to

---

23. See Clayton, *Mind and Emergence*, vi.

24. For a reductionist version, see Kim, *Physicalism, or Something Near Enough*, 14; see further, McLaughlin, "Varieties of Supervenience," 16–59.

25. The key scholars in the development of the concept have been Hilary Putnam and Jerry Fodor. See Putnam, *Language, and Reality*, 429–40 and Fodor, "Special Sciences," 97–115.

26. See Murphy and Brown, *Did My Neurons Make Me Do It?*, 204.

27. Murphy, "Nonreductive Physicalism: Philosophical Issues," 132–35.

28. That is, to speak of mental property (or any property for that matter) is to speak of causal efficacy (in other words: if mental events do not "do" anything, why speak of them at all!). It was formulated by Alexander, *Space, Time and Deity*, 2:8.

have causal powers; *to be real, new, and irreducible, therefore, must be to have new, irreducible causal powers.*[29]

Kim rightly concludes that apart from downward causation mental causation is not explicable. Because of this—and two related reasons, namely, rejection of causal overdetermination[30] and causal closure[31]—Kim rejects as incoherent the whole notion of nonreductive physicalism.[32] But doing so, as said, he clarifies helpfully the main resources available and necessary for the antireductionist program.

Let us now consider the potential of a nonreductive physicalist proposal as set forth by some leading Christian scholars.

Why Nonreductive Physicalism is a Move Towards the Right Direction but does not Take Us Far Enough

There are lasting values in nonreductive physicalism that need to be carefully preserved. The foundational key value simply is the importance of physicality.[33] Beyond that, nonreductive physicalism is fairly successful in negotiating between the full embrace of the most recent scientific data concerning human behavior and the essentials of Christian (religious) intuitions. That said, it is not difficult to see the basic philosophical dilemma of nonreductive physicalism and that its claim for *physicality* as the ultimate base and explanation is its Achilles' heel: "say yes, and you seem to end up with a reductive physicalism; say no, and you aren't really a physicalist after all."[34]

In this context one cannot avoid facing the problem common to all physicalists, namely, that of the higher mental capacities, consciousness, including self-consciousness. Wittgenstein's challenges to materialists still call for a response: "The idea of a process in the head, in a completely

---

29. Kim, *Supervenience and Mind*, 350; see also Kim, "Making Sense of Emergence," 5.

30. Kim, "Non-Reductivist's Troubles with Mental Causation," 208.

31. Kim, "Non-Reductivist's Troubles with Mental Causation," 209.

32. Kim, "Myth of Nonreductive Materialism," 242–60; Kim, "Non-Reductivist's Troubles," 208. Later in his evolving thinking Kim has come to grant the possibility and even need of a kind of mental causation—as long as the reductionist program is not thereby thwarted. Kim, *Physicalism, or Something Near Enough*, 9. On page 5, he calls this view "conditional physical reductionism."

33. See Brown, "Conclusion: Reconciling Scientific and Biblical Portraits of Human Nature," 223.

34. Clayton, *Mind and Emergence*, 130. No wonder J. Kim considers nonreductive physicalism internally incoherent. See Kim, *Mind in a Physical World*.

enclosed space, makes thinking something occult."[35] One way to highlight the distinctive nature of mental life is to speak of "intentionality,"[36] that is, "aboutness," referring to something else. This aboutness-relationship is dramatically different from a causal relationship.[37] It is hard to contest what the philosopher of mind Jerry Fodor observed: "Nobody has the slightest idea how anything material could be conscious."[38] Titles such as *How Matter Becomes Imagination*[39]—even though written by senior neuroscientists, one of whom is a Nobel Laureate—simply promise too much. No human researcher can know, as Thomas Nagel so famously argued, 'what it's like to be a bat.'"[40]

Furthermore, as surprising as it may sound, it seems to me to me that from a (natural) scientific perspective it is less than clear that physicalism is the right or even the best choice. It seems to many that current science is moving away from what "physical" (or material) used to mean. The physicist Arnold E. Sikkema notes that a key problem of nonreductive physicalism is "that it elevates the *composition* of entities as though what things are made of is of ultimate concern to a discussion of their ontology." As is well known, in the theory of relativity mass is nothing else but a form of energy (in relation to the speed of light); in quantum mechanics, treating subatomic entities as particles is complementary to regarding them as probability waves; and so forth.[41] The point here is that matter/physicality has become very elusive, virtually "non-material." And even if nonreductive physicalists would respond (as I guess they might) that the point of nonreductive physicalism is not on the composition, I think Sikkema's question calls for an answer.

The bottom line is this: what is matter/physicality? Is it totally different from the mental? If mental events, particularly consciousness, morality, and religiosity are but materially based processes, then the "matter" we speak of has little or nothing in common with our current scientific understanding! It may be, as the Jesuit scientist William Stoeger surmises, that the neuroscientific investigation pushes us to radically reconsider and change

---

35. Ludwig Wittgenstein, *Philosophical Grammar*, §64. Similarly, Wittgenstein, *Zettel*, §605.

36. For the groundbreaking work on intentionality we owe to the phenomenologist philosopher Edmund Husserl; see Spear, "Husserl on Intentionality and Intentional Content."

37. Clayton, "Neuroscience, the Person, and God: An Emergentist Account," 191.

38. Jerry Fodor, *Times Literary Supplement*, 3 July 1992, 5–7, quoted in Clayton, *Mind and Emergence*, 112.

39. Subtitle in Edelman and Tononi, *Universe of Consciousness*.

40. Clayton, *Mind and Emergence*, 111–12.

41. Sikkema, "Physicist's Reformed Critique," 23–24.

what "physical/material" and "non-physical/non-material" may mean.[42] In any case, as is well known, "matter" is not a well-defined scientific concept (whereas "mass" and "energy" are).[43] We even need a new vocabulary to speak of the mind and the mental. We probably cannot say the mental is "immaterial" or "non-physical" because that would cut off its deep integration with the brain (any more than we can say the mental is material). Would terms such as "trans-material/-physical" communicate that best?

The main point for my purposes is simply this: perhaps the premature jump onto the physicalist bandwagon by Christian scholars may not be as philosophically and scientifically advantageous as previously thought. There are also some urgent religious and theological reasons for continuing the quest. Beyond the obvious, that from the theological and religious point of view many would find it very difficult to think of ontology merely in terms of a staunch physicalist claim,[44] is the deeper claim that even for nonreductive physicalists who are not atheists, physicalism is only the penultimate option. All theistic traditions consider the Ultimate to be spirit/-ual, certainly that is case for all Abrahamic faiths. In this light, I feel sympathies for the philosopher-theologian Philip Clayton's preference for a "monism" that is not physicalist in itself although it takes physicality most seriously. He argues that we should not assume that the "entities postulated by physics complete the inventory of what exists" while insisting that "[r]eality is ultimately composed of one basic kind of stuff."[45] Rather, "recognizing the physical as one aspect among others will help develop a more fully orbed philosophy of science, recognizing the importance of the different methodologies of inquiry that rightfully play roles in the other scientific disciplines, rather than focusing on what some regard as the highly problematic ontology of the entities of mechanics due to their lying so far beyond imagination."[46] With these cautions and insights in mind, let us try our hand at a tentative constructive proposal for how to best understand the nature of human nature in light of theological, philosophical, and scientific contours.

---

42. Stoeger, "Mind-Brain Problem," 132.

43. Stoeger, "Mind-Brain Problem," 133–35; see also Heller, "Adventures of the Concept of Mass and Matter," 15–35.

44. Sikkema, "Physicist's Reformed Critique of Nonreductive Physicalism and Emergence," 22.

45. Clayton, *Mind and Emergence*, 4.

46. Sikkema, "Physicist's Reformed Critique," 26.

MULTIDIMENSIONAL MONISM: TOWARDS A HOLISTIC, PLURALISTIC, AND UNIFIED ACCOUNT OF HUMAN NATURE

Multidimensional Monism: Main Ideas and Intuitions

I argue that human beings are "psychosomatic unities rather than dual beings composed of a spiritual soul housed within a material body."[47] Indeed, as Tom Wright reminds us, we should talk about "differentiated unity": "Paul and the other early Christian writers didn't reify their anthropological terms. Though Paul uses his language with remarkable consistency, he nowhere suggests that any of the key terms refers to a particular 'part' of the human being to be played off against any other. Each *denotes* the entire human being, while *connoting* some angle of vision on who that human is and what he or she is called to be."[48]

But isn't a proposal like that still dualist? Or to put it in another way: Are all notions of dualism to be carved out once and for all? I doubt it. It seems to me that all views which take the mental as real (existent) and which also therefore assume its causal efficacy, end up being property dualists of a sort. Certainly nonreductive physicalism is, similarly to emergent monism. It seems to me the Thomistic view, although it has by and large funded substance ontology,[49] can be tweaked to express the best intuitions of property dualism. What also comes to mind here is the physicist Roger Penrose's idea of the mental as "conscious substance"; it speaks of consciousness (which he also dares to call "soul") in a way that clearly belongs under property dualism.[50] Somewhat similarly, the philosopher of mind David Chalmer's idea of the "information states" in terms of "the double-aspect principle" which is based on the "observation that there is a direct isomorphism between certain physically embodied information spaces and certain *phenomenal* (or experiential) information spaces"[51] represents property dualism of some sort.[52]

---

47. Polkinghorne, "Anthropology in an Evolutionary Context," 93.

48. Wright, "Mind, Spirit, Soul and Body."

49. Just consider this statement from *Summa Contra Gentiles* 2.69.2: "body and soul are not two actually existing substances; rather, the two of them together constitute one actually existing substance."

50. Penrose, *Emperor's New Mind*.

51. Chalmers, "Facing Up to the Problem of Consciousness," 200–219.

52. Chalmers, *Conscious Mind*, 305. In response to Chalmer's proposal, see the rejoinders in Shear, *Explaining Consciousness*.

In systematic theology, Moltmann's vision of "a *perichoretic* relationship of mutual interpenetration and differentiated unity"[53] and Pannenberg's "personal unity of body and soul"[54] speak the same language. The ethicist Niebuhr's associating the "self" with body but reluctance to reduce self to the bodily, reflects the same intuitions.[55] If I understand correctly "emergent dualism," it argues that having had the mental to emerge, it becomes a property on its own.[56] With all its deviations from classical Christian tradition, American Process philosophy's monistic dipolarism represents yet another form of property dualism.[57] In sum: for every nonreductionist, the distinction, yet not separation, between the physical and mental is unavoidable in philosophical, theological, and scientific discussion.

Furthermore, I argue that the reality of mental life cannot be had without a (strong) theory of emergence, as explained above. It not only saves the mental but also helps establish its causal efficacy. This "radical kind of emergence"[58] holds robustly to the mind's downwards and whole-part causation. Strong emergence "is consistent with the neuroscientific data and the data with the constraints on brain functioning. At the same time, it has the merit of conceiving of mental activity in terms of mental causation, which accords well with our own experience of mental agency."[59] A good example here is how to best speak of human "personhood"; it can never be a matter of merely analyzing and investigating biological and physical processes. The physical explanation never captures "me," the person, *qua* person, but rather as an object of study.[60]

With the tight, in many ways indistinguishable, interdependency and communion between the physical and mental in mind, the British physicist-priest Polkinghorne suggests "dual-aspect" monism as a fitting concept to describe the holistic account of human nature. The emphasis on *monism* indicates that the classical metaphysical options of materialism, idealism, and Cartesian dualism are unsatisfactory in light of the current multilayered,

---

53. Moltmann, *God in Creation*, 258–60 (259); he also speaks of the unity between body and soul in terms of covenant (260).

54. Main heading in Pannenberg, *ST* 2:181.

55. See Niebuhr, *Self and the Dramas of History*, 26.

56. See Hasker, *Emergent Self*. Cf. the "integrative dualism" of Charles Taliaferro in *Consciousness and the Mind of God*.

57. See further, Hartshorne, "Compound Individual," 193–220; for a short discussion, see Barbour, "Neuroscience, Artificial Intelligence, Human Nature," 275–80.

58. Van Gulick, "Reduction, Emergence and Other Recent Options," 1–34.

59. Clayton, *Mind and Emergence*, 139.

60. For comments, see the section titled "Person-Based Explanations and the Social Sciences" in Clayton, *Mind and Emergence*, 144–48.

complex, and dynamic understanding of reality, including human nature. Dual-aspect monism "acknowledge[s] the fundamental distinction between experience of the material and experience of the mental but which would neither impose on reality a sharp division into two unconnected kinds of substance nor deny the psychosomatic unity of human beings." A useful way for him to illustrate the nature of dual-aspect monism is quantum theory's idea of complementarity (superposition principle), which allows for two different/distinct states simultaneously. The main point about the *dual-aspect* nature is to argue that "there will be entities, such as stones, whose nature is located wholly at the material pole, and other entities, such as ourselves, who are 'amphibians,' participating in both kinds of polar experience," namely, mental and material.[61]

Polkinghorne also reminds us of the obvious difference between the material and noetic/mental: whereas the former is "a world of process, characterized by temporality and becoming," the latter is "everlasting, in the sense that such truths just *are* and do not evolve." These two "worlds," however, are "complementary aspects of a larger created reality" and hence illustrate the duality that goes beyond material versus mental: "it must also embrace becoming/being and everlasting/temporal." Humanity belongs to both, and therefore, "a fully integrated metaphysics" is needed in which "the multiplicity of experience leads us to an account of considerable richness and subtlety."[62] The potential liability of the dual-aspect monism is that it may make the mental less than real and merely a matter of perspective or experience.[63] The dual-aspect monist, however, doesn't have to be liable to this weakness.

That is not yet the whole story. Both the basic intuition of the undifferentiated psychosomatic unity and dual-aspect monism imply more, as Clayton puts it: "We need multiple layers of explanatory accounts *because* the human person is a physical, biological, psychological, and (I believe also) spiritual reality, and because these aspects of its reality, though interdependent, are not mutually reducible." The term "ontological pluralism" may best describe this approach.[64] Moltmann's creative nomenclatures "spirit-body," "spirit-*Gestalt*," "spirit-soul," as complementary metaphors, echoes this.[65] The German systematician Michael Welker warns us of the reductionism

---

61. Polkinghorne, *Faith, Science and Understanding*, 95–97.

62. Polkinghorne, *Faith, Science and Understanding*, 98.

63. This is clearly the case in Velmans, "Making Sense of Causal Interactions between Consciousness and Brain," 75.

64. Clayton, *Mind and Emergence*, 148.

65. Moltmann, *God in Creation*, 262–64.

with regard to fixating on one particular aspect, either physicalist or mentalist. Whereas scientists fear the latter, humanists tends to fear the former. "There are simply too many anthropological insights and burning questions in social and cultural studies and in the natural sciences that cannot be hosted by this model." Not only the sciences but also biblical theology point to multidimensionality.[66] Prophetically, one may want to say, already decades ago in Paul Tillich's theology, multidimensionality came to the fore—the inorganic, organic, psychic, and spiritual as the fundamental dimensions of the human.[67] Similarly, the practical theologian Don S. Browning has for years developed a robust theology of the multidimensionality of human nature (with a view to discerning moral goods and values).[68]

Is my proposal then something similar to "neutral monism"?[69] Not only because that nomenclature carries a philosophical history that I do not want to identify myself with but also because in the final analysis it leaves so much unexplained (such as, how do we then have the multiplicity of features and properties we have?), I find Clayton's "emergentist monism"[70] quite a comfortable label. It may also be named "property pluralism."[71] Ted Peters's "emergent holism" would also fit the bill.[72]

What Kind of Monism?

But why not physical monism? Above I have expressed my reservations about nonreductive physicalism and will not repeat them here. While I greatly appreciate Jaegwon Kim's honesty when, as a staunch physicalist, he admits, "Physicalism is not the whole truth, but it is the truth near enough,"[73] I also think any authentic physicalism ultimately leads to "ontological physicalism," according to which all there is, is physical[74]—and that I do not take

---

66. Welker, "Theological Anthropology," 319; so also Barbour, "Neuroscience, Artificial Intelligence, and Human Nature."

67. Tillich, *Systematic Theology*, 2:22–23.

68. Browning, *Fundamental Practical Theology*, 94–109, 139–70 lists the dimensions into which there is no need to go in detail here. For a short statement, see Browning, "Human Dignity, Human Complexity, and Human Goods."

69. For a useful discussion with sources, see Stubenberg, "Neutral Monism."

70. That is also the view of Peacocke, "Sound of Sheer Silencey," 219.

71. Clayton, "Neuroscience, the Person, and God," 212; Roger W. Sperry means something similar in his *Science and Moral Priority: Merging Mind, Brain, and Human Values*.

72. Peters,. "Resurrection of the Very Embodied Soul," 305.

73. Kim, *Physicalism, or Something Near Enough*, 6.

74. Kim, *Physicalism, or Something Near Enough*, 150.

as a credible option. Unlike some theistic naturalists (W. Wildman, among others), I am convinced that only *non*theistic materialist naturalism can stay content with physicalism all the way. The reason is simply this: strictly speaking, ontological physicalism can only be penultimate for a theist.

Hence, it seems to me that multidimensional monism, as argued in this project, fits better the key belief in Christian faith (and I guess, other theisms as well) of the complex unity of the finite world as God's creation. While exhibiting various properties as a result of rich creative divine work, the notion of the "unity of nature," as distinct from the infinity of the Creator God (who is Spirit), tells us all creatures share a common nature (however complex and multidimensional that may be).[75]

More precisely: What does theology have at stake in this debate on ontology? Clayton rightly notes that "[i]f one holds that all mental phenomena are only expressions of physical causes or are themselves, at root, physical events, then one has (at least tacitly) advanced a theory of the human person that is pervasively physical. It then becomes extremely unclear (to put it gently) why, *from the perspective of one's own theory of the human person*, a God would have to be introduced at all (except perhaps as a useful fiction)."[76] Now, that does not of course mean that a Christian physicalist couldn't introduce God. But the point is that a truly physical *anthropological* account does not make it any easier than any other version of human nature; God has to be introduced "from outside," after all.

Clayton lays out the options well: "If a theologian espouses physicalism, she may be forging an alliance with the majority worldview within the neurosciences, but she may also be giving up the most interesting rapprochement between theology and the sciences of the person just as she approaches that debate's most decisive issue." (Similarly, of course, traditional dualism may easily stall the dialogue with sciences.[77]) Perhaps, then, even in terms of dialogue (although theological convictions can never be primarily based on their usefulness), the best way for theology is to insist on the necessity but insufficiency of physical explanation.

When viewed from a historical perspective, not only the *opening* but also the full endorsement of nonmaterialist, in other words, idealist ontology has been the dominant position among Christians and other theists (both mono- and polytheists). The late American Reformed Paul K. Jewett expresses succinctly this sentiment: "To be materially conditioned

---

75. See also Clayton, "Neuroscience, the Person, and God," 209–10.

76. Clayton, "Neuroscience, the Person, and God," 204.

77. Clayton, "Neuroscience, the Person, and God," 204.

as conscious selves is not to be materially constituted as such."[78] Not only Idealist philosophers such as Kant, Fichte, Hegel, Schelling, and numerous others,[79] but virtually all such thinkers from antiquity to recent times have been Idealists of a sort; similarly most cultures in the Global South, particularly in Africa;[80] so also are the *advaita* (nondualistic) schools of Indian philosophy); and so forth. This suggestive listing alone would justify keeping the door open to nonphysicalist monism. It seems to me that Christian theology would do well to be cautious in going full-blown into physicalism because "we are in great danger of phrasing the discussion in such a way that the deepest and most significant issues of human existence simply never appear on the screen."[81]

The British philosopher-theologian Keith Ward has recently suggested another version of dual-aspect theory that he names "dual-aspect idealism" and situates between Cartesian dualism and physicalisms of all sorts (while taking physicalism very seriously). A student of Gilbert Ryle, who coined the term "ghost in the machine" ridiculing Descartes's dualism and turn to the inner self, Ward rightly contends that because "mind and consciousness are different from, something over and above, molecules and matter . . . they are not at all ghostly."[82] Indeed, he reminds us how radically different Idealism is from the physicalism/materialism of contemporary naturalism, in its claim that "the material world . . . exists as an environment created by a primordial mind in which finite minds can exist in mutual self-expression and interaction. . . . It totally reverses the modern myth that minds are by-products of a purely material evolutionary process, completely determined by physical events in their bodies and brains."[83] At the same time, he also reminds us how vastly different contemporary materialism is through the lens of force fields, quantum theory, and string theory.[84] Now, as mentioned, Ward is not drawn to dualism *per se*; instead, he represents a property dualism of a sort.

What Process philosophy is calling the "inner" life of the physical, Polkinghorne names dual-aspect monism, and the Oxford philosopher Horace Romano Harré, dual-side theories (of monism), all point to the same

---

78. Jewett, *Who We Are*, 9 (italics removed).

79. For an important discussion from the perspective of anthropology, see Martin and Barresi, *Rise and Fall of Soul and Self*, 185–90.

80. See Kapolyo, *Human Condition* and Mbiti, *Concepts of God in Africa*.

81. Hefener, "Imago Dei: The Possibility and Necessity of the Human Person," 81.

82. Ward, *More Than Matter*, 10.

83. Ward, *More Than Matter*, 57.

84. Ward, *More Than Matter*, ch. 2.

direction. While not Idealist thinkers *per se*, they do think that even "material" processes somehow are not completely void of some kind of teleology and that the universe is more like an organism rather than a machine.[85] Ward refers to the human embryo: as much as current science eschews any notions of vitalism or (Aristotelian) teleology, we expect it to become an adult person, a highly complicated obviously purposeful process.[86]

The minimalist statement about human nature, going back to the beginning of this section, is then psychosomatic pluralistic unity. The nomenclature "pluralistic unity" also points to the need to dare to "confuse" and go beyond established categories (while holding to the best insights of each) such as idealism, physicalism, and monism.[87] Multidimensional monism is one such emerging proposal for continuing discussion and critique. With the shift away from traditional substance dualism (notwithstanding property dualism of some sort), the question arises of whether to continue using the term "soul" at all. That question we take up next.

What about "Soul"?

Among the current advocates of nondualist accounts of human nature, including Christian nonreductive physicalists, the term *soul* has become a virtual anathema. By implication, it also happens often that all uses of that term, even if they are not using it in the substance dualistic context, are deemed suspicious. While that attitude is understandable, constructive theologians should also exercise some critical faculties here. I do not consider it wise, let alone necessary, to leave behind the ancient term of *soul*, even if traditional dualism is let go. The reasons to continue using the term *soul* are the following: First, similarly to so many other terms whose meaning has changed, the theologians' task is to help the faithful to grasp its redefinition. Just consider the term *creation*. As much as its meaning has changed after the embrace by theology of contemporary natural sciences' view of the evolvement of cosmos, its deepest intuitions have stayed intact. (That said, theologians also must be careful not to change the term's meaning at their own wish as often happened in Classical Liberalism when, say, the whole possibility of Jesus's bodily resurrection was categorically denied.)

Second, the term *soul* is so widely and frequently used in the biblical canon—and consequently, everywhere in Christian tradition—that its dismissal seems to be totally unfounded and counterproductive as it may

85. Ward, *More Than Matter*, 81–83 (81).
86. Ward, *More Than Matter*, 83–84 (84).
87. Ward, *More Than Matter*, 102–3.

cause the rejection of the proposal itself without further investigation. Third, there is also the interfaith consideration: although different religious traditions may mean different things when using the term, the cancellation in Christian tradition would not only look awkward and confusing to others but also seriously hinder dialogue. Fourth, blaming the use of "soul" (because of its close connection with substance dualism) for all kinds of ills in Christian life, say an anti-body attitude or isolationist spirituality or escapist eschatology, misses the main point, which is that most any conception of human nature may foster negative or positive spiritualties or orientations of religious life (just differently).

The late American Reformed theologian Ray S. Anderson offers useful guidelines for the systematic use of the term *soul*. Although my own constructive proposal of human nature does not exactly match his, these guidelines serve well regarding the term. First, "soul" does not denote a "substance or entity residing in the body" but rather the "whole person, especially the inner core of human personal life as created and upheld by God" (to which should be added that no less is body and other aspects of the multidimensional human being also upheld by God). Second, the terms body, soul, and spirit are not analytic distinctions but rather functional and overlapping with each other. Third, even though Christians have a firm hope for life eternal in the resurrected body as the gift of God, soul—no more than anything else in the human being—is not immortal by nature.[88] Fourth, as a result, rather than saying that the human person "has a soul," it is better to say that the "person is soul."[89]

Regardless of the terminological choice, all deviations from traditional dualism face the important questions of how to speak of an afterlife and continuation of personal identity. Although full discussion belongs to Christian eschatology, short notes are in order here.

What about Afterlife and Identity?

So, how to think of afterlife in the post-Cartesian-dualism world? In other words, does it mean that leaving behind traditional talk about the soul and its disembodied existence means leaving behind the idea of life everlasting? No, it does not. Christian tradition never affirmed the immortality of the soul (as in Platonic philosophy) nor that only one part of the human person will be saved for eternity. In fact, in early theology, notwithstanding terminological (and at times, material) inconsistency, the divinity of the soul and,

---

88. Anderson, *On Being Human*, 182–83 (182). See Harris, *Raised Immortal*, 237.
89. Anderson, *On Being Human*, 186.

hence, its intrinsic capacity to survive beyond death, was rightly rejected and replaced by belief in eternal life as the gift of God.[90] Furthermore, the hope for the resurrection was established for the whole person, not only for the soul.[91]

What about the continuity of personal identity? This has to be looked at from two complementary perspectives. Theologically speaking, guaranteeing the identity is the task of God, not ours.[92] Scientifically and philosophically speaking, identity is a task belonging to the human person, lasting all of one's life, embedded in growth and development in all areas, including personal development and social context. Embodied memory serves here an important role.[93] Whereas in this life, there is always the form of a timely sequence with its broken moments, when God's eternity comes to swallow the finite life, that "will represent the *totality* of our earthly existence."[94]

Polkinghorne correctly notes that in itself the soul's "role as the carrier of human identity is almost as problematic within life as it is beyond death." The continuity cannot be a matter of material continuity since atoms are in constant flux through wear and tear. Perhaps the best way to speak of the continuity of identity is in terms of "the almost infinitely complex, information-bearing pattern in which the matter of the body is organized at any one time. This surely is the meaning of the soul."[95] Based on the foundational Christian teaching of the human being as the image of God, we have to say that "[w]hat gives us an identity that does not die is not our nature, but a personal relationship with God."[96] Embodied, the soul does not carry in itself the powers of natural immortality. "As far as science can tell the story, the pattern that is a person will dissolve with that person's death and decay."[97] This proposal seems to correspond to contemporary scientific understandings of information or the way complex systems could be understood—and all living beings are systems of some kind.[98] Aquinas's hylomorphic account of human nature is also based on these intuitions.

90. Pannenberg, *ST* 3:571.

91. See Peters, "Resurrection of the Very Embodied Soul?" 322–25.

92. Peters, "Resurrection of the Very Embodied Soul?" 316.

93. Pannenberg, *ST* 3:562; for the importance of memory, see Augustine, *Confessions*, 10.17.

94. Pannenberg, *ST* 3:561; see also Peters, "Resurrection of the Very Embodied Soul?" 324.

95. Polkinghorne, "Anthropology in an Evolutionary Context," 98; see also Polkinghorne, "Eschatology: Some Questions and Some Insights from Science," 38–41.

96. Zizioulas, "Doctrine of the Holy Trinity," 58.

97. Polkinghorne, "Anthropology in an Evolutionary Context," 99.

98. Polkinghorne, *God of Hope*, ch. 9.

Now, seen from the theological point of view, this does not, however, mean that therefore when the person dies, that is all there is. Utilizing the concept of information, it can be stated that what the older soul theory rightly intuited was that "the faithful God will remember the pattern that is me and re-embody it in the eschatological act of resurrection." I couldn't agree more with Polkinghorne, who continues: "In making this assertion, I want to affirm the intrinsically embodied character of human being, without supposing that the flesh and blood of this world represents the only possible form that embodiment might take."[99] While I understand why Christian nonreductive physicalists—with justification—underline the importance of death's finality to combat the obvious misconception in which the soul were to possess natural powers of immortality and its independence,

I also find the "gap" theory—that is, between my personal death and the final resurrection there is "nothing of me"—problematic from the systematic theological point of view. Not that I have any doubts whatsoever concerning the capacity of the Creator to re-create *ex nihilo* the resurrected person who has faced physical death (that belief is no more difficult than believing that in the first place the person was given the gift of life). Nor do I think that positing a "soul" is needed to guarantee continuity between this life and the life to come, because, simply put, making the soul the locus of continuity doesn't really explain much in the first place! My reservations lie elsewhere, namely, in the complex and mutually conditioned continuity vs. discontinuity relationship between life on Earth and life in the resurrected body as well as between my own personal eternal destiny vs. that of the whole cosmos. If the gap theory is followed, both of these themes, crucial to a systematic theological negotiation of eschatological consummation, may be frustrated.

IN LIEU OF CONCLUSIONS: REMAINING TASKS AND QUESTIONS

Calling this short writing an "essay" has been intentional. Its etymological roots (in Latin and old French) go back to ideas of "attempt," "trial," or "testing." These terms accurately express my intention here. I have attempted tentatively to imagine a credible systematic/constructive theological account of the nature of human nature in critical and sympathetic dialogue with neurosciences, philosophy of mind, and the best of theological traditions, past and current. Even when distinguishing my proposal from others, I am not thereby denying deep indebtedness to their insights.

99. Polkinghorne, "Anthropology in an Evolutionary Context," 99–100.

A suggestive, tentative *essai* does not lend easily into hardcore conclusions! I would rather like to highlight some pertinent tasks for continuing collaboration:

The question of the biblical teaching on human nature is still without final clarification. While I feel sympathetic to some biblical scholars' view that in the first place the Bible is not seeking to instruct us in anthropology, I also believe that we need more work in clarifying particularly the meaning (to contemporary theology) of the apparent "phenomenological" dualism—or dualist rhetoric—of particularly of the New Testament. Is it merely a matter of ancient way of speaking?

Having mentioned that my own discipline, namely systematic (doctrinal) theology is a late-comer to the kind of interdisciplinary conversation in theological anthropology common in some other doctrinal loci, particularly the doctrine of creation, I wonder what is the reason for it? Is it because there is a default assumption that these kinds of questions of theological anthropology are best handled in the philosophy department? Or is there unwillingness among the systematicians to seek for collaboration?

Concerning the nature of monism I am suggesting, namely neither strictly speaking physicalist nor (necessarily, at least penultimately) idealist, I am looking forward to much interdisciplinary investigation concerning the meaning of those very concepts, namely "matter" and "mental." What if—as looks probable in light of where natural sciences' accounts of cosmos are going—the divide between the physical and mental becomes obsolete (at least in some sense); would that re-orient the theological talk about the nature of human nature? We also need continuing reflection on how the "mental" posited of humanity may be related to the "mental" in the whole cosmos.

CHAPTER 16

A Christian Vision of the "End" of Cosmos and Life

Towards a Constructive Eschatology for the Contemporary World

INTRODUCTION: THE OMNIPRESENCE OF THE VISIONS OF "END" IN SOCIETY, RELIGIONS, AND SCIENCES

As PROBLEMATIC AND CONTESTED as the role of eschatology, the doctrine of Last Things, maybe in contemporary mainstream Christian theology, the visions of "end" and consummation are not missing either in cultural, scientific, or religious conjectures. Call it "eschatology" or not, the "end" seems to be of high interest everywhere.

In the general sense of the term, it can be said that "eschatology" is not limited exclusively to the religious sphere. Just think of the growing concern, at times anxiety, in secular culture over the impending "end"—either of our planet or of human life.[1] Indeed, it seems obvious that "[e]very culture has an eschatology; it is part of our inescapable human attempt to make sense of the world."[2] Although these secular visions are not distinctively religious, they tend to feature structural similarities with religions, as is evident for example in the Marxist tripartite outline of the world's history: "A primal

---

1. See Körtner, *End of the World*, 1–22.
2. Gillman, *Death of Death*, 21.

state of innocence, followed by a period of social tension, which is, in turn, supplanted by a new era of harmony, the communist society of the future."[3]

Some kind of eschatological outlook can be discerned in many recent predictions of the future of human civilization in sociopolitical thought. How else to think of the (in)famous proposal of Francis Fukuyama at the time of the collapse of Soviet Communism, ominously titled *The End of History and the Last Man*? With a neoconservative confidence in the final victory of free-market capitalism and its version of democracy over other political ideologies, Fukuyama took it as the most developed and final stage of evolution, finally leading into peace as democracy's supremacy is discerned by all.[4]

Not surprisingly, this "right-wing" vision of the inevitable progress of history toward freedom was harshly contested by the ideological left. In the neo-Marxist manifesto of Michael Hardt and Antonio Negri, *Empire*, freedom is defeated by the empire, which replaces nation-states and even national conflicts with a new transnational global order, indeed an absolute and violent one. The new combined world rulers are international agencies and organizations from the UN to the World Bank and the alliance of rich nations, along with the "superpower" (USA).[5] The sequel by the same authors, written after 9/11, titled *Multitude: War and Democracy in the Age of Empire* (2004), further diagnoses reasons for the failure of the dream of progress. In sum: whatever one thinks of these various scenarios for the future, it appears that "eschatology" dies hard even in the secular realm.[6]

Back to religions. Although the Christian theologian has to be careful when speaking of "eschatology" as a pan-religious theme, it is true that all world religions express a concern over mortality, and all of them also envision some form of life after death. Furthermore, religions embrace beliefs not only about the origins but also about the "end" (or at least cycles of beginning and ending) of the whole of the cosmos. As diverse as these beliefs and symbols may be, it is clear that some kind of common denominator exists. That said, insofar as eschatology is "the study of the final end of things, the ultimate resolution of the entire creation," then it applies much more easily to "theistic religions that hold to a doctrine of creation and a linear

---

3. Gillman, *Death of Death*, 21, attributing the idea to Herberg, *Judaism and Modern Man*, 230–31.

4. Fukuyama, *End of History and the Last Man*.

5. Hardt and Negri, *Empire*.

6. Hardt and Negri, *Multitude*.

view of history and that believe that creation will come to a final end than to nontheistic traditions, particularly Buddhism."[7]

Recall that "Buddhist scriptures regularly refer to 'beginningless *saṁsāra*,' a cycle of birth and death of the universe (as well as of the individual) for which no starting point can be discerned. Nor is there an end, for Buddhists share with members of other Indian religions (notably the Hindus and the Jains) the idea that the universe passes through an unending series of cycles of manifestation and nonmanifestation."[8] Add to that the general observation that "[c]ultures that view time as an endless succession of repetitive cycles . . . develop only 'relative eschatologies,' because the concept of an ultimate consummation of history is alien to them."[9] Again, Buddhism is a grand example; this principle applies also to Hinduism. All that said, eschatology persists among religions in one form or another.

Nor are sciences immune to eschatological conjectures. Indeed, the picture painted of the "end" in sciences is not complicated: it leads to eventual decay and annihilation.[10] As is well-known, three basic options are available on the basis of Einstein's theory: if an open universe, then the process of expanding eventually leads to "freeze"; if "closed," the expansion will reach the culmination point and eventually "contract" until it results in "fry," the big crunch; and if a "flat" curvature, as in the first scenario, it will expand (forever) and finally reach "freeze."[11] Most all scientists in recent years have become convinced that the open universe is the correct guess and that its expansion is accelerating ever and ever more rapidly.[12]

In light of omnipresence of the visions of the "end" in cultural, religious, and scientific consciousness, the gradual eclipse of eschatology as a stated doctrine in Christian theology is counterintuitive. It calls for some critical assessment.

THE RISE AND ECLIPSE OF ESCHATOLOGY IN CHRISTIAN TRADITION

In distinctively Christian forms of eschatology, marked shifts have taken place in history. For the earliest followers of Christ, the intense expectation

---

7. Walls, *Oxford Handbook of Eschatology*, 4. The now classic study is Eliade, *Myth of the Eternal*.
8. Nattier, "Buddhist Eschatology," 151.
9. Werblowsky, "Eschatology," 2834.
10. For details, see ch. 2 in Kärkkäinen, *Hope and Community*.
11. Russell, *Time in Eternity*, 56–59 (and the extensive documentation therein).
12. See Russell, *Time in Eternity*, 59–60.

of the imminent return of their Lord was just that—*intense*; the (early) patristic church continued this focus.[13] Apocalyptic enthusiasm flourished in diverse forms. Even such intellectually oriented writers as the apologists of the second century employed urgent eschatological warnings and visions in their defense of the faith before the unbelieving world.[14] Although the eschatological hope waned some after the establishment of Christendom and its amillennialism, in no way did it die out. Indeed, more often than not, particularly in the Middle Ages and all way to the Reformation era, eschatological-apocalyptic imagination fueled spirituality.

By the time of modernity, eschatological "hope" had lost its meaning among the intelligentsia.[15] Kant's focus on religion's effect on morality undoubtedly helped the nineteenth-century liberal Protestants and others to reduce faith to the subjective and moral dimensions. And even the "rediscovery" of eschatology at the turn of the twentieth century in liberal New Testament scholarship (Johannes Weiss, Albert Schweitzer, and others) hardly signaled a robust interest in the *theological* significance of the end times. Not only did these scholars not believe the content of the New Testament claims regarding eschatology, but they were more keen on apocalypticism and, most ironically, its naive but totally mistaken application by Jesus and the disciples!

Simultaneously, though for different reasons, dismissal—or even an aggressive disavowal—of eschatological hope was funded by other leading philosophical and cultural figures. As is well known, L. Feuerbach took the human desire for life after death as a form of egotism.[16] He completely misunderstood the essence of Christian eschatological hope, as he took it as the denial of true human existence, particularly physicality.[17] The Freudian rejection of (religious) imagination of the afterlife merely as a (neurotic, or at least immature) form of an illusion attracted many followers.[18]

The Freudian interpretation sticks well with the contemporary naturalist worldview. The famed early twentieth-century British atheist philosopher Bertrand Russell opined that "[a]ll the evidence goes to show that what we regard as our mental life is bound up with brain structure and organized bodily energy. Therefore it is rational to suppose that mental life ceases

---

13. A massive resource is Daley, *Hope of the Early Church*.

14. Just consider the influential early second-century writings, the *Apocalypse of Peter* and *Epistle of the Apostles*, which discuss extensively end-time events.

15. See further Pannenberg. *Systematic Theology*, 3:532–45.

16. Feuerbach, *Essence of Christianity*, 170–84 particularly.

17. For details and sources, see Schwarz, *Eschatology*, 176–77.

18. Freud, *Reflections on War and Death*, 19.

when body ceases."[19] Philosophers such as Anthony Flew continued their persistent critique, targeting any belief in an afterlife and personal survival after death. He found logically and rationally failing the attempts by ancient philosophers, Christians and other believers, as well as those who consider near-death experiences, to establish the possibility of personal survival.[20]

No wonder that in much of post-Enlightenment theology any talk in the line of tradition about the "end" lacked content and became marginalized. The work begun by A. Schweitzer and other liberals was picked up in the latter part of the twentieth century by the (in)famous American Jesus Seminar. The late Marcus J. Borg advocated a totally noneschatological interpretation of Jesus and took the kingdom of God as merely a this-worldly entity.[21]

Some leading systematic theologians similarly dismissed or radically revised eschatology. There is almost no mention of eschatological themes in Gordon Kaufman's *In Face of Mystery: A Constructive Theology*, with the exception of a few unnuanced, hasty rebuttals of what he considers the traditional view of the judgment of God.[22] The *Cambridge Companion to Postmodern Theology* contains no entry on eschatology—the index does not even list the term! Virtual opposition to traditional eschatology comes from many quarters of women's, particularly feminist, green, and other liberation theologians. Some leading feminist pioneers have charged the (Christian) hope for afterlife (or "personal immortality," as it is sometimes put) to be "a patriarchal concept arising predominantly from the male psyche," while others argue that it necessarily neglects the destiny of the nonhuman creation and the cosmos.[23]

Similarly, consistent opposition to all notions of the consummation of God's kingdom after the book of Revelation has come from various types of postmodern philosophers, particularly on the more deconstructionist side on the old continent. If for Derrida "eschatology" is endless postponement without any arrival of the "Messiah,"[24] for his (former) colleague Gilles Deleuze and those like-minded, eschatology signals the threat of totality and homogenization.[25]

---

19. Russell, *Why I Am Not a Christian*, 45.

20. For an accessible account, see Flew, "Logic of Mortality," 171–87.

21. See Borg, *Jesus, A New Vision*; for criticism, see Witherington, *Jesus, Paul, and the End of the World*.

22. See Kaufman, *In Face of Mystery*, 409.

23. Karras, "Eschatology," 243–44.

24. Derrida, "Hospitality, Justice, and Responsibility," 70.

25. Deleuze, "Nietzsche and Saint Paul," 36–53.

SOME ATTEMPTS AT REDISCOVERY AND RECONCEIVING OF ESCHATOLOGY

It is not that all twentieth-century theological movements are willing to ignore eschatology. There is also the desire to reconceive it. Some nuanced and creative contemporary alternatives have been put forth to construct a viable eschatological vision. One of the most sophisticated revisions comes from the soil of process theology's deeply panentheistic and in many ways immanentist conception of God: therein God (in his two "dimensions," the consequent and primordial)[26] provides the "lure" for the future events but is not the one who guarantees an eschatological solution in any certainty.[27] There is neither an *ex nihilo* beginning (as God emerges with the cosmos) nor a final eschaton.

Furthermore, rather than resurrection hope for humanity, there is (in the original Whiteheadian process philosophy) an idea of "objective immortality," that is, some kind of nonpersonal recollection of us in divine memory. Even the post-Whiteheadian attempts by some recent process theologians (Marjorie Hewitt Suchocki and others) to frame that "memory" in terms of "subjective immortality" are a far cry from the personal resurrection of the body of classical Christianity.[28]

Another marked reorientation of eschatology is the feminist theologian Kathryn Tanner's "Eschatology without a Future" proposal, which resonates with the this-worldly approach of much of New Testament scholarship, although Tanner's reasons are theological and scientific. The main reason has to do with the obvious fact that the natural sciences' bleak picture of all life, and the cosmos itself, seems to be heading eventually toward annihilation; hence, these scientific "end-time scenarios conflict with the future-oriented, this-worldly eschatology"[29] of traditional Christianity.

Yet another highly important—as revisionist as it may be—eschatological restatement is the late John Hick's 1976 magnum opus, *Death and Eternal Life*. Mapping a huge domain of ideas among various religious traditions and in the tradition of Christian theology, he sets forth a creative synthesis between some living Asiatic faiths and a Judeo-Christian vision. He also staunchly opposes the prevailing naturalistic rebuttal of religious eschatologies: "In contrast to it," Hick states, "it seems to me that the claim of the religions that this life is part of a much larger existence that transcends

---

26. Griffin, "Process Eschatology," 297, with the citation from Whitehead, *Process and Reality*, 527.
27. See Cobb, *Christ in a Pluralistic Age*, chs. 15 and 16.
28. See Griffin, "Process Eschatology," 295–307.
29. Tanner, "Eschatology without a Future," 222.

our lifespan as animal organisms, whether through the continuation of individual consciousness or through participation in a greater transpersonal life, is very likely to be true." He further argues, "this is not ruled out by established scientific findings or by any agreed philosophical arguments."[30]

Although the present essay cannot follow the material proposals of these and related revisionist eschatologies, it acknowledges their desire not to leave behind the theology of the "end." Coming closest to the current proposal's intuitions are the many contemporary proposals that stay closely linked with the best of Christian tradition even when they seek to challenge and revise them. To a brief presentation of those we turn next before outlining our own constructive vision.

THE RISE OF CONSTRUCTIVE CHRISTIAN ESCHATOLOGIES

In the midst of the dismissal and radical reworking of the doctrine of last things, some leading contemporary theologians have helped rediscover eschatology and even put it at the center of theological conversations. Barth's classic rediscovery of eschatology is routinely mentioned as the clarion call: he claimed that without eschatology, no theology is worth its salt. That he was not able to materially deliver the promise does not make his initial call any less valuable.

The publication of German Reformed theologian J. Moltmann's *Theology of Hope* in the mid-1960s launched a new movement called "theology of hope."[31] For him, eschatology is the "first" chapter of Christian theology. Another German, the Lutheran W. Pannenberg, talks about the "causal priority of the future"[32] and makes the surprising and counterintuitive claim of "the present as an effect of the future, in contrast to the conventional assumption that past and present are the cause of the future."[33] Because of that, for Pannenberg the concept of anticipation of the future became a leading theme: the historical resurrection of Jesus Christ as a "proleptic" event makes Christian hope confident (albeit not yet fully determined) of the coming eschatological consummation on which ultimately hinges the truth of the Christian message.[34]

---

30. Hick, *Death and Eternal Life*, 15.

31. Moltmann, *Theology of Hope*.

32. So named by Russell, *Time in Eternity*, 117–19.

33. Pannenberg, *Theology and the Kingdom of God*, 54, cited in Russell, *Time in Eternity*, 118.

34. For a fine synopsis, see Russell, *Time in Eternity*, 119–22.

A Christian Vision of the "End" of Cosmos and Life   259

Several Americans have joined the turn to the future, including the two Lutherans, Ted Peters, with his concept of "retroactive ontology" materially repeating Pannenberg's futuristic causality,[35] and Robert W. Jenson, to whom God's true "triune identity" can be known in the course of history's unfolding toward consummation, in which process God shows his faithfulness.[36] Yet another American, the Anabaptist Thomas N. Finger, not only makes room for eschatology in his doctrinal presentation but even gives it the primary place by making it the leading theme.[37]

The British Anglican New Testament scholar N. T. Wright has labored for decades not only with issues such as resurrection but also, more recently, with the biblical basis of future hope. That I have had to critique him for a less than satisfactory vision of the "ultimate" consummation does not mean that his proposal would not have made a significant contribution.[38] He has been recently joined by another senior New Testament expert, A. Thiselton.[39]

Some leading science-religion experts, particularly the British physicist-priest John Polkinghorne and the American physicist-theologian Robert J. Russell, in collaboration with systematicians such as the German Michael Welker, have done groundbreaking work in helping rediscover the centrality of eschatology after the advent of modern science. And so forth. This is to say that with all the push toward ignoring eschatology in some theological quarters, in others it is alive and well.

Now, if there is a call and place for a constructive Christian eschatology for the third millennium—in a world plagued with secularism, religious enthusiasm, and the power of sciences—what might that doctrine look like? To our constructive vision we turn next.

ON THE CONDITIONS OF A COMPREHENSIVE CHRISTIAN ESCHATOLOGY

Although the equivalent of the term "eschatology," the Latin *de novissimis* ("the last things"), was used much earlier, only at the time of Protestant orthodoxy, in the *Loci theologici* (1610–1621) of the Lutheran Johann Gerhard, did the topic receive a full-scale treatment.[40] A few decades later the

35. Peters, *Anticipating Omega*.
36. Jenson, *The Triune Identity*.
37. Finger, *Christian Theology*.
38. See my *Hope and Community*, ch. 10 particularly.
39. Thiselton, *Life after Death*.
40. Gerhard, *Loci theologici* (1610–1621), devotes no fewer than two of nine books to the detailed discussion of eschatological topics (books 8 and 9).

term *eschatologia* itself was used in the last volume of another Lutheran scholastic, Abraham Calov's *Systema locorum theologicorum* (1655–1677).

But what is the "end" eschatology speaks of? A notoriously polyvalent term, "end" can mean both completion (that is, coming or bringing to an end)[41] and fulfillment (as in the Greek term *telos*). Both meanings are present in the Christian eschatological expectation.[42] P. Tillich saw this in his highly nuanced discussion of "the kingdom of God as the end of history," minding the dual nature of the term "end" as completion and fulfillment.[43] Stating that although "[p]ast and present meet in the present, and both are included in the eternal 'now,' . . . they are not swallowed by the present," he added that the future reference is not thereby ignored.[44] This sounds good and correct. Where Tillich goes astray, however, is when he argues that "the fulfillment of history lies in the permanently present end of history," leading to the disappointing thesis that, therefore, ultimately "[t]he eternal is not a future state of things; it is always present."[45] To say that the eternal is not a future state of things is of course true in one sense; eternity is "much more" than a temporal state of things; however, to say that alone (in Tillich's system) means that there is not a future in the sense that traditional eschatology intuits.[46] Tillich's abandonment of the future, final fulfillment of God's kingdom is but an example of the wide trend in the twentieth-century eclipse of future-oriented eschatology.[47]

Contemporary eschatology has to try to strike a radical balance between the New Testament type of enthusiastic hope for the coming of God's righteous rule and the fact that, simply put, "we are no longer a young religion looking forward to the imminent coming of Christ, as the members of the nascent church did in the first centuries."[48] As the German Lutheran theologian Hans Schwarz puts it, "we must guard against two frequent temptations: undue restraint and a travelogue eschatology."[49] It is instructive to note that while on the one hand the Christian Bible has eschatological-apocalyptic sections, and even a whole book devoted to the

---

41. I. Kant famously problematized the idea of "end" in this sense and rightly intuited that the idea of time coming to an end greatly challenges our mental powers. See Kant, "End of All Things," 221–22.

42. See Pannenberg, *Systematic Theology*, 3:586–87.

43. Tillich, *Systematic Theology*, 3:394.

44. Tillich, *Systematic Theology*, 3:395–96.

45. Tillich, *Systematic Theology*, 3:396, 400.

46. So also Pannenberg *Systematic Theology*, 3:587.

47. For details, see Pannenberg, *Systematic Theology*, 3:588–89.

48. Schwarz, *Eschatology*, xii.

49. Schwarz, *Eschatology*, 247.

topic in the New Testament, the church also wisely left out from its canon such wildly speculative and fantasy-oriented pieces of literature as the Book of Enoch and the Apocalypse of Paul.[50]

Seeking for a middle path between the two extremes, however, should not frustrate or push into the margins the radical nature of eschatological hope: "Eschatological faith has about it an undeniable defiance of commonsense appearances. In the face of suffering, violence, and seemingly hopeless injustice and tragedy, it is bold to believe that these are not the deepest and truest realities."[51] Particularly resurrection, "requires of faith something even more terrible than submission before the violence of being and acceptance of fate, and forbids faith the consolations of tragic wisdom; it places all hope and consolation upon the insane expectation that what is lost will be given back, not as heroic wisdom (death has been robbed of its tragic beauty) but as the gift it always was."[52]

When negotiating a radical middle path towards the dynamic vision of the "end" in its two-fold sense explicated above, three essential aspects should be integrated tightly into any constructive eschatology:

- first, the hope not only for the human future but also for the transformation and renewal of all creatures and the cosmos itself;
- second, hope for both persons and communities, including the whole of humanity; and third,
- hope for both the afterlife and the life-before-afterlife.

THE DOMAIN AND HORIZON OF A CONSTRUCTIVE ESCHATOLOGY FOR THE PLURALISTIC WORLD

At the very center of Christian hope, Pannenberg rightly reminds us, is "participation in the eternal life of God.... [And all] else that is related to it, including the resurrection of the dead and the last judgment, is a consequence of God's own coming to consummate his rule over his creation." This "future of God's kingdom," the "epitome of Christian hope,"[53] encompasses all of creation, not only humans, nor merely Earth—but the whole vast cosmos. This is the proper framework for eschatology. This widest horizon,

---

50. Schwarz, *Eschatology*, 247.

51. Walls, introduction to *Oxford Handbook of Eschatology*, 5.

52. Hart, *Beauty of the Infinite*, 392, as cited in Walls, *Oxford Handbook of Eschatology*, 6.

53. Pannenberg, *Systematic Theology*, 3:527.

however, has not been at the center of Christian eschatology. Indeed, what happened early in Christian theology was that personal eschatology became the focus of the Christian hope. And the concept of the kingdom of God was soon marginalized.

Even worse, when employed, its meaning was reduced mainly to hope for the personal resurrection of the body. Communal and cosmic horizons were marginalized. A telling example can be found in the eighth-century (Eastern) doctrinal manual *The Orthodox Faith* by John of Damascus, in which the whole concept of the kingdom is missing and individual resurrection is made the defining theme. The same is true of Western doctrinal presentations from Lombard's *Distinctions* all the way to the Reformation and Protestant Scholasticism. Even classical liberalism's rediscovery of the kingdom of God ended in an immanentist and personalist interpretation.[54]

Only in twentieth-century theology have the centrality and comprehensive nature of eschatology been rediscovered, including not only the personal but also the communal. But even here, a key weakness can still be discerned: the lack of a cosmic orientation. Whereas Barth succeeded in helping rediscover the centrality of eschatology to theology, only in the theologies of Rahner, Moltmann, and Pannenberg, among others, have the implications of what we know of the vastness of the cosmos—in terms of size, "age," and expansion—begun to emerge as integral themes. But even in them the *cosmic* orientation is still by and large in the making.

The development of a viable constructive eschatology for the sake of the religiously pluralistic and secular culture of the globalizing world, as already mentioned above, has to be linked to the following spheres:

1. personal and communal hope
2. human and cosmic destiny
3. present and future hope

Personal and Communal Hope

A systematically crucial problem for constructive eschatology is negotiating personal and communal hopes (ultimately relating to the whole human race) not only as parallel with each other but also as mutually linked. Only such an eschatology that can successfully envision "the perfecting of individual life after death . . . with the consummation of humanity and world

---

54. For details and sources, see Pannenberg, *Systematic Theology*, 3:527–30.

in the kingdom of God" will suffice.[55] Unless one is willing to go with the idea of physical death as an immediate entrance to God's eternity (without any "intermediate time"), a way has to be found to link one's own death and bodily resurrection with the rest of humanity. The theological options are these: "*Either* we expect full and real personal salvation at death even though this minimizes what takes place at the end, allowing for it nothing decisive for individual fulfillment and giving it the significance of an addition, since everything decisive has taken place already; *or* we expect the real decision and salvation to come only at the last day, though this is to play down death as access to Christ, as decision, as purifying, and as transformation."[56]

In the Old Testament and Jewish tradition, the communal hope lay in the forefront and the individual emerged only later gradually. Even when the hope for individuals developed, it was not divorced from but rather integrated into the hope for all of humanity. The Christian church adopted this view and faced the task of even expanding it with the inclusion of gentiles into the hope for a common destiny. In comparison, the pagan hope of the immortality of the soul (as in Plato) has no reference to the whole of humanity, only to the individual. Nor is the contemporary secular hope for the completion of human dreams in an ideal society, as expressed particularly in Marxism, successful in conceiving this utopia as for the whole of humanity; it only deals with those currently living; those who have passed away will totally miss it. The idealist philosopher Gotthold Lessing clearly understood that in his *Education of the Human Race* and was led to the idea of reincarnation for its solution.[57]

The solution of Christian tradition to this dilemma is based on the trinitarian faith, particularly on pneumatological resources. Similarly to the related locus of soteriology and ecclesiology, it is the Spirit's work to "lift us" up in filial relationship with Jesus Christ, the Savior, but not only as individuals without an integral link with others, but rather as members of the same "body" whose "head" is Christ. This "ecstatic" (as in "standing outside one's self") work of the Spirit is of course already at work in a different manner in creation, linking all creatures to the rest of creation.[58]

---

55. Pannenberg, *Systematic Theology*, 3:546.
56. Pannenberg, *Systematic Theology*, 3:547, emphasis in original.
57. See Pannenberg, *Systematic Theology*, 3:546–50.
58. Pannenberg, *Systematic Theology*, vol. 3:551–52.

Human and Cosmic Destiny

Although he himself failed to carry out the program, Tillich's demand that the basic dilemma of any eschatology—the relationship between the individual and collective hope—should not be "separated from the destiny of the universe"[59] is definitely pointing in the right direction. Christian hope of the eschatological consummation includes the whole of God's creation, "the integration of the real history of human beings with the nature of the earth."[60] This holistic and "earthly" eschatological vision is masterfully expressed by the American Anabaptist theologian Thomas A. Finger: "Since the new creation arrives through God's Spirit, and since it reshapes the physical world, every theological locus is informed by the Spirit's transformation of matter-energy."[61] Christ's resurrection through the life-giving Spirit is already a foretaste of the "transformation of matter-energy" in new creation, "a transformation of the present nature beyond what emergence refers to."[62] The pneumatologically loaded eschatological openness of creation points to the final consummation in which matter and physicality—no more than time—are not so much "deleted" as transformed, made transcendent, so to speak.[63]

Present and Future Hope

The present and future are linked tightly with each other through the presence of the Spirit: "By the Spirit the eschatological future is present already in the hearts of believers. His dynamic is the basis of anticipations of eschatological salvation already in the as yet incomplete history of the world."[64] This is a corrective to merely this-worldly "eschatologies," whether those of classical liberalism and other Enlightenment-driven traditions or contemporary eco-feminist (and some liberationist) views. It is also a defeat of those fundamentalist and other otherworldly eschatological visions that end up being escapist and dismissive of work toward improving the current world.

The "already" and "not yet" (of the arrival of the kingdom of God) and the "continuity" versus "discontinuity" (between new creation and

---

59. Tillich, *Systematic Theology*, 3:418.
60. Moltmann, *God in Creation*, xi.
61. Finger, *Contemporary Anabaptist Theology*, 563.
62. Russell, *Cosmology*, 37.
63. Russell, *Cosmology*, 37–38.
64. Pannenberg, *Systematic Theology*, 3:552.

this world) templates hold the present and future in dynamic tension and mutual conditioning. R. Russell summarizes it succinctly: "Eschatologies such as these view the new creation not as a replacement of the present creation—i.e., not as a second *ex nihilo*—nor as the mere working out of the natural processes of the world. Instead eschatology involves the complete transformation of the world by a radically new act of God beginning at Easter and continuing into the future."[65]

FINAL REFLECTIONS: ON THE DIFFICULTY AND CHALLENGES OF DOING ESCHATOLOGY

This essay has argued that eschatology, a proper vision of the "end," *telos* of cosmos, life, and humanity is an essential part of a constructive Christian theology for the sake of the pluralistic world in which secularism, religions, and sciences compete and rule. To its own detriment, modern theology abandoned this robust biblically-based vision for an elusive, mainly this-worldly account of Christian hope.

The limited space of the essay has only allowed the sketching of a rough outline of a comprehensive Christian vision of future for all aspects of God's vast, (almost) infinite creation. In keeping with the nature of an *essai*, a sketch rather than an overly schematized system, this one main point has been repeated: a new kind of vision for the doctrine of the "Last Things" is needed. In addition to its comprehensive nature, it has to deal with a number of complicated and complex issues, including the cosmic, communal, and personal implications of Christ's resurrection; the proper conception of the transition from "here" to "there," that is, how to imagine the continuity-*versus*-discontinuity between the conditions of the current world and the world-to-come particularly in light of the Christian embodied hope of the resurrected body; and so forth.[66]

While doing that intellectually demanding work, the constructive theologian would do well to heed to Moltmann's brilliant, although obvious observation. Any claim for *logos*, "teaching," "doctrine," "principle" about eschaton, events yet-to-happen, is quite a precarious assertion![67] Therefore, he recommends, we should instead speak of "the believing hope."[68] That

---

65. Russell, "Cosmology and Eschatology," 567.

66. In my *Community and Hope*, Part 1 such a comprehensive Christian vision has been set forth in a critical-sympathetic dialogue with the whole of Christian tradition, past and present, natural sciences, and four living faith traditions.

67. Moltmann, *Theology of Hope*, 16–17.

68. Moltmann, *Theology of Hope*, 19–22.

kind of discourse cannot be merely—and not always even primarily—analytic and doctrinal as much as that goal should be kept in mind. To speak of eschatology is to employ also suggestive, metaphorical, and testimonial resources.

No wonder much of the New Testament teaching on eschatology, as the late American Baptist theologian James McClendon put it, comes to us in the form of "word pictures," "words that present visual scenes."[69] Hence, McClendon recommends "eschatological picture thinking" as a methodological guide: therein the theologian engages various biblical-theological (and historical) pictures of God's eschatological rule to show that eschatology is both an image of the end and a directive for the church's present: eschatology is concerned "with what lasts and with what comes last."[70] Similarly, the Jewish theologian Neil Gillman says: "All eschatologies are imaginative constructs. They must be imaginative not only because they deal with events that no human has ever beheld, but even more because these events will inaugurate an age which is properly timeless."[71]

Add to those caveats yet another obvious one, namely, the vast size of the observed cosmos as we now know it. Speaking of its "end" and "destiny"—which we must attempt in contrast to earlier anthropocentric (and our-planet-centered) approaches—in light of its immensity should lead us into humble, tentative, and suggestive concepts. Not only that, but there is yet another layer of challenges to any serious talk about eschatology, what the Italian liberationist Vítor Westhelle names as its liminality, in three interrelated senses of the term—ontologically, ethically, and epistemologically:

> Eschatology is a discourse on liminality, on that which is different in an ontological, ethical and also epistemological sense. Ontologically, because it addresses the question of an Other reality, as different as the reality of God is from this world; ethically, because it pertains to a different code for morality, as different as the Sermon on the Mount is from all our ethical systems and moral prescriptions; epistemologically, because eschatology is also about the liminality of our accepted epistemic régimes, i.e., that there are other, often-suppressed "knowledges" beyond the commonly accepted noetic realm of the academy.[72]

---

69. McClendon, *Doctrine*, 75–77, 92; the latter quoted phrase is from Murphy, "Resurrection Body," 205.

70. McClendon, *Doctrine*, 44, 75.

71. Gillman, *Death of Death*, 25.

72. Westhelle, "Liberation Theology," 312–13.

These words of caution, however, are not to be taken in terms of stifling the theology of the "end." They are meant to be a constant reminder of the extreme caution the eschatologist should exercise when proposing constructive ideas. Although theologians should be quick to acknowledge the limits of human language and intellectual powers, they should also not capitulate before the bar of reason. Consider what A. McGrath, a leading expert on religion-science dialogue, states: "From a Christian perspective, the horizons defined by the parameters of our human existence merely limit what we can see; they do not define what there is to be seen."[73]

Theological imagination, as much as it has to be anchored in the wider human pursuit of truth, should bravely, though also carefully, rush in where angels fear to tread. Modern and contemporary theologians have so much feared the fame of the fool that they also often lacked the rewards of the discovery of the radically new and unanticipated.

---

73. McGrath, *Brief History of Heaven*, 1.

CHAPTER 17

The Greening of the Spirit

Towards a Pneumatological Theology of the Flourishing of Nature

THE ROLE OF SACRED TRADITIONS IN THE PRESERVATION OF NATURE: TENTATIVE CLARIFICATIONS

IF, AS SEEMS CLEAR to many in the beginning of the new millennium, "[e]nvironmental pollution is considered to be our world's most dangerous, and constant, threat,"[1] this raises the question for the theologian of the role of religions in relation to the impending eco-catastrophe.[2] I am convinced that not only "[h]uman beliefs about the nature of ecology are the distinctive contribution of our species to the ecology itself," but also that, importantly, "[r]eligious beliefs—especially those concerning the nature of powers that create and animate—become an effective part of ecological system."[3] Here we have a new challenge and opportunity for all religions and theologies to consider the threat that only recently has become global in its force, namely, the state of the environment.[4]

---

1. International Conference on Environmental Pollution and Remediation, July 15–17, 2013, Toronto, Canada, n.p., http://icepr2013.international-aset.com/index.htmlo.

2. In this essay, "pollution" is used as an inclusive umbrella term denoting all types of harm on environment by humans (whether directly or indirectly). The essay builds on and draws heavily from my forthcoming *Creation and Humanity*, ch. 8.

3. Sullivan, *Hinduism and Ecology*, xi.

4. Tucker and Grim, *Hinduism and Ecology*, xvii (xv–xxxii); Foltz, *Islam and Ecology*, xxxviii.

It is noteworthy that, unlike the past, currently most religions make claims to being "green" and routinely appeal to their sacred Scriptures in support of the claim.[5] The theologian, however, should exercise proper caution. To begin with: is it really the case that we should assume that conservation of the environment be on the forefront of sacred traditions and can expect the ancient Scriptures to be ready resources for third-millennium needs for green thinking?[6] Indeed, it is not as much a matter of what the ancient scriptures of each tradition is saying about nature at face value, but rather, whether—in keeping with the deepest theological and spiritual teachings—an ecofriendly hermeneutics is feasible and available within that tradition.[7] Rightly the Muslim writer Craig Phillips concludes: "Though we tend to read our scriptures anthropocentrically, we must reflect on the fact that our scriptures are not anthropocentric, and nor are they ecocentric."[8]

Be that as it may, it is also noteworthy that while religions' voice is widely dismissed in public conversations concerning the care of environment, at the same time the sacred traditions are by default blamed for many environmental ills, at times even regarded as *the* reason for the rape of nature.[9] As flawed historically, hermeneutically, and analytically, as is the (in)famous essay by Lynn White, "The Historical Roots of Our Ecological Crisis," at least it has been able to fuel self-critical soul-searching[10] and constructive responses among religious traditions. The issue of the role of Christianity and other religions in the suffering of nature will be discussed below.

Having clarified religions' role in relation to the environment, let us now delve into the theological work. The next section seeks to clarify the reasons the Judeo-Christian tradition, against its better knowledge, for too long tended to be either anti-environmentalist or at least failed to live up to its theological ideals. The rest of the essay, then, moves into constructive

---

5. For an important current resource, see the theme issue edited by Thottakara, "Ecology and World Religions," 9–120. Continuously updated information, resources, and discussions can also be drawn from the official website of the Alliance of World Religions and Conservation, http://www.arcworld.org/. The organization claims to be "secular" but to be helping faith traditions cultivate a keen awareness of the habitat at large.

6. See further Hütterman, *Ecological Message of the Torah*, 11. For a seasoned comment, see Sallie McFague, "Ecological Christology," 35.

7. See Foltz, "Islamic Environmentalism: A Matter of Interpretation, 249.

8. Phillips, "Green Creation," 6. He refers to Katz, "Faith, God, and Nature," 164.

9. White, "Historical Roots of Our Ecological Crisis," 1203–7. For a rebuttal and response from an Islamic perspective, see Foltz, "Islamic Environmentalism," 249. From a Jewish perspective, see Lamm, *"Faith and Doubt,"* 162–85.

10. Afrasiabi, "Toward an Islamic Ecotheology," 281.

work and seeks to find theological resources from both pneumatology and eschatology to develop a theology in support of the greening of creation.

ON JUDEO-CHRISTIAN TRADITION NOT BEING INHERENTLY ANTI-ENVIRONMENTALIST

A persistent myth when it comes to religion-environment conversation has to do with the alleged radical difference between Asiatic and Abrahamic traditions, namely, that whereas "Eastern religions promote a sense of harmony between human beings and nature. . . . the religions of the West . . . [are to be blamed for] promoting the separation of human beings and nature and encouraging acts of domination, exploitation, and control."[11] That charge, which appears in different forms in literature, however, is mistaken on two accounts. First of all, even a superficial knowledge of Buddhism and Hinduism, to name the most obvious Asiatic traditions, reveals that the attitude towards conservation of the environment is a highly complicated and difficult issue for Asiatic traditions. Rather than cosmo- or environment-centered, both traditions are deeply anthropocentric as their goal is the release from ignorance (differently conceived in each tradition). They are escapist rather than conservationist because of the "appearance" nature of reality (that is, what we see is not the "real" world, but rather, the real is beyond the seeming God-world dualities) and the cyclical worldview.[12]

Secondly, without setting up any kind of contest between religions, let it suffice to remark that the alleged anthropocentrism of the Judeo-Christian traditions[13] (which might lead to lack of efforts for caring for nature) is more than healed and corrected by weighty well-known theological resources such as God's charge to men and women to act as responsible vice-regents on behalf of other creatures and creation; the covenant spirituality of the Hebrews that binds human beings to God, other humans, and nature; the incarnational Christology of the Christian Scriptures in which Christ is the agent of creation and appears in created reality; the related sacramental

---

11. Eckel, "Is There a Buddhist Philosophy of Nature?," 327; Eckel himself is not condoning the statement. A typical unfounded commendation of Asiatic-traditions' opinion, without any scriptural or theological support (and obviously without any knowledge of the traditions themselves), can be found Snyder, *Practice of the Wild*, 10.

12. A detailed discussion of the environmental resources and obstacles in Hinduism and Buddhism (along with Abrahamic traditions) can be found in ch. 8 of my *Creation and Humanity*.

13. Callicott and Ames, "Introduction," 3–4.

theology in which God's grace is embodied; the expectation of the eschatological renewal of the heavens and earth; and so forth.[14]

That said, it is also important for contemporary Christian theology to acknowledge that the "ecological crisis of the modern world has its starting point in the modern industrial countries," which were shaped by Christian influence.[15] While this is not to put blame on Judeo-Christian religion per se because the most critical influence for dominating and exploiting nature comes from secular sources, particularly from the Enlightenment[16]—and as is well known, destruction of nature has been at least as rampant in atheistic lands[17]—it means that for too long a time Christian theology did not sufficiently clarify the ecological implications of its creation theology. As a result, it contributed passively, so to speak, to the abuse of God's creation.

Christian theology should have reminded itself more often that the mandate in Gen 1:26–27 for humanity to act as God's faithful vice-regents does not justify abuse but rather is a call to responsible service on behalf of God's good creation.[18] Regretfully, the command to "subdue the earth" was too often taken in its literal sense in Christian tradition. Although there is the minor alternative "green" tradition in Christianity that includes mystics and saints to whom nature had intrinsic value and human dominion represented stewardship and care for creatures, in the main Christian tradition, greatly influenced by Greek philosophical movements (particularly Stoicism), nature was conceived to have been made for humans and their benefit. As a result, it was seen through a utilitarian lens; humanity's relation to nature was based on a hierarchical, dualist view emphasizing difference rather than solidarity.[19]

It is precisely as the image of God, reflecting the characteristic of Creator, that in Judeo-Christian tradition the human being is placed in the world as steward, accountable to God.[20] Rather than superiority, humanity

---

14. I was inspired by Tucker and Grim, "Series Foreword," xxv.

15. Moltmann, *Spirit of Life*, 20.

16. It can also be shown historically that the domination of nature has its roots deeply in pre-Enlightenment Renaissance humanism and other related movements in which the *human being* rather than all creatures is put on a pedestal. Bauckham, *Living with Other Creatures*, 47–58. See also ch. 3 in my *Creation and Humanity*.

17. Indeed, removing God from the center and the introduction of anti-Christian influences has caused much of the abuse and distancing from nature. See Kerr, *Immortal Longings*, 163; more widely in Borgmann, *Power Failure*.

18. See Welker, *Creation and Reality*, 60–73.

19. For an excellent analysis, see Bauckham, *Living with Other Creatures*, ch. 2.

20. Pannenberg, *Anthropology in Theological Perspective*, 79; Fisher, *Human Significance*, 40–42.

should exhibit solidarity with creation to which it also belongs.[21] Indeed, says the Orthodox Zizioulas, humanity is called to exercise its priestly vocation on behalf of creation, and the "human being is not fulfilled until it becomes the 'summing up of nature,' as priest referring the world back to its Creator."[22] In the Christian vision, "[a]ll creatures on this earth find their way to one another in the community of a common way, a common suffering and a common hope."[23] There is a continuity between the human and nature, and Christ died and was resurrected not merely for humans but for nature as well.[24]

Currently it is often suggested that in order to exploit these rich theological resources listed above in the service of environmental care, Christian theology should make a shift towards speaking of nature as divine. A growing number of ecologically minded religionists seem to believe that the virtual divinization of nature is necessary in order to foster an attitude of care. The ecofeminist Starhawk is a striking example. While her call to treat nature as "Goddess" does not mean envisioning "a being somewhere outside of this world," it still is an invitation to see nature as inherently divine.[25] Is that so? Although in particular the many mystical spiritual traditions of both the Christian East and West have approached creation with a deep reverence and sense of holiness,[26] theological tradition has refrained from speaking of nature as divine. Rightly so, because divinization blurs the boundary line between the Creator and creatures.[27] It is neither necessary nor useful, therefore, to divinize nature.

What about calling nature a sacrament?[28] While there are sacramental elements in nature, calling nature a sacrament extends the meaning of that technical spiritual/theological term in a way that is a categorical mistake. Rather than being a sacrament, the special conveyor of salvific grace, nature—including creatures embedded in nature's web—hopes for the final

---

21. See Clifford, "When Being Human Becomes Truly Earthly," 173–89; Ruether, *Gaia and God*, 19–22 particularly.

22. As paraphrased by Fisher, *Human Significance*, 152 with quotation from Zizioulas, "Preserving God's Creation," 2. Cf. Clark, *Biology and Christian Ethics*, 269.

23. Moltmann, *Way of Jesus Christ*, 273.

24. Moltmann, *Way of Jesus Christ*, 273.

25. Starhawk, *Dreaming the Dark*, 11; see also her *Spiral Dance*.

26. For medieval mystical reverence of nature, see Dreyer, "Advent of the Spirit: Medieval Mystics and Saints," 123–62.

27. So Hall, *Imaging God*, 48; Fisher, *Human Significance*, 37–40.

28. Cf. Wallace, "Crum Creek Spirituality," 121–37; for discussion, see Daecke, "Profane and Sacramental Views of Nature," 127–40.

redemption according to the biblical promise (Rom 8:19-26).[29] Neither divine nor a sacrament, in theological perspective, "[n]ature remains sacred in the sense that it belongs to God, exists for the glory of God, even reflects the glory of God, as humans also do."[30] The de-divinizing of nature affirms creation as *creation*, finite and vulnerable, as well as valuable because of its goodness.[31]

THEOLOGICAL RESOURCES FOR HEALING AND FLOURISHING OF CREATION

The task of an ecological constructive Christian theology is twofold: on the one hand, it has to clarify and help avoid ways of thinking and speaking of nature as creation that are detrimental to her survival and well-being. On the other hand, it also has to search for resources—theological insights, metaphors, approaches—that can help foster the flourishing and continuing *shalom* of God's creation.

Based on a trinitarian theology of creation, two interrelated themes will be brought into conversation here: the Spirit's work for continuous healing of creation and the eschatological hope for final redemption, culminating in God's Sabbath-rest of eternal delight and consummation. It is highly promising that a growing number of theologians and religious communities are engaging the task of both theological reflection and ecologically sustaining activities in pursuit of a similar kind of vision.

An Ecological Pneumatology: The Vulnerability and Healing of Creation

Rich pneumatological resources in service of environmental care are hidden in various mystical traditions of the Christian church. The mystical vision intuits the link between the Holy Spirit and the flourishing of nature,[32] going back even to biblical traditions.[33] Just recall the medieval saint Hildegard of Bingen's metaphor of the "Greening of the Spirit"—which occasioned the

29. Materially similarly, Pannenberg, *Systematic Theology*, 2:137-38.
30. Bauckham, *Living with Other Creatures*, 13.
31. See further, Bauckham, *Bible and Ecology*.
32. For the importance of nature-based metaphors applied to the Spirit, see Fatula, *Holy Spirit*, 2-3 and passim; see also Moltmann, *Spirit of Life*, ch. 12, for an extensive discussion of various nature metaphors for the Spirit.
33. For the beauty of the earth described through the sensibilities of the Spirit's presence on the Day of Pentecost, see Fatula, *Holy Spirit*, 33-34.

title for this essay—St. Bernard of Clairvaux's symbol of the Spirit as the "living water,"[34] or Thomas Aquinas's poems of "Warming Fire" and "Light."[35] Theology that is still done mostly in the Global North has much to learn in this regard from her counterparts in the Global South. The Korean Methodist J. Y. Lee's distinctive pictures of the Spirit as "cloth" or "weaver" invoke images of protection and care,[36] which also supplements the predominantly masculine God language with female images of the Spirit.[37]

Named in the creed as *vivificantem* (the "vivifier" or life-giver), the Holy Spirit is not only the divine energy-information-life-force that brings about and sustains life, the Spirit is also the source of flourishing, thriving, prospering, blooming, blossoming.[38] Theologically speaking, the "Spirit is the ecstasy that implements God's abundance and triggers the overflow of divine self-giving,"[39] a gift of endless divine hospitality encompassing the whole "fellowship" of creation.[40]

Instead of invoking pantheistic, semi-pagan resources, increasingly utilized in many ecological and "Green" pneumatologies of nature, the moderate Catholic Feminist E. Johnson's *Women, Earth, and Creator Spirit* resonates well with a responsible panentheistic[41] Christian way of envisioning the role of the Spirit in the healing of the ecosystem:

> [T]he Spirit's encircling indwelling weaves a genuine solidarity among all creatures and between God and the world.... When things get broken, which can happen so easily, this divine creative power assumes the shape of a rejuvenating energy that renews the face of the earth (Ps 104:30). The damaged earth, violent and unjust social structures, the lonely and broken heart—all cry out for a fresh start. In the midst of this suffering the Creator Spirit, through the mediation of created powers, comes, as the Pentecost sequence sings, to wash what is unclean; to pour water upon what is drought-stricken; to heal what is

---

34. See Dreyer, "Advent of the Spirit," 123–62.
35. In Donahoe, *Early Christian Hymns*, 156–59.
36. Lee, *Trinity in Asian Perspective*, 104; for other metaphors, see Kim, *Holy Spirit in the World*, 181.
37. Boff, *Holy Trinity: Perfect Community*, 92; Comblin, *Holy Spirit and Liberation*, 49; Müller-Fahrenholz, *God's Spirit*, 26.
38. Johnson, *Women, Earth and Creator Spirit*, 42.
39. Pinnock, *Flame of Love*, 49–50.
40. Johnson, *Women, Earth*, 44.
41. In my *Trinity and Revelation*, part 2, I develop and argue for "Classical Panentheism," a middle way between Classical Theism and more radical contemporary panentheistic versions.

hurt; to loosen up what is rigid; to warm what is freezing; to straighten out what is crooked and bent.[42]

With the eco-pneumatologist M. I. Wallace, I wish to retrieve a central but neglected Christian theme—the idea of God as carnal Spirit who imbues all things—as the linchpin for forging a green spirituality responsive to the environmental needs of our time." This gives "hope for a renewed earth . . . founded on belief in God as Earth Spirit, the compassionate, all-encompassing divine force within the biosphere who inhabits earth community and continually works to maintain the integrity of all forms of life.[43]

While Wallace himself develops that idea in a troublingly robust panentheistic manner, at times flirting with soft forms of pantheism, that doesn't have to be the case. The statement can be aligned with the deepest intuitions of classical Christian tradition in which the omnipresence of the almighty, transcendent God, is so deeply imbued with the created reality that there is no place to hide from the divine presence (Ps 139). Differently from typical misunderstandings, "spirit" (*ruach, pneuma*) in the biblical understanding is not something opposed to "earthly" or "bodily," but rather the divine life-energy penetrating and permeating all created reality.[44] Importantly, the Bible uses metaphors of the Spirit that are taken from nature, such as the "animating breath," "the healing wind," "the living water," and "cleansing fire."[45] To speak of the "earthen spirit"[46] is not to undermine the divine uniqueness of the Spirit, but rather to speak of the divine infinity in which finite and infinite are both transcended and embraced simultaneously.

In Green theology, the Holy Spirit can also be depicted in terms of the "Wounded Spirit."[47] Wallace points out: "If Spirit and earth mutually indwell each other, then God as Spirit is vulnerable to loss and destruction insofar as the earth is abused and despoiled."[48] This is all good and useful. Where some eco-theologies take a dangerous and mistaken course is in speaking of the cosuffering of the Triune God in terms of deicide, the "death of god." Although the rhetoric warning that "the specter of ecocide raises the risk of

42. Johnson, *Women, Earth*, 43. See also Daneel, "African Independent Church," 143–66.

43. Wallace, *Fragments of the Spirit*, 7.

44. Moltmann, *Spirit of Life*, 225–26; see also 40.

45. Wallace, *Fragments of the Spirit*, 8; for other nature metaphors from the Bible, see Wallace, *Finding God in the Singing River*, 6–9.

46. For this term I am indebted to Wallace, "Christian Animism," 203–6.

47. Wallace, "Green Face of God, 450–53.

48. Wallace, "Green Face," 451.

deicide"[49] is just that—*rhetoric*—behind it are highly problematic theological and scientific assumptions. In light of current cosmological knowledge, it does not make sense at all to make any kind of link between what happens in one tiny, little planet in the margins of one of the galaxies among billions of other galaxies and Almighty Creator! For the Creator of this vast universe, the implications of even the most dramatic nucleocatastrophe are nil! Theologically, after even thousands of qualifications, to imply that the Creator's own creation could be a threat to the Creator, in any sense of the word, is simply absurd. In order to maintain the theologically pregnant meaning of Triune God's deep imbuement of the cosmos through and in the Spirit, this kind of suspicious rhetoric should be exposed and corrected.

In biblical traditions, the Spirit of God is not only messianic but also eschatological. The Spirit's presence points to the arrival of God's future, the promised shalom and Sabbath. To that we turn next.

The Eschatological Sabbath-Rest: The Jewish-Christian Vision of Shalom

In the biblical testimony, God "completed" creative work on the day of Sabbath (Gen 2:2), having first judged everything "very good" (1:31). In this light it is highly curious that Christian tradition speaks of six days of creation as if the seventh day, Sabbath, were meaningless. As a result, "[t]he resting God, the celebrating God, the God who rejoices over his creation, receded into the background." And yet, according to the biblical and Jewish intuition, "it is only the Sabbath which completes and crowns creation."[50]

Sabbath is not only looking back, it is also an eschatological feast as it "opens creation for its true future. On the Sabbath the redemption of the world is celebrated in anticipation." The institution of the year of Jubilee (Lev 25:8–55) continues and expands the Sabbath's rest and *shalom*.[51] The Sabbath is itself the presence of eternity in time, and a foretaste of the world to come.[52] As such it anticipates the arrival of the final *shalom*, "the beginning

---

49. Wallace, "Green Face," 452.

50. Moltmann, *God in Creation*, 6, 276. For important reflections from a First Nations perspective, see Woodley, *Shalom and the Community of Creation*, ch. 1 particularly.

51. The Jubilee also reminds us of the need to give rest to the fields and ground. A corollary lesson is the need to keep in mind economic and social justice when thinking of Shalom: while the pollution of nature is not solely the function of economic considerations, much of it is. See further, Bergmann, *Creation Set Free*, ch. 5 particularly.

52. Moltmann, *God in Creation*, 276.

of that peace with nature which many people are seeking today, in the face of the growing destruction of the environment."[53]

Sometimes it is surmised that the Christian eschatological hope would lead to the dismissal of hope for the rest of creation. This is not the case. The Cambridge philosopher-theologian Janet M. Soskice rightly notes that if "there is no hope of the triumph of God's justice on earth, no point in praying that God's kingdom will come and will be done on *earth* as it is in heaven."[54] That is because we will be "redeemed *with* the world, not *from* it."[55] It is rather Platonic dualism that has served as the source of gnosticism, escapism, and political irresponsibility.[56] Those dualities[57] should be eliminated and corrected in light of the expectation of the coming of God's universal rule in the new creation. Rightly, the American philosopher Kevin Corcoran writes that "we human beings have been made from the mud and dirt—God-blessed, God-loved, and God-embraced mud and dirt—and made for life in an equally earthy environment."[58] God's kingdom includes this whole world inasmuch as "God's reconciling, redemptive, and restorative activity takes place within the natural, material world. This is the theater of God's redemptive activity, the theater of God's kingdom."[59]

It is of utmost importance that contemporary Christian theology include in its eschatological vision not only humanity's *shalom* but also all other creatures' flourishing and rest from sufferings. Let it suffice to refer to biblical key passages such as Rom 8:23–26, among others. That said, it is also important to add that the inclusion of all creatures and all creation under the grand eschatological vision does not mean virtually eliminating the distinctive nature of humanity created in God's image and the unique religious ends for men and women—as is the stated goal in some new animal theologies. David Slough's systematic theology *On Animals* oddly argues that no more than the particularity of the incarnation (Jesus as Jewish male) can be interpreted as excluding gentiles and females does it exclude non-human creatures, animals, from "salvation."[60] Although this deeply flawed

---

53. Moltmann, *God in Creation*, 277.
54. Sockice, "Resurrection and the New Jerusalem," 57.
55. Moltmann, *Spirit of Life*, 89 (italics in original).
56. Moltmann, *Trinity and the Kingdom of God*, 89–90.

57. The discussion of "dualism" is often hampered by philosophically and historically inaccurate and misleading statements. A major theological study would be needed for a comprehensive picture.

58. Corcoran, "Thy Kingdom Come (On Earth)," 67.
59. Corcoran, "Thy Kingdom Come (On Earth)," 67.

60. Clough, *On Animals*, ch. 3. Even worse, he opines Christ's humanity does not really mean *humanity* but rather "created reality" (Kindle# 16-82, 316–82). Furthermore,

(albeit obviously well-meant) reasoning, should be rejected, its basic plea for making the Christian eschatological vision include all creation should be robustly supported.

IN LIEU OF CONCLUSIONS: SOME THEOLOGICAL TASKS FOR THE FUTURE

"Green" theology should not be an optional task for the like-minded and interested but rather, as Moltmann rightly states it, Christian theology of creation should be thoroughly "ecological."[61] Indeed, all theologies of creation are ecological in the sense that even without acknowledging it, they guide the attitudes of the faithful—similarly to what can be said of the "political" nature of each ecclesiology (church members do something "political" even if they claim to be a-political!). As discussed above, it took Christian theology a long time to become consciously ecological, and at times its silence or uncritical alliance with non-Christian viewpoints made it anti-ecological.

A continuing dialogue with natural sciences is a necessary task and asset in this pursuit. Although theology should never be merely the recipient of science's ever-new insights—the dialogue is rather a two-way process in which both parties speak to and challenge each other—no credible theology of creation and ecology can be constructed currently without deep investigation of scientific resources.

Similarly, the current pluralistic and globalized world calls for a continuing hospitable dialogue among religions. As discussed briefly in the first section, sacred traditions have an integral relation to the environment. Although they differ quite radically in their environmental resources, challenges, and potential, they have much to learn from each other.

Finally, as a systematic and constructive theologian, I look forward to a long-term interdisciplinary dialogue and collaboration with other theologians in pursuit of a coherent, dynamic, and sensitive theology of the "Greening of the Spirit."

---

distancing himself from all contours of theological tradition, he surmises that the *need* for redemption of animals is based on their moral responsibility, even sinfulness, although differently from humans, and so forth.

61. This is consistent theme in Moltmann, *God in Creation*.

Bibliography

Afrasiabi, Kaveh L. "Toward an Islamic Ecotheology." In *Islam and Ecology: A Bestowed Trust*, edited by Richard C. Foltz et al., 281–96. Cambridge: Center for the Study of World Religions, 2003.

Alexander, Kimberly Ervin. "The Pentecostal Healing Community." In *Toward a Pentecostal Ecclesiology: The Church and the Fivefold Gospel*, edited by John Christopher Thomas, 183–206. Cleveland: CPT, 2010.

Alexander, Samuel. *Space, Time, and Deity*. 2 vols. Toronto: Macmillan, 1920.

Althouse, Peter. "Ascension—Pentecost—Eschaton: A Theological Framework for Pentecostal Ecclesiology." In *Toward a Pentecostal Ecclesiology: The Church and the Fivefold Gospel*, edited by John Christopher Thomas, 225–47. Cleveland: CPT, 2010.

Anderson, Allan. *Spreading Fires: The Missionary Nature of Early Pentecostalism*. London: SCM, 2007.

Anderson, Ray. *On Being Human*. Pasadena: Fuller Seminary Press, 1982.

Anderson, Sybol Cook. *Hegel's Theory of Recognition: From Oppression to Ethical Liberal Modernity*. London/New York: Continuum, 2009.

Aquinas, Thomas, Saint. *Summa Contra Gentiles, Books I and II*. Edited by The Aquinas Institute. Steubenville: Emmaus Academic, 2019.

———. *Summa Theologica*. https://www.newadvent/org/summa.

Archer, Kenneth J. "The Fivefold Gospel and the Mission of the Church: Ecclesiastical Implications and Opportunities." In *Toward a Pentecostal Ecclesiology: The Church and the Fivefold Gospel*, edited by John Christopher Thomas, 7–43. Cleveland: CPT, 2010.

———. "Pentecostal Hermeneutics: Retrospect and Prospect." *Journal of Pentecostal Theology* 4 (1996) 63–81.

———. "Pentecostal Story: The Hermeneutical Filter for the Making of Meaning." *Pneuma: The Journal of the Society for Pentecostal Studies* 26 (2004) 36–59.

Archer, Kenneth J., and Lee Roy Martin. "Pentecostal Hermeneutics: Retrospect and Prospect." In *Pentecostal Hermeneutics*, 131–48. Leiden: Brill, 2013.

Armstrong, D. M. *A Materialist Theory of the Mind*. 2nd ed. New York: Routledge, 1993.

Asamoah-Gyadu, J. Kwabena. *African Charismatics: Current Developments Within Independent Indigenous Pentecostalism in Ghana*. Leiden: Brill, 2006.

———. "Christian Education in the Modern African Church: Maturity, Growth and the Spirituality of Ghanaian Pentecostal/Charismatic Movements." In *Teaching to Make Disciples: Collected Papers of the 30th Annual Meeting of the Society for Pentecostal Studies*. Tulsa: Oral Roberts University, 2001 (unpublished).

Augustine, Daniela C. "The Empowered Church: Ecclesiological Dimensions of the Event of Pentecost." In *Toward a Pentecostal Ecclesiology: The Church and the Fivefold Gospel*, edited by John Christopher Thomas, 157–82. Cleveland: CPT, 2010.

Badham, Paul, and Linda Badham, eds. *Death and Immortality in the Religions of the World*. New York: Paragon, 1987.

Baird, Justus. "Case for Multifaith Education." In *A Lifelong Call to Learn*, edited by Robert E. Reber and D. Bruce Reber, 245–60. Herndon: Alban Institute, 2010.

Baker-Fletcher, Karen. *Dancing with God: The Trinity from a Womanist Perspective*. St. Louis: Chalice, 2006.

Balia, Daryl, and Kirsteen Kim, eds. *Edinburgh 2010 Witnessing to Christ Today*. Oxford: Regnum, 2010.

Balthasar, Hans Urs von. "The Unknown Lying Beyond the Word." In *Exploration in Theology III: Creator Spirit*, 105–16. San Francisco: Ignatius, 1993.

Barbour, Ian G. "Neuroscience, Artificial Intelligence, and Human Nature: Theological and Philosophical Reflections." *Zygon: Journal of Religion and Science* 34 (1999) 361–98.

Barnhill, David Landis, and Roger S. Gottlieb, eds. *Deep Ecology and World Religions: New Essays on Sacred Ground*. Albany: State University of New York, 2001.

Barrett, Clive, ed. *Unity in Process: Reflections on Receptive Ecumenism*. London: Darton, Longman & Todd, 2012.

Barth, Karl. *Church Dogmatics*. Vol. I. Edinburgh: T. & T. Clark, 1956.

———. *Church Dogmatics*. Vol. III. Edinburgh: T. & T. Clark, 1960.

Bauckham, Richard. *The Bible and Ecology: Rediscovering the Community of Creation*. Waco, TX: Baylor University Press, 2010.

———. *Living with Other Creatures: Green Exegesis and Theology*. Waco, TX: Baylor University Press, 2011.

Bediako, Kwame. *Christianity in Africa: The Renewal of a Non-Western Religion*. Edinburgh: Edinburgh University Press, 1995.

Bergmann, Sigurd. *Creation Set Free: The Spirit as Liberator of Nature*. Grand Rapids: Eerdmans, 2005.

Berkhof, Hendrikus. *The Doctrine of the Holy Spirit*. Atlanta: John Knox, 1964.

Bickle, John. "Multiple Realizability." In *The Stanford Encyclopedia of Philosophy*, edited by Edward N. Zalta, n.d. https://plato.stanford.edu/entries/multiple-realizability/.

Bielfedlt, Dennis D. "The Ontology of Deification." In *Caritas Dei: Beiträge zum Verständnis Luthers und der gegenwärtigen Ökumene*, edited by Oswald Bayer, Robert W. Jenson and Simo Knuuttila, 90–113. Helsinki: Luther-Agricola-Gesellschaft, 1997.

Blue, Ken M. *Authority to Heal*. Downers Grove, IL: InterVarsity, 1987.

Bobrinskoy, Boris. *The Mystery of the Trinity. Trinitarian Experience and Vision in the Biblical and Patristic Tradition*. Crestwood: SVS, 1999.

Boesak, Allen. *Farewell to Innocence: A Socio-Ethical Study on Black Theology and Black Power*. Maryknoll, NY: Orbis, 1977.

Boff, Leonardo. *Holy Trinity, Perfect Community*. Translated by Phillip Berryman. Maryknoll, NY: Orbis, 2000.

———. *Trinity and Society*. Maryknoll, NY: Orbis, 1988.

Boonyakiat, Satanun. "A Christian Theology of Suffering in the Context of Theravada Buddhism in Thailand." PhD diss., Fuller Theological Seminary, School of Theology, 2009.
Borg, Marcus J. *Jesus, a New Vision: Spirit, Culture, and the Life of Discipleship*. San Francisco: Harper & Row, 1987.
Borgmann, Albert. *Power Failure*. Grand Rapids: Baker, 2003.
Boyd, Gregory A. *God at War: The Bible and Spiritual Conflict*. Downers Grove, IL: InterVarsity, 1997.
———. *Satan and the Problem of Evil: Constructing a Trinitarian Warfare Theodicy*. Downers Grove, IL: InterVarsity, 2001.
Bradnick, David. "Spirits and the Stars: A Spirit-Filled Cosmology." In *Interdisciplinary and Religio-Cultural Discourses: Loosing the Spirits*, edited by Veli-Matti Kärkkäinen et al., 213–26. London: Palgrave, 2013.
Brown, Robert McAfee. "The 'Preferential Option for the Poor' and the Renewal of Faith." In *Churches in Struggle: Liberation Theologies and Social Change in North America*, edited by William K. Tabb, 7–17. New York: Monthly Review, 1986.
Brown, Warren S. "Conclusion: Reconciling Scientific and Biblical Portraits of Human Nature." In *Whatever Happened to the Soul? Scientific and Theological Portraits of Human Nature*, edited by Warren Shelburne Brown et al., 213–28. Minneapolis: Fortress, 1998.
Browning, Don. *Fundamental Practical Theology*. Revised. Minneapolis: Fortress, 1995.
———. "Human Dignity, Human Complexity, and Human Goods." In *God and Human Dignity*, edited by R. Kendall Soulen and Linda Woodhead. Grand Rapids: Eerdmans, 2006.
Brunner, Emil. *The Misunderstanding of the Church*. London: Lutterworth, 1953.
Bulgakov, Sergius. *The Comforter*. Grand Rapids: Eerdmans, 2004,
Burgess, Richard H. "Nigerian Pentecostal Theology in Global Perspective." *PentecoStudies* 7 (2008) 29–63.
Byrd, Joseph. "Paul Ricoeur's hermeneutical Theory and Pentecostal Proclamation." *Pneuma: The Journal of the Society for Pentecostal Studies* 15 (1993) 203–14.
Callicott, J. Baird, and Roger T. Ames, eds. "Introduction: The Asian Traditions as Conceptual Resource for Environmental Philosophy." In *Nature in Asian Traditions of Thought: Essays in Environmental Philosophy*, edited by J. Baird Callicott and Roger T. Ames, 1–21. Albany: State University of New York Press, 1989.
———. *Nature in Asian Traditions of Thought: Essays in Environmental Philosophy*. Revised. Albany: State University of New York Press, 1989.
Calvin, John. *Calvin's Commentaries*. Calvin Translation Society. Grand Rapids: Christian Classics Etherial Library, n.d. https://www.ccel.org/ccel/calvin/commentaries.i.html.
———. *Institutes of the Christian Religion*. Translated by Henry Beveridge. Grand Rapids: Eerdmans, 1990. https://www.ccel.org/ccel/calvin/institutes.html.
Caputo, John, and Michael Scanlon, eds. *God, the Gift and Postmodernism*. Bloomington: Indiana University Press, 1999.
Cargal, Timothy B. "Beyond the Fundamentalist-Modernity Controversy: Pentecostals and Hermeneutics in a Postmodern Age." *Pneuma: Journal of the Society for Pentecostal Studies* 15 (1993) 163–87.
Carpenter, Harold. "Tolerance or Irresponsibility: The Problem of Pluralism in Missions." *Advance* 31 (1995) 19.

Carroll, William E. "Aquinas on Creation and the Metaphysical Foundations of Science." *Sapientia* 54 (1999) 69–91.

Case, Shirley Jackson. *The Origins of Christian Supernaturalism*. Chicago: Chicago University Press, 1946.

Castelo, Daniel. "The Improvisational Quality of Ecclesial Holiness." In *Toward a Pentecostal Ecclesiology: The Church and the Fivefold Gospel*, edited by John Christopher Thomas, 87–104. Cleveland: CPT, 2010.

Cerillo, Augusto. "Interpretive Approaches to the History of American Pentecostal Origins." *Pneuma: The Journal of the Society for Pentecostal Studies* 19 (1997) 29–52.

Chalmers, David J. *The Conscious Mind: In Search of a Fundamental Theory*. Revised. New York: Oxford University Press, 1997.

———. "Facing Up to the Problem of Consciousness." *Journal of Consciousness* 2 (1995) 200–219.

Chan, Simon. "'An Asian Review,' review of Jürgen Moltmann's *The Spirit of Life: A Universal Affirmation*." *Journal of Pentecostal Theology* 4 (1994) 35–40.

———. "Jesus as Spirit-Baptizer: Its Significance for Pentecostal Ecclesiology." In *Toward a Pentecostal Ecclesiology: The Church and the Fivefold Gospel*, edited by John Christopher Thomas, 139–56. Cleveland: CPT, 2010.

———. "Mother Church: Toward a Pentecostal Ecclesiology." *Pneuma: The Journal of the Society for Pentecostal Studies* 22 (2000) 177–208.

Chandngarm, Saeng. *Arriyasatsee [The Four Noble Truths]*. Bangkok: Sangsan, 2001.

Chapple, Christopher Key, and Mary Evelyn Tucker, eds. *Hinduism and Ecology: The Intersection of Earth, Sky, and Water*. Cambridge, MA: Harvard University Press, 2000.

Cho, David Yonggi. *When I Am Weak, Then I Am Strong*. Vol. 3. A Sermon Series. Seoul: Logos, 2003.

Chopp, Rebecca S. "Latin American Liberation Theology." In *The Modern Theologians*, edited by David Ford, 409–25. Oxford: Blackwell, 1997.

Clark, Stephen R. L. *Biology and Christian Ethics*. New York: Cambridge University Press, 2000.

Clayton, Philip. "God and World." In *The Cambridge Companion to Postmodern Theology*, edited by Kevin J. Vanhoozer, 203–18. Cambridge: Cambridge University Press, 2003.

———. "The Impossible Possibility: Divine Causes in the World of Nature." In *God, Life, and the Cosmos: Christian and Islamic Perspectives*, edited by Ted Peters et al., 249–80. Surrey: Ashgate, 2002.

———. *Mind and Emergence: From Quantum to Consciousness*. Oxford: Oxford University Press, 2004.

———. "Neuroscience, the Person, and God: An Emergentist Account." In *Neuroscience and the Person: Scientific Perspectives on Divine Action*, edited by Robert J. Russell et al., 181–214. Notre Dame: University of Notre Dame Press, 2004.

———. "The Spirit in Evolution and in Nature." In *Interdisciplinary and Religio-Cultural Discourses: Loosing the Spirits*, edited by Veli-Matti Kärkkäinen et al., 187–96. London: Palgrave, 2013.

———. "Toward a Theory of Divine Action that Has Traction." In *Scientific Perspectives on Divine Action: Twenty Years of Challenge and Progress*, edited by Robert John

Russell et al., 85–110. Vatican City and Berkeley: Vatican Observatory and Center for Theological and the Natural Sciences, 2008.

Clifford, Anne M. "When Being Human Becomes Truly Earthly: An Ecofeminist Proposal for Solidarity." In *In the Embrace of God: Feminist Approaches to Theological Anthropology*, edited by Ann O'Hara Graff, 173–89. Eugene, OR: Wipf & Stock, 2005.

Clooney, Francis X. *Theology after Vedānta: An Experiment in Comparative Theology*. Albany: State University of New York Press, 1993.

———. *Comparative Theology: Deep Learning across Religious Borders*. Oxford: Wiley-Blackwell, 2010.

———. "Comparative Theology: A Review of Recent Books (1989–1995)." *Theological Studies* 56 (1995) 521–50.

Clough, David L. *On Animals: Volume I: Systematic Theology*. New York: Bloomsbury T. & T. Clark, 2012.

Cobb, John B. *Christ in a Pluralistic Age*. Philadelphia: Westminster John Knox, 1975.

Comblin, José. *The Holy Spirit and Liberation*. Maryknoll, NY: Orbis, 1989.

Cone, James H. *A Black Theology of Liberation*. 2nd ed. Maryknoll, NY: Orbis, 1986.

Cooper, John W. *Body, Soul, and Life Everlasting: Biblical Anthropology and the Monism-Dualism Debate*. 2nd ed. Grand Rapids: Eerdmans, 2000.

Corcoran, Kevin. "Thy Kingdom Come (On Earth): An Emerging Eschatology." In *Church in the Present Tense: A Candid Look at What's Emerging*, edited by Jason Clark et al., 59–74. Grand Rapids: Brazos, 2011.

Corduan, Winfried. *A Tapestry of Faiths: The Common Threads Between Christianity and World Religions*. Downers Grove, IL: InterVarsity, 2002.

Cousins, Emily. "Mountains Made Alive: Native American Relationship with Sacred Land." *Cross Currents* 46 (1996) 497–510.

Cox, Harvey. *Fire From Heaven: The Rise of Pentecostal Spirituality And The Reshaping Of Religion In The 21st Century*. Cambridge: Da Capo, 2001.

———. "A Review of *Pentecostal Spirituality: A Passion for the Kingdom* by Steven J. Land." *Journal of Pentecostal Theology* 5 (1994) 3–12.

Crutchfield, James P., et al. "Chaos." In *Chaos and Complexity: Scientific Perspectives on Divine Action*, edited by Robert John Russell et al., 35–44. Notre Dame: Notre Dame University Press, 1996.

Cummings, Robert W. "Unto You Is the Promise: A Personal Testimony." Lucknow: Lucknow, 1941.

Cunningham, David S. *These Three Are One: The Practice of Trinitarian Theology*. Cambridge: Blackwell, 1998.

———. "The Trinity." In *The Cambridge Companion to Postmodern Theology*, edited by Kevin J. Vanhoozer, 186–201. Cambridge: Cambridge University Press, 2003.

D'Costa, Gavin. *The Meeting of Religions and the Trinity*. Maryknoll, NY: Orbis, 2000.

Dabney, D. Lyle. "Who Do You Say I Am? Pneumatological Discourse and the Question of Human Identity." Presented at the John Templeton Foundation Symposium, "Pneumatology: Exploring the Work of the Spirit from Contemporary Perspectives," New York, November 12, 2004 (unpublished).

Daecke, S. M. "Profane and Sacramental Views of Nature." In *The Sciences and Theology in the Twentieth Century*, edited by Arthur R. Peacocke. Notre Dame: University of Notre Dame Press, 1986.

Daley, Brian E. *The Hope of the Early Church: A Handbook of Patristic Eschatology.* Grand Rapids: Baker Academic, 2002.

Daneel, M. L. "African Independent Church Pneumatology and the Salvation of All Creation." *International Review of Mission* 82 (1993) 143–66.

Dau, Isaiah Majok. *Suffering and God. A Theological Reflection on War in the Sudan.* Nairobi: Paulines Publications Africa, 2002.

Davis, John R. *Poles Apart: Contextualizing the Gospel in Asia.* Bangalore: Theological Book Trust, 1998.

Davis, Stephen T., et al., eds. *The Resurrection: An Interdisciplinary Symposium on the Resurrection of Jesus.* New York: Oxford University Press, 1997.

Dayton, Donald W. *Theological Roots of Pentecostalism.* Grand Rapids: Zondervan, 1987.

De Kock, Wynand J. "The Church as a Redeemed, Un-Redeemed, and Redeeming Community." In *Toward a Pentecostal Ecclesiology: The Church and the Fivefold Gospel*, edited by John Christopher Thomas, 47–68. Cleveland: CPT, 2010.

De Nys, Martin J. *Hegel and Theology.* New York: T. & T. Clark, 2009.

Del Colle, Ralph. "Postmodernism and Pentecostal-Charismatic Experience." *Journal of Pentecostal Theology* 17 (2000) 97–116.

Deleuze, Gilles. *Essays Critical And Clinical.* Translated by D.W. Smith and M.A. Greco. Minneapolis: University of Minnesota Press, 1997.

Derrida, Jacques. *Given Time: 1. Counterfeit Money.* Chicago: Chicago University Press, 1995.

———. "Hospitality, Justice, and Responsibility: A Dialogue with Jacques Derrida." In *Questioning Ethics: Contemporary Debates in Philosophy*, edited by Richard Kearney and Mark Dooley, 65–83. London: Routledge, 1999.

Donahoe, Daniel Joseph. *Early Christian Hymns, series 2.* Middletown. Donahoe, 1911.

Dooley, Mark, et al., eds. "Hospitality, Justice, and Responsibility: A Dialogue with Jacques Derrida." In *Questioning Ethics: Contemporary Debates in Continental Philosophy*, 65–83. London/New York: Routledge, 1999.

Dowey, Edward A., Jr. *Knowledge of God in Calvin's Theology, 3rd Ed.* Grand Rapids: Eerdmans, 1994.

Dretske, Fred I. *Explaining Behavior: Reasons in a World of Causes.* Cambridge, MA: MIT, 1988.

Dreyer, Elizabeth A. "An Advent of the Spirit: Medieval Mystics and Saints." In *Advents of the Spirit: An Introduction to the Current Study of Pneumatology*, edited by Bradford E. Hinze and D. Lyle Dabney, 123–62. Milkauwee: Marquette University Press, 2001.

Dufourmantelle, Anne, and Jacques Derrida. *Of Hospitality.* Stanford: Stanford University Press, 2000.

Dunn, James D. G. *The Theology of Paul the Apostle.* Grand Rapids: Eerdmans, 1997.

———. "Towards the Spirit of Christ: The Emergence of the Distinctive Features of Christian Pneumatology." In *The Work of the Spirit: Pneumatology and Pentecostalism*, edited by Michael Welker, 3–26. Grand Rapids: Eerdmans, 2006.

Dupuis, Jacques. *Jesus Christ at the Encounter of World Religions.* Maryknoll, NY: Orbis, 1991.

———. *Toward a Christian Theology of Religious Pluralism.* Maryknoll, NY: Orbis, 1997.

Dyrness, William A., et al., eds. *Global Dictionary of Theology: A Resource for the Worldwide Church*. Downers Grove, IL: IVP Academic, 2008.

Eckel, Malcolm David. "Is There a Buddhist Philosophy of Nature?" In *Buddhism and Ecology: The Interconnection of Dharma and Deeds*, edited by Mary Evelyn Tucker and Duncan Ryuken Williams, 327–49. Cambridge: Center for the Study of World Religions, 1998.

———. "Perspectives on the Buddhist-Christian Dialogue." In *The Christ and the Bodhisattva*, edited by Donald S. Lopez Jr and Steven C. Rockefeller, 43–62. Albany: State University of New York, 1987.

Edelman, Gerald M., and Giulio Tononi. *A Universe Of Consciousness: How Matter Becomes Imagination*. New York: Basic, 2000.

Edwards Jr., O. C. "Meanings of Full Communion: The Essence of Life in the Body." *Speaking of Unity* 1 (2005) 9–35.

Edwards, Denis. "The Discovery of Chaos and the Retrieval of the Trinity." In *Chaos and Complexity: Scientific Perspectives on Divine Action*, edited by Robert John Russell et al., 157–75. Notre Dame: Notre Dame University Press, 1996.

Eliade, Mircea. *The Myth of the Eternal Return: Or, Cosmos and History*. Translated by Willard R. Trask. Princeton: Princeton University Press, 1971.

Erickson, Millard J. *God in Three Persons: A Contemporary Interpretation of the Trinity*. Grand Rapids: Baker, 1995.

Ervin, Howard M. "Koinonia, Church and Sacraments: A Pentecostal Response." A Pentecostal Position Paper Read at the International Roman Catholic-Pentecostal Dialogue in Venice, August 1–8, 1987 (unpublished).

Evans, James H. *We Have Been Believers: An African-American Systematic Theology*. Minneapolis: Fortress, 1992.

Farley, Wendy. *Tragic Vision and Divine Compassion: A Contemporary Theodicy*. Louisville: Westminster John Knox, 1990.

Fatula, Mary Ann. *The Holy Spirit: Unbounded Gift of Joy*. Collegeville, MN: Liturgical, 1998.

Feuerbach, Ludwig. *The Essence of Christianity*. Translated by George Eliot. New York: Harper and Brothers, 1957.

Fiddes, Paul. *Participating in God. A Pastoral Doctrine of the Trinity*. Louisville: Westminster John Knox, 2000.

Finger, Thomas N. *Christian Theology: An Eschatological Approach*. Nashville: Thomas Nelson, 1985.

Fisher, Christopher L., ed. *Human Significance in Theology and the Natural Sciences: An Ecumenical Perspective with Reference to Pannenberg, Rahner, and Zizioulas*. Eugene, OR: Pickwick, 2010.

Flanders, Christopher L. "About Face: Reorienting Thai Face for Soteriology and Mission." PhD Diss., Fuller Theological Seminary, School of Intercultural Studies, 2005.

Flew, Anthony. "The Logic of Mortality." In *Death and Immortality in the Religions of the World*, edited by Paul Badham and Linda Badham, 171–87. New York: Paragon, 1987.

Fodor, Jerry. "Special Sciences (Or: The Disunity of Science as a Working Hypothesis)." *Synthese* 27 (1974) 97–115.

Foltz, Richard C. "Introduction." In *Islam and Ecology: A Bestowed Trust*, edited by Richard C. Foltz et al., xxxvii-xviii. Cambridge, MA: Harvard University Press, 2003.

———. "Islamic Environmentalism: A Matter of Interpretation." In *Islam and Ecology: A Bestowed Trust*, edited by Richard C. Foltz et al. Cambridge: Center for the Study of World Religions, 2003.

Foltz, Richard C., et al., eds. *Islam and Ecology: A Bestowed Trust*. Cambridge: Center for the Study of World Religions, 2003.

Fredricks, James L. *Faith Among Faiths: Christian Theology and Non-Christian Religions*. New York: Paulist, 1999.

Freud, Sigmund. *Reflections on War and Death*. Translated by A. A. Brill and Alfred B. Kuttner. New York: Moffat, Yard and Co., 1918.

Fukuyama, Francis. *The End of History and the Last Man*. New York: Free, 1992.

Geivett, Douglas R., and W. Gary Phillips. "A Particularist View: An Evidentialist Approach." In *Four Views on Salvation in a Pluralistic World*, edited by Dennis L. Ockholm and Timothy R. Phillips, 211–44. Grand Rapids: Zondervan, 1995.

Gifford, Paul. *Ghana's New Christianity, New Edition: Pentecostalism in a Globalising African Economy*. Bloomington: Indiana University Press, 2004.

Gilkey, Langdon. "Cosmology, Ontology, and the Travail of Biblical Language." *The Journal of Religion* 41 (1961) 194–205.

Gillman, Neil. *The Death of Death*. Woodstock: Jewish Lights, 2000.

Goergen, Donald J. "The Quest for the Christ of Africa." *African Christian Studies* 17 (2001). http://www.sedos.org/english/goergen.htm.

González, Justo L. *Mañana: Christian Theology from a Hispanic Perspective*. Nashville: Abingdon, 1990.

Gozzano, Simone, and Christopher S. Hill, eds. *New Perspectives on Type Identity: The Mental and the Physical*. New York/Cambridge: Cambridge University Press, 2012.

Graff, Ann O'Hara, ed. *In the Embrace of God: Feminist Approaches to Theological Anthropology*. Eugene, OR: Wipf & Stock, 2005.

Graham, Stephen Ray, ed. "Christian Hospitality and Pastoral Practices in a Multifaith Society: An ATS Project, 2010–2012." *Theological Education* 47 (2012) 1–10.

Green, Joel B. *Body, Soul, and Human Life: The Nature of Humanity in the Bible*. Grand Rapids: Baker Academic, 2008.

Gregersen, Niels Henrik. "Special Divine Action and the Quilt of Laws: Why the Distinction between Special and General Divine Action Cannot be Maintained." In *Scientific Perspectives on Divine Action: Twenty Years of Challenge and Progress*, edited by Robert John Russell et al.,179–99. Vatican City and Berkeley: Vatican Observatory and Center for Theological and the Natural Sciences, 2008.

———. "Three Types of Indeterminacy." In *The Concept of Nature in Science and Theology*, edited by Niels Henrik Gregersen et al., 165–86. Geneva: Labor et Fides, 1997.

Grenz, Stanley J. "Community & Relationships." http://www.stanleyjgrenz.com/articles/talk_mag.html.

———. *Rediscovering the Triune God: The Trinity in Contemporary Theology*. Minneapolis: Fortress, 2004.

———. *The Social God and Relational Self: A Trinitarian Theology of the Imago Dei*. Louisville: Westminster John Knox, 2001.

———. *Theology for the Community of God*. Grand Rapids: Eerdmans, 1994.

Grieve, Wolfgang, ed. *Justification in the World's Context*. Documentation 45. Geneva: LWF, 2000.
Griffin, David Ray. "Process Eschatology." In *The Oxford Handbook of Eschatology*, edited by Jerry L. Walls, 295–307. New York: Oxford University Press, 2007.
Grislis, Egil. "Luther and the Turks." *The Muslim World* 64/3 (1974): 180–93.
Guinness, Os. *Fit Bodies, Fat Minds: Why Evangelicals Don't Think, and What to Do About It*. Grand Rapids: Baker, 1994.
Gunton, Colin. *Father, Son and Holy Spirit. Essays Toward a Fully Trinitarian Theology*. New York: T. & T. Clark, 2003.
———. *The One, the Three and the Many: God, Creation, and the Culture of Modernity*. Cambridge: Cambridge University Press, 1993.
———. *The Triune Creator: A Historical and Systematic Study*. Grand Rapids; Eerdmans, 1998.
Gutiérrez, Gustavo. *Essential Writings*. Edited by James B. Nicholoff. Minneapolis: Fortress, 1996.
Haddad, Yvonne Yazbeck, and Wadi Z. Haddad, eds. *Christian-Muslim Encounters*. Gainesville: University Press of Florida, 1995.
Haight, Roger. *Christian Community in History*, vol. 2: *Comparative Ecclesiology*. New York/London: Continuum, 2005.
———. *Ecclesial Existence*, vol. 3 of *Christian Community in History*. New York/London: Continuum, 2008.
Hall, Douglas J. *Imaging God: Dominion as Stewardship*. Grand Rapids: Eerdmans, 2004.
———, ed. *God and Human Suffering: An Exercise in the Theology of the Cross*. Reprint edition. Minneapolis: Fortress, 1987.
Han, Sang-Ehil. "Christian Hospitality and Neighborliness." http://docs.ats.edu/uploads/resources/publications-presentations/chapp-reports/pentecostal-theological-seminary.pdf.
Han, Sang-Ehil, et al. "Christian Hospitality and Pastoral Practices from an Evangelical Perspective." *Theological Education* 47 (2012) 11–31.
Hanh, Thich Nhat. *Living Buddha, Living Christ*. New York: Riverhead, 1994.
Hardt, Michael, and Antonio Negri. *Empire*. Cambridge, MA: Harvard University Press, 2000.
———. *Multitude: War and Democracy in the Age of Empire*. New York: Penguin, 2004.
Harper, Brad, and Paul Louis Metzger. *Exploring Ecclesiology: An Evangelical and Ecumenical Introduction*. Grand Rapids: Brazos, 2009.
Harris, Murray J. *Raised Immortal: Resurrection and Immortality in the New Testament*. Grand Rapids: Eerdmans, 1983.
Hart, David Bentley. *The Beauty of the Infinite: The Aesthetics of Christian Truth*. Grand Rapids: Eerdmans, 2003.
Hartshorne, Charles. "The Compound Individual." In *Philosophical Essays for Alfred North Whitehead*, edited by F. S. C. Northrup. New York: Russell & Russell, 1967.
Hasker, William. *The Emergent Self*. Ithaca: Cornell University Press, 2001.
Haught, John F. *Is Nature Enough? Meaning and Truth in the Age of Science*. Cambridge/New York: Cambridge University Press, 2006.
Hefener, Philip. "Imago Dei: The Possibility and Necessity of the Human Person." In *The Human Person in Science and Theology*, edited by Niels Henrik Gregersen et al., 73–94. Issues in Science and Theology. Grand Rapids: Eerdmans, 2000.

Hegel, G. W. F. *The Phenomenology of Mind*. San Francisco: Harper Torch, 1967.
Heim, S. M. *The Depth of the Riches. A Trinitarian Theology of Religious Ends*. Grand Rapids: Eerdmans, 2001.
Heller, Michael. "Adventures of the Concept of Mass and Matter." *Philosophy in Science* 3 (1988) 15–35.
Herberg, Will. *Judaism and Modern Man;: An Interpretation of Jewish Religion*. New York: Farrar, Straus and Young, 1951.
Heschel, Abraham J. *The Prophets*. New York: Harper & Row, 1962.
Hess, Mary. "The Pastoral Practice of Christian Hospitality as Presence in Muslim-Christian Engagement: Contextualizing the Classroom." *Theological Education* 47 (n.d.) 7–12. http://docs.ats.edu/uploads/resources/publications-presentations/chapp-reports/luther-seminary.pdf.
Hessel, Dieter T., and Rosemary Radford Ruether, eds. *Christianity and Ecology: Seeking the Well-Being of Earth and Humans*. Cambridge: Center for the Study of World Religions, 2000.
Hick, John. *Death and Eternal Life*. Louisville: Westminster John Knox, 1994.
Hietamäki, Minna. "Recognition and Ecumenical Recognition—Distinguishing the Idea of Recognition in Modem Ecumenism." *Neue Zeitschrift für systematische Theologie und Religionsphilosophie* 56 (2014) 454–72.
Hill, Graham. *Salt, Light, and a City: Introducing Missional Ecclesiology*. Eugene, OR: Wipf & Stock, 2012.
Hinlicky, Paul R. "Theological Anthropology: Toward Integrating *Theosis* and Justification by Faith." *Journal of Ecumenical Studies* 34 (1997) 44–47.
Hinze, Bradford E., and D. Lyle Dabney, eds. *Advents of the Spirit: An Introduction to the Current Study of Pneumatology*. Milwaukee: Marquette University Press, 2001.
Hollenweger, Walter J. "After Twenty Years' Research on Pentecostalism." *International Review of Missions* 75 (1986) 3–12.
———. "The Critical Tradition of Pentecostalism." *Journal of Pentecostal Theology* 1 (1992) 7–17.
———. *The Pentecostals*. Peabody: Hendrickson, 1988.
———. "Verheissung und Verhängnis der Pfingstbewegung." *Evangelische Theologie* 53 (1993) 265–88.
Honneth, Axel. *Disrespect: The Normative Foundations of Critical Theory*. Malden: Polity, 2007.
———. *The I in We: Studies in the Theory of Recognition*. Malden: Polity, 2012.
———. *The Struggle for Recognition: The Moral Grammar of Social Conflicts*. Cambridge: Polity, 1995.
Hütterman, Aloys. *The Ecological Message of the Torah: Knowledge, Concepts and Laws with Made Survival in a Land of Milk and Honey Possible*. Atlanta: University of South Florida, 1999.
Imasogie, Osadolor. *Guidelines for Christian Theology in Africa*. Achimota: Africa Christian, 1993.
Imbelli, Robert. "The Unknown Beyond the Word: The Pneumatological Foundations of Dialogue." *Communio* 24 (1997) 326–35.
Ingram, Paul O., and David R. Loy. "The Self and Suffering: A Buddhist-Christian Conversation." *Dialog* 44 (2005) 98–107.

Inoue, Naoki. "Spirit and Spirits in Pantheistic Shintoism: A Critical Dialogue with Christian Panentheism." In *Interdisciplinary and Religio-Cultural Discourses*, edited by Veli-Matti Kärkkäinen et al., 55–70. Grand Rapids: Eerdmans, 2006.

Isasi-Díaz, Ada María. *En la Lucha [In the Struggle] A Hispanic Women's Liberation Theology*. Minneapolis: Fortress, 1993.

Jantzen, Grace. *Becoming Divine: Towards a Feminist Philosophy of Religion*. Bloomington: Indiana University Press, 1999.

Jenson, Robert W. *Systematic Theology. Vol. 1. The Triune God*. New York: Oxford University Press, 1997.

———. *The Triune Identity: God According to the Gospel*. Philadelphia: Fortress, 1982.

Jewett, Paul K. *Who We Are: Our Dignity as Human: A Neo-Evangelical Theology*. Grand Rapids: Eerdmans, 1996.

John Paul II. *Apostolic Letter On The Christian Meaning Of Human Suffering: Salvifici Doloris*. Boston: St. Paul Editions, 1984. https://www.vatican.va/content/john-paul-ii/en/apost_letters/1984/documents/hf_jp-ii_apl_11021984_salvifici-doloris.html.

Johns, Jackie David. "Pentecostalism and the Postmodern Worldview." *Journal of Pentecostal Theology* 7 (1995) 73–96.

Johnson, Elizabeth. *She Who Is: The Mystery of God in Feminist Theological Discourse*. New York: Crossroad, 1993.

———. *Women, Earth, and Creator Spirit*. New York: Paulist, 1993.

Johnston, Robert K. "Art and the Spiritual." In *Interdisciplinary and Religio-Cultural Discourses*, edited by Veli-Matti Kärkkäinen et al., 85–96. Grand Rapids: Eerdmans, 2006.

Jones, Lindsay, ed. *Encyclopedia of Religion*. 2nd ed. 15 vols. Detroit: Macmillan Reference USA, 2004.

Kalu, Ogbu U. "Preserving a Worldview: Pentecostalism in the African Maps of the Universe." *Pneuma: The Journal of the Society for Pentecostal Studies* 24 (2003) 110–37.

———. "*Sankofa*: Pentecostalism and African Cultural Heritage." In *The Spirit in the World: Emerging Pentecostal Theologies in Global Contexts*, edited by Veli-Matti Kärkkäinen, 135–52. Grand Rapids: Eerdmans, 2009.

Kamppuri, Hannu T., ed. *Dialogue between Neighbours: The Theological Conversations between the Evangelical-Lutheran Church of Finland and the Russian Orthodox Church 1970–1986*. Helsinki: Luther-Agricola Society, 1986.

Kant, Immanuel. "The End of All Things." In *Religion and Rational Theology*, translated and edited by Allen W. Wood and George di Giovanni, 221–22. Cambridge: Cambridge University Press, 2001.

Kapolyo, Joe M. *The Human Condition*. Downers Grove, IL: InterVarsity, 2005.

Kärkkäinen, Veli-Matti. "Are Pentecostals Oblivious to Social Justice? Theological and Ecumenical Perspectives." *Missionalia* 29 (2001) 387–404.

———. "Christian as Christ to the Neighbor." *International Journal of Systematic Theology* 6 (2004) 101–17.

———. "The Church as Charismatic Fellowship: Ecclesiological Reflections from the Pentecostal-Roman Catholic Dialogue." *Journal of Pentecostal Theology* 18 (2001) 100–21.

———. "The Church as the Fellowship of Persons: An Emerging Pentecostal Ecclesiology of *Koinonia*." *PentecoStudies* 6 (2007) 1–15.

---. "A Constructive Christian Theology for the Pluralistic World: Author's Introduction of the Project and a Response to Reviewers." *Dialog. A Journal of Theology* 59 (2020) 370–78.

---. *Creation and Humanity*. Grand Rapids: Eerdmans, 2015.

---. "Dialogue, Witness, and Tolerance: The Many Faces of Interfaith Encounters." *Theology, News and Notes* 57 (2010) 29–33.

---. "The Ecumenical Potential of Theosis: Emerging Convergences between Eastern Orthodox, Protestant, and Pentecostal Soteriologies." *Sobornost/Eastern Churches Review* 23 (2002) 45–77.

---. "Evangelical Theology and the Religions." In *The Cambridge Companion to Evangelical Theology*, edited by Timothy Larsen and Daniel J. Treier. New York: Cambridge University Press, 2007.

---. "'Evil, Love and the Left Hand of God': The Contribution of Luther's Theology of the Cross to Evangelical Theology of Evil." *Evangelical Quarterly* 79 (2002) 215–34.

---. "The Holy Spirit and Justification: The Ecumenical Significance of Luther's Doctrine of Justification." *Pneuma: The Journal of the Society for Pentecostal Studies* 24 (2002) 26–39.

---. *Holy Spirit and Salvation: The Sources of Christian Theology*. Louisville: Westminster John Knox, 2010.

---. "Introduction: Pentecostalism and Pentecostal Theology in the Third Millennium: Taking Stock of the Contemporary Global Situation." In *The Spirit in the World. Emerging Pentecostal Theologies in Global Contexts*, edited by Veli-Matti Kärkkäinen, xiii–xviii. Grand Rapids: Eerdmans, 2008.

---. *An Introduction to the Theology of Religions: Biblical, Historical and Contemporary Perspectives*. Downers Grove, IL: IVP Academic, 2003.

---. "Justification as Forgiveness of Sins and Making Righteous: The Ecumenical Promise of a New Interpretation of Luther." *One in Christ* 37 (2002) 32–45.

---. "March Forward to Hope: Yonggi Cho's Pentecostal Theology of Hope." *Pneuma* 28 (2006) 253–63.

---. "Missiology, Pentecostal and Charismatic." In *New International Dictionary of Pentecostal and Charismatic Movements*, edited by Stanley M. Burgess and Eduard M. van der Maas, 877–85. Grand Rapids: Zondervan, 2002.

---. "Mission, Spirit, and Eschatology: An Outline of a Pentecostal-Charismatic Theology of Mission." *Mission Studies* 16 (1999) 73–94.

---. *One With God: Salvation as Deification and Justification*. Collegeville: Liturgical, 2004.

---. "Pentecostal Hermeneutics in the Making: On the Way from Fundamentalism to Postmodernism." *The Journal of the European Pentecostal Association* 18 (1998) 76–115.

---. "Pentecostal Missiology in Ecumenical Perspective: Contributions, Challenges, Controversies." *International Review of Mission* 88 (1999) 207–25.

---. "Pentecostal Pneumatology of Religions: The Contribution of Pentecostalism to Our Understanding of the Work of God's Spirit in the World." In *The Spirit in the World. Emerging Pentecostal Theologies in Global Contexts*, edited by Veli-Matti Kärkkäinen, 155–80. Grand Rapids: Eerdmans, 2008.

---. *Pneumatology: The Holy Spirit in Ecumenical, International, and Contextual Perspective*. Grand Rapids: Baker Academic, 2002.

———. "'The Re-Turn of Religion in the New Millennium': Pentecostalisms and Postmodernities." *Swedish Missiological Themes* 95 (2007) 469–96.

———. "Salvation as Justification and Deification: The Ecumenical Potential of a New Perspective on Luther." In *Theology Between West and East: Honoring the Radical Legacy of Professor Dr. Jan M. Lochman*, edited by Frank Macchia and Paul Chung, 59–76. Lanham: University Press of America, 2002.

———. "Theology of the Cross: A Stumbling Block to Pentecostal-Charismatic Spirituality." In *Spirit and Spirituality: Essays in Honour of Russell P Spittler*, edited by Wonsuk Ma and Robert P. Menzies, 150–63. New York: T. & T. Clark, 2004.

———. "Theologies of Religions." In *Evangelical Interfaith Dialogue* 1 (2010) 3–7.

———. "Theologies of Religions." In *Witnessing to Christ in a Pluralistic World: Christian Mission among Other Faiths*, edited by Lalsingkima Pachuau and Knud Jørgensen, 110–18. London: Regnum, 2011.

———. *Toward a Pneumatological Theology: Pentecostal and Ecumenical Perspectives on Ecclesiology, Soteriology and Theology of Mission*, ed. Amos Yong. Lanham, Boston, and New York: University Press of America, 2002.

———. "Toward a Pneumatological Theology of Religion: Pentecostal-Charismatic Contributions." *International Review of Mission* 41 (2002) 187–98.

———. *The Trinity: Global Perspectives*. Louisville: Westminster John Knox, 2007.

———. *The Trinity and Religious Pluralism. The Role of the Doctrine of the Trinity in Christian Theology of Religions*. Burlington: Ashgate, 2004.

———. *Trinity and Revelation*. Grand Rapids: Eerdmans, 2014.

———. "'Truth on Fire': Pentecostal Theology of Mission and the Challenges of a New Millennium." *Asian Journal of Pentecostal Theology* 3 (2000) 33–60.

———. "The Working of the Spirit of God in Creation and in the People of God: The Pneumatology of Wolfhart Pannenberg." *Pneuma: The Journal of the Society for Pentecostal Studies* 26 (2004) 17–35.

Kärkkäinen, Veli-Matti, Kirsteen Kim, and Amos Yong, eds. *Interdisciplinary and Religio-Cultural Discourses on a Spirit-Filled World: Loosing the Spirits*. New York: Palgrave Macmillan, 2013.

Karras, Valeria A. "Eschatology." In *The Cambridge Companion to Feminist Theology*, edited by Susan Frank Parsons, 243–55. New York: Cambridge University Press, 2002.

Katz, Eric. "Faith, God, and Nature: Judaism and Deep Ecology." In *Deep Ecology and World Religions: New Essays on Sacred Ground*, edited by David Landis Barnhill and Roger S. Gottlieb, 153–67. Albany: State University of New York, 2001.

Kaufman, Gordon. *In Face of Mystery: A Constructive Theology*. Cambridge, MA: Harvard University Press, 1993.

Keller, Catherine, and Laurel C. Schneider eds. *Polydoxy: Theology of Multiplicity and Relation*. New York: Routledge, 2011.

Kelly, Gerard. "A New Ecumenical Wave." Presented at the National Council of Churches Forum, Canberra, July 12, 2010. http://www.ncca.org.au/index.php/faith-and-unity/46-a-new-ecumenical-wave/file.

Kelsey, David H. "On Human Flourishing: A Theocentric Perspective." Paper presented at the Yale Center for Faith and Culture Consultation on God's Power and Human Flourishing, New Haven, CT, May 23–24, 2008.

———. *Eccentric Existence: A Theological Anthropology*. 2 vols. Louisville: Westminster John Knox, 2009.

Kerr, Fergus. *Immortal Longings: Versions of Transcending Humanity*. Notre Dame: University of Notre Dame Press, 1997.
Kim, Grace Ji-Sun. *The Holy Spirit, Chi, and the Other: A Model of Global and Intercultural Pneumatology*. New York: Palgrave Macmillan, 2011.
Kim, Jaegwon. "Making Sense of Emergence." *Philosophical Studies* 95 (1999) 3–36.
———. "The Myth of Nonreductive Materialism." In *The Mind-Body Problem: A Guide to the Current Debate*, edited by Richard Warner and Tadeusz Szubka, 242–60. Cambridge: Blackwell, 1994.
———. *Mind in a Physical World: An Essay on the Mind-Body Problem and Mental Causation*. Cambridge, MA: MIT, 1998.
———. "Non-Reductivist's Troubles with Mental Causation." In *Mental Causation*, edited by John Heil and Alfred Mele. New York: Clarendon, 1993.
———. *Physicalism, or Something Near Enough*. Princeton: Princeton University Press, 2005.
———. *Supervenience and Mind*. New York: Cambridge University Press, 1993.
Kim, Kirsteen. *The Holy Spirit in the World: A Global Conversation*. Maryknoll, NY: Orbis, 2007.
———. "The Potential of Pneumatology for Mission in Contemporary Europe." *International Review of Mission* 95 (2006) 334–40.
Kim, Sebastian C. H. "Spirits of the Political: Theological Engagement in the Public Sphere." In *Interdisciplinary and Religio-Cultural Discourses*, edited by Veli-Matti Kärkkäinen et al., 125–40. Grand Rapids: Eerdmans, 2006.
Kolb, Robert, et al., eds. *The Oxford Handbook of Martin Luther's Theology*. Reprint edition. Oxford: Oxford University Press, 2016.
Körtner, Ulrich. *The End of the World: A Theological Interpretation*. Louisville: Westminster John Knox, 1995.
Kovel, Joel. *History and Spirit: An Inquiry into the Philosophy of Liberation*. Boston: Beacon, 1991.
Küng, Hans. *The Church*. Garden City, NY: Doubleday, 1976.
Küppers, Bernd-Olaf. "Understanding Complexity." In *Chaos and Complexity: Scientific Perspectives on Divine Action*, edited by Robert John Russell et al., 93–105. Notre Dame: Notre Dame University Press, 1996.
Kusalasaya, Karuna. *Buddhism in Thailand: Its Past and Present*. Bangkok: Mental Health, 2001.
Kuzmic, Peter, and Miroslav Volf. "Communio Sanctorum: Toward a Theology of the Church as a Fellowship of Persons." A Pentecostal Position Paper Read at the International Roman Catholic-Pentecostal Dialogue, Riano, Italy, May 21–26, 1985 (unpublished).
Joint Working Group between the Roman Catholic Church and the World Council of Churches. *The Nature and Purpose of Ecumenical Dialogue*. Geneva: World Council of Churches, 2005.
———. *Reception: A Key to Ecumenical Progress*. Geneva: World Council of Churches, 2014. https://www.oikoumene.org/en/resources/documents/commissions/jwg-rcc-wcc/ninth-report-of-the-joint-working-group.
LaCugna, Catherine Mowry. *God for Us: The Trinity and Christian Life*. San Francisco: Harper, 1991.
Lai, Whalen W. "Tillich on Death and Suffering: A Key to Buddho-Christian Dialogue." *Journal of Ecumenical Studies* 28 (1991) 566–80.

Lak, Yeow Choo. "Preface." In *Doing Theology with the Spirit's Movement in Asia*, edited John C. England and Alan J. Torrance, vi–vii. Singapore: ATESEA, 1991.

Lamm, Norman. *Faith and Doubt: Studies in Traditional Jewish Thought*. New York: Krav, 1972.

Land, Steven J. *Pentecostal Spirituality: A Passion for the Kingdom*. Sheffield: Sheffield Academic, 1993.

Larsen, Timothy, and Daniel J. Treier, eds. *The Cambridge Companion to Evangelical Theology*. New York: Cambridge University Press, 2007.

Lee, Jung Young. *The Trinity in Asian Perspective*. Nashville: Abingdon, 1996.

Lee, Maurice, and Miroslav Volf. "The Spirit and Church." *Conrad Grebel Review* 18 (2000) 20–45.

Lim, David, and Steve Spaulding, eds. *Sharing Jesus Holistically with The Buddhist World*. Pasadena: William Carey Library, 2013.

Lim, Timothy T. M. "Ecclesial Recognition: An Interdisciplinary Proposal." PhD diss., Regent University School of Divinity, 2014.

Lohse, Bernhard. *Martin Luther's Theology: Its Historical and Systematic Development*. Minneapolis: Fortress, 1999.

López Rodriguez, Dario Andres. "The Redeeming Community." In *Toward a Pentecostal Ecclesiology: The Church and the Fivefold Gospel*, edited by John Christopher Thomas, 69–83. Cleveland: CPT, 2010.

Lopez, Donald S., Jr, and Steven C. Rockefeller, eds. *The Christ and the Bodhisattva*. Albany: State University of New York, 1987.

Lord, Andrew M. "The Voluntary Principle in Pentecostal Missiology." *Journal of Pentecostal Theology* 17 (2000) 81–95.

Lorgunpai, Seree. "The Book of Ecclesiastes and Thai Buddhism." *Asia Journal of Theology* 8 (1994) 155–62.

Lossky, Vladimir. *The Mystical Theology of the Eastern Church*. Yonkers: SVS, 1976.

Louis, Gabriel Reuben. "Response to Wonsuk Ma." Presented at the Asia Pacific Theological Association, Pune, India, n.d. http://www.pctii.org/cyberj/cyberj4/louis.html.

Luther, Martin D. *Heidelberg Disputation*. Translated by Aaron T. Fenker. Independently published, 2018.

———. *The Large Catechism*. Translated by F. Bente and W. H. T. Dau. St. Louis: Concordia, 1921. https://www.ccel.org/ccel/luther/large_cat/files/large_catechism.html.

———. *Luther's Small Catechism with Explanation—1991 Edition*. St. Louis: Concordia, 2008.

———. *Luther's Works*. Edited by Jaroslav Pelikan et al. 75 vols. St. Louis: Concordia, 1955.

———. *Martin Luthers Werke [Scrhiften]*. 73 vols. Kritische Gesamtausgabe. Weimar: Hermann Böhlau, 1883. http://www.theologische-buchhandlung.de/weimar.htm.

———. *Psalmenvorlesungen 1513/15 (Ps 1–84)*. Vol. 3. Die Deutsche Bibel. Weimar: Hermann Böhlau, 1885.

———. *The Smalcald Articles*. Translated by F. Bente and W.H.T. Dau. Champaign, IL: Project Gutenberg, 1995. https://www.gutenberg.org/files/273/273-h/273-h.htm.

Lutheran World Federation, and Roman Catholic Church. *Joint Declaration on the Doctrine of Justification*. Grand Rapids: Eerdman, 2000.

Ma, Wongsuk. "Toward an Asian Pentecostal Theology." Presented at the Asia Pacific Theological Association, Pune, India, n.d. http://www.pctii.org/cyberj/cyberj1/wonsuk.html.

Ma, Wonsuk, and Robert P. Menzies, eds. *Spirit and Spirituality: Essays in Honour of Russell P Spittler*. New York: T. & T. Clark, 2004.

Macchia, Frank D. *Baptized in the Spirit: A Global Pentecostal Theology*. Grand Rapids: Zondervan, 2006.

———. "The Church of the Latter Rain: The Church and Eschatology in Pentecostal Perspective." In *Toward a Pentecostal Ecclesiology: The Church and the Fivefold Gospel*, edited by John Christopher Thomas, 248–59. Cleveland: CPT, 2010.

———. "Sighs Too Deep for Words: Towards a Theology of Glossolalia." *Journal of Pentecostal Theology* 1 (1992) 47–73.

———. "Tongues as a Sign: Towards a Sacramental Understanding of Pentecostal Experience." *Pneuma: The Journal of the Society for Pentecostal Studies* 15 (1993) 61–76.

MacKay, Donald MacCrimmon. *The Clock Work Image: A Christian Perspective on Science*. Downers Grove, IL: InterVarsity, 1974.

Mannermaa, Tuomo. *Christ Present in Faith: Luther's View of Justification*. Minneapolis: Augsburg Fortress, 2005.

———. *Kaksi rakkautta: Johdatus Lutherin uskonmaailmaan*. Helsinki: Suomen Teologisen Kirjallisuusseura, 1995.

———. "Theosis as a Subject of Finnish Lutheran Research." *Pro Ecclesia* 4 (1995) 37–48.

———. "Why is Luther so Fascinating? Modern Finnish Luther Research." In *Union with Christ: The New Finnish Interpretation of Luther*, edited by Carl Brateen and Robert Jenson, 1–20. Grand Rapids: Eerdmans, 1998.

Martin, Lee Roy. *Pentecostal Hermeneutics: A Reader*. Leiden: Brill, 2013.

Martin, Raymond, and John Barresi. *The Rise and Fall of Soul and Self: An Intellectual History of Personal Identity*. New York: Columbia University Press, 2008.

Masao, Abe. "Suffering in the Light of Our Time, Our Time in the Light of Suffering." *The Eastern Buddhist* 27 (1994) 1–13.

Matei, Eugen. "The Practice of Community in Social Trinitarianism: A Theological Evaluation with Reference to Dimitru Staniloae and Jürgen Moltmann." PhD diss., Fuller Theological Seminary, 2004.

Mbiti, John S. *African Religions and Philosophy*. New York: A. Prager, 1969.

———. *Concepts of God in Africa*. 2nd ed. London: SPCK, 1986.

———. *Introduction to African Religion*. London: Heinemann Educations, 1975.

McClendon, James William. *Systematic Theology, Vol. 2: Doctrine*. Nashville: Abingdon, 1994.

McDaniel, Jay. "The God of the Oppressed and the God Who Is Empty." *Journal of Ecumenical Studies* 22 (1985) 687–702.

McDermott, Gerald R. *Can Evangelicals Learn from World Religions?: Jesus, Revelation Religious Traditions*. Downers Grove, IL: IVP Academic, 2000.

McDonnell, Kilian. "The Determinative Doctrine of the Holy Spirit." *Theology Today* 39 (1982) 142–61.

———. *The Other Hand of God: The Holy Spirit as the Universal Touch and Goal*. Collegeville, MN: Liturgical, 2003.

———. "Pneumatology Overview." *CTSA Proceedings* 51 (1996) 188–98.

———. "Theological Presuppositions in Our Preaching about the Spirit." *Theological Studies* 59 (1998) 219–35.
McFague, Sallie. "An Ecological Christology: Does Christianity Have It?" In *Christianity and Ecology: Seeking the Well-Being of Earth and Humans*, edited by Dieter T. Hessel and Rosemary Radford Ruether. Cambridge: Center for the Study of World Religions, 2000.
McGrath, Alister E. *A Brief History of Heaven*. Malden: Wiley-Blackwell, 2003.
———. *A Scientific Theology*. Vol. 2: *Reality*. Grand Rapids: Eerdmans, 2002.
McLaughlin, Brian. "Varieties of Supervenience." In *Supervenience: New Essays*, edited by Elias E. Savellos and Umit D. Yalcin, 16–59. New York: Cambridge University Press, 1995.
McNamara, Patrick. *Where God and Science Meet: How Brain and Evolutionary Studies Alter Our Understanding of Religion: Where God and Science Meet*. 3 vols. Westport: Praeger, 2006.
Melanchthon, Philipp. *The Augsburg Confession and the Apology of the Augsburg Confession with Key Historical Documents*. Edited by Concordia Publishing House. St. Louis: Concordia, 2020. https://bookofconcord.org/augsburg-confession/.
———. *Melanchthon on Christian Doctrine: Loci Communes, 1555*, edited by Clyde L. Manschreck. New York: Oxford University Press, 1965.
Menzies, William W. "Reflections on Suffering: A Pentecostal Perspective." In *Spirit and Spirituality: Essays in Honour of Russell P Spittler*, edited by Wonsuk Ma and Robert P. Menzies, 141–49. New York: T. & T. Clark, 2004.
Meyer, Harding. "Anerkennung—ein 'Ökumenischer Schlüsselbegriff.'" In *Dialog und Anerkennung: Hanfried Krüger zu Ehren*, edited by Peter Manns, 25–41. Frankfurt am Main: Lembeck, 1980.
Miller, Albert. "Pentecostalism as a Social Movement." *Journal of Pentecostal Theology* 4 (1996) 97–144.
Mittelstadt, Martin W. *The Spirit and Suffering in Luke-Acts: Implications for a Pentecostal Pneumatology*. New York: Bloomsbury Academic, 2004.
Miyahira, Nozomu. *Towards a Theology of the Concord of God: A Japanese Perspective on the Trinity*. Carlisle: Paternoster, 2000.
Mobley, Gregory. "Taking Interfaith Off the Hill: Revelation in the Abrahamic Traditions." *Theological Education* 47 (n.d.) 1–6. http://docs.ats.edu/uploads/resources/publications-presentations/chapp-reports/andover-newton-theological-school.pdf.
Moltmann, Jürgen. *The Church in the Power of the Spirit: A Contribution to Messianic Ecclesiology*. London: SCM, 1977.
———. *The Crucified God*. Translated by R.A. Wilson. Minneapolis: Fortress, 1993.
———. *Experiences in Theology: Ways and Forms of Christian Theology*. Minneapolis: Fortress, 2000.
———. *God in Creation*. Translated by Margaret Kohl. Minneapolis: Fortress, 1993.
———. *The Spirit of Life: A Universal Affirmation*. Translated by Margaret Kohl. Minneapolis: Fortress, 1992.
———. *Theology of Hope*. Translated by James W. Leitch. Minneapolis: Fortress, 1993.
———. *The Trinity and the Kingdom*. Translated by Margaret Kohl. Minneapolis: Fortress, 1993.
———. *The Way of Jesus Christ*. Translated by Margaret Kohl. Minneapolis: Fortress, 1993.

Morales, Erwin. "Vector Fields as the Empirical Correlate of the Spirit(s): A Meta-Pannenbergian Approach to Pneumatological Pluralism." In *Interdisciplinary and Religio-Cultural Discourses: Loosing the Spirits*, edited by Veli-Matti Kärkkäinen et al., 227–42. London: Palgrave, 2013.

Moreland, J. P., and Scott B. Rae. *Body and Soul: Human Nature the Crisis in Ethics*. 3rd ed. Downers Grove, IL: IVP Academic, 2000.

Müller-Fahrenholz, Geiko. *God's Spirit: Transforming a World in Crisis*. New York: Continuum, 1995.

Murphy, Nancey. *Beyond Liberalism and Fundamentalism. How Modern and Postmodern Philosophy Set the Theological Agenda*. Valley Forge: Trinity, 1996.

———. *Bodies and Souls, or Spirited Bodies?* New York: Cambridge University Press, 2006.

———. "Divine Action in the Natural Order: Buridan's Ass and Schrödinger's Cat." In *Chaos and Complexity: Scientific Perspectives on Divine Action*, edited by Robert John Russell et al., 340–42. Notre Dame: Notre Dame University Press, 1996.

———. "Emergence, Downward Causation, and Divine Action." In *Scientific Perspectives on Divine Action: Twenty Years of Challenge and Progress*, edited by Robert John Russell et al., 111–31. Vatican City and Berkeley: Vatican Observatory and Center for Theological and the Natural Sciences, 2008.

———. "Introducing Receptive Ecumenism." *The Ecumenist: A Journal of Theology, Culture, and Society* 5 (2014) 1–7.

———. "Nonreductive Physicalism: Philosophical Issues." In *Whatever Happened to the Soul? Scientific and Theological Portraits of Human Nature*, edited by Warren Shelburne Brown et al., 127–48. Minneapolis: Fortress, 1998.

———. "The Resurrection Body and Personal Identity: Possibilities and Limits of Eschatological Knowledge." In *Resurrection: Theological and Scientific Assessments*, edited by Michael Welker et al., 202–18. Grand Rapids: Eerdmans, 2002.

Murphy, Nancey, and George F. R. Ellis. *On the Moral Nature of the Universe: Theology, Cosmology, and Ethics*. Minneapolis: Fortress, 1996.

Murphy, Nancey, and Warren S. Brown. *Did My Neurons Make Me Do It? Philosophical and Neurobiological Perspectives on Moral Responsibility and Free Will*. Oxford: Oxford University Press, 2007.

Murray, Paul D., ed. *Receptive Ecumenism and the Call to Catholic Learning: Exploring a Way for Contemporary Ecumenism*. Oxford: Oxford University Press, 2008.

Muthukan, Pin. *Buddha-Sart (Buddhalogy)*. Vol. 2. Bangkok: Mahamakut Buddhist University Press, 1992.

Nasr, Seyed Hossein, ed. *Islamic Spirituality: Manifestations*. New York: Crossroad, 1997.

Nattier, Jan. "Buddhist Eschatology." In *The Oxford Handbook of Eschatology*, edited by Jerry L. Walls, 151–69. New York: Oxford University Press, 2007.

Newlands, George, and Allen Smith. *Hospitable God: The Transformative Dream*. Surrey: Ashgate, 2010.

Niebuhr, Reinhold. *The Self and the Dramas of History*. New York: Scribner's, 1955.

Ockholm, Dennis L., and Timothy R. Phillips, eds. *Four Views on Salvation in a Pluralistic World*. Grand Rapids: Zondervan, 1995.

Oden, Patrick. "Chaos or Completion: The Work of Spirits in History." In *Interdisciplinary and Religio-Cultural Discourses: Loosing the Spirits*, edited by Veli-Matti Kärkkäinen et al., 71–84. London: Palgrave, 2013.

Ogbonnaya, A. O. *On Communitarian Divinity. An African Interpretation of the Trinity*. New York: Paragon, 1994.
Oladipo, Caleb Oluremi. *The Development of the Doctrine of the Holy Spirit in the Yoruba (African) Indigenous Christian Movement*. Frankfurt: Peter Lang, 1996.
Onyinah, Opoku. "Deliverance as a Way of Confronting Witchcraft in Contemporary Africa: Ghana as a Case Study." Asian Journal of Pentecostal Studies 5 (2002) 107–34.
———. "Pentecostal Healing Communities." In *Toward a Pentecostal Ecclesiology: The Church and the Fivefold Gospel*, edited by John Christopher Thomas, 207–24. Cleveland: CPT, 2010.
Panikkar, Raimundo, and R. R. Barr. *The Silence of God: An Answer of the Buddha*. Maryknoll, NY: Orbis, 1989.
Pannenberg, Wolfhart. *Anthropology in Theological Perspective*. Translated by Matthew J. O'Connell. Philadelphia: Westminster, 1985.
———. "Christian Morality and Political Issues." In *Faith and Reality*. Philadelphia: Westminster, 1997.
———. "Contingency and Natural Law." In Pannenberg, *Towards a Theology of Nature: Essays on Science and Faith*, edited by Ted Peters, 72–122. Louisville: Westminster John Knox, 1993.
———. "God as Spirit—and Natural Sciences." Zygon: Journal of Religion and Science 36 (2001) 783–94.
———. *Systematic Theology*. Translated by Geoffrey W. Bromiley. 3 vols. Grand Rapids: Eerdmans, 1991.
———. *Theology and the Kingdom of God*. Translated by Richard John Neuhaus. Philadelphia: Westminster, 1969.
Parsons, Susan Frank, ed. *The Cambridge Companion to Feminist Theology*. New York: Cambridge University Press, 2002.
Peacocke, Arthur R., ed. "Prologue: Naturalism, Theism, and Religion." In *All That Is: A Naturalistic Faith for the Twenty-First Century*, edited by Philip Clayton. Minneapolis: Fortress, 2007.
———. *The Sciences and Theology in the Twentieth Century*. Notre Dame, IN: University of Notre Dame Press, 1986.
———. "The Sound of Sheer Silence: How does God Communicate with Humanity." In *Neuroscience and the Person: Scientific Perspectives on Divine Action*, edited by Robert John Russel et al., 235–40. Vatican City and Berkeley: Vatican Observatory and Center for Theological and the Natural Sciences, 1999.
———. "The Sound of Sheer Silence: How Does God Communicate with Humanity." In *Neuroscience and the Person: Scientific Perspectives on Divine Action*, edited by Robert J. Russell et al., 215–47. Notre Dame: University of Notre Dame Press, 2004.
———. *Theology for a Scientific Age: Being and Becoming—Natural, Divine, and Human*. Minneapolis: Fortress, 1993.
Pelikan, Jaroslav. *The Emergence of the Catholic Tradition (100-600)*. Vol. 1 of *The Christian Tradition: A History of the Development of Doctrine*. Chicago: Chicago University Press, 1971.
Pelikan, Jaroslav, and Helmut T. Lehman, eds. *Luther's Works*. Minneapolis: Fortress, 2002.

Penrose, Roger. *The Emperor's New Mind: Concerning Computers, Minds, and the Laws of Physics*. New York: Oxford University Press, 2016.

Peters, Ted. *Anticipating Omega: Science, Faith, and Our Ultimate Future*. Göttingen: Vandenhoeck & Ruprecht, 2006.

———. "The Heart of the Reformation Faith." *Dialog: A Journal of Theology* 44 (2005) 6–14.

———. *God as Trinity. Relationality and Temporality in Divine Life*. Louisville: Westminster John Knox, 1993.

———. *God—The World's Future: Systematic Theology for a Postmodern Era*. Minneapolis: Fortress, 1992.

———. "Resurrection of the Very Embodied Soul?" In *Neuroscience and the Person: Scientific Perspectives on Divine Action*, edited by Robert J. Russell et al., 305–26. Notre Dame: University of Notre Dame Press, 2004.

Peura, Simo. "Christ as Favor and Gift: The Challenge of Luther's Understanding of Justification." In *Union with Christ: The New Finnish Interpretation of Luther*, edited by Carl Brateen and Robert Jenson, 42–69. Grand Rapids: Eerdmans, 1998.

Phillips, Craig. "Green Creation: Comparative Ecological Theology in the Bible and Qur'ān." *Journal of Comparative Theology* 2 (2011) 4–20.

Pinnock, Clark H. *Flame of Love: A Theology of the Holy Spirit*. Downers Grove, IL: InterVarsity, 1996.

———. *A Wideness in God's Mercy: The Finality of Jesus Christ In A World Of Religions*. Grand Rapids: Zondervan, 1992.

Plantinga, R. J. "God So Loved the World: Theological Reflections on Religious Plurality in the History of Christianity." *Calvin Theological Journal* 39 (2004) 275–302.

Pohl, Christine D. *Making Room: Recovering Hospitality as a Christian Tradition*. Grand Rapids: Eerdmans, 1999.

Poirier, John C., and Lewis, B. Scott. "Pentecostal and Postmodernist Hermeneutics: A Critique of Three Conceits." *Journal of Pentecostal Theology* 15 (2006) 3–21.

Polish, Daniel F. "The Buddha as a Lens for Reading Koheleth / Ecclesiastes." *Journal of Ecumenical Studies* 43 (2008) 370–82.

Polkinghorne, John. "Anthropology in an Evolutionary Context." In *God and Human Dignity*, edited by R. Kendall Soulen and Linda Woodhead, 89–103. Grand Rapids: Eerdmans, 2006.

———. *Faith, Science and Understanding*. New Haven, CT: Yale University Press, 2001.

———. *God of Hope and the End of the World*. New Haven, CT: Yale University Press, 2002.

———. "The Laws of Nature and the Laws of Physics." In *Quantum Cosmology and the Laws of Nature: Scientific Perspectives on Divine Action*, edited by Robert J. Russell et al., 437–48. Vatican City/Berkeley: Vatican Observatory and Center for Theological and the Natural Sciences, 1993.

———. "Metaphysics of Divine Action." In *Chaos and Complexity: Scientific Perspectives on Divine Action*, edited by Robert John Russell et al., 97–109. Notre Dame: Notre Dame University Press, 1996.

———. *Quarks, Chaos and Christianity: Questions to Science and Religion*. New York: Crossroad, 2005.

———. *Reason and Reality: The Relationship between Science and Religion*. Philadelphia: Trinity, 1991.

———. *Science and Creation: The Search for Understanding*. Boston: New Science Library, 1989.

———. *Science and Providence: God's Interaction with the World*. West Conshohocken: Templeton, 2005.

———. "Wolfhart Pannenberg's Engagement with the Natural Sciences." *Zygon: Journal of Religion and Science* 34 (1999) 151–58.

Polkinghorne, John, and Michael Welker, eds. *The End of the World and the Ends of God: Science and Theology on Eschatology*. 1st ed. Harrisburg, PA: Trinity, 2000.

Pontifical Council for Promoting Christian Unity. "Evangelization, Proselytism and Common Witness: Final Report of the Dialogue." *Information Service N. 97 (1998/ I–II), 38–56* 97 (I–II 1998) 38–56.

Popper, Karl. "Natural Selection and the Emergence of Mind." *Dialectica* 32 (1978) 339–55.

Prenter, Reginald. *Spiritus Creator: Luther's Concept of the Holy Spirit*. Philadelphia: Muhlenberg, 1953.

Prichard, Rebecca Button. *Sensing the Spirit: The Holy Spirit in Feminist Perspective*. St. Louis: Chalice, 1999.

Prigogine, Ilya, and Isabelle Stengers, *Order Out of Chaos: Man's New Dialogue with Nature*. Toronto: Bantam, 1984.

Putnam, Hilary, ed. *Philosophical Papers, Vol. 2: Mind, Language and Reality*. New York: Cambridge University Press, 1979.

Rahula, Walpola. *What the Buddha Taught: Revised and Expanded Edition with Texts from Suttas and Dhammapada*. Revised. New York: Grove, 1974.

Ray, Darby Kathleen, ed. *Theology That Matters: Ecology, Economy, and God*. Augsburg Fortress, 2006.

Richie, Tony. "Demonization, Discernment, and Deliverance in Interreligious Encounter." In *Interdisciplinary and Religio-Cultural Discourses: Loosing the Spirits*, edited by Veli-Matti Kärkkäinen et al., 171–86. London: Palgrave, 2013.

Rickabaugh, Brandon L. "Responding to NT Wright's Rejection of the Soul: A Defense of Substance Dualism." Presented at the The Society of Vineyard Scholars Conference, Minneapolis, MN, April 28, 2012.

Robeck, Cecil M. *The Azusa Street Mission and Revival: The Birth of a Global Movement*. Nashville: Thomas Nelson, 2006.

———. *The Azusa Street Mission and Revival: The Birth of the Global Pentecostal Movement*. Nashville: Thomas Nelson, 2017.

———. "National Association of Evangelicals." In *The New International Dictionary of Pentecostal and Charismatic Movements*, edited by Stanley M. Burgess and Eduard M. van der Maas, 922–25. Grand Rapids: Zondervan, 2002.

———. "Pentecostal Origins from a Global Perspective." In *Together in One Place: Theological Papers from the Brighton Conference on World Evangelization*, edited by Harold D. Hunter and Peter. D. Hocken. Sheffield: Sheffield Academic, 1993.

Robinson, John A. T. *The Body: A Study in Pauline Theology*. London: SCM, 1952.

Rodríguez, Rubén Rosario. *Racism and God-Talk: A Latino/a Perspective*. New York: New York University Press, 2008.

Roozen, David A. "Curriculum Development Project: Educating Clergy for a Multifaith World," Association of Theological Education CHAPP Program, 2012. http://www.ats.edu/uploads/resources/publications-presentations/chapp-reports/hartford-theological-seminary.pdf.

Ruether, Rosemary R. *Gaia and God: An Ecofeminist Theology of Earth Healing*. San Francisco: HarperCollins, 1992.
Rusch, William G. *Reception: An Ecumenical Opportunity*. Philadelphia: Fortress, 1988.
Russell, Bertrand. *Why I Am Not A Christian and Other Essays on Religion and Related Subjects*. New York: Simon and Schuster, 1957.
Russell, Letty M. *Just Hospitality: God's Welcome in a World of Difference*. Louisville: Westminster John Knox, 2009.
Russell, Robert John. "Challenges and Progress in 'Theology and Science': An Overview of the VO/CTNS Series." In *Scientific Perspectives on Divine Action: Twenty Years of Challenge and Progress*, edited by Robert John Russell et al., 3–56. Vatican City/Berkeley: Vatican Observatory and Center for Theological and the Natural Sciences, 2008.
———. "Cosmology and Eschatology." In *The Oxford Handbook of Eschatology*, edited by Jerry L. Walls, 563–80. New York: Oxford University Press, 2007.
———. *Cosmology: From Alpha to Omega: The Creative Mutual Interaction of Theology and Science*. Minneapolis: Fortress, 2008.
———. *Time in Eternity: Pannenberg, Physics, and Eschatology in Creative Mutual Interaction*. Notre Dame, IN: University of Notre Dame Press, 2012.
Russell, Robert John, et al., eds. *Scientific Perspectives on Divine Action: Twenty Years of Challenge and Progress*. Vatican City/Berkeley: Vatican Observatory and Center for Theological and the Natural Sciences, 2008.
Ryan, Thomas. "Gethsemani II: Catholic and Buddhist Monastics Focus on Suffering." *Buddhist-Christian Studies* 24 (2004) 249–51.
Saarinen, Risto. "Anerkennungstheorien und Ökumenische Theologie." In *Ökumene—Überdacht (Quaestiones Disputate 259)*, edited by Thomas Bremer, 237–61. Freiburg: Herder, 2013.
———. *Faith and Holiness: Lutheran-Orthodox Dialogue 1959-1994*. Göttingen: Vandenhoeck & Ruprecht, 1997.
———. *God and Gift: An Ecumenical Theology of Giving*. Collegeville, MN: Liturgical, 2005.
———. "Lutheran Ecclesiology." In *Routledge Companion to the Christian Church*, edited by Gerard Mannion and Lewis S. Mudge, 171–73. New York: Routledge, 2012.
———. "Quantum Physics in Philosophical and Theological Perspective." In *Physics, Philosophy and Theology: A Common Quest for Understanding*, edited by Robert J. Russell et al., 343–74. Vatican City: Vatican Observatory, 1988.
———. "The Third Dimension of Faith." *Dialog: A Journal of Theology* 44 (2005) 15–16.
Saunders, Nicholas. *Divine Action and Modern Science*. Cambridge: Cambridge University Press, 2002.
Schebera, Richard. "Comparative Theology: A New Method of Interreligious Dialogue." *Dialogue and Alliance* 17 (2003) 7–18.
Schwarz, Hans. *Creation*. Grand Rapids: Eerdmans, 2002.
———. *Eschatology*. Grand Rapids: Eerdmans, 2000
Second Vatican Council. *Dogmatic Constitution on the Church (Lumen Gentium)*. In *The Documents of Vatican*, edited by Walter M. Abbott II ed., 15–96. New York: Guild, 1966.
Segesvary, Victor. *L'Islam et La Réforme: Étude Sur l'attitude Des Réformateurs Zurichois Envers l'Islam, 1510-1550*. Lanham: University Press of America, 1998.

Segundo, Juan Luis. *The Liberation of Theology*. Maryknoll, NY: Orbis, 1976.
Shear, Jonathan, ed. *Explaining Consciousness: The Hard Problem*. Reprint ed. Cambridge, MA: MIT, 1999.
Sheppard, Gerald T. "Pentecostalism and the Hermeneutics of Dispensationalism: The Anatomy of an Uneasy Relationship." *Pneuma: The Journal of the Society for Pentecostal Studies* 6 (1984) 5–34.
Shults, F. LeRon. *Reforming the Doctrine of God*. Grand Rapids: Eerdmans, 2005.
———. "Theological Responses to Postmodernities or Tending to the Other in Late Modern Missions and Ecumenism." Presentation for the Nordic Institute for Missiological and Ecumenical Research Annual Meeting at the University of Abo, Turku, Finland, August 19–22, 2007.
Sikkema, Arnold E. "Physicist's Reformed Critique of Nonreductive Physicalism and Emergence." *Pro Rege* 33 (2005) 20–32.
Silcock, Jeffrey G. "Luther on the Holy Spirit and His Use of God's Word." In *The Oxford Handbook of Martin Luther's Theology*, edited by Robert Kolb et al., 294–309. Oxford: Oxford University Press, 2014.
———. "Luther on the Holy Spirit and His Use of God's Word." In *The Oxford Handbook of Martin Luther's Theology*, edited by Robert Kolb et al., 294–309. Reprint ed. Oxford: Oxford University Press, 2016.
Simmer-Brown, Judith. "Suffering and Social Justice: A Buddhist Response to the Gospel of Luke." *Buddhist-Christian Studies* 16 (1996) 99–112.
Simons, Menno. *Reply to Gellius Faber (1552)*. In *The Complete Writings of Menno Simons (c. 1496–1561)*, edited by H. S. Bender, 623–27. Scottsdale, AZ: Herald, 1956.
Slade, Stanley David. "The Theological Method of Juan Luis Segundo." PhD diss., Fuller Theological Seminary, 1979.
Slomp, Jan. "Calvin and the Turks." In *Christian-Muslim Encounters*, edited by Yvonne Yazbeck Haddad and Wadi Z. Haddad, 126–42. Gainesville: University Press of Florida, 1995.
Smart, Ninian, and Steve Konstantine. *Christian Systematic Theology in a World Context*. Minneapolis: Fortress, 1991.
Smith, James K. A. "What Hath Cambridge to Do with Azusa Street? Radical Orthodoxy and Pentecostal Theology in Conversation." *Pneuma: The Journal of the Society for Pentecostal Studies* 25 (2003) 97–114.
Smyth, John. *Principles and Inferences Concerning the Visible Church*. In *The Works of John Smyth, Fellow of Christ's College 1594-8*, edited by W. T. Whitley, 1:249–68. Cambridge: Cambridge University Press, 1915.
Snyder, Gary. *The Practice of the Wild*. San Francisco: North Point, 1990.
Sobrino, Jon. *Spirituality of Liberation: Toward Political Holiness*. Maryknoll, NY: Orbis, 1988.
Sockice, Janet Martin. "Resurrection and the New Jerusalem." In *The Resurrection: An Interdisciplinary Symposium on the Resurrection of Jesus*, edited by Stephen T. Davis et al., 41–58. New York: Oxford University Press, 1997.
Solivan, Samuel. *Spirit, Pathos and Liberation: Toward an Hispanic Pentecostal Theology*. Sheffield: Sheffield Academic, 1998.
Spear, Andrew D. "Husserl on Intentionality and Intentional Content." In *Internet Encyclopedia of Philosophy: A Peer-Reviewed Academic Resource*, 2011. http://www.iep.utm.edu/huss-int/.

Sperry, Roger. *Science and Moral Priority*. New York: Columbia University Press, 1983.

"The Spirit at Work in Asia Today: A Document of the Office of Theological Concerns of the Federation of the Asian Bishops' Conferences." FABC Paper no. 81 (1998) 23.

Spittler, Russell P. "Spirituality, Pentecostal and Charismatic." In *The New International Dictionary of Pentecostal and Charismatic Movements*, edited by Stanley M. Burgess and Eduard M. van der Maas, 1096–1102. Grand Rapids: Zondervan, 2002.

Starhawk. *Dreaming the Dark: Magic, Sex, and Politics*. Boston: Beacon, 1982.

———. *The Spiral Dance: A Rebirth of the Ancient Religion of the Great Goddess*. San Francisco: Harper & Row, 1979.

Stibbe, Mark W. G. "A British Appraisal." Review of Jürgen Moltmann's *The Spirit of Life: A Universal Affirmation*." *Journal of Pentecostal Theology* 2 (1994) 5–16.

Stoeger, William J. "Conceiving Divine Action in a Dynamic Universe." In *Scientific Perspectives on Divine Action: Twenty Years of Challenge and Progress*, edited by Robert John Russell et al., 225–47. Vatican City/Berkeley: Vatican Observatory and Center for Theological and the Natural Sciences, 2008.

———. "'Epistemological and Ontological Issues Arising from Quantum Theory.'" In *Quantum Mechanics: Scientific Perspectives on Divine Action*, edited by Robert J. Russell et al., 81–98. Vatican City/Berkeley: Vatican Observatory and Center for Theological and the Natural Sciences, 2001.

———. "The Mind-Brain Problem, the Laws of Nature, and Constitutive Relationships." In *Neuroscience and the Person: Scientific Perspectives on Divine Action*, edited by Robert J. Russell et al., 129–46. Notre Dame: University of Notre Dame Press, 2004.

Stubenberg, Leopold. "Neutral Monism." In *The Stanford Encyclopedia of Philosophy*, edited by Edward N. Zalta, n.d. http://plato.stanford.edu/archives/spr2010/entries/neutral-monism.

Sullivan, Francis A. *Salvation Outside the Church: Tracing the History of the Catholic Response*. New York: Paulist, 1992.

Sullivan, Lawrence E. "Preface." In *Hinduism and Ecology: The Intersection of Earth, Sky, and Water*, edited by Christopher Key Chapple and Mary Evelyn Tucker. Cambridge, MA: Harvard University Press, 2000.

Taliaferro, Charles. *Consciousness and the Mind of God*. New York: Cambridge University Press, 1994.

Tanner, Kathryn E. *Economy of Grace*. Minneapolis: Fortress, 2005.

———. "Eschatology without a Future." In *The End of the World and the Ends of God: Science and Theology on Eschatology*, edited by John Polkinghorne and Michael Welker, 222–38. Harrisburg, PA: Trinity, 2000.

———. "Workings of the Spirit: Simplicity or Complexity?" Presented at the John Templeton Foundation Symposium, "Pneumatology: Exploring the Work of the Spirit from Contemporary Perspectives," New York, NY, November 12, 2004.

Tappert, Theodore G., trans. The Book of Concord: The Confessions of the Evangelical Lutheran Church. Philadelphia: Fortress, 1959.

Tappert, Theodore G. *The Book of Concord: The Confessions of the Evangelical Lutheran Church*. Philadelphia: Fortress, 1959.

Taylor, Charles. "The Politics of Recognition." In *Multiculturalism: Examining the Politics of Recognition*, edited by Amy Guttmann, 25–74. Princeton: Princeton University Press, 1994.

———. *A Secular Age*. Cambridge, MA: Harvard University Press, 2007.

Tennent, Timothy C. *Christianity at the Religious Roundtable*. Grand Rapids: Baker, 2002.

———.*Theology in the Context of World Christianity: How the Global Church Is Influencing the Way We Think about and Discuss Theology*. Grand Rapids: Zondervan, 2007.

World Council of Churches. *The Church: Towards a Common Vision*, Faith and Order Paper 214. Geneva: World Council of Churches, 2013.

The Pontifical Council for Promoting Christian Unity. "Evangelization, Proselytism and Common Witness: Final Report of the Dialogue." *Information Service N. 97 (1998/I-II), 38–56* 97 (I–II 1998) 38–56.

Thiselton, Anthony C. *Life after Death: A New Approach to the Last Things*. Grand Rapids: Eerdmans, 2011.

Thomas, John Christopher. "Pentecostal Theology in the Twenty-First Century." *Pneuma: The Journal of the Society for Pentecostal Studies* 20 (1998) 3–19.

Thottakara, Augustine. "Ecology and World Religions." *Journal of Dharma* 26 (2001) 9–120.

Thurman, Robert A.F., trans. *Vimalakīrti Nirdeśa Sutra*. The Pennsylvania State University, 1976. http://www2.kenyon.edu/Depts/Religion/Fac/Adler/Reln260/Vimalakirti.htm.

Tillich, Paul. *Future of Religions*. New York. Harper & Row, 1966.

———. *Systematic Theology, Vol. 1*. Chicago: University of Chicago Press, 1973.

———. *Systematic Theology, Vol. 2: Existence and the Christ*. Chicago: University of Chicago Press, 1975.

———. *Systematic Theology, Vol. 3: Life and the Spirit: History and the Kingdom of God*. Chicago: University of Chicago Press, 1976.

Tracy, David. "Comparative Theology." In *The Encyclopedia of Religion*, edited by Mircea Eliade and Charles J. Adam, 14:444–46. New York: Macmillan, 1987.

Tracy, Thomas F. "Particular Providence and the God of the Gaps." In *Chaos and Complexity: Scientific Perspectives on Divine Action*, edited by Robert John Russell et al., 291–324. Vatican City/Berkeley: Vatican Observatory and Center for Theological and the Natural Sciences, 1995.

———. "Special Divine Action and the Laws of Nature." In *Scientific Perspectives on Divine Action: Twenty Years of Challenge and Progress*, edited by Robert John Russell et al., 249–83. Vatican City and Berkeley: Vatican Observatory and Center for Theological and the Natural Sciences, 2008.

Tucker, Mary Evelyn, and Duncan Ryuken Williams, eds. *Buddhism and Ecology: The Interconnection of Dharma and Deeds*. Cambridge: Center for the Study of World Religions, 1998.

Tucker, Mary Evelyn, and John Grim. "Series Foreword." In *Hinduism and Ecology: The Intersection of Earth, Sky, and Water*, edited by Christopher Key Chapple and Mary Evelyn Tucker. Cambridge, MA: Harvard University Press, 2000.

Van Gulick, Robert. "Reduction, Emergence and Other Recent Options on the Mind/Body Problem: A Philosophical Overview." *Journal of Consciousness Studies* 8 (2001) 1–34.

Vandervelde, George. "Justification and Deification—Problematic Synthesis: A Response to Lucia Turcescu." *Journal of Ecumenical Studies* 37 (2001) 73–78.

Vasanthakumar, Michael Solomon. "An Exploration of the Book of Ecclesiastes in the Light of Buddha's Four Noble Truths." In *Sharing Jesus Holistically with The Buddhist World*, edited by David Lim and Steve Spaulding. Pasadena: William Carey Library, 2013.

Velmans, Max. "Making Sense of Causal Interactions between Consciousness and Brain." *Journal of Consciousness Studies* 9 (2002) 69–95.

Venerable Phra Dhammapitaka, (P.A. Payutto). *Tri-Luk (Three Characteristics of Existence)*. Bangkok: Buddhadhamma Foundation, 2004.

Villafañe, Eldín. *The Liberating Spirit: Toward an Hispanic American Pentecostal Social Ethic*. Grand Rapids: Eerdmans, 1993.

Volf, Miroslav. *After Our Likeness: The Church as the Image of the Trinity*. Grand Rapids. Eerdmans, 1998.

———. "Materiality of Salvation: An Investigation in the Soteriologies of Liberation and Pentecostal Theologies." *Journal of Ecumenical Studies* 26 (1989) 447–67.

———. "'The Trinity Is Our Social Program': The Doctrine of the Trinity and the Shape of Social Engagement." *Modern Theology* 14 (1998) 403–23.

———. "Unity, Diversity, and Apostolicity: Any Hopes for Rapprochement between Older and Younger Churches?" In *Believing in Community: Ecumenical Reflections on the Church*, edited by Peter de Mey, 487–506. Leuven: University of Leuven, 2013.

———. *Work in the Spirit: Toward a Theology of Work*. Eugene, OR: Wipf & Stock, 2001.

Wallace, Mark. "Christian Animism, Green Spirit Theology, and the Global Crisis Today." In *Interdisciplinary and Religio-Cultural Discourses*, edited by Veli-Matti Kärkkäinen et al., 197–212. Grand Rapids: Eerdmans, 2006.

———. "Crum Creek Spirituality: Earth as a Living Sacrament." In *Theology That Matters: Ecology, Economy, and God*, edited by Darby Kathleen Ray, 221–37. Minneapolis: Fortress, 2006.

———. *Finding God in the Singing River*. Minneapolis: Fortress, 2005.

———. *Fragments of The Spirit: Nature, Violence, And The Renewal Of Creation*. New York: Continuum, 1996.

———. "The Green Face of God: Recovering the Spirit in an Ecocidal Era." In *Advents of the Spirit: An Introduction to the Current Study of Pneumatology*, edited by Bradford E. Hinze and D. Lyle Dabney, 444–64. Milwaukee: Marquette University Press, 2001.

Walls, Jerry L., ed. *The Oxford Handbook of Eschatology*. New York: Oxford University Press, 2007.

Ward, Graham. *The Postmodern God: A Theological Reader*. Oxford: Blackwell, 1997.

Ward, Keith. "Divine Action in an Emergent Cosmos." In *Scientific Perspectives on Divine Action: Twenty Years of Challenge and Progress*, edited by Robert John Russell et al., 285–98. Vatican City/Berkeley. Vatican Observatory and Center for Theological and the Natural Sciences, 2008.

———. *More Than Matter? What Humans Really Are*. Grand Rapids: Eerdmans, 2010.

———. "'Personhood, Spirit, and the Supernatural.'" In *All That Is: A Naturalistic Faith for the Twenty-First Century*, edited by Philip Clayton, 152–62. Minneapolis: Fortress, 2007.

———. *Religion and Community*. Oxford: Clarendon, 2000.
———. *Religion and Revelation: A Theology of Revelation in the World's Religions*. Oxford: Clarendon, 1994.
Wariboko, Nimi. "Spirits and Economics." In *Interdisciplinary and Religio-Cultural Discourses*, edited by Veli-Matti Kärkkäinen et al., 141–54. Grand Rapids: Eerdmans, 2006.
Warrington, Keith. "Healing and Suffering in the Bible." *International Review of Mission* 95 (2006) 154–64.
Warrior, Robert Allan. "Canaanites, Cowboys and Indians: Deliverance, Conquest and Liberation Theology Today." *Christianity and Crisis* 49 (1989) 261–65.
Welker, Michael. *Creation and Reality*. Minneapolis: Fortress, 2000.
———. *God the Spirit*. Minneapolis: Fortress, 1992.
———. "The Spirit in Philosophical and Theological Perspectives." Presented at the John Templeton Foundation Symposium, "Pneumatology: Exploring the Work of the Spirit from Contemporary Perspectives," New York, November 12, 2004 (unpublished).
———. "Theological Anthropology versus Anthropological Reductionism." In *God and Human Dignity*, edited by R. Kendall Soulen and Linda Woodhead, 317–30. Grand Rapids: Eerdmans, 2006.
Wells, Harold. "The Holy Spirit and Theology of the Cross: Significance for Dialogue." *Theological Studies* 53 (1992) 476–78.
Wenk, Matthias. "The Church as Sanctified Community." In *Toward a Pentecostal Ecclesiology: The Church and the Fivefold Gospel*, edited by John Christopher Thomas, 104–35. Cleveland: CPT, 2010.
Werner, Dietrich, et al., eds. *The Handbook of Theological Education in World Christianity: Theological Perspectives, Regional Surveys, Ecumenical Trends*. London: Regnum, 2010.
Westhelle, Vitor. "Liberation Theology: A Latitudinal Perspective." In *The Oxford Handbook of Eschatology*, edited by Jerry L. Walls, 311–27. New York: Oxford University Press, 2007.
White, Lynn, Jr. "The Historical Roots of Our Ecological Crisis." *Science* 155 (1967) 1203–7.
Whitehead, Alfred North. *Process and Reality*. Edited by David Ray Griffin and Donald W. Sherburn. New York: Free, 1978.
Wiebe, Phillip H. *God and Other Spirits: Intimations of Transcendence in Christian Experience*. Oxford: Oxford University Press, 2004.
Wildman, Wesley J. "The Divine Action Project, 1988–2003." *Theology and Science* 2 (2004) 31–75.
Wildman, Wesley J., and Robert John Russell. "Chaos: A Mathematic Introduction with Philosophical Reflections." In *Chaos and Complexity: Scientific Perspectives on Divine Action*, edited by Robert John Russell et al., 49–90. Notre Dame: Notre Dame University Press, 1996.
Wiles, Maurice. "Religious Authority and Divine Action," In *God's Activity in the World: The Contemporary Problem*, edited by Owen C. Thomas, 181–94. Chico: Scholars, 1983.
Williams, Andrew Ray. *Washed in the Spirit: Toward a Pentecostal Theology of Water Baptism*. Cleveland: CPT, 2021.

Williams, Delores S. *Sisters in the Wilderness: The Challenge of Womanist God-Talk.* Maryknoll, NY: Orbis, 1993.

Wink, Walter. *Engaging the Powers: Discernment and Resistance in a World of Domination.* Minneapolis: Fortress, 1992.

———. *Naming the Powers: The Language of Power in the New Testament.* Minneapolis: Fortress, 1984.

Winkler, Lewis. *Contemporary Muslim and Christian Responses to Religious Plurality: Wolfhart Pannenberg in Dialogue with Abdulaziz Sachedina.* Eugene, OR: Pickwick, 2011.

Witherington, Ben, III. *Jesus, Paul and the End of the World.* Downers Grove, IL: IVP Academic, 1992.

Wittgenstein, Ludwig. *Philosophical Grammar.* Berkeley: University of California Press, 1974.

———. *Zettel.* Edited by G. E. M. Anscombe and G. H. von Wright. Translated by G. E. M. Anscombe. 1st ed. Berkeley: University of California Press, 1970.

Woodley, Randy. *Shalom and the Community of Creation: An Indigenous Vision.* Grand Rapids: Eerdmans, 2012.

Wright, N. T. "Mind, Spirit, Soul and Body: All for One and One for All; Reflections on Paul's Anthropology in His Complex Contexts." Presented at the Society of Christian Philosophers Eastern Meeting, March 18, 2011. http://www.ntwrightpage.com/Wright_SCP_MindSpiritSoulBody.htm.

Yong, Amos. *Beyond the Impasse: Toward a Pneumatological Theology of Religions.* Grand Rapids: Baker Academic, 2003.

———. *Discerning the Spirit(s): A Pentecostal-Charismatic Contribution to Christian Theology of Religions.* Sheffield: Sheffield Academic, 2000.

———. *In the Days of Caesar: Pentecostalism and Political Theology.* Grand Rapids: Eerdmans, 2010.

———. "The Many Tongues of the Spirit? Interpreting Veli-Matti Kärkkäinen's *A Constructive Christian Theology for [a] Pluralistic World.*" In *Christian Theology in the 21st Century: Engaging with Veli-Matti Kärkkäinen's Project in Constructive Theology for a Pluralistic World,* edited by Patrick Oden, Peter G. Heltzel, and Amos Yong. Lanham: Lexington/Fortress, forthcoming.

———. *Pneumatology and the Christian-Buddhist Dialogue: Does the Spirit Blow through the Middle Way?* Leiden/Boston: Brill, 2012.

———. *The Spirit of Creation: Modern Science and Divine Action in the Pentecostal-Charismatic Imagination.* Grand Rapids: Eerdmans, 2011.

———. "A Spirit-Filled Creation? Toward a Pneumatological Cosmology." In *The Spirit of Creation: Modern Science and Divine Action in the Pentecostal-Charismatic Imagination,* 173–225. Grand Rapids: Eerdmans, 2011.

———. "The Spirit(s) the Heaven Above and the Earth Beneath: Toward a Theology of Creation in Pentecostal and Pneumatological Perspective." Presented at the John Templeton Foundation Symposium. Pneumatology: Exploring the Work of the Spirit from Contemporary Perspectives," New York, November 12, 2004.

———. *The Spirit Poured Out on All Flesh: Pentecostalism and the Possibility of Global Theology.* Grand Rapids: Baker Academic, 2005.

———. *Theology and Contemporary Critical Theory.* New York: St. Martin's, 2000.

———. "The Turn to Pneumatology in Christian Theology of Religions: Conduit or Detour?" *Journal of Ecumenical Studies* 35 (1998) 437–54.

———. "Whither Evangelical Theology? The Work of Veli-Matti Karkkainen as a Case Study of Contemporary Trajectories." *Evangelical Review of Theology* 30 (2006) 60–85.

York, Donald G. "The Spirit in Evidence: Stories of How Decisions are Made." In *The Work of the Spirit: Pneumatology and Pentecostalism*, edited by Michael Welker, 205–20. Grand Rapids: Eerdmans, 2006.

Yun, Koo D. *The Holy Spirit and Ch'i (Qi): A Chiological Approach to Pneumatology*. Eugene, OR: Pickwick, 2011.

Zimmermann, Jen. *Incarnational Humanism: A Philosophy of Culture for the Church in the World*. Downers Grove, IL: InterVarsity, 2012.

Zizioulas, John D. *Being as Communion: Studies in the Personhood and Church*. Crestwood: SVS, 1985.

———. "The Doctrine of God the Trinity Today: Suggestions for an Ecumenical Study." In *The Forgotten Trinity 3: A Selection of Papers Presented to the British Council of Churches Study Commission on Trinitarian Doctrine Today*, edited by Alasdair I. C. Heron, 19–21. London: British Council of Churches/CCBI, 1991.

———. "The Doctrine of the Holy Trinity: The Significance of the Cappadocian Contribution." In *Trinitarian Theology Today: Essays on Divine Being and Act*, edited by Christoph Schwöbel, 44–60. Edinburgh: T. & T. Clark, 1995.

———. "Human Capacity and Human Incapacity: A Theological Exploration of Personhood." *Scottish Journal of Theology* 28 (1975) 401–47.

———. "On Being a Person: Towards an Ontology of Personhood." In *Persons, Divine and Human*, edited by Christoph Shwöbel and Colin Gunton, 33–46. Edinburgh: T. & T. Clark, 1991.

———. "Preserving God's Creation: Three Lectures on Theology and Ecology: Lecture One." *King's Theological Review* 12 (1989) 1–5.

———. "The Teaching of the 2nd Ecumenical Council on the Holy Spirit in Historical and Ecumenical Perspective." *Credo in Spiritum Sanctum* 1 (1983) 42–47.

Zwemer, Samuel M. "Calvinism and the Missionary Enterprise." *Theology Today* 7 (1950) 206–16.

Zwi Werblowsky, R. J. "Eschatology: An Overview." In *Encyclopedia of Religion*, edited by Lindsay Jones, 148–51. Detroit: Macmillan Reference USA, 2004.

Index

A
Abraham, 53, 212, 295
Adam, 212, 222
Africa, 8–9, 16–17, 44, 117, 158, 165, 246, 280, 286, 288–89, 294, 297
  African Economy, 286
African American, 52–54, 117, 156, 285
African Charismatics, 199, 279
African cultures, 23
African Independent Church, 149–50, 275, 284
African Interpretation, 297
African Religions, 9, 113, 213, 294
African theologies, 8, 16, 199, 279, 286
  African folk religions, 5
afterlife, 201, 234, 248, 255–56, 261
American Process theology, 157, 242
Anabaptists, 88–90, 110, 122, 224–25
analogies, 23, 85, 137–38, 140
  master-slave, 126
  principle Augustine's, 137
  psychological, 136–37
  social, 46
angels, 7–8, 15, 44, 97, 203, 267
animism, 193
Augustine, 22, 28, 57, 107, 134–41, 179, 197, 249, 280, 303

B
Black theology, 53–54, 280, 283
blessings, 165, 208, 215
Bodhisattva, 202, 209, 285, 293

Boonyakiat, Satanun 193, 195–96, 200–203, 208, 281
brain, 63, 233, 240, 242–44, 246, 295, 304
Buddha, 192–96, 200–203, 297–99, 304
Buddhism, xxii, 29, 34–35, 191–93, 195–96, 198, 201, 203, 205, 209–11, 254, 270, 281, 285, 292
  Buddhist Eschatology, 254, 296
Buddhist-Christian Dialogue, 196, 285
Buddhists, 35, 191, 193, 195–96, 200–201, 206, 208–11, 254, 293

C
Calvin, John, xiv, 14, 110, 121, 124, 212–27, 281
Calvinism, 213, 226, 307
Cappadocians, 134–36, 138, 179, 307
Catholicism, 13, 102, 104, 107–8, 112, 118–20, 122–24, 127, 161, 171, 174, 182–84, 186–87, 300, 302
  ecclesiology, 117
  theologians, 123, 174–75, 189
  theology, 103, 117, 122, 175
  tradition, 5, 115, 297
catholicity, 28, 123
causal influence, 62, 237
  possible, 73
causal influence downwards, 237
causality, 60, 63–64, 68, 70–72, 235, 237–38, 258, 292, 296
  whole-part, 63

causal powers, 235, 237–38
   irreducible, 238
   new, 237
change, 3, 40, 105, 107, 128–29, 135, 148, 195, 237, 239, 247
   effective social, 160
chaos, 64–66, 70, 75, 283, 285, 296, 298–99, 305
   order out of, 64
charismatic movements, 149–50, 290, 299, 302
charisms, xx, 27, 88–89, 91–93, 166
children, 81, 86, 91, 125, 185, 205, 207, 209–10, 225
Christ, 22–24, 81–85, 91–92, 101–5, 107–9, 111–13, 115–16, 118–20, 122–25, 168, 170–75, 178–84, 206–7, 220–23, 225
   ascended, 24, 27
   ascension of, 24, 27
   body of, 92, 130, 160, 184
   indwelling of, 103, 105
   lordship of, 93, 164
   real presence of, 104, 109
   resurrection of, 74–75
   risen, 143, 182–83
   saving work of, 179, 182
Christendom, 199, 255
Christian animism, 13, 275, 304
Christian doctrine, xxii, 4, 31, 175–76, 178, 189, 212, 232, 295
Christian East, 4, 12, 51, 110, 133, 135, 137–43, 171, 272
Christian experience, 198–99, 202, 207
Christian hospitality, 38–39, 286–88
Christianity, 31–32, 34, 140–41, 158–59, 193, 196, 225, 227, 269, 271, 283, 285, 295, 298, 305
Christian-Muslim encounters, 171, 176, 182, 187, 287, 301
Christians, 32–33, 37, 105–8, 113–15, 173–74, 176–78, 183, 185–87, 189–92, 195–96, 200–202, 206, 208, 256, 264–65
Christian theology of religions, 32, 172, 176, 181, 183, 291, 306
Christian tradition, 4–5, 15, 17, 48, 51, 53, 56, 196–98, 200–201, 205, 247–48, 254, 258, 263, 297–98
Christian vision, 58, 191–92, 201–2, 206, 252–53, 255, 257, 259, 261, 263, 265, 267, 272
Christology, xxi, 14, 16, 56, 80, 139, 172, 175, 178–81, 183
   incarnational, 270
church, 19–28, 84–88, 92–96, 113–25, 127–28, 130–31, 159–61, 163–66, 174–75, 184–85, 187–88, 225–27, 279–85, 292–95, 302–5
   apostolic, 28, 127
   early, 94, 151, 255, 284
   independent, 116, 149
church life, 49, 131, 165
Classical Liberalism, 4, 14, 60, 171, 247, 264
Classical Theism, 46, 71, 74, 197, 274
Clayton, Philip, 13, 59–62, 69, 158, 237–40, 242–45, 282, 297, 304
Clooney, Francis X., 32–34, 36, 283
communion, 27, 43, 45–47, 49–53, 55, 57, 79, 81, 112, 114–15, 127, 129–31, 135, 166–67, 184–86
communion theology, 44, 46, 49, 137, 184
community, xxi–xxii, 24–25, 34–36, 46, 48–50, 52, 57–58, 81, 91–94, 115, 124–27, 131–32, 158–60, 207, 304–5
comparative theology, xxii, 31–34, 36, 125, 131–32, 283, 298, 300, 303
compassion, 204, 209–10
Cone, James, 54, 283
Confucian traditions, 9, 11, 208
consciousness, 137, 148, 181, 194, 206, 218, 237–39, 241–42, 246, 282, 285, 301–2, 304
constructive theology, xxi, xxv, 31, 52, 58, 115, 157, 247, 256, 265, 273, 278, 290–91, 306
consubstantiality, 135, 141–42
consummation, 177, 252, 256, 259, 262, 273
   final, 72, 264

contemporary theology, 12–13, 15, 26, 43–44, 46, 152, 173, 197, 214, 251, 286
context, xv–xvi, xx, xxiii, 22, 53–54, 64, 69, 72–73, 122–23, 126, 183, 186–87, 237–38, 301, 303
continuity, 28, 110, 124, 157, 170, 179, 188, 194, 249–50, 264, 272
cosmologies, 3, 5–6, 16–18, 56, 70, 72, 210, 232, 262, 264–65
cosmology, and eschatology, 265, 300
cosmos, 7–8, 10–12, 16, 73, 75, 170–71, 247, 250–51, 253, 256–57, 261–62, 265, 270, 282, 285
   spirit-filled, 13
cosmotheandrism, 174
covenant, 81, 119, 222, 242
creation, 10–14, 26, 69–72, 75, 94–96, 179, 185–86, 242–43, 253–54, 261, 263–64, 270–74, 276–78, 299–300, 304–7
   doctrine of, 12, 26, 197, 232, 251, 253, 271, 278, 306
   new, 56, 75, 179, 264–65, 277
creator, xviii, 8, 10, 69, 71, 78, 80, 86, 217–20, 222, 227–28, 245, 250, 271–72, 276
cultures, 14, 27, 30, 77, 87, 94–95, 150, 152, 158, 167, 246, 252, 281, 287, 296
   ancient, 15
   secular, 252, 262

D

Dabney, Lyle, 171, 179, 183, 188, 283–84, 288, 304
D'Costa, Gavin, 174, 184, 186–87, 283
death, 80, 82, 108, 112, 168, 182–83, 186, 192, 205–6, 222–23, 249, 252–56, 259, 261–63, 285–86
defeat, 123–24, 235, 237, 264
defense, 142, 236, 255, 299
deification, 101–5, 111, 280, 290–91, 304
   idea of, 106, 110
   ontology of, 109
deity, 52, 135, 139, 141, 143, 178, 181, 215, 219, 221, 237, 279
Derrida, Jacques, 47–48, 256, 284

despair, 152, 207
destiny, 202, 256, 264, 266
   personal eternal, 250
destruction, 169, 271, 275, 277
determinism, 60, 62, 64–68, 73–74
Dhamma, 192, 285, 299, 303
dialogical engagement, 30, 33, 35, 196
dialogue, xix, xxii, 34–36, 38, 40, 102–4, 111–13, 171–72, 178, 185–90, 196, 284, 288–90, 299–300, 305–6
dignity, 160, 235, 289, 298
discernment, 8–9, 154, 187, 189, 299, 306
disciples, xvii, xx, 81, 209, 255
discipleship, 48, 281
discipline, 29, 31–32, 121, 251
   academic, 33–34
   scientific, 240
   theological, 172
Dispensationalism, 163, 301
dissolution, 63, 75
diversity, xv–xvi, xix, 17, 30, 36, 52, 115, 117, 126–27, 130, 150, 175, 181, 186–87, 304
   celebrated, xix
   community in, 50
   cultural, xvi, 36
   global, 30
   growing, 34
   religious, 33, 36–37
divine, overflow of, 10, 274
divine action, xiii, 58–59, 61, 63–76, 282–83, 285–86, 292, 296–98, 300, 302–6
   metaphysics of, 67, 298
   miraculous, 73
   multifaceted, 67, 71
   objective, 75
   profound, 75
divine acts, 59–61, 65, 69, 72–73
   affirming, 60
   non-interventionist, 62
   real, 60
   salvage, 60
   special, 61
   subjective, 60
divine acts obsolete, 60

divine intervention, 61, 198, 227
divinization, 113
　virtual, 272
divorce, 174, 190
doctrine, 4, 13–14, 17, 19, 43–44, 57, 84, 138–39, 173, 176, 252, 254, 258–59, 265–66, 297
dreams, 97, 151, 155, 253, 263
dualism, 16, 62, 67, 152, 156–57, 231–34, 241, 246, 251, 271, 277
　emergent, 236, 242
　integrative, 242
　nature-history, 60
　phenomenological, 251
　property, 241–42, 246–47
　traditional, 231, 235, 245, 247–48
dukkha, 192–95, 203

E
earth, 5, 11, 80, 82, 85–86, 165, 167, 219, 221–22, 271–75, 277, 282–83, 288–89, 302–4, 306
ecclesiality, 28, 115–16, 119–20, 122–23, 129–30
ecclesiology, xxi, xxiv, 4, 20–22, 25–26, 28, 118, 131, 141, 152, 160, 291, 293, 295, 305
ecology, xiv, xxi, 7, 268–69, 271, 273–74, 278–80, 282, 285–86, 288, 295, 299, 302–5, 307
economics, 13, 50, 87, 94–96, 182, 194
ecumenism, xxii–xxiii, 22, 37–38, 104, 107, 112–13, 115–16, 118–19, 121, 123, 125, 127–32, 134, 287, 290
embodiment, 80, 156–57, 159, 250
　principle of, 153, 157
emergence, 5, 31, 62–63, 193, 236–40, 242–43, 264, 282, 284, 292, 296–97, 301, 303
　constant, 130
　open-system, 236
　radical kind of, 242
　theory of, 236–37, 242
emotions, 156, 232
enjoyment, 194, 199
environment, 13, 64, 246, 268–70, 277–78

eschatological, 23, 156, 181, 254–55, 261, 264, 273, 276
eschatology, 4, 23–24, 56, 161, 249, 252–62, 264–66, 270, 287, 290–91, 294, 296, 299–300, 302, 304–5
　constructive, xiv, 252, 261–62
　consummation, 56, 75, 130, 250, 264
　dispensational, 163
　dispensationalist, 165
　escapist, 248
　feast, 130, 276
　kingdom, 24, 48, 266
　outlook, 163, 253
　renewal, 26, 179
　revisionist, 258
　traditional, 256
　travelogue, 260
　visions, 255, 257, 264, 277
eternal life, 47, 84, 106, 168, 249, 257–58, 261, 288
Europe, 9, 19, 30, 163, 224
evangelicals, 95, 114, 163, 227, 287, 293, 299, 302
　contemporary, 226–27
evangelists, xvii, 25, 219
evil, 8, 15, 105, 158, 195–97, 216, 224, 281, 290
　powers, 17
evil spirits, 7–8, 167, 188
evolution, 11, 13, 56, 78, 253, 282
existence, xviii, 26, 69, 80, 149, 193–96, 201–3, 209, 214–16, 218, 227, 236, 257, 303–4
expectation, xvi, 47, 160, 163, 198, 208, 254, 260–61, 271, 277
experience, 37, 86, 148, 154–56, 161, 167, 198, 200, 213, 242–43, 294, 305
　common, 161
　contemporary charismatic, 170
　polar, 243
　psychological, 233
　public, 13
　religious, 155, 164, 174, 233
　subjective, 105, 109
　transformative, 151

turn to, 154
unmediated spiritual, 89

F
fairness, 49, 89, 110, 218, 233
faith, 32–34, 36–37, 75, 101–5,
    107–14, 117, 186–87, 189–90,
    222–23, 255, 261, 291, 293–94,
    297–98, 300
  true, 86, 104
Father, 23, 26–27, 45–47, 51–52,
    57–59, 78–79, 81–82, 84–86,
    133–43, 167, 173–74, 177–81,
    184–85, 205, 222
fear, xviii, 37, 61, 68, 74, 80, 89, 123,
    219, 225–26, 244
fellowship, 27, 40, 49, 57–58, 94,
    124–25, 127, 160, 184, 212, 274
filioque, 133, 138–43
First Nations, 54
Fivefold Gospel, xiii, 20–21, 23, 28,
    279–80, 282, 284, 293–94, 297,
    305
  ecclesiology, 20–21, 24
flesh, 79–80, 106, 165, 198, 206, 250,
    306
flourishing, 36, 45, 55–56, 95, 273–74,
    277
foundationalism, 154, 189
freedom, 16, 40, 46, 52, 74, 95, 102,
    158, 164, 180, 185, 190, 253
  absolute, 95
  authentic, 53
  inviting, xviii
  sovereign, 185
Fukuyama, Francis, 253, 286
Full Gospel, 20–21, 24, 28, 150
fundamentalism, 60, 148, 152–53,
    157, 163–64, 281, 290, 296
fundamentalists, 89, 163, 165, 264

G
Gautama Buddha, 192–94, 196, 203,
    209
gender, 22, 156
gifts, 24–25, 27, 45, 47–49, 58, 86,
    90–93, 106–8, 160, 177, 179, 184,
    187, 298, 300
  charismatic, 90

  distinctive, 166
  fivefold ministry, 24
  pure, 48
  spiritual, 87–89, 92, 157, 166
Global North, 6, 8–10, 12, 27, 37, 50,
    165, 206, 274
Global South, 8–9, 11, 16–17, 23, 50,
    83, 95, 158, 165, 246, 274
glossolalia, 24–25, 155, 160–61, 294
God, xvii–xxii, 3–16, 43–65, 67–75,
    78–83, 90–95, 101–13, 176–90,
    196–203, 205–8, 213–27, 256–
    66, 269–77, 280–87, 294–305
  biblical, 173, 177, 204, 221
  essence of, 47, 57, 106, 219
  gift of, 187, 248–49
  knowledge of, 177, 182, 203, 214,
    216–20, 222, 227–28
  mercy of, 93, 222
  true, 215–16, 220, 222, 225
  union with, 104
goodness, 47, 58, 80, 105–6, 197, 201,
    217, 273
gospel, xx, 26, 28, 80–81, 86, 117,
    120–22, 162, 164, 183, 206, 208,
    210, 222–23, 225
grace, 48, 85, 90, 92, 106–7, 110, 113,
    182, 211–12, 271, 289, 302
growth, 80, 129, 158, 164, 198, 249,
    279

H
happiness, 16, 194–95
healing, 23, 25–26, 88, 92, 149, 151,
    155, 157, 160, 167–69, 198, 200,
    203–5, 207–10, 273–74
  community, 24
  continuous, 273
  instantaneous, 73
  love, 46
  mental-physical, 17, 96, 157
health, 157, 165, 292
heart, xvii, xx, 48–49, 57, 86, 89–90,
    103–5, 108, 151, 155, 157, 160,
    205–6, 215–16, 221
heaven, 6, 26, 70, 85, 147–49, 154–55,
    212, 215, 219, 267, 271, 277, 283,
    295
Hegel, 11, 126, 246, 279, 288

Hildegard, 10, 273
Hinduism, xxii, 29, 34–35, 37, 113, 148, 164, 192, 254, 268, 270, 282, 302–3
history, xvi–xvii, 13, 26, 46–47, 59–62, 77, 138, 140–42, 172–74, 177–78, 253–54, 260, 285–87, 296–97, 302–3
　universal, 59
holiness, 21, 86, 101–2, 123, 187, 272, 300
holism, 16, 21, 67, 70, 152–53, 157, 164, 233–34, 241, 264
　emergent, 244
Holy Spirit, xvi–xvii, 9–10, 13–14, 83–87, 90, 133–35, 140–42, 160–61, 167–71, 181–85, 187–89, 206–7, 273–75, 292, 297–99
homogeneity, 6, 187, 256
honor, xiii–xiv, 35, 50, 118, 225
hospitality, 17, 45, 47–49, 52, 54–55, 58, 208, 256, 284, 300
　divine, 48–49, 52, 57, 274
human beings, 8, 12, 48, 55–57, 78, 82, 105, 186, 194–95, 203, 241, 243, 264, 270, 277
human flourishing, xiii, 16, 43, 45, 54–57, 291
humanity, xxi, 12–13, 44, 46, 136–37, 140, 214, 218, 231–32, 234, 261–63, 265, 270–72, 277, 297
human nature, nature of, xiv, xxv, 34–35, 79, 195, 208, 214, 231–34, 238, 240–45, 247–51, 280–81, 296

I
idealism, 242, 246–47
identity, 40, 51, 78, 82–83, 125, 129, 150, 163, 177–78, 181, 248–49
idols, 221–22, 225
image, 25, 27, 32, 78, 81, 137, 140, 185–86, 188, 214, 220, 266, 271, 274, 277
imagination, 7, 28, 130, 239–40, 255, 266, 285
　eschatological-apocalyptic, 255
imago dei, 44, 137, 154, 176, 287

immortality, 216, 233–34, 248, 250, 263, 280, 285, 287
　natural, 249
　objective, 257
　personal, 256
　subjective, 257
incarnation, 80, 135–36, 138, 173, 177, 182, 277
inclusiveness, 16, 21–22, 44, 52, 54, 115–16, 162, 164
　mutual, 46
indeterminacy, 64–65, 68, 286
individualism, 21, 50, 81, 166
　religion of, 165
individuality, 158–59, 173
　biological, 185
indwelling, 72, 109, 181, 275
infinity, 71, 245
injustice, 54, 197, 202, 204, 261
innocence, 52, 253, 280
inspiration, 4, 37, 51–52, 163
integration, xv, 240, 264
intelligence, 9, 137, 232
interdisciplinary conversation, dynamic, 231
interdisciplinary work, xxii, 17, 61, 232–33, 251, 278, 284, 293, 301
interreligious dialogue, 29–30, 38–39, 131, 171, 299–300
Islam, xxii, 5, 29, 32, 34–35, 87, 149, 171–72, 183, 213, 223, 226, 279, 286, 300
Islam-Christian encounter, 171

J
Jesus, 24–26, 56–58, 77–79, 81, 140–41, 168, 173, 177–78, 180–81, 183, 255–56, 277, 282, 284, 301
Judaism, 34–35, 81, 87, 172, 177, 212, 222, 224–25, 253, 263, 269, 276, 286, 288, 291
justification, 16, 21, 84, 101–5, 107–8, 111–13, 128, 250, 287–88, 290, 294, 298
justification and theosis, xiii, 101–5, 107, 109, 111, 113

K
kamma, 193–94, 201, 203, 206, 209

kingdom, 49, 58, 170, 173–75,
  180–81, 184–85, 188, 197, 256,
  260, 262, 277, 283, 293, 295
knowledge, xix, 37, 40, 62, 78, 109,
  155, 173, 203, 214, 216–19, 223,
  266, 270, 288
koinonia, 27, 140, 160–61, 166, 285,
  289

L
language, xviii–xix, 30, 77, 108, 155,
  220, 237, 241–42, 267, 299
  masculine God, 274
  sign, 75
Latin America, 8–9, 44, 53, 165, 204,
  282, 299
laws, 14, 63–64, 67–70, 74, 111–12,
  193–94, 202, 219, 286, 288
  natural, 68, 73–74
  nature's, 73
  physical, 74
liberation, 14, 16, 44, 52, 54, 156,
  191–92, 196, 200, 203–6, 209–11,
  274, 283, 301, 304
  theologies, 14, 16, 44, 51–53, 148,
  202, 204, 266, 281, 305
life, 7–13, 15–16, 54–56, 79–82,
  85–87, 157–60, 167–68, 194,
  201, 208, 248–50, 252–53, 257,
  273–75, 281–82
love, xvii, xx, 10–11, 45, 47–48, 50,
  52–53, 105–7, 122, 124, 126, 137,
  139, 197, 204–6
Luke, 79, 112, 125, 181, 206–8, 301
Lumen Gentium, 27, 116, 122, 300
Luther, Martin, 22, 47, 70, 82, 84–90,
  102–11, 197, 205, 212–13, 223,
  227, 290–91, 293–94, 298, 301
Lutheran
  Church, xiii, 87, 90, 92, 95, 102–3,
  107, 116, 121, 128, 293, 302
  theologies, 83–84, 87, 90, 101, 103,
  106–7, 111, 113, 116, 120–21,
  150, 260, 300
Lutheranism and Eastern Orthodoxy,
  110

Lutherans, xxi, 14, 83–84, 86–88, 91,
  95, 101–2, 108, 112, 115, 117,
  122, 128, 212, 258–59

M
Macchia, Frank, 21, 23–25, 27, 151,
  161, 166, 291, 294
Mahayana Buddhism, 10, 37, 191,
  202–3, 209, 211, 296
Mainline Protestants, 23, 28, 89, 118,
  120
Marxism, 263
materialism, 158, 236, 238, 242, 246
matter, 17, 19, 56–57, 69, 71, 79–80,
  121, 123, 239–40, 242–43,
  246–47, 249, 251, 269, 285–86
  decisive, 84
  informed, 71
  spirit-less, 71
mediator, 69, 174, 213, 215, 217–18,
  220–22, 226–27
Melanchthon, Philip, 94, 103, 212, 295
mental causation, 235, 237–38, 242,
  292
metaphors
  nature-based, 273
  soteriological, 112
metaphysics, 12, 15, 109, 236, 243
methodology, 4, 6, 8, 10, 12, 14, 16,
  18, 20, 22, 24, 26, 28, 30, 34
mind, 31, 62–63, 125–26, 137, 209–
  10, 215, 218–21, 227, 235–36,
  238, 240–42, 246, 292, 298–99,
  302–3
ministry, 4–5, 23, 25, 81, 86–89,
  91–95, 115–16, 156–57, 161, 164,
  179–80, 182, 187–88, 204, 208
  apostolic, 210
  healing, 151, 204, 210
miracles, 59, 73–75, 89, 91, 151,
  209–10
missiology, 161, 164–66, 192, 198–99,
  290
mission, xx, xxiv, 20–21, 23, 27–28,
  159, 161, 164, 166–68, 181, 279,
  281, 284–85, 288, 290–92
modernist, 17, 23, 35

modernity, 6, 147–48, 155, 158, 164, 183, 255, 279, 287
Moltmann, Jürgen, xviii–xxi, 11–12, 16, 34–36, 49, 58, 71–72, 124–25, 142, 157, 197, 242–43, 264–65, 271–73, 275–78
money, 165, 237
monism, 233, 235–36, 240–44, 246–47, 251, 283, 302
- multidimensional, xiv, 231–33, 235, 237, 239, 241, 243, 245, 247, 249, 251
- nonphysicalist, 246
- physical, 231, 244

Montanism, 88
mothers, 11, 77, 124, 209, 218
multiplicity, 68, 152, 243–44, 291
Murphy, Nancey, 60–61, 63–66, 234–35, 237, 266, 296
Muslims, 37, 148, 171, 178, 182–83, 185–86, 189–90, 192, 213, 223–25
- evangelizing, 226
- theology, 32, 187, 225, 227

mutuality, 26, 46, 49, 52, 72, 123, 143, 265
mutual participation, 40, 58, 72, 119, 136, 210, 242, 246
mystery, 9, 51, 72, 122, 142, 200, 202, 256, 280, 291

N
naturalisms, 7, 73, 75, 246, 297
natural sciences, xxii, 10, 12, 61, 74, 244, 247, 251, 257, 265, 278, 283, 285–86, 296–300, 302–4
nature, 13, 27–29, 58–67, 69–70, 74–76, 78, 80, 134–36, 248–49, 264–65, 268–77, 280–83, 285–86, 297–99, 302–4
- corrupt, 216
- fallen, 108
- multifaceted, 65, 200

neighbor, 22, 101, 103, 108, 205, 289
neuroscience, xiv, 231, 235–36, 239, 242, 244–45, 250, 280, 282, 297–98, 302

Non-Interventionist Objective Divine Action, 61–63, 65, 67–69, 73, 75–76
nonreductive physicalism, 232, 235–41, 244, 296, 301

O
offices, 25, 27, 85, 94, 117, 120–21, 302
ontology, 60, 109, 139, 239–40, 245, 286
- idealist, 245
- incarnational, 157
- large funded substance, 241
- realistic, 109
- retroactive, 259

openness, xvi, 22–23, 34, 61, 63, 67–68, 73, 76, 129, 157, 160, 164
order, 45, 58, 64–66, 69, 94, 101, 121–22, 138, 167, 173, 210, 218–19, 221, 299, 303
origins, 10, 12, 108, 135, 137, 140–41, 143, 151, 190, 193, 197, 221, 253, 282
Orthodox and Reformed Churches, 142
Orthodox Churches, 22, 26, 28, 112, 141, 180
orthopathos, 204–5
orthopraxis, 204

P
pacifism, 89, 121
pain, 136, 182, 192–94, 198, 204–5, 208
- emotional, 195
- people's, 209
- sharing, 197

panentheism, 46, 71–72, 74, 157, 257, 274
Pannenberg, Wolfhart, xviii–xxii, 12, 51–52, 70–71, 114, 124, 136–37, 141–43, 176–77, 184–85, 188–89, 232–33, 249, 258, 260–64
participation, 23, 27, 94, 101, 103–5, 258, 261
particles, 12, 217, 239
pastors, xvii, xxii, 25, 94, 121
pedagogy, 30–31, 36, 39

Pentecost, 20, 24, 26–27, 84, 91, 94, 96, 143, 179, 184, 273, 279–80
Pentecostalism, xiv, 20–22, 26, 28, 147–59, 162–67, 192, 198–99, 204, 284, 286, 288–91, 295, 301, 306–7
   communities, 20, 150, 157, 159–61, 165–66, 199, 207
   ecclesiology, xiii, 19–23, 25, 27, 279–80, 282, 284, 294, 297
   spirituality, 21, 150–51, 155, 160, 163, 165, 199, 209, 283
   theologians, 20–21, 24, 153, 155, 160, 165, 199
   theology, 19, 22, 24, 26, 156, 164, 199, 205, 282–84, 288–91, 293–95, 298, 302–4
Pentecostals, xiv, xvi, 23–24, 26–28, 117, 119, 148–51, 154–56, 159–61, 164–66, 198–200, 204–7, 279, 293–95, 305–6
personhood, 45–46, 58, 74, 126, 173, 242, 304, 307
persons, 35–36, 46, 104–5, 135–36, 138–39, 158–61, 173, 178–80, 206, 222–23, 234, 242, 244–45, 248–50, 297–98
phenomenology, 31, 63, 126, 131, 193, 239, 288
philosophy, xiv, 5, 9, 15, 31, 73, 109, 232, 250, 280, 284, 288, 294, 300–302, 307
   contemporary, 126, 232
physicalism, 232–40, 244–47, 292
   ontological, 244–45
   reductive, 238
physicality, 233–34, 238, 240, 255, 264
physics, 12, 66–67, 232, 240, 298, 300
piety, 4, 155, 214, 218
pluralism, 3, 6, 31–32, 38, 114, 164, 172, 174–75, 180, 236, 241, 247, 262, 281
pneumatology, xiii–xiv, xvi, xx–xxi, 3–11, 13–17, 95, 169–72, 175–76, 178–81, 188–90, 268, 270, 283–84, 290–92, 304–7
   green, 274

Polkinghorne, John, 12, 65–67, 75–76, 170–71, 187, 241, 243, 249–50, 298–99, 302
postmodernism, xiv, 5–6, 23, 49, 147–49, 152–59, 162–63, 167, 171, 188–89, 281–82, 290–91, 296, 298, 301
   people, 3, 152, 154–56, 158–59, 256
postmodernitism, and pentecostalisms, 153, 162, 166–67
powers, 3–4, 6, 8–10, 12, 14–18, 24, 26–27, 47, 55–56, 124–25, 173, 181, 187, 205–7, 306
   creative, 10, 274
   spiritual, 5, 8, 95–96, 198
prayer, 24, 59, 73–74, 94, 120, 151, 203, 221, 277
preaching, 84–85, 117–18, 122–23, 125, 160, 178–80, 222, 295
process philosophy, 246, 257, 287
promise, 17, 20, 24, 57, 61, 67, 118, 125, 128, 172, 179, 236, 239, 283, 290
prophetic, 24, 88, 92, 97, 148, 151, 157, 197, 205, 222
   failed, 147
Prosperity Gospel, 91, 165
Protestantism, 13, 88, 104, 116–17, 122–24, 142, 152, 171–72, 212–14, 290
providence, 65, 67, 70–71, 75, 299
   general, 59
   special, 59, 61
   wonderful, 215

Q

quantum physics, 62, 64–66, 68–70, 75–76, 232, 239, 243, 246, 282, 298, 300, 302

R

racism, 14, 22, 54, 299
   white, 53
Radical Orthodoxy, 152–53, 155, 157
redemption, 22, 25, 171, 179, 186, 197, 206, 273, 276, 278
   final, 56, 273
redemptive suffering, 197, 204–6, 209, 211

reductionism, 4–5, 15, 60, 235–36, 243
  causal, 236
  conditional physical, 238
  methodological, 236
  modernist, 15
  ontological, 236
relationality, 44, 46, 58, 62, 136, 139, 143, 158, 177, 186, 298
  dynamic, 52
  mutual, 50, 57
relationship, 31–32, 46, 50, 57, 60, 71–73, 107, 111, 142–43, 166–67, 179–80, 182, 185, 205, 208
  body-mind, 151
  causal, 66, 239
  integral, 85, 175, 182, 184, 207
  personal, 74, 249
religions, 31–37, 55–56, 147–49, 151–52, 164, 169–90, 209, 212–23, 225–28, 233, 252–54, 268–70, 289–91, 297–300, 305–7
religiosity, 5, 56, 167, 213–14, 221, 226–27, 236, 239
religious traditions, 31–33, 55–56, 176, 192, 205, 209, 248, 257, 269, 294
resurrection, 75, 81, 84, 181–83, 244, 249–50, 257, 259, 261, 277, 284, 287, 296, 298, 301
  bodily, 234, 247, 263
  final, 250
  historical, 258
  personal, 257, 262
revelation, xxi, 34–35, 39, 45–46, 51, 71, 78, 163, 173, 176, 187, 225–26, 291, 294–95, 305
  continuing, 157
  general, 217
  new, 225
  special, 217, 219
revival, 156, 162, 299
righteousness, 104, 107–8, 112
  of Christ, 107–8
  of God, 105, 108
  human, 108
Roman Catholicism, 15, 112–13, 128, 150, 171–72, 292–93

Ruether, Rosemary Radford, 272, 288, 295, 300
Russell, Robert John, 47, 49, 52, 61–66, 68, 72, 254, 256, 258–59, 264–65, 282–83, 285–86, 296–98, 300, 302–5

S
Sabbath, 273, 276
sacramentality, 89, 118, 121, 156, 160, 272
sacraments, xiv, 24–25, 28, 84, 87, 89–90, 94, 101, 114–25, 127, 129, 131, 141, 160–61, 272–73
saints, 106, 124, 160, 271–72, 279, 284
salvation, 3–4, 7–8, 14, 16–17, 21, 23, 56, 85–87, 101–5, 107–13, 165, 182–84, 203, 221–23, 290–91
  doctrine of, 4, 110, 113, 141–42
  history, 13, 59, 177
  materiality of, 156, 158, 165, 304
sanctification, 16, 21, 24, 85–86, 96, 102–3, 150
Sarah, 53
Satan, 15, 197, 224, 281
savior, 24, 80, 150, 180, 202–3, 206, 223, 227, 263
Schleiermacher, Friedrich, 60, 69, 214
sciences, xiv, 60, 65–66, 94–95, 240, 242–45, 249, 252, 254, 278, 282–83, 285–88, 297–300, 302, 305
  paradigms, 3, 7
  political, 126
scientists, 17, 60, 68–69, 77, 231, 244, 254
scriptures, xx, 4, 15, 37, 49, 85, 90, 122, 138, 159, 163–64, 219–20, 223, 227, 269
secularism, xxii, 95, 259, 265
self, 47, 158–59, 194, 203, 233, 242, 246, 288, 294, 296
  inner, 246
self-consciousness, 126, 173, 233, 238
service, 15, 22, 44, 48, 79, 81, 92–93, 96, 130, 156, 188, 199, 272–73
  humble, 93
  responsible, 127, 271
shalom, 273, 276–77, 306

shame, 206, 218
Shiva, 181
sickness, 16, 73, 156, 192, 207, 209
signs, 58, 75, 89, 94, 160, 185–86, 294
    classic Protestant, 122
    manifest, 222
    missionary, 25
    tongues as a, 161
    visible, 89
sinfulness, 48, 80, 103, 202, 278
sins, 16, 56, 79, 96, 101, 110, 112, 178, 196–98, 201–2, 206–7, 222–23, 290
    forgiveness of, 16, 84, 112, 204, 212
    greatest, 96
    power of, 108, 112
    structural, 202
social justice, 156, 165, 276, 289, 301
society, 7, 13–14, 17, 45–46, 49, 51, 55, 87, 94–96, 126, 160, 185, 199, 296, 299
sociology, 33, 131, 151, 158
sorrows, 79, 81, 194
soul, xiv, 11, 23, 68, 165, 233–35, 241–42, 246–50, 281, 283, 286, 294, 296, 299, 306
space, 11, 64, 69, 126, 158, 172, 232, 237, 279
    enclosed, 239
    limited, 265
speech, 155, 171, 203, 220–21
    liberative, 53–54
spirit, 3–14, 16–17, 22–24, 26–28, 68–72, 84–92, 94–96, 133–43, 163–90, 204–5, 271–77, 280–84, 288–92, 294–97, 301–7
    of Christ, 142, 173, 181, 284
    Christology, 16, 26, 173, 181, 184
    earthen, 13, 243, 275, 305
    of God, 3, 9–10, 14, 16, 18, 26, 57, 71, 83, 86, 88, 95, 174, 179, 189
    of life, 7–8, 11–12, 16, 71, 84, 96, 157, 271, 273, 275, 277, 282, 295, 302
    role of, 4, 7, 12, 16, 71, 83, 85, 87, 90, 94–95, 161, 181, 263
    of Truth, 141
spiritual discernment, 185, 188

spirituality, 9, 14, 16, 80, 87, 128, 149–51, 154, 163–64, 193, 199, 291, 294–95, 302
story, 140, 152, 159, 162, 183–84, 205, 209, 243, 249, 307
structures, xviii, 4, 30, 44, 64, 71, 129–30, 202, 217–18, 220
    new, 62–63, 130, 236
    nonhierarchical, 149
    oppressive, 160
    particular, 121
    social, 96, 274
submission, 81, 208, 220, 261
subordinationism, 49, 139, 180
substances, 45–46, 84–85, 105, 139, 241, 243, 248
    conscious, 241
    ontology of, 51
suffering, 49, 52, 182, 191–211, 261, 269, 274, 277, 281, 284, 288, 292, 294–95, 300, 305
supernatural, 5, 73–74, 226, 304
survival, 53, 273, 288
systematicians, 35, 157, 231–32, 251, 259
Systematic Theology, xv–xvi, xxiii–xxiv, 8, 12, 14, 50–52, 62–64, 68, 70–74, 124, 136–37, 184–85, 260–64, 297–98, 303
systems, 15, 63–64, 236, 249
    chaotic, 67, 70
    closed, 63
    closed physical, 59
    complex, 64, 249
    ethical, 266
    humanistic, 203
    political, 14
    schematized, 265
    theological, 8

T

teachers, xvii, 24, 35, 81, 85, 121, 209
    ancient Christian, 80
teaching, xvii–xviii, xxiv, 20, 26, 29, 39, 89, 92, 94, 134, 138, 212–13, 216, 219, 226
    creative interfaith, 39
    function, 24, 104
    gift, 25, 269

teaching (continued)
  scriptural, 71, 78
  theology, xxiv, 29–31, 36–39,
    286–88, 295, 305
temporality, 243, 298
temptations, 4, 79, 167, 201
Tertullian, 84, 119, 221
testimony, 49, 86, 179, 188, 220, 224
Thailand, 9, 30, 35, 191–93, 195–96,
    201–2, 206, 209, 281, 292
  Buddhism, 192–93, 209, 211, 293
  Christians, 191, 193, 202, 208, 211
  students, 30
themes, 23–25, 27–28, 47, 83, 87, 125,
    131, 153, 191–92, 196, 198–99,
    205–6, 208, 211, 250
theologians, 7–8, 11, 14, 17, 34–37,
    50–51, 54, 65, 69, 73, 76–77,
    171–72, 176, 247, 266–69
  contemporary, xviii, 24, 45, 56, 139,
    166, 173–74, 178, 267
theology, xiv–xx, xxii–xxv, 8–13,
    19–21, 32–38, 50, 53, 58–60, 103,
    105–7, 109–11, 138–42, 231–35,
    278–87, 289–307
  anthropology, 110, 188, 227, 232,
    244, 251, 283, 288, 291, 305
  of the cross, 197–99, 204, 206
  early, 50, 54, 177, 233, 248
  green, 275, 278
  modern, 15, 50, 60, 154, 265, 304
  perspective, 62, 126, 181–82, 187,
    227, 271, 273, 297, 300, 305
  reflection, 179, 206, 228, 273, 284
  of religions, xxi, 31–32, 164, 172,
    175, 179–80, 182, 188–89,
    212–14, 222, 226–27, 290, 306
  and science, 61, 300, 305
  traditions, 14, 20, 30, 33, 70,
    139–40, 202, 233, 250, 272, 278
theosis, xiii, 101–13, 142, 290, 294
Theravāda Buddhism, xiv, 35, 37, 191,
    193, 202–3, 206, 209–11, 281
Tillich, Paul, 8, 14, 31, 54, 73, 244,
    260, 264, 292, 303
tongues, 89, 151, 155, 160, 163, 166,
    294, 306
totality, 231, 249, 256

traditions, xv–xvi, 18, 28–29, 31–35,
    37, 84–85, 87, 115, 128–29, 134–
    35, 137–38, 141–43, 210–11,
    256–57, 269–70
  biblical, 273, 276
  sacred, 268–69, 278
transcendence, 70, 74, 143, 178, 186,
    190, 218, 264, 305
transformations, 3, 6, 75, 193, 261,
    263–65
Trinitarianism, 49–50, 70–71, 134–35,
    139, 170–74, 176, 179, 181, 184,
    188–90, 307
trinitarian theology, 25–26, 43, 57,
    69–70, 134, 138–40, 175, 186,
    273, 283, 286, 288, 307
  Spirit-Christology, 26–27
  teaching, 84, 137
trinity, 43–47, 49–52, 57–58, 70–71,
    83–84, 133–43, 171–80, 185–86,
    189–90, 197, 280, 285–86,
    291–93, 295–99, 304
tritheism, 139, 178
Triune God, 23–24, 44, 46–47, 49–50,
    52, 58, 69, 71–72, 86, 88, 95–96,
    118, 139–40, 173–75, 184–87
trust, 35, 152, 167, 204, 279, 286
truth, xx, 33, 35, 40, 58, 105–6, 139,
    141–42, 152, 187–88, 194–95,
    223, 226, 243–44, 287
  absolute, 148
  basic, 113

U
United States, 30, 53, 117, 161, 163
unitive, xiii, 3, 5, 7–9, 11, 13, 15, 17,
    64
unity, xiv, 87, 92–93, 114–15, 117,
    119, 121, 123–27, 129–31,
    133–37, 143, 179, 186, 280, 285
universe, 8, 10, 59, 64, 66, 69–70,
    72–74, 80, 239, 247, 254, 276,
    285, 289, 296

V
value, xix, 32–33, 71, 80, 125–26, 147,
    153, 157, 165, 214, 218, 220, 227,
    238, 244
Vatican II, 122, 174–75, 182

violence, 17, 32, 54, 78, 186, 225, 253, 261, 274, 304
visions, 17, 22, 58, 83, 94–96, 114–15, 151, 155, 210, 252, 254–55, 259, 265, 273, 280
Volf, Miroslav, 14, 44, 51, 57, 94, 117–20, 131, 140, 156, 160, 165, 184, 292–93, 304

W
water, 11, 26, 85, 162, 209, 225, 274, 282, 302–3, 305
Welker, Michael, xiv, 181–83, 187, 232, 244, 271, 284, 296, 299, 302, 305, 307
West, 12, 37, 133–35, 137–39, 141–43, 199, 270, 272, 291
Western theology, 50, 141
wholeness, 165–66, 194
Wink, Walter, 5, 14–15, 306
wisdom, xix, 25, 47, 92, 105–6, 160, 189, 193, 209, 214, 217, 221–22, 261
  human, 222
  theological, 133
witnessing, 165, 280, 291
Womanist theology, 53, 280, 306
women, xvii, xx, 10, 16, 35, 40, 44, 48–49, 78–81, 161, 208–10, 214–15, 270, 274–75, 277
work, xvi–xviii, xxii–xxv, 5–6, 10–11, 20–21, 86–87, 94–95, 107–8, 164, 174–76, 179, 185–89, 263–65, 301–2, 304–7
  comparative, 131
  good, 102–3, 108
  outward, 136, 179
world, xviii–xx, 46–49, 59–65, 67–73, 148–51, 164–65, 167–71, 184–85, 215–20, 264–66, 270–72, 276–77, 289–90, 298–302, 305–7
  contemporary, xiv, 155, 191, 252
  globalizing, 38, 262
  physical, 74, 157, 238, 264, 292
  spirit, 17, 199
World Council of Churches (WCC), 30, 37, 127–28, 292, 303
world religions, 29, 31, 39, 164, 175, 227, 253, 269, 279–80, 283–86, 288, 291, 294–95, 303
worldview, 5, 46, 192, 245, 289
  contemporary naturalist, 255
  cyclical, 270
  dynamic, 164
  organic, 158
worship, 121, 124, 127, 138, 151, 156, 160, 162, 186, 203, 215–16, 225
wrath, eternal, 212
Wright, NT, 68, 181, 241, 259, 306

Y
Yong, Amos, xxiii–xxiv, 6, 10, 12–13, 164–65, 169, 172, 175, 179–80, 188, 198, 291, 306

Z
Zizioulas, John, 27, 43, 45–46, 51, 184, 249, 272, 285, 307

www.ingramcontent.com/pod-product-compliance
Lightning Source LLC
Chambersburg PA
CBHW030432300426
44112CB00009B/959